John Thein

Christian anthropology

John Thein

Christian anthropology

ISBN/EAN: 9783742892621

Manufactured in Europe, USA, Canada, Australia, Japa

Cover: Foto ©Lupo / pixelio.de

Manufactured and distributed by brebook publishing software (www.brebook.com)

John Thein

Christian anthropology

CHRISTIAN ANTHROPOLOGY

BY

Rev. JOHN THEIN

Pastor of St. Martin's Church, Liverpool, O.

WITH AN INTRODUCTION BY

PROF. CHAS. G. HERBERMANN, PH.D., LL.D.

SECOND EDITION.

NEW YORK, CINCINNATI, CHICAGO
BENZIGER BROTHERS

INTRODUCTION.

The Church has taught for ages that between the truths of revelation and the truths of science there can be no conflict. The Vatican Council has solemnly repeated this teaching. On the other hand some men famed for scientific learning and some famed for unscientific bluster proclaim that between faith and science no reconciliation is possible. Educated Catholics may well ask, How are such assertions possible? Still it is not hard to find the explanation. If we could ascertain at once what are the truths of science and what are the truths of revelation their comparison would end the controversy. But what are the truths of science? Science has no infallible mouthpiece. The ablest and sincerest men of science may be mistaken. Generations of scientists have fought in defence of error. For hundreds of years they taught that the sun moves and the earth is at rest. For centuries they spoke of heat and light as imponderable substances. Linnæus taught that species were immutable; Lamarck, the contrary. Cuvier, Von Baer, and Agassiz returned to the teaching of Linnæus, and now Darwin and Haeckel, reviving the views of Lamarck, proclaim the mutability of species. Who is right? Linnæus or Lamarck? Cuvier or Haeckel? When does a scientific theory become a scientific theorem, a scientific truth? Can one great name safeguard us against error? There is not a distinguished scientist alive who will say in cold blood, "I cannot err." Is the consensus of all men of science a guarantee that their teaching is scientific truth? The history of Ptolemy's theory bids us be prudent in our answer. Surely it is more than hazardous to maintain that a theory or view against which are raised some of the weightiest voices in science is, without possibility of error, the scientific truth.

And what are the truths of revelation? Some scientific oracles, not content with defining the truths of science, insist upon defining for us the truths of religion. No doubt they are very kind; but really we must decline their Grecian gifts. We look to the Church to tell us what are revealed truths. Reasonable men will find this reasonable. When the Church has spoken, we know what revealed truth is. But there are hundreds of opinions on dogma and morals which the Church has neither approved nor condemned; there are thousands of Biblical texts the meaning of which she has not defined. To be sure, we have the opinions of theologians, we have what is called the received interpretation of the Scriptures, which is often but another word for theological opinion. But the views of theologians, however learned and holy, are not, of necessity, revealed truths. For scholars, who are not controversial scientists, it is not always easy to decide what are the truths of revelation.

Since, then, it is neither easy to find the truths of science nor to find the truths of revelation in every case, it follows that it is difficult to compare them with each other. The prudent scholar, therefore, will not commit himself hastily to the proposition that there is between them an irrepressible conflict. Where religion and science seem to be at variance— and during the past half century scientists (not science) have propounded many views seemingly at variance with Scripture—he will first ascertain whether the dicta of scientists are the truths of science, and next whether the assumed meaning of the Bible has been officially set forth by the Church. The former he will ascertain by inquiring whether the views in question are unanimously held by all reputable authorities in science or whether weighty voices are raised in contradiction; the latter he will easily ascertain by an appeal to Church History. If he finds that the Church has defined nothing in the premises, he may examine what is the most probable and the best supported theological opinion.

Father Thein, in the present work, has followed the prudent, reasonable method we have just sketched. He has been an enthusiastic student of science, deeply interested in its progress. To anthropology above all—the science of man—he has given years of study and research. With patient toil and vigilant eye he has delved in biological, geological, and archæological books and periodicals for whatever could throw light on the nature, the origin, and the early history of man. At the same time he has never lost sight of the teachings of Scripture and the Church. But Father Thein never saw the irreconcilable conflict between science and religion which some writers see all around them. In his book he offers to us the fruits of his studies. He sets down the most important facts and theories in modern anthropology. He constantly cites the great masters of anthropological science. He discusses the views of modern thinkers, frequently by laying before the reader the divergent opinions of other thinkers of acknowledged merit. He gives title and page for his references. Thus, while freely giving his own opinion on the points at issue, he enables the reader to judge for himself what is and what is not demonstrated scientific truth.

Father Thein's presentation of the theological side of the controversy is safe and conservative. It is based on the writings of such authorities as the Abbé Vigouroux, Professor Hettinger, the Jesuits Pianciani, Brucker, Cornely, Knabenbauer, Hummelauer, and other contributors to the "Stimmen aus Maria-Laach," "La Controverse," and the "Revue des Questions Scientifiques."

Though the reader may not in every instance agree with the author's judgments, Thein's "Christian Anthropology" is a mine of information, eminently useful to educated Catholics. It is a store-house of knowledge on every-day questions of scientifico-religious controversy, and a monument of learning, of study, and of research.

CHARLES GEORGE HERBERMANN.

PREFACE.

THE condition of the world to-day is known. Everywhere we see infidelity rising up against God's revelation. The weapons which in former centuries were shattered and rendered useless, are diligently searched for in the ruins of the past, and are refurbished with new phrases and shibboleths, in order to be employed once more in the warfare against Christianity. New objections are invented against the Christian religion. Men of science dig into the depths of the earth, and into the history of all times and nations, to find new weapons against Christ's Church. What history does not furnish is supplied by falsehood and misrepresentation.

The Sacred Scriptures have been the special target of infidelity. It is against them that rationalistic criticism directs the full force of its efforts. This has been the case since the foundation of the Church. From the moment paganism became acquainted with them it ridiculed them. Apion, the grammarian, mocked them in Egypt, and an unknown painter derided them at Pompeii.[1] After the religion of Christ had gained its first victories the attacks increased; at the present hour they are numberless, and the Bible for many is nothing but a heap of contemptible fables. Christianity is declared to be a tissue of absurdities.

The scientific arguments against the Scriptures, formerly rare and without much weight, have grown more numerous and important in our days, on account of the extraordinary progress of science. The adversaries of Holy Scripture dis-

[1] In 1883 there was discovered at Pompeii a caricature of the Judgment of Solomon, related in the Third Book of Kings, iii. 26, 27.

play and develop them, in order to break down both Faith and Revelation. In the name of geology, they attack the Biblical account of the creation of the world, pretending that it is irreconcilable with geological discoveries; in the name of astronomy, they maintain that Moses and other inspired writers attribute to the earth a role in the universe to which it has no rightful claim; in the name of paleontology, they strive to remove the origin of our globe and of man far beyond the limits hitherto assigned to them; in the name of natural history, they charge the Sacred Scriptures with many errors.

The foregoing lines characterize in general the spirit of the modern materialistic and rationalistic schools. Entirely imbued with this spirit, the men belonging to these schools were forced by the logic of their principles to degrade man to a mere animal, to "the first among the anthropoids."

Man, according to the modern evolutionary theory advanced by the school of Haeckel, is a purely chemical product of matter, of atoms; his soul is only the activity of the nerves and the brain. Like the rest of the world, man's existence has really no aim or purpose—"his origin is from the morass, he is wading for a short while in the morass, and again will become part of the morass." Such is the morassy circle of man's destination. The summary of the materialistic doctrine is this: Between man and the irrational animal there is no essential difference—man is simply a more happily organized animal; he differs from the animal not in kind, but in degree. The human soul is a temporary quality of the brain, a result of man's development; it has no substantial existence. Between the reason of man and the instinct of the animal there is no essential difference, but merely a difference of degree; man, like the animal, is the sum of corporal dispositions and external influences; hence the spiritual life of the individual is absolutely, completely, and eternally annihilated by death. This is the highest wisdom of modern materialistic anthropology! Karl Vogt, the Professor of Geneva, cries out: "*Let any man overthrow this doctrine if he can!*"

Well, though we may not succeed in refuting all its details, we will show, at least, its inward groundlessness.

Professor Huxley, borrowing from the inspired Book, which he rejects, one of its most striking figures, seems to pity those who "waste their lives in wishing to put the new and generous wine of science into the old utricles of Judaism." But we can assure Mr. Huxley, and prove to him, that the new wine of science, noble and generous as it may be, will keep just as well, yea, much better, in the old utricles of Judaism than in his own utricles or in those of his adherents. For these old Jewish utricles have become, by a Testament, in good and due form, the utricles of Christianism; and just as the tumultuous waters of the ocean will be maintained in their old bed, which the hand of God has dug for them, so also will "the new wine of science," with all the immense progress of the natural sciences, be kept safe and pure in the utricles of the New Testament of Christianity.

Our book is entitled "Christian Anthropology," in contradistinction to materialistic anthropology. The latter stands in direct opposition to the former, and is not bounded by the same horizon, and has not the same extent. The narrow, smothering, and often unhealthy dimensions of a theatre are sufficient for materialistic anthropology. It is an isolated branch of zoölogy—a chapter taken from natural history. Observation, material experiments, manipulation, the scalpel, the microscope, statistics, measurements of the skull and the skeleton—this is all. In it there is no question of a soul, and the name of God is not even mentioned. The physical, physiological, and pathological characters of man, the viscera, the muscles, the bones, are counted, and labelled with a flourish; not even a convolution of the brain, a deformation of its bony envelope, is omitted; all are minutely described. To materialistic anthropology man is the human animal, with patterns for all races and for all countries. This constitutes its entire science, and from this is drawn a conclusion worthy of its premises: "Man is a mammal, whose organization, needs, sicknesses are most complicated; an animal whose brain and wonderful functions have attained the highest degree of development. As such, he is subject to the same laws as the rest of animals; as such, he also shares their fate."

Christian anthropology, on the contrary, embraces the entire man, the soul as well as the body. It notes the great difference between man and the beast; it considers his intellectual and moral qualities as well as his anatomical and physiological characters, and, therefore, man's origin, nature, place in creation, antiquity, unity, immortality, future life. Such is the complete plan of our "Christian Anthropology."

Who will dispute the importance of the above questions?—questions so much and often so vehemently discussed in our days?—questions the importance of which our Holy Father, Pope Leo XIII., so well understands when he writes:

"The times in which we live require a knowledge which embraces not only the sacred sciences, but also the philosophical sciences, enriched by physical and historical discoveries. . . . For the philosophical sciences our Encyclical Letter '*Æterni Patris*' has pointed the road and the correct method. A great number of eminent minds have made beautiful and fruitful discoveries; it becomes us the less to ignore them, as unbelievers make use of this daily progress in order to forge arms against the truths of revelation. Therefore, he who defends the Faith must devote himself to the study of the natural sciences more than in the past" (*Encyc. Letter*, Feb. 15, 1882). Our late Plenary Council of Baltimore enjoins the same duty.

The above words are especially addressed to the priest, but where is the layman, the student, or the professional man who should not feel sufficiently interested in these questions to acquaint himself more or less with the scientific subjects so often brought before him? Where is the man who is not likely to meet them every day, at every step, in a book, in a periodical, in a newspaper, in society, on his travels, in his ordinary relations with the world, even in the bosom of his own family? Questions, assertions, denials formulated in big-sounding words, accredited more or less by those whom the world calls "savants." Questions which, alas! only too often are likely to trouble and to destroy his belief, the peace of his heart.

But it is especially the priest who should possess a more or less thorough knowledge of these scientific subjects, which are so often and so vigorously debated nowadays. Difficulties, arguments on a new discovery, on scientific phenomena, against revealed truth, present themselves sooner or later to every priest in the exercise of his ministry; they are propagated in books with high-sounding titles, in cheap and popular reviews and magazines; by swarms of demi-savants, or even by children who frequent the schools; they may come up at any moment, perhaps unconsciously, in the bosom of Christian families or even in a lesson of the Catechism.

Nowadays the priest who knows only his dogmatic and moral theology may be surprised and confounded by objections formulated in entirely new language, supported by pretended fact or by a discovery wrongly interpreted. If a priest is ignorant or little acquainted with the weapons and methods modern men of science make use of to break down and destroy the Christian religion, he must not be astonished that his theology, his scholastic methods of argumentation, are not always sufficient to remove the uncertainty of the victim of pseudo-scientific fascination, who comes to him with his doubts and his cruel anxieties.

The ordinary Christian may perhaps be able to rest content without inquiry and study; he may hold fast in simplicity and in faith to the teaching of his Church, and may not suffer himself to be shaken in his belief by all the objections of human science; but deliberate ignorance would be sinful in a theologian and priest, and worthy of blame in one who wishes to be considered a man of education.

Again, it is impossible for theology to maintain her rank as queen among the sciences if she proudly or timidly isolates herself. She may, indeed, keep her royal rank, but what avails a royalty which is acknowledged by no subject?

Religion has suffered immensely, and faith is completely extinct in many, because they read infidel and rationalistic literature, and because there are none to instruct them in the truth. Do we exaggerate? Is our assertion unfounded? If the optimist could step outside of his sphere and throw a glance at the inside of the materialistic camp, he would soon convince himself of the necessity of studying the schemes and doings of the men who triumphantly cry out that "astronomy takes the roof from over the head and geology the ground from under the feet of the old faith;" who describe the discoveries in the sphere of natural science in particular as "the knell of the Mosaic cosmogony;" who tell us that the Biblical accounts, especially that of the creation of the earth and man, are "senseless" and a "lie."

If such an optimist should look a little more closely and descend into the inferior regions of the intellectual and doctrinal revolution, his discoveries would be no less striking, no less alarming. The freethinkers of the factory, of the workshop, have also their logic, and a brutal logic it is. The materialistic doctrines of our time have torn from their hearts the belief in a God, their faith in a heaven and a hell. "Very well," they cry out aloud, "we want our heaven here upon earth." "Do you want to make man happy?" says one of the materialistic chiefs; "go to the source of all happiness, of all pleasures—to the senses." "We do not want self-denial," says another; "all we want is enjoyment, nymph-dances, nectar and ambrosia! If the world had never believed in a God, how much happier would it be!" "They speak to us about heaven," says a third one, "about a future life; science has proved that there is no such thing, that it is an idle fancy, an illusion, and a lie. We do not want heaven; we do not want a future life. All we want is hell, with all the voluptuousness that precedes it." In the face of such doctrines it would be sinful and criminal to remain idle, to look on. It is the duty of all, but especially of the priest, to inquire into the remedy that may help to stem the tide of infidelity.

Unfortunately, our English Catholic literature furnishes us with very few of these remedies; upon questions of profane science we have hardly any works whereby we could instruct ourselves or others. And what is to be more regretted, perhaps, is the fact that Catholics, as a rule, have little appreciation of this kind of literature. Very few of our Catholic publishers are willing to risk the publishing of a scientific work, even if an author offers his work for nothing. Such works have so limited a sale that the publisher fears to lose money in getting out the book.

With regard to this point, non-Catholic literature is far ahead of us, both in America and Europe. Its publishers have no trouble whatsoever in selling their books. They get out edition after edition, and the public reads them greedily. Unfortunately, many of these works are far from being scientific, in the true sense of the word. The most of them are more or less saturated with modern rationalism, if not with materialism. While there are still authors who seek to defend Faith and Revelation, the number of scientific writers is very small whose works are free from meddling with religion, as scientific works ought to be, and many an author is so imbued with prejudice that he never fails, when the occasion offers, to aim side-blows at the Church and her doctrine. Certainly this is much to be regretted, for no Catholic can conscientiously read such books.

We have tried, as much as possible, to keep the present work free from the faults mentioned. The facts stated herein are not mere assertions, but are based upon empirical knowledge. The reader will find that we quote authors of different nationalities and creeds—Catholics and non-Catholics, rationalists and materialists. Our sole aim is to combat the errors and the false doctrines of the two latter schools, to defend Faith and Revelation against modern rationalism and materialism.

For this purpose we do not rely so much on our own arguments as on those of authors who can speak with professional authority. In fact, the details of the subjects developed in this book have been drawn from standard and, mostly, recent works; from authors who have studied and written on the subjects herein treated. If we have not always given proper credit, we beg the author's indulgence.

In conclusion, we beg leave to say that if this book prove a source wherein the Catholic, but especially my brother priests, can find something wherewith to stem the tide of infidelity, I shall feel happy; if it give rest to some souls or restore the peace of their heart, troubled by false science, I shall consider this as my greatest earthly reward for the many hours and years spent on this work.

THE AUTHOR.

CONTENTS.

INTRODUCTION, ... 3
PREFACE, ... 7
TABLE SHOWING THE SUCCESSIVE APPEARANCE OF LIVING THINGS IN SUCCESSIVE GEOLOGICAL PERIODS, . . . 23

CHAPTER I.

ORIGIN OF LIFE AND ITS DEVELOPMENT.

The teaching of Faith and Revelation on the origin of life.—Can science answer this question?—Spontaneous generation.—Its history.—There is no spontaneous generation.—Experiments by Pasteur and others.—Was the first living germ brought upon earth by an aerolite?—Monism.—Did the "moneron" of Professor Haeckel ever exist?—The famous Bathybius.—Experiment by Professor Moebius.—Huxley at the Congress of the British Association.—Observations of Milne-Edwards and John Murray.—Haeckel defends a lost cause.—Monism in flagrant contradiction to experimental method and scientific evidence.—Conclusion. 27

CHAPTER II.

DARWINISM AND MONISM.

Positive science and the development of life.—Successive and progressive Evolution.—The system of Darwin and Haeckel.—Darwin's book on the "Origin of Species."—Criticism of Darwinism.—Darwinism restricted within certain limits is not necessarily in conflict with the Bible.—However, it is an anti-Genesis in its tendencies.—Definition of

Genus, Species, and Variety.—Variability is limited.—It never touches what is essential in the species.—Embryology. — Comparative anatomy. — Rudimentary organs.—Atavism.—"Natural selection" does not explain what it pretends to explain.—Both geology and paleontology confirm the permanency of species.—Neither the flora nor the fauna have changed.—Acknowledgment of Huxley.—Hybridization.—Hybrids do not perpetuate themselves.—Species are unchangeable.—The breeder and the florist may produce varieties, but God alone can create species.—Account and criticism of Haeckelianism.—Comparison with Darwinism.—Monism incapable of establishing the filiation of species and the origin of man.—The truth victorious. 55

CHAPTER III.

ORIGIN OF MAN.

What is man?—Whence does he come?—Different methods followed to arrive at the knowledge of man.—Man's origin and nature.—Teachings of Faith.—Scientific certainties.—Harmony between Faith and true science.—Pseudo-scientific systems.—Man's immediate ancestor.—Professor Mivart's theory.—Can it be maintained?—Conclusion. . . . 111

CHAPTER IV.

MAN AND BEAST.

Is man merely a perfected animal?—Darwin's "struggle for life."—How does it correspond with the wisdom, order, and omnipotent power of God?—The assumed change of inferior species into superior ones, by the struggle for life, does not explain their origin.—It is impossible to explain the origin of man from an ape by the struggle for life.—How did the last monkey acquire the faculty of thinking, speaking, walking on two legs, etc.?—No trace of a higher development is found in any animal species.—If species changed in former times, why does this not happen in historical times?—Darwin's "struggle for life" is purely imaginary. 135

CHAPTER V.

MAN AND BEAST.—Continued.

The structure of man and that of the ape.—Two kinds of distinctive characters.—Physical characters.—The head.—The brain.—The foot and the hand.—Bodily development.—Rudimentary formations.—Embryological development.—Universality.—Senses.—Psychological characters.—Reason.—Liberty.—Language. — Results of language.—Genius.—The Tasmanians.—Sense of shame.—Conclusion. 150

CHAPTER VI.

MAN AND BEAST.—Concluded.

Instinct and intelligence.—Difference between the intelligence of man and that of the animal.—Objections and answers.—The animal has passions and affections like man.—Man is not the only animal that can speak.—Self-consciousness. — Individuality. — Abstraction. — Belief in God.—Sense of beauty.—Moral sentiment.—Destructive criticism of Darwinism by Professor Virchow. 182

CHAPTER VII.

THE STATE OF PRIMITIVE MAN.

Infidelity and the state of primitive man.—Man's primitive state was not a state of savagery.—His state is one of degradation and degeneration.—Savages in Europe during the last century.—The Fuegeans.—The Veddahs of Ceylon.—Andamans.—Hottentots.—Bushmen.—Shameless exaggerations.—A people in the mere natural state discovered nowhere.—The paradisiac state and original happiness mentioned in the myths of all the nations.—Civilization in Asia when barbarism prevailed over Europe.—Really progressive development possible only through Christianity.—Man could not rise by his own powers from the state of savagery or from that of a helpless child to higher perfection.—It was unworthy of God to place man in the world a savage or a harmless child.—Only materialists believe this. 206

CHAPTER VIII.

THE ANTIQUITY OF MAN AND BIBLICAL CHRONOLOGY.

The antiquity of man and modern chronologists.—Are their calculations reconcilable with the accounts given by Genesis?—The genealogical tables.—Three lessons.—Consequences resulting from Biblical chronology.—Impossibility of fixing the date of man's creation.—Mankind very probably over 8000 years old.—New difficulty.—Supposed omissions in the genealogical tables.—Proofs of this supposition.—Admitting such omissions, mankind dates back more than 8000 years.—The ten Chaldean antediluvian kings.—The value of the Chaldean sar.—Tabular view.—Theory of P. Bourdais.—Conclusion. 233

CHAPTER IX.

THE ANTIQUITY OF MAN AND GEOLOGY.

The claims of science.—Antiquity of man according to geology.—Alluvions.—Peat-moors.—Stalagmites.—Antiquity of man according to physical geography.—Antiquity of man as inferred from climatic changes.—These changes are exaggerated.—Valuable hints from ancient writers.—Antiquity of man as indicated by changes in the fauna.—Alleged prehistoric animals.—We cannot draw a line between the age of the mammoth and that of the reindeer.—Man contemporary with many extinct animals.—Tertiary and quaternary man.—The age of the acerotherium, halitherium, and elephas meridionalis.—Quaternary man.—What is tertiary and what is quaternary?—Powerful catastrophes.—Antiquity of man judged by the progress of his industry.—Five types of primitive man.—The ages of stone, bronze, and iron are not consecutive.—No necessity of extra-scientific hypotheses.—Conclusion. 255

CHAPTER X.

THE ANTIQUITY OF MAN AND THE CHRONOLOGIES OF INDIA, CHINA, EGYPT, AND CHALDEA.

PAGE

Chronology of India.—Its great chronological pretensions are not justified.—Chronology of China.—Facts against the credibility of the Chinese chronology.—Chronology of Egypt.—Increasing difficulties in face of new information from the monuments.—Chief authorities.—Contradictory accounts.—The monumental lists.—Chaldea and Assyria offer more precise chronological figures.—Canons or eponymous lists.—The account from the cylinder of Nabonidos.—If it is correct, even the chronology of the Septuagint is too short.—Conclusion. 330

CHAPTER XI.

THE UNITY OF THE HUMAN SPECIES.

Importance of the subject.—La Peyrère, the inventor of polygenism.—His system.—Criticism.—The Preadamites.—Historical side of the question.—The strongest polygenists are found in the United States.—The polygenists confound races with species.—Influence of climate and heredity.—The classification of the human species is not yet settled.—The influence of climate and heredity upon man's body is unquestionable.—Examples. 355

CHAPTER XII.

THE UNITY OF THE HUMAN SPECIES.—Continued.

Preliminary remarks.—Color of the skin.—Dr. Malpighi's discovery.—Causes of different pigments in races.—Character of the hair.—Form of the skull.—Custom of some peoples to give the skull a certain form.—No part of the human body is more subject to change than the skull.—Causes.—Examples.—Cardinal Wiseman and the first series of generations.—Measurements of the skull.—Relation between talent and cranial capacity.—Volume of the brain.—Relation between intelligence and weight of the brain.—Comparative study of the human skeleton.—Different languages no argument against monogenism.—Rapid increase of mankind.—Geographical objections against monogenism.—Origin of the Polynesians.—Of the Americans.—Conclusion. 376

CHAPTER XIII.

SPECIFIC UNITY OF MANKIND.

Preliminary remarks.—Anatomical organization of man.—Inner organs.—Man not confined to one kind of food.—Interracial fecundity.—Examples.—Man a cosmopolite.—All men endowed with intelligence and reason.—All are social beings.—All endued with speech and free-will.—All are religious.—American Indians.—Negroes.—Conclusion. . . . 423

CHAPTER XIV.

THE DELUGE AND THE TRADITIONS OF MANKIND.

Meaning of the word deluge.—The Biblical account of the Deluge of Noe confirmed by universal tradition.—Traditions in Asia.—Egypt.—Chaldea.—The account of Berosus.—Its striking resemblance with that of Genesis.—Is Ararat Armenia?—Poem of Izdhubar claimed to be anterior to Abraham.—Comparison.—Legends of the Deluge among other nations.—Account of the Arameans.—Hindoos.—Iranians.—Aryan races.—American traditions.—Conclusion. 436

CHAPTER XV.

GEOLOGY AND THE DELUGE.

Geology has no facts that are at variance with the tradition of the Deluge.—Geological facts.—Erratic rocks.—Bone caves.—Osseous breccias.—Tufaceous limestone.—Geology confirms the Deluge.—Universality of the Deluge.—Three systems.—First, absolute universality.—Second: restricted universality.—This system is not in contradiction with the Sacred Text.—Arguments in its favor.—Important question.

—Third: more restricted universality.—The Deluge did not cause the death of certain Mongolian and Ethiopian races.— Can such a view be maintained?—Conclusion. 460

CHAPTER XVI.

CAUSES OF THE DELUGE. ANSWERS TO OBJECTIONS.

Why natural science cannot bring serious objections against the Deluge.—Linguistic and zoölogical objections.— Size of the ark and number of animal species.—Positive experiments.—Re-peopling of the earth by animals.—Causes of the Deluge.—Torrential rains.—Invasion of seas.—Subterraneous fountains.—Upheavals and depressions.—Combination of the different systems.—Conclusion. 481

CHAPTER XVII.

MAN'S COMPONENT ELEMENTS. THE EXISTENCE OF THE SOUL.

Definitions. —Life.—Life-spring. — Soul.—Organism.— Vegetative, sensitive, and intellectual life.—The highest form of life, the soul, appears in man.—The essence of the principle of life.—What is an organism?—Without accepting a soul-principle, we cannot explain organism.—Nature of the human soul.—Teachings of Holy Scripture.—Three steps in the creation of man.—The distinction between the body and the soul and the intimate union of the two clearly expressed in Holy Scripture.—Hebrew psychology.—Man's soul is not a complex of his corporal organs.— Mental diseases prove nothing against the existence of the soul.—From corporal indications no certain conclusions can be drawn on the condition of the soul. 496

CHAPTER XVIII.

THE IMMORTALITY OF THE SOUL AND ITS FUTURE LIFE.

What will be the fate of man's soul after death?—Views of materialists.—Did the Hebrews believe in the immortality of the soul?—The Book of Wisdom.—Daniel.—Notions the Hebrews had of the soul's duration.—The Chaldeans also, the ancestors of the Hebrews, believed in the immortality of the soul.—Funeral customs and burial places.—Proof of the Babylonian belief in another life.—Descent of Ishtar into Hades.—Egyptian belief in another life.—Proofs of the Hebrew belief in the immortality of the soul.—Sheol of the souls.—Belief of other nations.—Etruscans.—Iranians.—Indians.—Greeks.—Romans.—Ancient Germans.—Other nations.—Immortality clearly revealed.—Future life and the idea of God.—What is death?—Nothing can be annihilated.—Only two things possible with regard to the human soul.—Life the fundamental law of creation.—Without a future life man would be the most lamentable of beings.—Man's destiny from the standpoint of Christian doctrine.—Three factors.—Virtue must be rewarded and vice punished.—This world does not sufficiently reward virtue or punish vice.—Conclusion. 524

TABLE

SHOWING THE SUCCESSIVE APPEARANCE OF LIVING THINGS IN SUCCESSIVE GEOLOGICAL PERIODS.

For the better understanding of certain facts treated in this book we give the following table, compiled from the second edition of the "Manual of Paleontology" of Prof. Alleyne Nicholson, one of the greatest living authorities on ancient life in Great Britain. It shows the succession of plant and animal life in the world as far as at present known. The oldest rocks are naturally placed last, the others in the order of superposition.

CENOZOIC, OR NEW LIFE.

POST TERTIARY (that is, from the Tertiary up to the present era).—Man, sheep and goats, cave lions, huge kangaroos.

PLIOCENE.—Swordfish, walrus, hares. The Tertiary vegetable world (including the rocks to the Eocene) was very much the same as it now is in hot and temperate climates.

MIOCENE.—Oxen, elephants, bears, land tortoises (one in India 20 feet long and 7 feet broad), sloths, whales, sperm-whales, dolphins, rhinoceros, tapirs, camels, seals. Beasts of prey abounded. Beavers. Lichens.

EOCENE.—Deer. Beasts of prey begin. Dogs, rats, mice, bats, lemurs, animals related to the horse, to the pig, to the tapir, to the whale. Snakes, crocodiles. Mammalia begin to abound. Sturgeon. Frogs and toads, newts and salamanders. Pillworts.

MESOZOIC, OR MIDDLE LIFE.

- CRETACEOUS (CHALK).—Fishes with bony skeletons begin to appear. True sharks, huge lizards (75 feet long in some cases), crocodiles (America), gigantic extinct reptiles of the lias continue. Toothed birds. No mammalia are found as yet in chalk. First certain appearance of trees like the trees of our own temperate regions—the oak, beech, fig, poplar, walnut, willow, alder, etc.; also palms.
- OOLITE, OR JURASSIC (of which lias are the lowest rocks).—Fourteen small mammals found in the upper beds of oolite. A single specimen (the earliest) of a bird. Turtles, lizards. In lias and oolite, gigantic extinct reptiles, the ichthyosaurus, plesiosaurus, megalosaurus, pterodactyle, and many others in great numbers. In lower oolite, oldest known crab. Three or four small marsupial quadrupeds.
- TRIASSIC.—Three or four mammals found in the uppermost beds. Footprints, "in great part or wholly the work of reptiles." Crocodiles. A great animal, half reptile, half bird. Marked change in the vegetation as compared with that of the permian and carboniferous periods. Abundance of cycads.

PALÆOZOIC, OR ANCIENT LIFE.

- PERMIAN.—First undoubted remains of a reptile, the protosaurus. Turtles and tortoises. Vegetable world nearly related to that of the coal measures: ferns, cone-bearing trees, etc.
- CARBONIFEROUS (coal, limestone, etc.).—Sea snails, scorpions, spiders, millipedes, winged insects. The limestone in many places, over large areas and for a thickness of many yards, is almost entirely made up of the remains of stone lilies (crinoidea). The footprints of the cheirotherium (handbeast). Vertebræ of a large creature believed to be allied to a frog. Vegetable world much the same as that of the Devo-

nian rocks: fungi, cone-bearing trees, flowering plants, etc., as in the Devonian, gigantic mosses and horsetails.

DEVONIAN.—Winged insects. This is the age of armored fishes, the scales ganoid or enamelled and hard as bone, forming a true armor. Plants abundant. Cone-bearing trees, ferns, tree ferns, club mosses, horsetails, trees allied to our hardwood trees. Representatives of almost all the great groups of plants which grow at present flourished in this age.

SILURIAN.—Starfish, sea-urchins, creatures allied to sharks, stone lilies, tribolites. Bivalve shells related to oysters, cockles, etc., abound.

LOWER SILURIAN.—Worm-like creatures, cuttlefish, creatures allied to nautilus, corals, zoophites, stone lilies. Seaweeds, ferns, horsetails, club mosses, a cone-bearing tree (allied to the pines), trees allied to the conebearers and to cycads.

CAMBRIAN.—Stone lilies, bivalve shells, shells like whelks, limpets, etc. Crustaceans of a low type allied to shrimps. Possibly seaweeds.

HURONIAN.—

LAURENTIAN.—Eozoon. It is, however, greatly questioned whether this is an organism.

CHRISTIAN ANTHROPOLOGY.

CHAPTER I.

ORIGIN OF LIFE AND ITS DEVELOPMENT.

The teaching of Faith and Revelation on the origin of life.—Can science answer this question?—Spontaneous generation.—Its history.—There is no spontaneous generation.—Experiments by Pasteur and others.—Was the first living germ brought upon earth by an aerolite?—Monism.—Did the "Moneron" of Professor Haeckel ever exist?—The famous Bathybius.—Experiment by Professor Moebius.—Huxley at the Congress of the British Association.—Observations of Milne-Edwards and John Murray.—Haeckel defends a lost cause.—Monism in flagrant contradiction to experimental method and scientific evidence.—Conclusion.

THE origin of life and its development is a subject of vital interest to all. Still if questioned: What is life in itself? we must confess that we know no more about it than we know of matter in itself. However, we know something of the properties of matter, and also know something about the laws of life and its development. These questions have been frequently discussed in our day; their importance is so apparent that we shall devote the present and the following chapter to them, in order to show the wild, reckless, and fallacious theories of some modern scientists, who make use of every primordial organism, to escape acknowledging God as the Origin and Creator of all life.

1. FAITH AND THE ORIGIN OF LIFE.—What are the teachings of Faith with regard to the origin of life? The first chapter of Genesis tells us that life had a beginning, that God created the vegetable world and the different kinds of animals, and, lastly, that He created a man and a woman, in a manner different from that in which He created other beings or things. In the account of the Deluge we are told that all men on earth were destroyed except Noe and his family, and that all mankind is descended from the three sons of Noe. Thus the origin, the first cause of life, is the same as the origin and first cause of all things. If we are asked: Is life due to immediate creation—to a special intervention of God, or is it the result of an initial state—an effect of laws primitively established, developed under favorable circumstances, determined by the Creator? we answer: Faith does not prescribe, nor the Bible teach anything in regard to this. The dogma of creation is simple, clear, and comprehensive; but it leaves a vast field open to human investigation and to the researches of biology, geology, and paleontology.

2. SCIENCE AND THE ORIGIN OF LIFE.—Can science give us unquestioned information on the origin of life? Can it offer definite teachings? Yes, it knows two things with certainty; first, life did not always exist on earth, it had a beginning; secondly, it is a law, proved by experiment, that every living being comes from a being endowed with life. Geology and paleontology prove a condition of the earth when life did not and could not exist. They affirm with certitude that there has been an azoic period—that there is a primitive azoic, terrestrial crust.

The passage from death to life, from the inorganic to the organic on our globe, has a great scientific and doctrinal significance. It is the battle-field of materialism. It was so simple to affirm the eternity of matter, of force, of movement. But things changed greatly when materialists were brought face to face with the sensible, undeniable facts of observation and experiment. Then the difficulties of materialism became quite grave, for after the formidable problem of the origin of atoms came the no less formidable problem of the origin of life. For a second time atheistic monism found itself caught in its own trap; it must either acknowledge creative intervention, or discover an acceptable theory—a truly scientific theory—to replace it.

The scientists who are not afraid to acknowledge their inability to explain the origin of life on the globe, are not only by far the most numerous, but also those best authorized to speak on this subject. However, we will quote only from the masters of rationalistic science—the fathers of the materialistic school.

Tyndall, the orator of Belfast, is astonished, and regrets that Darwin and Spencer have slipped even slightly on the question of life. Nevertheless, the question has to be put, he adds; we expect a solution, and here it is: When we come to the bottom facts, life disengages itself from the material, all-powerful elements in the abyss of the past by some impenetrably mysterious action. Of course Tyndall does not slip "slightly" at all; his solution is only a little more difficult, but not any clearer, when he appeals to an impenetrable mystery.

"Science," says Huxley, "has no means to form an opinion on the commencement of life; we can only make conjectures, without any scientific character." Du Bois-Reymond, one of the foremost of the materialists in Germany, places the origin of life among the seven riddles which seem to defy experimental science. Virchow, answering Haeckel at the Congress of Naturalists, resumes the debate thus: "According to my opinion, we should simply acknowledge that in reality we know nothing on the question of the connection between the organic world and the inorganic. We cannot represent a hypothesis as a certainty, a problem as an established theory."[1] Finally Darwin has the courage to tell us "that there is a certain grandeur in considering life with all its properties, as it has been given at its beginning by the Creator."

3. SYSTEMS ON THE ORIGIN OF LIFE.—The diverse systems imagined to explain the appearance of life upon earth may be reduced to *spontaneous generation*, or *heterogeny*,[2] by which is meant the production of an organic individual without parents (Haeckel); that is, a brute body as antecedent, and a being endowed with life as consequent. This question has been studied from very different points of view. Some seek the solution of a purely scientific fact. Does spontaneous life exist in nature? An affirmative answer to this question does not of necessity exclude the idea of God, the idea of a primitive cause; the apparition of an organic being without parent, under favorable circumstances, might result from the special actions of the creative power. Faith and Christian philosophy are unconcerned in such an investigation, whatever the solution may be.

Others—the monists—set up a double theory, scientific and philosophical. They attempt to explain the origin of life without a God, through the mechanical,

---

[1] Cf. "Revue Scientifique," Dec. 8, 1887.

[2] The opposite of heterogeny is homogeny. The expression heterogeny is inexact; some prefer the word agenesy, or abiogenesis. The formula "spontaneous generation" is equally improper; it would be more correct to say: spontaneous production of life or of organized matter.

inherent forces of matter only. For them, the living atom is a spontaneous product or, rather, a necessary evolution of eternal matter. They deny every supernatural intervention of God, proximate or remote; they teach the "natural creation" of living beings.

These are two very different theses, which must be explained and discussed separately. Let us examine first the scientific problem. Is it possible to establish by observation or experiment the appearance of a living being not coming from a being already endowed with life? Positive and rationalist scientists answer: No. Only the latter make a reservation, pretending that what has not been established yet, may be established hereafter. We shall very soon learn the value of this pretension.

4. SPONTANEOUS GENERATION.—The history of the theory of spontaneous generation is very ancient and interesting. In the Biblical account of creation we read only that the origin of the vegetable and the animal world must be referred to the creative activity of God, and that God has taken measures for the reproduction and preservation of the various species of plants and animals. We are not told how the first organic beings originated, and still less how thenceforth the separate individuals should come into existence, whether by means of procreation from eggs and germs, or by other means also. The author of Genesis had no reason for entering into such scientific details.

5. HISTORY OF THE HYPOTHESIS OF SPONTANEOUS GENERATION.—The history of the errors taught in connection with the so-called doctrine of spontaneous generation is very well fitted to show us to what illusions the human mind is liable. Aristotle explains the origin of organized beings by three modes of generation: they are viviparous, that is, produce young alive and completely

formed; they are oviparous, or produce eggs from which come the young; and they result from spontaneous generation, that is, generation without parents. The description of the spontaneous generation of bees, by Virgil, in the Fourth Book of the Georgics, is well known. The fathers of the Church, and also the scholastics, believed in the spontaneous generation of a number of animals, and this belief was general up to a comparatively recent period.

The fathers and scholastics did not, however, derive this theory from the Bible; but as it was not opposed to the Bible, they took it quite naturally from ancient scientific writers, especially from Aristotle. We know that they asserted that not only midges, fleas, lice, and other vermin sprang simply from the earth, but also frogs, serpents, and mice; the eel, also, in which Aristotle could find no ovary, was supposed to have originated from slime. Even in the seventeenth century the learned Jesuit Athanasius Kircher gives regular recipes for bringing animals into existence: "Take as many serpents as you like, dry them, cut them into small pieces, bury these in damp earth, water them freely with rain-water, and leave the rest to the spring sun. After eight days the whole will turn into little worms, which, if fed with milk and earth, will at length become perfect serpents, and by procreation will multiply *ad infinitum*." Van Helmont indicated the proceedings necessary to produce frogs, leeches, scorpions, and mice. P. Buonanni (1638–1725) believed that certain woods by rotting in the sea would produce worms from which butterflies would be engendered, which would finish by transforming themselves into birds. Sebastian Munster (1489–1552) stated that in Scotland trees are found whose fruit, wrapped in the leaves, when it falls into the water at a seasonable time becomes a bird, called "the bird of the tree." Aldrovandi (1522-1605) also considered sea-ducks the products of certain trees.¹

6. SPONTANEOUS GENERATION A DREADFUL WEAPON.—Certainly, this doctrine of spontaneous generation furnishes a dreadful weapon to the materialists. Combined with "transformism," another doctrine of the materialistic school, it enables them—so they pretend, at least —to explain the present state of the organic world, without the intervention of the Creator. Indeed, if beings, however small they may be, arise spontaneously; if these beings can develop and produce, in the course of time, various and more complicated forms through a series of successive transformations, as is generally maintained nowadays, then the mystery which hangs over contemporary fauna and flora disappears, without having recourse to an exterior power.

Undoubtedly, there would yet remain more than one mystery to be solved. We might ask, for instance, whether the wonderful laws which govern nature do not necessarily presuppose a legislator? But materialism and atheism, which do not stop at such little difficulties, would not fail to trumpet forth their victory.

7. SPONTANEOUS GENERATION CONDEMNED BY EXPERIMENTAL SCIENCE.—Unfortunately for these doctrines, the assertion that matter organizes itself so as to produce life has been disproved in the progress of science. While transformism, pretty well shaken by recent inquiries and impartial observation, still retains a certain probability, which misleads the imaginations of many, spontaneous generation is formally and judicially condemned by experiment and rejected by the immense majority of savants, as contrary to the most positive results of observation.

¹ F. Hement, "L'Origine des Êtres Vivants," 1882, pp. 57-58; F. Hoppe-Seiler," Ueber die Entstehung der Lebenskräfte," pp. 15-20.

Its history is most interesting, for it shows how difficult it is to uproot the false doctrines which spring from incomplete science and conform to popular prejudice. When it had been proved that the relatively superior animals in the zoölogical series, for example, rats, fishes, and frogs, spring from parents similar to themselves by sexual generation, the adherents of spontaneous generation, obliged to abandon this ground, fell back upon another, less known at the time. They pretended that insects, at least, formed an exception to the general rule. They pointed to the bees which, though sexless, produce new swarms every year; the fleas, whose numberless families invade in a few days the young stalks of our rosebushes, the so-called entozoa, intestinal worms which appear without apparent cause in putrified meat, and those which develop in the fruit of our orchards and in the galls of our oaks without any one being for a long time able to give a reason for their appearance. But then came the naturalists of the seventeenth and eighteenth centuries: the Dutch Swammerdam, the Swiss Bonnet, the Italians Redi and Vallisnieri, whose ingenious observations obliged the adherents of spontaneous generation to retreat for a second time.

8. THE EXPERIMENTS OF BONNET, REDI, AND VALLISNIERI.—Bonnet proved that young bees all come from the eggs laid by a single individual, till then improperly called King, and since known by the name of Queen. Redi had no trouble in establishing that the worms which fill putrified meat owe their origin to eggs laid by flies, and that the worms themselves are nothing else than the larvæ of future flies. Vallisnieri discovered that the insects which infest our apples and pears are larvæ of a nocturnal butterfly, and result from the development of an egg introduced into the incipient fruit at the time of the blooming.

Bonnet, who had made the flea his special study, in his turn showed that this insect owed its astonishing fecundity, not to spontaneous generation, but to a peculiar mode of reproduction; to the strange fact that, during the season of heat, the flea gives birth to females only, all of which have the property of producing new females without previous sexual union. It has been calculated that, owing to this mode of reproduction, known under the name of *Parthenogenesis*, milliards of fleas can arise from one single individual in the course of one single season. But this wonderful fecundity, which each generation communicates to the following, disappears with the return of the cold in fall. The animal, heretofore viviparous, now becomes oviparous, and from its eggs come males and females, which, by their union at the return of the warm season, will give birth to an almost unlimited series of generations exclusively female.

Forced to acknowledge their error in the field of entomology, the adherents of spontaneous generation, or heterogeny, retreated upon the domain of the infinitely small animalcules. They pretended that infusoria and other microscopic animals can spring spontaneously, if not from inorganic matter, at least from organic elements which belonged to living beings.

In defence of this argument they fell back on the unknown. On account of the imperfect means of investigation, it could not be shown that reproduction does not take place in this manner. However, the laws of analogy pointed rather to the opposite opinion. Until proof to the contrary was furnished, we had the right to believe that the mode of reproduction established for the other beings of the zoölogical series applies equally to those inferior beings which can not be directly observed.

9. THE EXPERIMENTS OF SPALLANZANI AND PASTEUR.—The opinion of the heterogenists would have been legit-

imate, had it been based upon correct facts. But, instead of being favorable to this opinion, observation has always opposed it. The experiments made since the last century by Spallanzani went far to prove that infusoria develop in a liquid only as long as this liquid is in communication with the air; from which it is natural to conclude that they are the product of germs·contained in the atmosphere.

However, these first experiments were not absolutely conclusive. While Spallanzani succeeded in hindering the appearance of infusoria of a superior order, he failed, in spite of all his precautions, to check the appearance of animalcules of extreme smallness. It needed the labors of Pasteur to solve the question in a definite manner.

The experiments of this famous savant began in the year 1858. Provoked in some way by two zoölogists, Professors Pouchet and Jolly, the one at Rouen, the other at Toulouse, Pasteur demonstrated to his colleagues of the Academy of Sciences that no organized being, however small, developed in a liquid when the germs existing in neighboring bodies are completely shut out. For this purpose it was sufficient to raise the temperature of the liquid to 100° R. and to cork up the bottle which contains it with gun-cotton or amianthus. The latter substance, while permitting the outside air to penetrate during the cooling, will keep back solid particles and, with them, the germs of living beings. Under these conditions, if the experiment is performed with some skill, not only no animalcules will develop in the liquid, but this liquid, though suitable for fermentation, will never change.

Here is Huxley's description of some of Pasteur's experiments:

"Pasteur fixed in the window of his room a glass tube,

in the centre of which he had placed a ball of gun-cotton. . . . One end of the glass tube was, of course, open to the external air, and at the other end of it he placed an aspirator, a contrivance for causing a current of the external air to pass through the tube. He kept this apparatus going for four-and-twenty hours, and the result was that a very fine dust was gradually deposited at the bottom of it. That dust, on being transferred to a stage of a microscope, was found to contain an enormous number of starch grains. . . . But besides these, Pasteur found also an immense number of other organic substances, such as spores or fungi, which had been floating about in the air, and had got caged in this way. Pasteur also took one of these vessels of infusion, which had been kept eighteen months without the least appearance of life, and, by a most ingenious contrivance, he managed to break it open and introduce such a ball of gun-cotton, without allowing the infusion or the cotton ball to come into contact with any air but that which had been subjected to red heat; and in twenty-four hours he had the satisfaction of finding all the indications of what had been hitherto called spontaneous generation. . . . He then took some decaying animal or vegetable substance . . . and filled a vessel having a long tubular neck with it. He then boiled the liquid, and bent that long neck into an S shape, or zig-zag, leaving it open at the end. The infusion then gave no trace of any appearance of spontaneous generation, however long it might be left, as all the germs in the air were deposited in the beginning of the bent neck. He then cut the tube close to the vessel, and allowed the ordinary air to have free and direct access; and the result of that was the appearance of organisms in it, as soon as the infusion had been allowed to stand long enough to allow of the growth of those it received from the air, which was about forty-eight hours. The result of Pasteur's experiments proved, therefore, in the most conclusive manner, that all the appearances of spontaneous generation arose from nothing more than from the deposition of the germs of organisms which were constantly floating in the air. To this conclusion, however, the objection was made that if that were the cause, then the air would contain such an enormous number of these germs that it would be a continual fog. But Pasteur replied that they are not there in anything like the number we might suppose, and that an exaggerated view has been held on the subject; he showed that the chances of animal or vegetable life appearing in infusions depend entirely on the conditions under which they are exposed. If they are exposed to the ordinary atmosphere around us, why, of course you may find organisms appearing early. But, on the other hand, if they are exposed to air from a great height, or from some very quiet cellar, you will often not find a single trace of life."[1]

10. DEATH-BLOW TO SPONTANEOUS GENERATION.— Many scientific men think that the doctrine of spontaneous generation of infusoria received its death-blow, as Huxley says, by these experiments of Pasteur. This, however, is going too far. No doubt, most of the leading savants of the present age declare themselves decidedly against the theory of spontaneous generation,[2] and one of the defenders of this theory admits that those who agree with him form only a small and unimportant party, and that "almost all eminent men of science" are opposed to it.

---

[1] Huxley, "On Our Knowledge of the Phenomena of Organic Nature," London, 1863, pp. 78 *seq.*

[2] Ehrenberg, R. Wagner, J. Müller, Liebig, Brown, Virchow, Schleiden, Unger, Herm, Hoffmann, F. Cohn, and others. In France, Flourens, M. Edwards, Pouchet, N. Jolly, Ch. Musset, C. Bernard, Dumas, and others.

11. ADHERENTS OF SPONTANEOUS GENERATION FOUND ONLY IN THE CAMP OF MATERIALISM.—If we still find more or less avowed sympathizers with the doctrine of spontaneous generation in the camp of contemporary materialists, this must not surprise us. To deny spontaneous generation means to confess and confirm the fact of original creation, and we can easily understand that for many modern scientists, entirely impregnated with a materialistic spirit and infatuated with its progress, this is a very bitter pill to swallow. Creation, they say, is a miracle, and, *a priori*, they declare the miracle impossible. It is useless to draw the conclusion.

Materialism does not understand that this kind of reasoning rests on a twofold error. In the first place, we may ask why a miracle should be impossible, seeing that He who laid down the laws of nature has also the power to restrict them, when and wherever He pleases. In the second place, it is false to assert that the creation of the first living being was a miracle properly speaking, because this creation was not against any law. The law which to-day governs the development of life commenced to exist only with the living being itself. Surely there could be no exception to a law that did not exist.

On the other hand, it would be a miracle were matter to organize itself, as the heterogenists wish us to believe, and bring forth beings without parents, for it is evident that would be contrary to the mode of reproduction established in the whole organic kingdom, wherever it has been possible to study it.

12. WHAT THE HETEROGENISTS CLAIM IN OUR DAYS.—From what we have said, the most prejudiced ought to acknowledge that the hypothesis of spontaneous generation has lost all probability and every claim to a scientific character since the famous experiments of Pasteur. Without admitting this absolutely,

most biologists no longer contend that truly spontaneous generation, that is, the production of an organized being from purely inorganic matter, is a matter of course. All they pretend in our days—and this is the meaning they attribute to the word heterogeny—is, that organisms of an inferior order, for instance, the so-called fungi or ferment cells, can arise from organic matter in a putrified state. This doctrine, in the eyes of the advocates of spontaneous generation, has not the value of the preceding one, because it does not explain the origin of life. If an organism can arise only from the putrified elements of a prior organism, the origin of life remains unexplained. How did the first organism appear?

To solve this really insurmountable difficulty, we are told that the first living germ was brought upon earth by an aerolite, that is, one of those small celestial bodies which circulate in space, and finally enter the sphere of attraction of our planet and fall on its surface. In fact, some savants claim to have recognized some mould on an aerolite, and conclude that this mould could only spring from the putrification of organic substances, and that this putrification supposes ferments;[1] that is, mono-cellular organisms. But this discovery, aside from being questionable, has not the importance attached to it, for even if mould were recognized on the aerolite in question, there was not found on it the least cell, the least living organism. Were there organisms in the aerolites, they, undoubtedly, would be destroyed either by the cold of space, or by the intense heat which the passage of these bodies through the atmosphere produces. It has been observed, indeed, that aerolites, im-

[1] Ferment or yeast consists of very small vegetable cells, which, when they are placed in a liquid exposed to the action of the air, multiply by budding and produce fermentation.

mediately after falling upon earth, were burning hot on their exterior surface, whilst their interior was below the freezing point. After all, if it could be proved that life was brought upon the earth by a celestial body, which seems impossible, the problem of life's origin would be shifted, but not solved. We could always ask: How did it first appear on the aerolite? Now, if spontaneous generation does not take place upon our globe, and we trust that we have proved sufficiently that it does not, there is nothing that authorizes us to assume that it takes place elsewhere.

The heterogenists driven to the wall, a certain number of naturalists of the materialistic school, to whom the idea of a Creator is revolting, and who, nevertheless, are obliged to acknowledge the improbability of the spontaneous generation of an organized being, claim that mineral matter could at least under favorable circumstances associate its elements in such a manner as to constitute one of those partly living substances which want nothing but organization in order to be endowed with real life, of which substances liquid albuminoid protoplasm, contained in vegetable cells, is a well-known example. This brings us to the theory of monism.

13. MONISM.—We observed before that the monists set up a double claim with regard to the origin of life: a scientific and a philosophical one. They attempt to explain life without a God. Their system is known under the name of monism (from the Greek "*monos*," sole, unique), and the aim of this theory is to reduce everything which exists to a unity; that is, to the material *atom*.

14. MONISM AN IMPROVEMENT ON DARWINISM.—Monism at bottom is merely a special form of materialism, an improvement on the doctrine of evolution. Darwin, who made transformism a popular theory, as we shall

see in our next chapter, never touched upon the question of how the first living thing came into being. Professor Haeckel, of Jena, thought that materialism had gained nothing, as long as we may believe in the creation of a single being, however small. Consequently, he made an attempt to solve the problem of the origin of life.

In reality, Haeckel's system does not contain any new ideas. Like all materialists, he supposes that matter, as well as the laws which govern its transformations, is eternal. In regard to life, he holds that its beginnings were the most humble we can imagine. On a certain day, at the end of the geological period, undoubtedly during the Laurentian epoch, some atoms of azote, carbon, oxygen, and hydrogen agglomerated together under exceptionally favorable circumstances, so that they constituted the first and most simple of organisms—the moneron.

15. WHAT THE MONERA ARE.—These monera, imaginary beings, which nobody, not excepting Haeckel, has ever seen, are organic beings of the most simple kind, so the German Professor tells us. Their entire body, which during life is at most as large as a pin's head, is nothing more than a shapeless, mobile lump of jelly (protoplasm). The monera cannot "exactly be called either plants or animals;" "strictly speaking, they do not deserve the name of organism at all,"[1] for they are not composed of organs, but consist entirely of shapeless, simple, homogeneous protoplasm. They propagate themselves by subdivision. When one of these little spheroids has attained a certain size by the assimilation of foreign albuminous matter, it falls into two or more pieces, which again, by simple growth, become like the parent body.

[1] Haeckel, "Natürliche Schöpfungsgeschichte," pp. 164. 305.

Although natural history is an experimental science, although it has no right to affirm anything except what it has verified by experiment, the Jena Professor nevertheless affirms the occurrence of spontaneous generation in nature in spite of the contrary testimony of experiment.

16. HAECKEL AND THE FIRST MONERA.—The first appearance of the monera is to Haeckel the proof of the reality of spontaneous generation. But the moneron, this living organism without form and without organs, produced only by the chemical combination of inorganic elements—this moneron is the product of Haeckel's imagination; it does not exist now, and never has existed. The most simple organisms known are not without form and structure; they have an organization sufficiently complicated; for instance, the *plasmas* of *myxomycetes*, as appears from the inquiries of Bary, Hofmeister, and other naturalists. Even the protoplasm of the highest cells present a distinct differentiation of solid and liquid in the form of ramifications of a mucous fluid, of small voids, etc. The *amœbæ*, which, so Haeckel tells us, are monera, possess not only a nucleus and a contractive vesicle, but produce in this nucleus small germinal grains, and in certain capsules elementary tissues, which probably indicate sexual difference.[1] Even the most simple of the monera, the *Protamœba primitiva*, which Haeckel describes as homogeneous and without nucleus—although the existence of amœbæ without nucleus is denied by other zoölogists—the *Protamœba primitiva*, to judge it by the drawing of Haeckel, is not homogeneous; it is a granulous substance, which thickens in the centre.[2]

[1] Gruf, "Verhandl. des Naturhistorischen Vereins des Rheinlands," vol. xxvii., p. 200.
[2] A. Wiegand, "Der Darwinismus," vol. ii., p. 456.

17. THE STORY OF THE BATHYBIUS.—It is true, Haeckel quotes the Bathybius as a moneron produced by spontaneous generation. The Bathybius plays an important role in the history of monism, and we must dwell on it for a few moments. Haeckel calls it "the most remarkable perhaps of all the monera." The famous English zoölogist, Huxley, discovered it in 1868, and named it Bathybius Haeckelii, in honor of the German transformist. Bathybius signifies "which lives in great depths," because this "protoplasm" was found in the ocean, at depths of 12,000 to 24,000 feet.

"There, among an innumerable multitude of polythalamias and radiolites, which people the fine calcareous mud of these abysses, the Bathybiuses exist in immense quantities. They are sometimes roundish, formless lumps of jelly, sometimes a gelatinous network covering fragments of stone and other objects. Their body, like that of the other monera, consists purely and simply of a plasma, without structure or protoplasm; that is, of one of those carbon albuminoid compositions which, through infinite modifications, form the essential and constant substratum of the phenomena of life in all organisms. . . . Lately some one has contested the existence of the Bathybius, but no one has proved that it does not exist." [1]

Haeckel here defends a lost cause. The Bathybius, "one of the chief supports of the modern theory of evo-

---

[1] Haeckel, "Natürliche Schöpfungsgeschichte," pp. 165, 166. Haeckel here reproduces what he had said in the first editions of his book, except the last phrase, which he added, and the interesting phrase which follows, that he suppressed: "Often small calcareous corpuscles, discoidals, cyclops, etc., englobed in these masses of mucosity (of the Bathybii), are very probably products of excretion." "Histoire de la Création," by Letourneau, p. 165.

lution,"[1] does not really exist; it has never existed. Huxley himself, who baptized it and gave it a fictitious existence, no longer believes in its reality. Here we quote his own words: "I fear the thing to which I gave that name is little more than sulphate of lime precipitated in a flocculent state from the sea-water through the strong alcohol in which the specimens of the deep sea soundings which I examined were preserved."[2] Du Bois-Reymond says, "Since then the scientific existence of the Bathybius Haeckelii has become as precarious as that of its supposed fossil model *Eozoon Canadense*."[3] The Bathybius exists only in the dark depths of scientific superstition.[4]

18. EXPERIMENTS OF MOEBIUS.—At the Congress of German Naturalists, held at Hamburg in 1876, Professor Moebius, of Kiel, delivered a discourse on the marine fauna and the expedition of the "Challenger," which he summed up as follows: "On the plains,—submarine plains, from 12,000 to 13,000 feet in depth—it was asserted, was spread the mysterious *Urschleim*, the Bathybius. . . . Unfortunately, the fates have proved the contrary. The Bathybius, which harmonizes so well with the modern ideas of the origin of life, proved to be only an artificial product, a precipitate of gypsum, dissolved in sea-water by the alcohol in which the preparation was preserved. Whenever any one has examined fresh preparations on board, it has been impossible to discover the least trace of the Bathybius."

There was a moment of profound astonishment in the

[1] Haeckel, "Le Règne des Protistes," p. 77. Haeckel, in this work (pp. 77, 78), relates at length the history of the Bathybius.
[2] Huxley, "Nature," 19th Aug., 1875.
[3] "Ueber die Grenzen des Naturkennens."
[4] Cf. Zittel, "Die Kreide, p. 27.

audience when Moebius, using such a simple recipe, made the Bathybius appear in a glass filled with seawater, by adding thereto a certain quantity of alcohol."

19. OBSERVATIONS MADE BY MILNE-EDWARDS.—Milne-Edwards, summing up the researches made on board the "Traveller," where, he was promised, nothing should be neglected in order to find and study the Bathybius, says: " . . . Often in the middle of the vessel we have seen this enigmatical substance; we submitted it to microscopic examination, and we came to the belief that the thing does not deserve the honor which has been bestowed upon it, and the eloquent pages which have been consecrated to it. The Bathybius is nothing but a mass of mucosities which the sponges and certain zoöphytes allow to escape on account of contact with fishing instruments. The Bathybius, which has taken up too much of the attention of the world of science, should therefore descend from his pedestal and return to his non-existence in the depths of the sea."[2]

And, nevertheless, we still meet transformists who obstinately defend this thing—amorphous mucus, soft jelly, precipitate of gypsum or of diluted lime—transformed by Haeckel into the main support of the modern theory of evolution.

20. STATEMENT OF JOHN MURRAY.—John Murray, a member of the "Challenger" expedition, says: "I have known an eminent naturalist who, passing his fingers inside the vessel, said it was alive with protoplasm, and that it was the Bathybius which gave to his fingers its glutinous and greasy sensation. . . . I have seen several savants losing their temper in my presence when I told them that a mistake had been

---

[1] Quoted in Haeckel, "Le Règne des Protistes," p. 93.
[2] "Séance de l'Institut," Oct. 15, 1882.

committed with regard to this subject, and that Huxley, Haeckel, and others had been led into error. And these are the men who reject, *a priori*, every metaphysical or religious belief as anti-scientific."

To finish with the Bathybius, let us add that this attempt of monism is the more unfortunate because, even if we admit the existence of "this most remarkable of the monera, endowed with all the vital properties—the main support of the modern theory of evolution," it would yet remain to be proved that it is the product of spontaneous generation. That question remains unanswered after, as well as before, the Bathybius.

21. LAST ARGUMENT OF MONISM.—The last argument of monism, the most handy, if not the most logical, is this: If inorganic matter cannot organize itself, owing to a combination of purely natural circumstances, we are obliged to have recourse to the supernatural, to the miracle, to God. Now, this is anti-scientific; this is impossible. The most certain results of experiment are counted for nothing, if they suggest the existence of God. The French translator of Haeckel, M. Soury, in one of his comments, frankly says: "According to many others, for they are unanimous on this point, there exists no other alternative to explain the origin of life. He who does not believe in spontaneous generation, or rather secular evolution of inorganic matter, must admit a miracle. This is a necessary hypothesis, which cannot be overthrown, either by arguments *a priori*, or by the experiments of the laboratory."[1] That is, it is superior to evidence, to philosophic reasoning, and to positive science. After all, "the limits of experiment are not those of nature; one must see scientific horizons beyond them; that which has not yet been established may be established at some future day." But what will

[1] Soury, Preface to "Preuves du Transformisme de Haeckel."

then become of the principle of induction, which alone allows us to generalize, to ascend to the laws of nature? What will become of science when possible facts are set up in opposition to real facts, to facts that have been established?

22. ONLY ONE CHOICE LEFT.—This necessity to choose between experimental, metaphysical, and religious certainty on the one hand, and the indispensable postulate of monism on the other, was solemnly proclaimed in presence of Haeckel himself, by his master, a man little suspected of mystical tendencies—Virchow: "Not a single positive fact is known which proves that an inorganic mass has transformed itself into an organic mass, and, nevertheless, if I do not wish to believe in a special Creator, I must have recourse to spontaneous generation; the matter is evident, *tertium non datur*. When we have once said, 'I do not admit creation, and I want an explanation of the origin of life,' we set up a first thesis; but whether we wish or not, we must come to the second: *Ergo*, I admit spontaneous generation. But we have no proof thereof; nobody has seen the production of organic matter; it is not the theologians, it is the savants who reject it. . . . If we have to choose between spontaneous generation and creation, to speak frankly, we savants (materialists) have a little preference for spontaneous generation. Ah! if only some demonstration would come to light. . . . But I think we have yet time to wait. . . . With the Bathybius disappeared our greatest hope of a demonstration."[1]

23. HAECKEL DOES NOT GIVE UP YET.—However, Haeckel does not wish to give up his pet theory. He reminds us that chemists have recently succeeded in doing what was asserted fifty years ago to be impossible: that is, in producing carbon compounds, or so-called

[1] "Revue Scientifique," Dec. 8, 1877.

"organic" substances, as urea, alcohol, acetic acid, and so on, from inorganic substances. "Therefore," he says, "there is every probability that sooner or later we shall succeed in producing artificially the protoid compounds or protoplasm itself. We may therefore assume that in nature also there may be formed from inorganic substances first some simpler carbon compounds, and from these protoplasm capable of life. If this exists, it only needs to individualize itself in the same way as the mother liquor of crystals individualizes itself, and we have the moneron."

But Haeckel himself admits that this must remain a pure hypothesis so long as it is not directly observed or repeated by experiments.[1] He adds, "that the process of the spontaneous generation of monera would in any case be very difficult to observe, and could hardly be verified with undoubted certainty, even if it still happened daily and hourly." But we answer, it cannot be difficult to repeat the process by means of experiment, if it be as simple as Haeckel makes it. "The special conditions of existence," under which conditions the Bathybius originates, according to Haeckel, may be artificially produced; but yet he has not responded to the challenge to fabricate a Bathybius.[2] Haeckel, if he studies carefully the experiments of Pasteur and Tyndall, will have to admit that the origin of monera by spontaneous generation is impossible.

Haeckel's theory that albuminous protoplasm can individualize itself into monera in the same way as the mother liquor of crystals individualizes itself in crystallization, is rather venturesome. Organic cells and crystals are essentially different, inasmuch as "the cell not

[1] "Natürliche Schöpfungsgeschichte," p. 309; cf. "Anthropologie," p. 377.
[2] "Ausland," 1870, 1091.

only grows from without, but primarily from within; it does not lose its activity like the crystal at the moment of its formation, but creates from within itself new forms like itself; and alike in its dimensions, its extent, and its duration in time, it is limited by its own individual formative and living impulse."[1] K. E. Baer says: "Organic bodies are not changeable, but they are the only things that change themselves. The crystal and the rock are, no doubt, also exposed to final destruction, but the destruction does not come from within; damp, heat, chemical and physical forces in general help to wear them away. Were they placed in an isolated spot in the universe, they would last forever; for what is lifeless cannot die—it is only destroyed by the outside world. On the other hand, organic bodies destroy themselves; they are not only subject to constant change, but their whole development is a progress towards death."[2]

After what has been said, we may surely conclude that recent researches have shown that the theory of spontaneous generation is inadmissible even in the case of the most simple and smallest organic being; or, in other words, it is scientifically proved that no organic being comes into existence by spontaneous generation. But may we not still assume that spontaneous generation did occur in the early periods of the world's history?

24. DID SPONTANEOUS GENERATION OCCUR IN EARLY PERIODS?—"Nowadays," says Burmeister, "when plenty of beings capable of reproduction exist everywhere, there is no need that new ones should form themselves from dead matter; and perhaps the material from which

[1] Huber, "Die Lehre Darwins," p. 14; Michaelis, "Haeckogonie," p. 100.
[2] Baer, "Reden," vol. i., 38.

they could form themselves is wanting, as by far the greater part of the organic materials now existing is already contained in living organisms, and the only provision for new individuals appears to be by means of procreation. But in the early ages of organization all this was different, and therefore the course of generation was probably different also."[1]

Haeckel reminds us that at the time when, after water first appeared in a liquid state on the cooled crust of the earth, organisms were first formed, the immeasurable quantities of carbon which we now find deposited in the coal measures existed in a totally different form: they were probably for the most part dispersed throughout the atmosphere in the shape of carbonic acid. The whole composition of the atmosphere, including even its density and electrical conditions, was therefore very different from what it is at present; and in like manner the chemical and physical nature of the primeval ocean— its temperature, density, saltness, etc. — must have differed widely from the present ocean; so that we cannot deny the supposition that at that time, under conditions quite different from those of to-day, spontaneous generation, which perhaps is now no longer possible, may have taken place.[2]

25. WE HAVE NO RIGHT TO SUPPOSE SPONTANEOUS GENERATION IN EARLY PERIODS.—However, even admitting this possibility which Burmeister and Haeckel assume, their supposition is not scientifically probable. Frohschammer justly says with reference to this: "As in these days, according to our experience, cells and germs only originate in organisms, we have no right to suppose, without certain proof and sure warrant, that it was different in early days, in the beginnings of organic

[1] Burmeister, "Geschichte der Schöpfung," p. 287.
[2] Haeckel, "Natürliche Schöpfungsgeschichte," p. 303.

nature. This is a principle which is generally insisted on in natural science at the present day, and which, therefore, ought not to be discarded in this case without very good reason."[1]

26. INDIGNANT WORDS OF QUENSTEDT.—Men of science can make no objection to the following indignant words of Quenstedt. He says:

"To the scientist, to understand means to *see*, and he can only draw conclusions on this basis. If, nowadays, even the smallest plant cannot come into existence without a germ, what thoughtful savant would venture rashly to assert that the whole beautiful vegetable and animal world, including man, has been generated *only* from dead earth? But to many the idea that the Creator has power to breathe life into the dead lump of clay is so unwelcome that they would rather embrace the wildest dreams in order to prove themselves apparently right. Yes, they say, it is very easy to explain why the earth *nowadays* brings forth no living creature: now it is in its old age; but when it was young things were different. It is amusing to hear these men, who usually subject to the sharpest criticism the slightest instinctive revolt of the mind against the abstract laws of nature, when they come to the beginnings of organic life, tell us how then, in the bosom of the formations, every speck of mud suddenly teemed with life, and describe the unwearied creative power of the dead earth. Here we have an instance of the narrowness of man's spirit; he believes that nothing can exist but what he can conceive. When philosophers go this length, we may perhaps pardon them; for if they could no longer think, what is left to them? As students of nature, however, we may draw conclusions only from accurate observations; but we must always define the limits, beyond which we

[1] "Das Christenthum," p. 64.

cannot go. If Unger is right in saying that not the meanest plant can spring from our soil without a germ, must not a sober investigator conclude that what cannot occur to-day under the existing laws of nature, can never have occurred? For it is upon this very fixity of these eternal laws that the whole structure of earthly knowledge rests."[1]

27. SUMMING UP OF THE QUESTION OF THE ORIGIN OF LIFE.—To sum up, monism, in its most complete, most recent, and most painfully elaborated expression, is both anti-scientific and anti-metaphysical, in flagrant opposition to experimental method and rational evidence. Berthelot's words seem to have been purposely written to describe the method of Haeckel and his adherents. He says:

"Positive science seeks neither the first cause nor the end of things, but it proceeds by establishing facts, through observation and experiment. . . . It compares them, it determines their relations from the more general facts which are in its possession, and this is its only guarantee of reality, verified by observation and experience. This is the chain of those relations which constitute positive science. . . . The ideal science (antiscience) has for foundation individual opinions and liberty."[2]

The Haeckelian monism is opposed to reason, for it implies a metaphysical contradiction. Creation being replaced by "the evolutional phases of eternal matter," we find ourselves face to face with the insoluble difficulty of the eternity of matter and of movement, or with a special force which would aggravate the difficulty by a new complication.

To the above we add the judgment of some eminent savants, which proves how the pretensions of materialism

[1] "Sonst und Jetzt," p. 233. [2] "Principes de la Science."

are disappearing before the experiments of science and logical deductions, like mist before a bright sun. And as often as those ingenious and shifting pretensions are brought forward as exact scientific results, they are overwhelmingly disproved by a more thorough application of science and reason. With regard to primitive generation, Quatrefages says:

"We see how careful these people, who brag about free science and claim for themselves its monopoly, who pretend to speak in the name of philosophy and reason only, should be in view of their instinctive aversion to revealed truth, which aversion leads them to reject every testimony, every doctrine, which is in any way connected with faith. It is they precisely who are the greatest, the most intolerant absolutists, and their infidel hypotheses, however venturesome they may be, are set up by them as dogmas."[1]

The following from Liebig, about the "apostles of materialism," is well known: "They are the opinions of amateurs, who, deriving their authority from their excursions on the limits of the domain of natural inquiry, explain to the ignorant and credulous public how the world and the life therein really arose, and how far man has gone in his experience of what is highest."[2] Even in their own camp words of warning are heard, for Virchow has to admit: "There is a materialistic as well as an ecclesiastical and idealistic dogmatism. Certainly the materialistic is the more dangerous, because it denies its dogmatic nature and puts on the cloak of science; because it presents itself as empirical, when it is only speculative, and because it wishes to extend the limits of natural inquiry to questions where it is evidently still incompetent."[3]

[1] "Revue des Deux Mondes," 1860, vol. xxx., p. 809.
[2] "Chemische Briefe," pp. 203, 209.
[3] "Archiv für Pathol. Studien," vol. ii., p. 9.

CHAPTER II.

DARWINISM AND MONISM.

Positive science and the development of life.—Successive and progressive evolution.—The system of Darwin and of Haeckel.—Darwin's book on the "Origin of Species."—Criticism of Darwinism.—Darwinism restricted within certain limits is not necessarily in conflict with the Bible.—However, it is an anti-Genesis in its tendencies.—Definition of genus, species, and variety.—Variability is limited.—It never touches what is essential in the species.—Embryology.—Comparative anatomy.—Rudimentary organs.—Atavism.—"Natural selection" does not explain what it pretends to explain.—Both geology and paleontology confirm the permanency of species.—Neither the flora nor the fauna have changed.—Acknowledgment of Huxley.—Hybridization.—Hybrids do not perpetuate themselves.—Species are unchangeable.—The breeder and the florist may produce varieties, but God alone can create species.—Account and criticism of Haeckelianism.—Comparison with Darwinism.—Monism incapable of establishing the filiation of species and the origin of man.—The truth victorious.

How did life manifest itself for the first time on the globe? How did it develop in the course of time? It is plain that these two questions are not the same. We have just criticized the systems, hypotheses, and errors which deal with the former question; it remains for us to study the difficult problems which relate to the latter: How did life develop after it had appeared on earth?

28. FAITH AND SCIENCE ON THE DEVELOPMENT OF LIFE.—Before entering on the discussion of this question, we must state that it includes no special reference to man;

the problem of anthropology is reserved for future discussion in the following chapters, where man's origin, natural history, and destiny are considered. The only point we are going to examine here is: How did life develop in the animal and vegetable kingdoms? Does faith tell us anything of this? What does it teach with regard to the development of organic beings, with regard to the successive manifestations of life on earth? Nothing.

What does science teach us in regard to the development of life? Has it anything certain to tell us on this subject? Yes, geology and paleontology, as we have mentioned before, show that since the beginning of life upon earth the organic ladder, both vegetable and animal, rises according to a law of constant progress, at least taken as a whole, if not in detail. Since what time has life begun to exist? Since what time has life begun to develop on our globe? Not only has science no certain answer to this question, but its estimates or guesses have no claims to probability, because it is very difficult to fix the duration of geological time, and every attempt to express it in figures must necessarily be based on the time that sedimentary rocks require for their formation. It is staggered by the fact that the natural forces, always identical in their essence, must have varied in their mode of action. All we know is, that the varied succession of the sedimentary layers and the unceasing transformation of the fauna and flora must have required considerable time. It is not too much to put it at millions of years.[1]

29. How Did Organic Life Develop?—All we have to keep in mind here is the fact, scientifically established by geology and paleontology, and affirmed by Genesis, that from the appearance of the first living beings until man's advent, life has developed according to a

[1] See Lapparent, "Traité de Géologie."

law of constant organic progress, taking it on the whole, if not in its details. How did this progressive development take place? It is very easy to understand the whole importance and interest of this question. There are two theories which strive to answer it. The first is the theory of independent, successive creations, that is, the direct intervention of the Creator, producing them in the different geological epochs. This is the traditional belief; it proclaims the fixity of the species; it is the prevalent view in our days, not only in Christian exegesis, but also in science; for experience shows that the transformation of the essential qualities of beings, and transition from one species to another, is contrary to the laws of nature. The second theory is the theory of the successive and progressive evolution by transformation of living organisms, which rests on the hypothesis of the variability of species. It must be taken in its true sense as taught, and we must be careful not to confound the general idea, or, as it is called, the "principle," of transformism, with particular conceptions or systems, such as brusque transformations, or evolution properly speaking, which owes its origin to Haeckel, or slow transformations through organic adaptation—the systems of Lamarck and Darwin.

30. HAECKEL'S SYSTEM.—The system of Haeckel is also called "monism." As we saw in the preceding chapter, he maintains that there exists throughout nature a great evolutionary process, which is one, continual, and eternal; that all the phenomena of nature, without exception, from the movement of the celestial bodies to the fall of a stone, from the growth of plants and animals to consciousness in man, take place in virtue of the evolutionary process according to one and the same law of causality; in short, that everything is reducible to the mechanism of the atom.[1]

[1] Haeckel, "Les Preuves du Transformisme," p. 16.

31. Darwin's System.—Darwin's system of descent, for which the special name transformism has been retained, explains the origin of organic species by slow, gradual, and successive transformations, so that, according to this theory, all the complex vegetable and animal organisms we see in nature come from simple organisms. It admits as the beginning of organic life only one primitive form, or, at most, a very small number of forms, from which all the present forms have descended. Finally, the "theory of selection" consists in attributing to the selection, which we are going to explain, the origin of species. It supposes the indefinite variability of species and their transmutability. Species are not original, they say; they are produced like the varieties which we observe every day in the same species, by changes and accidental modifications due especially to selection. These have afterwards become fixed in such a manner as to perpetuate themselves. It is this theory, explaining by mechanical causes the transformation of species, which is Darwinism pure and simple. The monists and transformists are generally Darwinists, but the real Darwinists are generally not monists or Haeckelists.

The history of science and philosophy does not, perhaps, furnish a parallel to the influence exercised by the transformist hypothesis in the latter half of the present century. To slur it over, or to set little value on its influence in this or other countries, would be against all the rules of apologetic tradition. Moreover, it is often misunderstood and falsely interpreted in its doctrinal consequences by believers and unbelievers; therefore a critical exposition of the principal contradictory theses, considered under their different aspects and in their relation to faith, will enable us to solve easily the objections drawn from Darwinism and to dispel the phantoms which some conjure up at every step.

32. ON WHAT NATURALISTS ARE AGREED.—The great naturalists agree well enough in defining species. To Lamarck, Cuvier, Buffon, and Karl Vogt, the species is the reunion of similar individuals, issued from parents which resemble them as they resemble each other; it is the individual repeated and continued indefinitely. But the agreement ceases as soon as there is question of tracing the origin of species. Are they invariable? Are they the results of creative acts? Must we admit the axiom of Linnæus: *Tot numeramus species quot ab initio creavit infinitum ens?* Are they variable? Can they descend by transformation from a small number of types or even from a single initial type? Is the permanency of the species absolute or only relative and temporary? Here you have in a nutshell the questions raised by transformism. The original conception, though still quite confused, the first rough drafting of the transmutation theory, is due to the natural philosopher Maillet. And among his successors Lamarck is the deepest, Goethe the keenest, Haeckel the most impious, Darwin the most ingenious and by far the most popular.

33. LAMARCK AND DARWIN.—" It is not useless," wrote Lamarck in his " Philosophie Zoologique," 1809, just half a century before Darwin's book," Origin of Species," appeared, 1859, "to inquire whether it is true that species have an absolute permanency, whether they are as ancient as nature, and whether they existed originally such as we observe them to-day, or whether, subject to the changes of surroundings which might take place, although very slowly, they have not changed in character and form in the lapse of time." Struck by the difficulty which the fixity of species presents—for they, so to say, pass the one into the other—Lamarck pronounced in favor of their

variability. In order to explain their successive transformations, he invokes three principal factors, namely: "The phenomena of adaptation or the influence of exterior circumstances, the changes of which bring on new needs, which can only be satisfied by appropriate modifications of the organism; heredity, the role of which is considerable, and in virtue of which every change produced in the organization of individuals is transmitted by way of reproduction to their descendants; time, a necessary condition for the transformation of species, for these modify themselves only slowly and by insensible gradations."

Being published at an unfavorable time, the ideas of Lamarck passed almost unnoticed. The discussion which, like an echo, arose between Bory de Saint Vincent and the famous Cuvier, twenty years later, served to bring them into notice. The theory of descent was rejected by almost all naturalists, and the belief in the immutability of species was general when Darwin's famous book on the "Origin of Species" appeared in 1859. The moment was favorable; the work was applauded by some and sharply combated by others. The work of the English naturalist was the starting-point of a movement in favor of the doctrine of descent, which generally goes under the name of Darwinism. Thus it is the theory of the English savant which it is especially important to know in order to understand the sense and the bearing of transformism, and as there is hardly any question that has been more frequently examined than this, we will give the leading points as briefly and clearly as possible.

34. LAMARCKISM PERFECTED BY DARWIN.—The first fact, which serves as a starting-point, are the established variations in the history of cultivated plants and domestic animals. Man transforms and improves breeds by

selective breeding; analogous variations manifest themselves under our eyes independently of any human interference. Other factors affecting variation are climate, the surroundings of flora and fauna, the greater or less abundance of light, heat, food, habits, sexual impressions, disuse of organs or development of organs, which bring on true atrophy or extraordinary development, perfecting one or more special organs or features until they become fixed and perpetuated, etc. Darwin has composed an entire code: laws of adaptation, laws of correlation, of growth, of variation, of inheritance, etc. It is a "luxury of wheelwork" and of words, which adds to its scientific prestige; it is a skilful amplification of Lamarck's first idea.

A second formula, which has made this theory popular, is the "struggle for life;" struggle for the existence of the individual, struggle for the perpetuity of the species. The struggle will be the more destructive, the closer species and individuals are to each other, having the same habits and the same needs. The most opposite varieties will have the greatest chance to live, and thus will tend more and more to separate themselves from the common type. It has been proved that vegetable and animal propagation tends to increase according to a geometric progression, whilst the means of subsistence increase only in an arithmetical proportion. The consequences of this disproportion are inevitable; the more feeble, the less favored by circumstances, of necessity disappear in the struggle for life; the stronger, those endowed with more vigor, alone will survive with the advantages acquired. This is "natural selection," this is the ray of light which has transformed science and lit up in its depths the problem of the progressive development of life; this is the God-machine which allows us to conceive of an end unconsciously pursued, infallibly attained

(Vogt, Haeckel), and which is to replace the God of the ancient faith for a more happy posterity!

The wonderful results of natural selection are transmitted and perpetuated, thanks to another great factor, another great law hardly contestable—heredity. The role of this third element is of prime importance; it explains the universal tendency in all forms of life to transmit and perpetuate themselves, as well as genealogical improvements and perfections. Finally, the Darwinian theory imperiously claims a last factor of unlimited power, which is absolutely essential, and never fails to intervene to explain the crucial difficulties it meets with in accounting for the production of the first man from that original prototype which was the fruitful parent of all life. That factor is *time*.

Such is in concise expression Lamarckism set forth and perfected by Darwin. The learned Englishman has enriched the original system with a great number of observations and experiments; he has completed it, or, in other words, transformed it, by introducing selection, which constitutes the characteristic factor of Darwinism. In the eyes of the public, and for a certain time, Darwin has supplanted Lamarck, whose superiority posterity will undoubtedly acknowledge.

Having set forth the leading points of the Darwinian theory, we shall now examine them more closely in detail, and after that we shall consider the doctrine of transformation as set up by Haeckel; our criticism, for want of space, must be short.

35. CRITICISM OF DARWINISM.—In the first place we may remark that Darwinism maintained within certain limitations is not necessarily in contradiction with the Bible. "Suppose that the theory of Darwin," says Reusch, "were demonstrated by incontestable proofs, and that—a thing I regard as impossible—the natural

sciences would prove that all species of plants and animals which have existed and which still exist can be reduced to a few primitive forms, would there be a contradiction between the Bible and the natural sciences? I do not believe it!"[1]

The Bible teaches that the universe is the work of a Creator, who has produced the world for a determinate end. This double truth can be reconciled with Darwinism, and the Darwinists generally admit this. Lyell, the eminent geologist, says: "The ensemble and succession of natural phenomena can only be the material application of a preconceived design, and if this succession of facts can be explained by transmutation, the perpetual adaptation of the organic world to new conditions leaves the argument in favor of a design, and consequently of a designer, as powerful as ever."[2]

Lamarck, who taught transformation before Darwin, expressly admitted the existence of God and His Providence.

"Among the false ideas to which the subject I am here examining has given place, I will quote the two principal. . . . The first leads most men to believe that nature and its supreme Author are synonymous terms. . . . It (nature) is in some manner only an intermediary between God and the physical universe for the execution of the divine will. . . . It has been supposed that nature itself is God. . . . Strange! men have confounded the watch with the watch-maker, the work with its author. Certainly this idea is illogical. . . . As regards the laws of nature, they are only the expression of the will which has established them, after having primitively combined them for the end He had proposed to Himself."[3]

[1] Reusch, "La Bible et la Nature," pp. 106, 109.
[2] Lyell, "Antiquity of Man."
[3] "Hist. Nat. des Anim. sans Vertèbres," 1835, pp. 258, 272, etc.

36. Genesis is Not in Formal Contradiction with the Theory of Natural Selection.—But Darwinism in itself does not exclude altogether the intervention of God in the creation of the world; on the contrary, more than once it speaks like the Bible. Even Haeckel is obliged to acknowledge the points of contact between Genesis and Darwinism. He says:

"In this Mosaic hypothesis of creation two of the most important and fundamental propositions stand out with remarkable clearness and simplicity: they are the idea of division of labor, or differentiation, and the idea of progressive development, of perfecting. Although these great laws of organic evolution, these laws which we shall prove to be the necessary consequence of the doctrine of descent, may be regarded by Moses as the expression of the activity of the Creator forming the universe, nevertheless we discover therein the beautiful idea of progressive evolution, of gradual differentiation from primitively simple matter. We can, therefore, pay a sincere and just tribute of admiration to the grand idea contained in the hypothetical cosmogony of the Jewish legislator, without being obliged to acknowledge, what some are pleased to call, divine manifestation."[1]

Thus Genesis, as Vigouroux rightly says, is not in formal opposition to the theory of natural selection, inasmuch as the latter is distinct from the theory of descent. Outside of the question of first cause and finality, Darwinism consists essentially in asserting a continual progress in the production of beings and a relation of filiation between different beings, the more perfect descending from the less perfect through a kind of generation. Of these two Darwinian ideas, the first one, that of progress, is Biblical: Moses shows us a very

[1] Haeckel, "Nat. Schöpfungsgeschichte," p. 40.

marked gradation in the creative work; the second, that of filiation, does not appear in the account of Moses, but one could not maintain that his language excludes it absolutely, at least if we receive it with certain limitations. Every day of creation is characterized by the production of a new species of beings, which receive their existence by the command of God. The most natural manner to understand this command is to see therein, not a transformation of that which existed already, but completely new productions. However, according to some, there is not one word in the Sacred Text which is opposed to the hypothesis of evolution; nothing is revealed of the particular manner in which the plants and the animals were produced. The only exception is man, whose creation Genesis describes in detail.

However, it appears to us difficult, continues Vigouroux, if not impossible, to explain Holy Scripture in the sense that all animals developed from plants and plants from minerals by way of transformation, as the adherents of the theory of descent pretend. Moses tells us that God created the plants and the animals "each after its kind." This simple affirmation seems to be the formal condemnation of transformism without limitation. But Darwinism proper does not go as far as absolute transformism. The English naturalist admits in both the vegetable and animal kingdoms the existence of several primitive types, not of one only, and his hypothesis can be reconciled with the language of Scripture; for when the latter tells us that animals were created by species, it does not determine the number of these species. Thus, there does not exist any radical incompatibility between the two explanations. At most, we may think that Darwin restricts too much the number of primordial species, but as he limits it only in a hypothetical manner, and as Genesis does not mention the number of species, agreement between the two in regard to this matter is far from being impossible; it is only one question more that the Scripture, like Darwin, leaves undecided.

If the plurality of primitive species be admitted, there is no longer any conflict in regard to their mutability. Darwin maintains that there are to-day species which have been derived from other species. Holy Scripture does not teach us anything on this question. It does not tell us whether this is so or whether it is not so; consequently, Scripture is not involved in this contention, and the same is true of the Church, which has not passed judgment on this matter. Therefore, we believe that those Darwinists who admit in the vegetable and animal kingdoms the existence of several primordial types created by God, from which have come by way of transformation and filiation the different existing species of the organic world, do not teach anything contrary to revealed doctrine. For example, M. Albert Gaudry, Professor at the Museum of Natural History, in Paris, is of opinion that secondary species are transmutable, but are derived from a certain number of primordial and irreducible classes, and this view is not in conflict with Genesis, because it admits the multiplicity of primitive types and does not exclude the Creator.

37. DARWINISM IS AN ANTI-GENESIS IN ITS TENDENCIES.—Hence, restrained or modified Darwinism is not in itself a contradiction of the Bible. It can, consequently, be maintained with the necessary restrictions by believing Catholics, as it is in fact by Mr. St. George Mivart and others. But if it is not in the strict sense opposed to Genesis, this theory is so by reason of its tendencies, and the manner in which most of its defenders support it. The number of orthodox Darwinists is indeed very small,

and the number of heterodox very large. Most of those who have embraced Darwinism go far beyond what it teaches; they accept transformism with all its shocking and impious consequences, as Darwin himself did in his last years. The theory of selection is for them an argument in favor of their thesis, an essential element of their system, an integral part of their doctrine, even the foundation of their hypothesis, without which the whole edifice they try to raise with so much pains and labor collapses. It is therefore useful to examine in detail the scientific value of this system.[1]

38. DEFINITION OF GENUS, SPECIES, AND VARIETY.— Darwinism, in the judgment of the most impartial and competent men, has made valuable improvements in natural history by determining the causes which produce varieties and breeds in the organic world,[2] but it goes astray when it tries to go beyond this. Its discoveries suffice to explain the origin of varieties, but not that of species. According to the definitions universally accepted by all savants before Darwin, *species* is a collection of individuals having the same essential qualities, issued from the same primitive pair, and having the power to reproduce themselves indefinitely. A group of species which have common characters takes the name of *genus*. The species is unchangeable in its essential characters, but its accessory characters can change under the influence of external agencies, and thus give rise to varieties and races. We call *varieties* a group of individuals of the same species which differs from the common type by accidental modifications of the species. These may be due to climate, food, unlimited range, exercise, impressions through the nervous system, breeding,

[1] Vigouroux, "Les Livres Saints," etc., vol. ii., pp. 593, 595.
[2] See Quatrefages, "Note sur Darwin," in the "Comptes Rendus de l'Académie des Sciences," vol. xciv., 1882, pp. 1216, 1219.

crossing, etc. These modifications are not essential and specific, but changeable and unstable. They generally affect size, color, and conformation. In virtue of the law of reversion, varieties naturally return to the primitive type, if extraneous causes do not force individuals of the same variety to couple in order to perpetuate their race conformably to the law of heredity. When the particular characters which constitute a variety become fixed and perpetuated in a constant manner, they form a *race*.

In order that so important a point as the classification of genus, species, and varieties may be better understood, we give an account of the system of Linnæus, which will be found instructive and interesting.

Linnæus combines the species which are most closely connected or allied into larger groups, which he calls *genera*. Since then it has become customary to connect the names of the genus and species together in the systematic enumerations of plants and animals. The domestic cat, for instance, is *Felis domestica;* the wild cat, *Felis catus;* the tiger, *Felis tigris;* the lion, *Felis leo;* the panther, *Felis pardus;* the jaguar, *Felis onca*. These six beasts of prey are therefore species of the genus *Felis*. In botany, in the same way, seven kinds of pine are called species of the one genus *Pinus:* the pine, *Pinus alba;* the fir, *Pinus prica;* the larch, *Pinus larix*, etc. Linnæus combines the genera which are most like each other into so-called orders, *ordines*, and the orders which resemble each other, into *classes*.

Of course, besides the resemblances which characterize all the individuals of a species, we find individual differences. If one egg does not exactly resemble another egg, still less are two horses, two dogs, etc., exactly alike. There is conformity in the essential qualities, which remain the same through all generations, and there is difference in the non-essential qualities.

The groups of individuals of the same species which resemble one another in non-essential characteristics, and which yet differ from the great mass of individuals, are called varieties, and if their peculiarities become hereditary they can propagate new races. Poodles, greyhounds, bulldogs, terriers, etc., for instance, are different breeds or races of the same species, dog; the dog, the wolf, the fox, etc., are different species of the genus *Canis—Canis domesticus, Canis lupus, Canis vulpes.* "The race," says Virchow, "forms a separate series within the species, which, however far we may go back, at some time branches off from the common root, and does not again amalgamate with it, but remains true to its own peculiarities; varieties, on the other hand, represent branches from the stem, which often repeat themselves, which occur, as it were, under the eyes of the observer, and sometimes produce progeny with the qualities of the original ancestors."[1] As, for instance, we find that flowers which regularly produce white blossoms sometimes produce red; while from the seeds of the latter, after a few generations, white flowers will spring again. Varieties and races have, therefore, been formed in the course of time; species, on the other hand, have existed from the beginning.

39. DARWIN ALWAYS AVOIDED DEFINING RACES AND SPECIES.—Such were the opinions of the old naturalists. Darwin, however, who proposed to explain the *origin of species*, as the title of his work indicates, has not only always evaded, but purposely avoided, giving a definition of races and species. This is a serious fault, and makes a bad break in his work; betrays embarrassment, and shows that his conclusions rest on equivocation. It is easy to see, nevertheless, by the manner in which he reasons, that the distinctions admitted by him between

[1] "Die Lehre Darwins," "Deutsche Jahrbücher," vol. vi., p. 341.

species and races do not appear to him well founded, and that these words are for him only two different names for one and the same thing. He says:

"Although entire libraries were written on the question whether this or that class is a species or a variety, a good or a bad kind, no naturalists can answer the question what a good or a bad species, properly speaking, is." He resumes: "Thus far no definite line was drawn either between kinds and species, between sub-species and expressed varieties, or between the latter and individual differences. Thus the individual differences form the first step to insignificant varieties, which then are changed (by natural selection) into striking varieties, sub-species, and kinds. Hence the expression 'species' is an arbitrary one, from which 'variety' only differs inasmuch as this is applied to more or less deviating and changing forms."[1]

Thus, according to Darwin, variety is a "rising species," as compared with the race; it does not differ by any important character from the species. Hence when he has explained the origin of races, he has at the same time explained the origin of species. The dispute between the Darwinists and their opponents may be reduced to one question, which covers the whole ground in dispute: Does a real difference exist between species and race? Darwin, in order to establish his thesis, should have commenced by proving that the transformation of species is a real fact, and only afterwards have shown how this transformation takes place. But he was careful to avoid venturing over this road, and preferred to evade the principle and draw the consequences therefrom. He occupied himself with explaining the fact which he continually pre-supposed without having established it. Now we shall follow him over the ground he has chosen to take.

[1] Darwin, "Origin of Species," ch. ii.

40. PROOFS BROUGHT FORWARD BY THE EVOLUTIONISTS.—The adherents of the system of evolution accumulate a number of proofs in detail, and from these they infer the identity of race and species. These proofs can all be reduced to three heads, namely: the variability of plants and animals, embryology, and comparative anatomy. Still, all these proofs are insufficient to substantiate the fact of the transformation of species; none of them establishes the passing of one species into another, which is absolutely necessary to demonstrate the Darwinian hypothesis.

41. (*a*) VARIABILITY.—That human intelligence and perseverance has obtained many extraordinary and astonishing results in the transformation of cultured plants and animals is a fact well known to all. We confess Darwin's contributions are invaluable in their way; they probably inaugurate a "new epoch in natural history;" they will serve to bring more order into the chaos of our scientific knowledge. But the case is far from being closed, the variability of species is far from being proved. Improved fruit-trees, ornamental, horticultural, and culinary plants, show singular and important changes of the vegetable organism, in their fruits, blossoms, stems, and leaves. In the animal world, also, man can produce not only new races, but also certain features, markings, development, formations, dwarfing, etc., that suit his caprice or afford him certain advantages. The pigeon fancier produces birds with short or with long beaks, crested or with plain heads, frilled or hooded, of all colors and markings. One can trace the dog in scores of types, sizes, and colors, varying widely in his most prominent characteristics. The horse, too, has undergone many important changes and improvements, furnishing numerous breeds for man's use and benefit. A bull of abnormal appearance in Paraguay became the

progenitor of a hornless race of cattle now quite popular among stockmen and farmers. The appearance of a hornless animal, followed by selective breeding, was the foundation of a new race. From a bandy-legged ram an American sheep-breeder raised a new race of sheep. We could multiply examples of variation in domestic animals, where some peculiar feature was taken for a starting-point, and was followed by selective breeding, until it became developed and fixed. We may even go further than experience would lead us, and assume with the Darwinists that all the domesticated races may be reduced to a primitive pair of each kind. But all these changes, however numerous and great they may be, do not justify Darwin in drawing the conclusion that there is no difference between race and species.

42. THE VARIABILITY OF SPECIES IS LIMITED.—The variability of species, according to the experience furnished by artificial breeding, has limits; neither the vegetable nor the animal kingdom ever passes these limits. The changes always bear only on accessory or acquired properties, and in no case do they touch what is characteristic and fundamental in the species. However persistent his efforts, however ingenious his experiments, man has never bred a dog out of a fox or a wolf, nor a swan out of a goose, although these animals are closely related. A pigeon or dog fancier may produce many races of pigeons or dogs, but however great or small the likeness between the several organs may be, he cannot change them to another species. In spite of all changes that have produced more than two hundred varieties, eleven races, and four clearly marked groups of pigeons from the primitive blue rock dove, as soon as man remits his selective breeding and his care, there is a return to the primitive type and markings. The same may be said of the dog; although there are twelve clearly marked

varieties of greyhounds alone, they and the bulldog may be traced to a common parentage, but not to different species.

Thus variability, in the first place, is limited. As Hartmann says:

"Every breeder knows that the first degrees of modification are the easiest to obtain; that all subsequent degrees are the more difficult to realize, the more they branch off from the normal type, and that every experiment of artificial breeding, in any of the directions open by nature, arrives at a limit where every attempt to push it further becomes fruitless. For example, since 1852 no new development in the dimensions of the gooseberry has been brought about, although there appears to be no reason why they do not become as thick as lemons, if variability were wholly unlimited."[1]

Again, M. Wiegand, Professor of Botany at Marburg, observes that natural variations are limited, both as regards quality and as regards quantity.

"The breeder would not dare attempt to obtain an inverted variety from the chicken, or from the spurred pigeon a yellow pigeon, or a blue lemon or orange or a yellow poppy from a garden poppy, or a rose having a hundred yellow leaves, because nature does not produce these modifications."[2]

From this it follows that if species is variable it is not transmutable. Though the characters which distinguish it can be modified to a certain degree, this modification never extends so far as to produce what it would be right to call a new species. Artificial selection alone proves the relative fixity of specific characters.

43. VARIETIES LEFT TO THEMSELVES RETURN TO THEIR PRIMITIVE TYPE.—To variability, as well as to

[1] "Le Darwinisme," p. 98.
[2] "Der Darwinismus und die Naturforschung," vol. i., p. 54.

the ocean, God has fixed a limit which it cannot pass; though it can modify, it cannot create. This is so true that the changes which are obtained by artificial selection are made permanent only by the constant intervention of an intelligence that must preside over their preservation. Nature is so conservative that in virtue of the law of reversion it returns to its primitive type as soon as the selector no longer interferes or contravenes its tendencies.

Darwin himself acknowledges that, in order to obtain new races, the breeders must exercise great intelligence, unremitted care, and constant attention. "Not one man in a thousand has accuracy of eye and judgment sufficient to become an eminent breeder. If gifted with these qualities, he studies his subject for years, and devotes his lifetime to it with indomitable perseverance, he will succeed and may make great improvements; if he wants any of these qualities, he will assuredly fail."[1]

If this is the case when the most energetic and the most intelligent will can hardly succeed in obtaining a somewhat new type, how is it possible to uphold the idea that nature, deprived of all direction, could bring forth the innumerable beings which people the globe from a few rudimentary types?

One day a strawberry-plant whose culture had greatly modified the leaves was brought to Linnæus. These, instead of being composed of three small leaves, had one. This strawberry-plant was preserved in the "Jardin des Plantes," and Duchène, a famous gardener of the time, saw it bloom and bear fruit. Then he tried to reproduce it by sowing its grains; in the third seed-bed he obtained a strawberry-plant whose leaves had recovered their natural character: they were trifoliates.[2]

[1] "Origin of Species," pp. 41, 42.
[2] L. Simon, "De l'Origine des Espèces," 1865, pp. 40, 41.

The same facts have been observed in animals. All this proves how constant the laws of nature are. Artificial races are factitious and conditional; they depend upon the climate, soil, regimen, alliances,¹ as well as on the regular and permanent care provided by the protective hand of man. If this hand is withdrawn, if conditions change, even old races degenerate and disappear: after having oscillated, like the pendulum of a clock, they return to their starting-point. "Natural selection," says P. Janet, a philosopher and freethinker, "is nothing else than the chance of Epicurus, and just as barren as this."

O. Heer, arguing from the results of his paleontological inquiries, says: "The origin of varieties is a secret, an enigma, about which we may guess, but which has not found its solution by the application of laws so far known."[2] Virchow, after having expressed himself in the same sense, continues, saying: "I only ask for proof whereby such a transformation is established; until this proof is furnished, I can admit only that it is probable. However, I was misled and deceived so often by probabilities, that I have learned to be more cautious in future and to wait until the facts are clearly proved."[3]

44. VARIABILITY NEVER AFFECTS WHAT IS ESSENTIAL IN SPECIES.—In the second place, variability never affects what is essential in species. For example, experiment allows us to bring about modifications in certain organs, but never the production of a new organ, even by means of the most refined artificial selection. "The gymnast," pointedly observes M. Janet, "has muscles more movable or less movable than other men.

[1] E. Hartmann, "Le Darwinisme," p. 69.
[2] O. Heer, "Die Urwelt der Schweitz," p. 603.
[3] "Correspondenzblatt,' 1871, p. 70.

Has he different muscles? Has he more? Are they differently arranged?"¹ Certain influences can produce physiological changes, but these changes never touch organic forms. The use or disuse of members favors their development or tends to incipient atrophy, but if they exercise an influence on the volume, the weight, and the structure of organs, they do not modify their form; and it is even more clear that atrophy never goes so far as wholly to suppress an organ. This Hartmann, himself a transformist, admits.² Variability, therefore, has only a limited power. It can produce durable effects only by exercising these powers within restricted limits; in other words, it can establish races, but not species.

45. (*b*) EMBRYOLOGY.—The Darwinists regard the argument from embryology as one of the strongest arguments in favor of their doctrine, but it is a sword which cuts both ways, and does not furnish conclusive proof in favor of Darwinism. Transformists consider the ensemble of embryonic facts as representative of the genesis of beings. The embryo is for them the animal itself less modified than it will be later on, and producing in its personal evolution the phases which the species has undergone in its gradual formation. What is conclusive in their favor, they think, is the extremely close resemblance which is remarked in the early phases of embryonic existence between animals that later on will be as different as reptiles, birds, and mammifers. Every animal comes from an egg and a primitive cell. The phenomena which pass within them towards the end are the same in all eggs. The segmentation and apparition of the first rudiments takes place in all living things in the same order and in the same manner.

¹ P. Janet, " Les Causes Finales," Paris, 1876, p. 381.
² Darwin, " Origin of Species," pp. 519, 532.

Embryology, according to Darwinism, offers us a short way to the complete history of the evolution of animal species. Every animate thing comes from an egg, *omne vivum ex ovo; omne ovum ex ovario;* every animate thing in a short time runs through these phenomena; and the multiple halting-places which their ancestors demanded in the course of nature are not known. Transformation alone is able to render an account of this singular phenomenon, which is therefore a proof in favor of transformation.

46. EVERY EGG DEVELOPS ONLY INTO ITS OWN TYPE OF LIFE.—This is, in substance, what the Darwinists claim, but all savants do not share this belief; several naturalists consider the evolutionists' argument from embryology to be poetic rather than scientific.[1] On what foundation is the supposition that the individual passes through all the phases of its race-history based? On no foundation whatsoever. These forms follow a development proper to each species, and are fixed when the characters of animal life direct them into a special form, which then remains invariable, and is never found in another animal species; or, in other words, "every egg develops only into its own distinct type of life. The growth always stops at the same place; the development always proceeds to a certain definite point, never falls below or passes beyond."

The ovules of mammals in their primitive state resemble one another, so that they cannot be physically distinguished, and, nevertheless, an ovule in the course of its development may become a horse, a dog, or a whale. Therefore, there must be in the ovule a special principle, a something which distinguishes its physical composition, although in the present state of our knowledge, and with the resources at present within our reach,

[1] B. B. Pussey, "Permanency and Evolution,' 1862, p. 92.

this escapes the eye of the naturalist; it being impossible to ascertain these physical differences on account of the imperfection of our senses. There is a moment, says Coste, the creator of embryology, when the organization of the superior animal reduces itself to the simplicity of the cell.

"The egg offers us the transitory image of this simplicity, for it has all the characters of the cell and develops in a similar manner. Like the latter, it is made up of an enveloping membrane and its cellular contents, but this contents, instead of undergoing the lot in store for the common cells, tends to move constantly towards the end of its high destination. Here, therefore, the analogy is *merely in the form or appearance;* the difference is *in the nature of the force* which animates this form and co-ordinates the materials thereof."[1]

47. THE FIRST SENSIBLE PROGRESS IN THE EVOLUTION OF THE EGG.—The first sensible progress in the evolution of the eggs of superior animals consists in the formation of the blastoderm, that is, of the general envelope of the skin of the new being. This gives to the embryo a certain likeness to the inferior animals, such as the medusæ and hydræ, in which the general envelope performs all the functions and in fact constitutes the grown-up organism. But, continues Coste:

"At one point of the blastodermic side a primitive or vertebral line appears quite early; of this inferior animals never reveal any trace, and it is precisely this that prevents our inferring that these resemblances have the character of identity. While expressing the idea of a general plan common to all beings, they exclude the possibility of a transformation under the influence of external agents."

[1] Coste, "Histoire du Developpement des Corps Organisés," vol. i., p. 17.

Agassiz confirms the assertions of the French Professor:

"It has been maintained in the broadest terms that superior animals pass, during their development, through all the phases which characterize inferior classes. Thus formulated, this proposition is entirely contrary to truth. . . . In their primitive condition the eggs of all animals are alike, but as soon as the embryo begins to show characteristic traits, these reveal such peculiarities that the type of the animal can be distinguished. It cannot be said, therefore, that there are phases in the development of an animal that do not lie within the lines of its evolution. At no moment of its development is a vertebrate an articulate or an animal resembling an articulate; at no instant is an articulate a mollusk, nor a mollusk a radiate, and *vice versa*. . . . No superior animal passes through phases representative of all the inferior types of the animal kingdom; it undergoes simply a series of modifications special to the animals of the order to which it belongs."[1]

Nay, more, as Agassiz has also established, the characters of its species manifest themselves before those of its order and before those of its genus, which is at direct variance with the genealogical succession of the transformists.

Finally, the fact alleged by the evolutionists is not a universal one, and has been greatly exaggerated. The cuts by which Haeckel has represented the different embryos in order to make them perceptible and to show their likeness when they first appeared, seemed to be a triumphant argument in favor of his thesis; but since then they have considerably lowered the reputation of this savant, and even cast suspicions on his good faith; for it is known and acknowledged in Germany to-day

[1] L. Agassiz, "Histoire Générale du Développement," etc., p. 18.

that these cuts are a falsification of the figures of Messrs. His and Semper.[1] The striking resemblances there depicted are, therefore, in reality the result of a fraud. It is certain, as Darwin himself admits, that all animals, without exception, do not pass through the different stages of their so-called ancestors.[2] But the laws of nature are general, and if the Darwinistic explanation of embryological development were correct, it would not admit of any exception. The law which governs the formation of animals in the first period of their existence is, therefore, not a proof of the truth of Darwin's system.[3]

48. (*c*) COMPARATIVE ANATOMY.—The third argument of the evolutionists is no more conclusive than the others. One of the chief reasons they advance in favor of their system, and one which strikes many minds as conclusive, is that which they draw from comparative anatomy; it is founded on the existence of many rudimentary, atrophied, and disused organs in animals. Darwin says:

"It would be difficult to name a superior animal in which there does not exist some part in the rudimentary state. In the mammifers, for instance, the males always possess rudimentary mammæ; in the serpents one wing of the lung is rudimentary; in the birds the bastard wing is so rudimentary that it is useless for flying. Is there anything more curious than the presence of teeth in the fœtus of the whale, which, when grown up, has no trace of these organs; or the presence of teeth which never pierce the gum in the upper jaw of a calf before its birth? . . . In the works of natural history they generally tell us that the rudimentary organs were created with a view to symmetry or to complete the

---

[1] See "Literarischer Handweiser," 1884, col. 20.
[2] Darwin, "Origin of Species," p. 503.
[3] Cf. Vigouroux, "Livres Saints," etc.

plan of nature. Now, this is merely a repetition of the fact, and no explanation.

"On the view of descent with modification, the origin of rudimentary organs is simple. . . . I believe that disuse has been the main agency; that it has led in successive generations to the gradual reduction of various organs, until they have become rudimentary—as in the case of the eyes of animals inhabiting dark caverns, and of the wings of birds inhabiting oceanic islands, which have seldom been forced by beasts of prey to take flight, and have ultimately lost the power of flying. . . . Rudimentary organs may be compared with the letters in a word still retained in the spelling, but become useless in the pronunciation, but which serve as a clue for its derivation. On the view of descent with modification, we may conclude that the existence of organs in a rudimentary, imperfect, or useless condition, or quite aborted, far from presenting a strange difficulty, as they assuredly do on the ordinary doctrine of creation, might even have been anticipated in accordance with the views here explained."[1]

Darwin, while explaining by atrophy the rudimentary organs, explains at the same time the striking similitude of forms which we remark under apparent diversity in the different species of animals actually existing. Without this system it is impossible, say the Darwinists, to discover by what strange coincidence the structure of the bones is so similar in the arm of man, in the wing of the bat, in the front leg of the horse and in the fin of the porpoise, and why the neck of the giraffe and that of the elephant contain the same number of vertebræ.[2]

49. ANATOMICAL SIMILARITY OF LITTLE IMPORTANCE.—In the first place, let us observe that anatomical

[1] Darwin, "Origin of Species," pp. 408–410.
[2] Quatrefages, "Ch. Darwin," p. 192.

similarity has not the importance which the Darwinists attribute to it. Resemblance in the skeletons of two animals is not sufficient at all to establish identity of species. The horse, the ass, the zebra, and the jiggetai are very different animals, and nevertheless they resemble one another so closely in their skeletons that it is impossible to distinguish them by their osteological characters alone. If these four species were buried together, paleontologists of the future would be obliged to reduce them to one. Louis Agassiz, the famous naturalist of Harvard University, far from finding an argument in favor of transformation of species from similarity in the structure of animals, on the contrary draws thence an argument in favor of creation.

"Nothing in the organic kingdom is of a nature to impress us so much as the unity of plan which appears in the structure of the most different types. From one pole to another under the meridians, mammifers, birds, reptiles, fishes, reveal one and the same plan of structure. This plan denotes abstract conceptions of the highest order; it surpasses by far the grandest generalizations of the human mind, and it needed the most laborious researches to enable man to form only an idea of it. Other no less wonderful plans appear in the articulata, the mollusks, the radiata, and in the different types of plants, and in spite of this logical relation, this wonderful harmony, this infinite variety in unity, these are represented to us as the result of forces to which belong neither the least spark of intelligence, nor the faculty of thinking, nor the power of combining, nor the notions of time or space! If anything in nature can place man above other beings, it is precisely the fact that he possesses these noble attributes. Without these gifts in a very high degree of excellence and perfection, none of the general traits of parentage which unite the great types of the animal and vegetable kingdoms could either be perceived or understood. How then could these relations be imagined, if not with the help of analogous faculties? If all these relations surpass the intellectual horizon of man, if man himself is only a part, a fragment of the total system, how could this system have been called into existence, if there was not a supreme intelligence, author of all things?"[1]

50. RUDIMENTARY ORGANS.—With regard to those "animals inhabiting dark caverns and having only rudimentary eyes, and the birds inhabiting oceanic islands which have lost the power of flying," we must say, that the ideas put forward by Darwin are borrowed from Lamarck, who tells us that the giraffe got its long neck by trying to stretch it out more and more in order to be able to reach the leaves of African trees. According to Darwin, also, the eyes of subterranean animals become continually smaller, because they have no occasion to make use of them in their dark dwelling-places. But if disuse reduces the size of the eyes by degrees, certainly there is a limit to their decrease, or else we should have eyeless animals inhabiting dark places. If Darwin's hypothesis be true, why are so many animals which live in the depths of the ocean provided with well-formed eyes? We instance the animals of which Mr. Thompson reports,[2] which at a depth of two miles have such perfect eyes that the remainder of the body might appear as only an appendix to them.

When Darwin considers the rudimentary organs as useless, he tells us something which is not by any

[1] L. Agassiz, "Rapportes des Animaux entre eux et avec le Monde Ambiant," "Revue des Cours Scientifiques," May 2, 1868, pp. 351, 352.   [2] "Nature," April 3, 1873.

means proved. Indeed, we are far from knowing perfectly the functions of all the parts of organized beings. It is therefore very possible that all rudimentary organs, like the wings of the apteryx, serve an end which is unknown to us,—we are ignorant of so many things! We should always say with Linnæus: *Deus omnisciens; legi aliquot ejus vestigia per creata rerum.*

The uniformity of plan adopted by the Creator in His works may very well explain the presence of organs without apparent use in some animals, whatever the transformists may say. God has impressed on them in some manner the seal of their parentage. Instead of being an argument in favor of evolution, remarks Agassiz, "does not the existence of a rudimentary eye discovered by Doctor J. Wyman in a fish (*amblyopsis spelæus*) of the Mammoth Cave of Kentucky, prove rather that this animal, like all others, has been created with all its peculiar characteristics by the fiat of the Almighty, and that this rudimentary eye has been left to it as a reminiscence of the general plan of structure on which is constructed the grand type to which it belongs?"

51. DARWINISM IS FAR FROM EXPLAINING WHAT IT ATTEMPTS TO EXPLAIN.—It is evident that Darwinism is far from explaining clearly the facts which it essays to explain. Every organic peculiarity, at least when it is well proved, should explain itself by its use. Now this is not the case, as Darwin himself acknowledges. There are upland geese with webbed feet which rarely or never go near the water.[1] On the plains of La Plata a woodpecker, the *Colaptes campestris*, has the feet of a climber and does not climb.[2] These are cases in which, if the Darwinian explanation were correct, certain organs should be atrophied through disuse. But it hap-

---

[1] Darwin, "Origin of Species," p. 177.
[2] Darwin, *op. cit.*, p. 176.

pens they are not. What should we conclude from this unless that the explanations of Darwin and his adherents are unsatisfactory and incomplete?

How many other facts are there which are equally mysterious to Darwinism? Thus it cannot explain the existence of the neuters, so numerous in beehives and ant nests. Nevertheless, this is a remarkable fact in natural history. Isolated cases in the animal kingdom are accidents, and consequently are explained without much difficulty; but here there is question of the regular and normal production of individuals, the organization of which transforms itself so as to assure sterility, although they came from ancestors that were fertile since the species existed. Here is a derogation from one of the most general rules of the organized world.[1] Darwin himself could find no satisfactory reason for this phenomenon nor for a great number of other facts.[2]

52. (*d*) ATAVISM.—Sometimes it happens that an animal, to whatever part of the zoölogical series it belongs, reproduces in an unexpected manner the traits of one of its ancestors, from which it is separated by several generations; this is what is called a case of "atavism." Transformists wish to explain resemblances which appear from time to time in the animal world, for instance in the mammifer, by heredity and affiliation with species of an inferior order, such as reptiles and fishes. Is this not going beyond the limits of induction? Hear what Conteyeau, a rationalist who denies both God and miracles, says: "Just like the arguments drawn from the embryonal state and rudimentary organs, those which the transformists borrow from atavism and monstrosities cannot reasonably be admitted, as long as the alleged facts regard exclusively varieties of the same species.

[1] Cf. Darwin, "Origin of Species," pp. 226 *seq.*
[2] Quatrefages, "Ch. Darwin," p. 164.

In all other cases they rather prove unity of plan. Indeed, it will be admitted without difficulty that accidental modifications of individuals look more or less alike among all the individuals of the group to which they belong. There is nothing unnatural in horses and asses having sometimes zebra legs, because, excepting the horse, all the species of the genus *Equus* (horse) are striped in various ways, but this does not prove at all, as is asserted, that they have a common ancestor with a striped robe."[1]

The theory of selection, therefore, does not clear up what it pretends to explain. It is far from removing all the veils which hide the secrets of nature. The arguments brought forward in its favor are not conclusive. Were they well founded, one could not help drawing therefrom at least the general truths of the system. But Darwin's theory offers, for the most part, only presumptions and probabilities. But were even these probabilities well supported, they would have to vanish before the light of facts. This is what we are now going to establish.

53. THE DARWINISTS DO NOT PRODUCE ONE ESTABLISHED FACT.—In all their discussions the Darwinists do not bring up as proof one established fact in support of their fundamental thesis. They maintain that species proceed from one another by way of descent, and they cannot show that it is a fact that a single species passed into another during the records of animal life. They draw inferences from the universal diversity of organic and inorganic things and from some particular abnormal productions. There is a hierarchy in beings; they assure us there is a genealogy; they establish resemblances, and affirm descent; they observe variability, and assert transmutability; they

[1] "Revue Scientifique," April 30, 1881.

conclude from the possibility of their system to its reality. However, as the scholastics say, very correctly, *a possibili ad actum non valet consecutio*. The possibility of a thing is far from explaining its existence; everything is possible, except what is self-contradictory. But science is the study of facts, not of possibilities; it is founded on observation and experience, and though it has the right to invent hypotheses, to bind together the phenomena observed, and thus establish a natural philosophy, it is only on condition of not contradicting the phenomena which we observe in the world, and of respecting the laws of nature, which we behold with our eyes in daily application. Every theory which is in opposition to the facts and the laws of nature must be rejected by the naturalist as unsound, and contrary to the principles and methods of science. Now the hypothesis of the mutability of species is in opposition to facts; this is what both history and experience attest.

54. HISTORY AND GEOLOGY.—History and geology, as high as one can ascend in the study of the past, confirm the permanency of species. Thus, in the ruins of Herculaneum and Pompeii, buried for more than 1800 years under lava from Mount Vesuvius, there was found in the house of a painter a collection of shells, and in the store of a fruit-dealer vessels full of chestnuts, olives, and nuts, all in a perfect state of preservation. These shells and fruits are nowise different from the same kinds of shells and fruits to-day. Aristotle described, more than 2000 years ago, a great number of plants and animals. His descriptions are exact and faithful pictures of the present species, and show that during the interval of time these species have undergone no perceptible change. In the course of the present century there were discovered in the tombs of ancient Egypt seeds of various plants and many species of em-

balmed animals, which had lived long before Aristotle, even as far back as the fourth Egyptian dynasty. These seeds and animals are the same as those of our day.

55. THE FAUNA OF ANCIENT EGYPT.—The same is the case with the plants and animals represented by the paintings, sculptures, and bas-reliefs that abound on the monuments of that country. Here are some examples: On the shores of the river Nile is found to-day an indigenous dog; formerly submissive to man, it is now free and nomadic. Thirty centuries of civilization, followed by a thousand years of barbarism, could not affect its nature nor cause it to undergo any change. These dogs, which are commonly called by the Hindoo name, *parias*, are altogether like those which are found embalmed in great numbers in the ancient tombs. The only and invariable sign for the word dog in all the hieroglyphic inscriptions is their picture. This indigenous type was not the only one which existed in the land of Menes and Sesostris. The greyhound, hunting-dog, and bulldog were also known, and their characteristic forms are exactly reproduced on bas-reliefs and paintings, which date back about 4000 years. We refer in particular to the figured scenes on the tomb of Roti, a famous sportsman who lived under the twelfth dynasty, more than 2000 years before Christ. On the most ancient monuments we hardly find anything but the hieroglyphic dog, which leads us to suppose that the other races were of foreign origin. It is not less curious that the greyhound and the bulldog were as distinct and characteristic at that time as they are to-day, and that these types have persisted without any notable change since the beginning of historical times, under the most diverse climates and most changeable conditions. With regard to the mastiff, properly speaking (*Canis laniarius*), it does not figure on the monuments of Egypt, but its

genealogy is very respectable, for its ancestors had already statues in Babylon and Nineve more than 600 years before Christ. Mr. Nott, in an interesting chapter treating of the " Monumental History of Dogs," [1] gives an engraving of a magnificent bas-relief found in the ruins of Babylon, and sculptured, as Oriental archæologists tell us, in the reign of Nabuchodonosor. It represents a fine mastiff, whose form and proportions, physiognomy and carriage are found again without any modification in the mastiff of to-day. There is here no question of mere resemblance, but of complete identity; and the identity is so marked that the Babylonian dog seems copied from a photograph of one of our most beautiful and useful watch-dogs. Thus certain types have perpetuated themselves without any change from the earliest times until our own days. Forty centuries at least have passed by without altering their general characteristics. Neither time, climate, habit, nor nourishment could efface the seal of nature.[2]

What is true with regard to dogs is equally true with regard to all other animals figured on the monuments of the valley of the Nile, as Cuvier attests: " I have carefully examined," he says, "the figures of animals and birds engraved on the numerous obelisks which came from Egypt, in the ancient city of Rome. All these figures, taken on the whole—and this alone could have been the object of attention for artists—bear a perfect resemblance to the species we see to-day. Every one can examine the copies thereof which Kircher and Zoega will furnish; without preserving the purity of

[1] This article forms a part of a remarkable chapter on hybridity, published in the beautiful work of Nott and Gliddon, " Types of Mankind."

[2] P. Broca, " Mémoire sur l'Hybridité," in the " Journal de la Physiologie de l'Homme," vol. i., pp. 444, 446.

the features of the animals, they yet offer very recognizable figures. It is easy to distinguish the ibis, vulture, screech-owl, falcon-hawk, the Egyptian goose, the lapwing, the ground-rail, the viper or asp, the ceraster, the Egyptian hare with its long ears, the hippopotamus, etc." Any Egyptologist unacquainted with fossil fauna will find Cuvier's account confirmed by an examination of the figures of birds and animals on the obelisk in the Central Park, at New York.

56. THE FLORA OF ANCIENT EGYPT.—The flora has no more changed than the fauna. With the flowers found in the tombs of Amenophis I., of the eighteenth dynasty, who lived over 3000 years ago, Schweinfurth has composed a magnificent herbal of samples for the museum of Boulak, and he has placed them alongside of modern specimens in order that the visitor may be enabled to compare them. The resemblance is such that the ordinary eye fails to detect any difference, either in form or color, without the written indications which make known their origin.[1]

Lacépède, therefore, correctly concluded from these facts, especially from the collection of mummified animals brought from Egypt by Geoffroy St. Hilaire:

"Never has there been anything brought to light to

---

[1] L. Drapeyron, "Revue de Géographie," 1882, vol. xi., p. 90. Cf. Kunth, "Recherches sur les Plantes dans les Tombeaux Egyptiens," by M. Passalacqua, in the "Annales des Sciences Naturelles," 1882, vol. viii., pp. 418, 423. "The fruits and fragments of plants," he says, on p. 418, "in the tombs of ancient Egypt almost all belong to vegetables which we meet to-day in those countries. The most scrupulous comparison of the analogous plants did not allow me to perceive any difference. Consequently, it appears to me to be proved that the vegetation of these two epochs is perfectly identical, and that since many centuries plants have not undergone any sensible change, either in their forms or in their structures."

decide better (the permanency of species), for here we have a great number of remarkable species which are several thousands of years old. It seems that the superstition of the ancient Egyptians was inspired by nature, with the view of leaving a monument of its history. This whimsical people, by embalming with such great care the animals which they had made the objects of their stupid adoration, have left us in their sacred grottos almost complete cabinets of zoölogy. . . . And when at present we satisfy ourselves with our own eyes what many species were about 3000 and more years ago, . . . we can hardly control our enthusiasm when we see animals preserved with their bones and hairs, and perfectly recognizable, which two or three thousand years ago had priests and altars in Thebes or in Memphis. But . . . let us confine ourselves to laying before you the inference from this portion of the collection made by citizen Geoffroy, namely, that these animals are perfectly similar to those of to-day."[1]

57. THE TERTIARY FAUNA.—Geology and paleontology permit us to go much further back into the past, far beyond the limits which history can reach, and their testimony is the same as that of ancient Egypt. Darwin has been obliged to acknowledge that the skeletons of animals have not changed since the glacial period. According to Agassiz, the southern extremity of Florida has been formed by the accumulations of the corals of tropical seas, and, if his calculations are correct, the formation of the coral reefs required no less a period than two hundred thousand years. Now when we compare the zoöphytes which formed the uppermost ledges of these reefs with those which formed their lowest strata, we cannot detect any difference between them.

Professor Marsh, our great American paleontologist,

[1] "Annales du Muséum," 11th year (1802), pp. 235, 236.

has up to the present time described from his great collection twenty-five different species of mammals from the tertiary formation. They are divided into fourteen kinds and seven families. All these families are equally represented by the European fauna.[1] Two scorpions from the silurian formation were discovered up to the present. The one was found by Torell, in 1884, on the island of Gothland; the other by Lesmahagon, also in 1884, in Scotland. Both greatly resemble the family of scorpions of our days. Besides the *Palæoblattina Douvilléi*, of which however only one wing was found, these scorpions are the only land animals which the silurian formation has produced thus far.[2] The archæopteryx is a fossil mesozoic bird, discovered by Andreas Wagner in 1861, in the lithographic slates of Solenhofen, in Bavaria. It is of the jurassic age, and is notable as the oldest known type of birds. A second species from the same formation and locality was named *Archæopteryx macrura* by Owen. The specific identity of the two can neither be affirmed nor denied, and their generic identity is only presumptive. A third and still more characteristic specimen is identical with the second, and has furnished many additional characters. When found at the beginning it was thought to form the transition between reptile and bird; now, however, it is proved to be really a bird. A specimen of this genus had a row of twelve teeth, of almost equal size, and about one millimetre long; its lizard-like tail was formed of twelve vertebræ, and it had separate metacarpal bones as well as a carinate sternum and other features of modern birds. In the wing were counted seventeen pinions, of which six or seven were flight-feathers; its long tail had many steerage-feathers.[3]

[1] "Jahrbuch der Naturwissenschaften," 1887–1888, pp. 333, 334.
[2] *Ibid.*, 1885–1886, p. 255.   [3] *Ibid.*, 1886–1887, p. 278.

Only very lately, two German savants, Professor Hosius and Dr. Marks, have shown that up to the present time the Westphalian chalk has furnished fifty-eight well-preserved fossil fishes, besides the teeth of at least thirteen flat and smelting gillaroos, so that the fishes found in the Westphalian chalk amount to seventy-one species. They all belong to the upper chalk and were sea-fish. They are representatives partly of the brackish-water fauna and partly of the sweet-water fish, whose nearest relatives still people the great rivers of South America and West Africa. It is a matter of interest that the Westphalian fish fauna shows the greatest agreement with the chalk fishes found at the foot of Mount Carmel, in Palestine, and near the city of Beyrout.[1]

58. THE TERTIARY FLORA.—C. von Ettingshausen established with certainty 129 species of the tertiary flora of Australia. True, there are many species which show an essential difference from the Australian flora of to-day, but there are also many whose forms are analogous to the flora now found in that country.[2] Peterson and Naumann gathered in Japan a great variety of fossil plants from the miocene, pliocene, and post-pliocene, *i.e.*, from the tertiary formation. Of these twelve belong to the tertiary flora of Alaska, fourteen are represented in Europe, and twelve were found in the Arctic regions. Its various representatives are still found to a greater or less extent in these countries.[3] Keilbach found in the peat strata, on the Elbe, near Lauenburg, which date from the diluvial time, twenty-two well-recognizable species of plants, and they are all still found in the same plain. The sea-thorn (*hippophaë rhamnoides*) found in the south of Sweden in the lime strata proves that this plant

[1] "Jahrbuch der Naturwissenschaften," 1885–1886, p. 256.
[2] *Ibid.*, 1887–1888, p. 336.
[3] *Ibid.*, 1889–1890, p. 370.

existed originally in Northern Europe in geological positions corresponding to the Alps, hence that it is an Alpine plant. Only at a later period did it wander from here to the coast, where it is still found in Sweden as well as in Northern Germany.[1]

The comparison of the flora of the glacial period with that of our time leads to the same results. There was discovered near Hohenhausen, in the canton of Zürich, in the midst of a peat marsh, quite a collection of the flora of these ages. These fossils are embedded in peat, whose formation, according to certain geologists, must have taken place between the two glacial epochs. The yew-tree, the wild pine, the larch, the birch, the maple, the nut-tree (two varieties), have been recognized as having existed in an age certainly anterior to ours. They have been compared with the same species as they now grow, and no difference has been found to exist between them. In a word, history and natural science prove the stability and permanency of species. The Darwinists cannot cite one historical instance of the transition of one species to another; their system is therefore in contradiction with the facts. Nature is not a "transformist," and Moses spoke the truth when he said that God created plants and animals according to their kind.

The transformists themselves have been obliged to acknowledge the force and certainty of the facts we bring forward in this chapter. They are forced to admit that there exists no positive proof of the transformation of one animal species into another. Even the fathers of the system, Huxley, Haeckel, and Darwin, admit this.

"According to Huxley, the structure of each animal is so well defined, so precisely marked, that in the present state of our knowledge no form can be offered as proof

[1] "Jahrbuch der Naturwissenschaften," 1886–1887, p. 356.

of transition from one group to another, from the vertebrates to the annelidæ, from the mollusks to the cœliacs; no more to-day than in ancient epochs, whose annals geology has studied. The positive proofs, the only certain and indisputable witnesses on which we count, are insufficient to establish any progressive modification of animals towards a type less embryonal, less generalized in a great number of groups of a long geological period. In these groups numerous variations manifest themselves very clearly, but progression, as generally understood, appears nowhere. The edifice of phylogeny, built on these hypotheses, must always, conformably to the nature of things, remain incomplete, full of voids, in part uncertain, and changing."[1]

"He who rejects these views on the imperfection of the geological record will rightly reject the whole theory. For he may ask in vain where are the numberless transitional links which must formerly have connected the closely allied or representative species found in the successive stages of the same great formation."[2]

59. DARWINISM AND PREHISTORIC TIMES.—It follows from the avowals of its own adherents that the theory of evolution is in contradiction with the best established facts of history and paleontology. Are these admissions not decisive, and have we not the right to conclude therefrom that the system is false and deceptive? However, the Darwinists do not acknowledge themselves beaten, even after these confessions; they say that what is not produced in historic times may have been produced in the prehistoric times—hundreds of centuries ago—although geology has not preserved any trace of these changes and revolutions. A system that is obliged to have recourse to the unknown, is no longer

[1] Haeckel," Natürliche Schöpfungsgeschichte," 7th ed. 1879, p. xxiv.
[2] Darwin, "Origin of Species," p. 319.

a scientific system; it does not rest on proofs, but on imagination. However, let us follow up the defenders of the variability of species on their own lines and show them by the light of natural history and experience that species such as they are constituted can never have changed.

60. THE STERILITY OF HYBRIDS PROVES THE FIXITY OF THE SPECIES.—To make the mutability of species, that is, the production of new species, possible, the products of the union of two different species should be able to perpetuate themselves indefinitely. Now, experience proves that this is not the case. "If the species change, hybridization would surely be the most direct and most efficacious means to operate the change. On the contrary, hybridization is the means which shows most completely the fixity of species."[1] All attempts made to produce new and permanent species by coupling two different species have been without success; all the efforts of the most skilful artificial selection fail, when opposed to the laws of nature. True, hybrids can be obtained, that is, individuals from parents of different species, such as the mule, the result of a union between a male ass and a mare, but these hybrids have not the faculty of perpetuating themselves.[2]

A species can vary almost indefinitely in the forms of its representatives without losing its fundamental fecundity and the faculty of reproducing itself in all its varied forms. The physiological separation of species, even of such as are very closely related, is clearly proven by the experiments of Darwin himself. He acknowledges that the struggle for existence and natural selection cannot explain the appearance of an organism. He

[1] Flourens, "Examen du Livre de M. Darwin sur l'Origine des Espèces," Paris, 1864, p. 91.
[2] Cf. A. Godron, "De l'Espèce et des Races," vol. i., p. 197 *seq.*

makes the same avowal when there is question of fecundity, which is supposed at a given moment to separate forms physiologically issued from the same stock and to transform them into distinct species.[1]

This sterility of hybrids furnishes a decisive proof in favor of the fixity of species. The adherents of variability have made vain efforts to contest the fact or to escape its consequences. It has been denied by Broca,[2] but maintained in a convincing manner by Quatrefages[3] and Blanchard. "A doubt exists for science," says the latter, "only with regard to the descent of some species very closely related. When one of the elements of production predominates, the other effaces itself; thus the independent character of specific types shows itself, and the impossibility to constitute a new and independent form."[4] "Nobody," says Quatrefages, "believes any longer in the fecundity of crosses between animals belonging to different classes or families."[5]

With regard to the vegetable kingdom, the experiments of M. Naudin, though an evolutionist himself, have established that hybrid plants cannot truly perpetuate themselves; after a certain number of generations they return naturally and spontaneously to the primitive type of the one or the other of the two original species.[6] Thus we can lay it down that in nature there is much less tendency to fuse species than to preserve the specific characters. This is demonstrated by the tendency which cultivated plants and domesticated ani-

[1] Quatrefages. "Note sur Ch. Darwin," in the "Comptes Rendus de l'Académie des Sciences," vol. xciv., 1882, p. 1221.
[2] Broca, "Mémoires Anthropologues," Paris, 1877, p. 242.
[3] Quatrefages, "L'Espèce Humaine," 6th ed., 1880, pp. 46, 61.
[4] Blanchard, "L'Origine des Êtres," in the "Revue des Deux Mondes," Oct. 1, 1874.
[5] Quatrefages, "Ch. Darwin," p. 234.
[6] Flourens, "Examen du Livre de Darwin," p. 92 *seq*.

mals have to return to their original forms.¹ We may therefore conclude with Flourens:

"There are two kinds of fecundity: first, a continued fecundity. This is characteristic of species. All varieties of horses, dogs, sheep, goats, etc., mingle and produce together with continued fecundity. Secondly, there is a limited fecundity. This is characteristic of the genus. When two distinct species, the dog and the jackal, the wolf and the dog, the ram and the goat, the ass and the horse, etc., are coupled, they produce offspring which will soon be barren; and this prevents any durable intermediate species from being established. The horse and the ass have been coupled for centuries, but the male and female mule do not produce any intermediate species; for centuries the goat and the ram have been coupled; they produce mongrels, but these mongrels have not given rise to an intermediate species. Scientists ask what is characteristic of genus; where can we find it? It lies in the two different kinds of fecundity. Continued fecundity marks species; limited fecundity marks genus."²

Finally, another fact which militates against the theory of evolution is, that the qualities of animals are immutable, whilst according to Darwin they ought to be changeable.

The characteristics of insects should have undergone some kind of transformation in the course of ages. But though they have been observed for many centuries, there is no modification, no progress in their instincts. The spider weaves its web to day in the same manner as it did in the time of Aristotle, and the ant gathers provisions just as it did in the time of Solomon.³

---

¹ O. Heer, "Le Monde Primitive de la Suisse," p. 763.
² "Examen du Livre de Darwin," pp. 113, 114.
³ For a more detailed refutation of Darwinism see Vigouroux, "Les Livres Saints et la Critique Rationaliste," 2d ed., Paris, 1886, pp. 537, 636; also Levand Lestrade, "Transformisme et Darwinism," Paris, 1885.

61. PLANTS AND ANIMALS SHOW THE PERMANENCY OF SPECIES.—The continued observation of plants and animals shows that the transformation of their essential qualities and the passing of one species into another are contrary to the laws of nature. History has established this cardinal point by every observation which has come under its domain. The Darwinists are unable to show or name a single specimen of a superior type issuing forth from an inferior one, or of one species being produced from a different species. There may be variations, nay, wide variations, within the species, but species is not transmutable in its nature and organism. The fact established by Darwin is this: natural selection, or, to speak more correctly, Divine selection, acting through the laws of nature which it has established, can produce new races. But Darwin's system is false, inasmuch as it confounds the species with the race; it applies to the former what belongs only to the latter. History and science agree in affirming with Genesis that species in the vegetable and animal world is primitive and irreducible. "*Naturæ semper est species et genus*," said Linnæus; "*culturæ sæpius varietas; artis et naturæ classis ac ordo.*" The breeder and the florist can produce varieties and races; God alone can create species.

Of the objections urged against Darwinism, the following is one of the most difficult to meet. The transformations assumed by Darwin are supposed to have been so slow that each species must have required a thousand, ten thousand, nay, perhaps a million of generations in order to be realized. These figures, multiplied by the thousands of species which succeed each other in the series since the beginning of life, would lead us to millions if not to milliards of years. "But," observes Conteyeau, a French savant, and himself a transformist, after his way, "before granting so freely these assumed periods of centuries, the Darwinist should first ask himself whether the earth and the sun, this wheel-work so indispensable to the development of life upon our planet, have lasted so long. Now, astronomers and physicists, who alone are competent to decide this question, do not seem to be disposed to make this concession."[1]

"All these deductions" (of the transformists), remarks Prof. Tait, "are cumulative; but a single fact is sufficient to overthrow the pretensions of Lyell and Darwin. We may state that it is a conclusion, demonstrated by natural philosophy, that the maximum of the past duration of animal life upon our globe can be approximately estimated at some ten to fifty millions of years at most, and that the future progress of science will never pass this estimate, but, on the contrary, will tend to reduce it more and more."[2]

In spite of the great admiration which Quatrefages has for the English naturalist, here is what he says of his system: "Darwin, as well as his predecessors, heap hypothesis upon hypothesis. Now, with the help of all these accessory theories, comparisons, and metaphors, is it possible to give an explanation of all the facts? No, for Darwin himself acknowledges repeatedly, 'I have the conviction, however, that objections like these have little weight, and that these difficulties are not insoluble.' But is this conviction a proof," continues Quatrefages, "or even an argument? . . . . It is to the judges appealed to by Darwin that I also address myself. It is to minds free from all prejudice, to competent, impartial, and intelligent men that I address the question, whether it is permitted, in matters of science, to regard personal conviction, or mere possibility, as proof,

[1] "Revue Scientifique," March 6, 1875.
[2] *Ibid.*

the unknown as an argument. . . . What is required first of all are facts, observations, and the results of experiments." [1]

A theory like Darwin's should at least have the merit of explaining the phenomena of the biological order. But Darwinism is incapable of explaining one of the most singular facts in natural history, namely, the existence of neutral individuals among bees and ants. For how can we understand the fact that fecund bees produce sterile bees, and this regularly and normally? Here is a deviation from one of the most general rules of the organized world. Besides, the fact is in clear contradiction to the most fundamental law of heredity laid down by Darwin and Lamarck.

62. ACCOUNT AND CRITICISM OF MONISM.—A theory intimately connected with Darwinism is Haeckel's monism, to which we already drew attention in the preceding chapter. Haeckel is the German Darwin; he is the culmination of the English Darwin—Darwin perfected. Indeed, the latter acknowledges the great services which Haeckel has rendered to his cause. "This naturalist," he says, "whose views on many points are much more complete than mine, has confirmed all the conclusions to which I have been led myself."

Haeckel, indeed, is more complete than Darwin; he has pushed the theory of evolution to its last consequences; he has reduced it to a coherent system; given by its means a universal explanation of the world and everything that exists, and opposed it to all the traditional explanations of the origin of things.

63. HAECKEL'S POSITION AMONG EVOLUTIONISTS.— A certain number of German transformists look upon Haeckel with some disfavor, and combat many of his

[1] "Ch. Darwin et ses Precurseurs," pp. 167, 170.

views which spring from the extravagant ideas he expresses in reducing everything to the moneron. He is the *enfant terrible* of the party, but nevertheless he received the approval of Darwin,[1] and it is not without justice that Haeckel answers his adversaries by claiming that he pushes his system to its logical conclusions, whilst they are satisfied to stop half-way. The English savant is full of reserve; he speaks of God, and tries to dispel the accusations of irreligion brought up against his system. The Jena Professor is more frank; he throws down the mask and deduces all the conclusions contained in the premises advanced by the theory of natural selection. Darwinism is rather a biological theory than a philosophical and religious system. Monism, on the contrary, is above all a materialistic explanation of the origin of things. Darwin occupies himself principally in answering the question *how*, and seeks the conditions of existence in what exists; Haeckel, before all, wants to know the *why*, and decides the question of cause and origin. Whilst the former does not formally exclude final causes, the latter makes light of them, and expressly rejects the action of an intelligent cause acting after a fixed plan in the work of the production of the world. He says:

"The theory of evolution set up by Darwin necessarily leads, when it is pursued to its logical consequences, to the admission of the monistic or mechanical conception of the world. Contrary to the dualistic or theological opinion, the mechanical theory regards the forms of both organic and inorganic nature as the products of natural forces. In every animal or vegetable species we behold not the materialized thought of a personal creator, but the transitory expression of a phase of the mechanical evolution of matter, the expression of a

[1] Cf. A. Wiegand, "Der Darwinismus," vol. ii., pp. 81, 82.

necessarily efficient cause, of a mechanical cause. While theological dualism sees in the wonders of creation only the arbitrary ideas of a capricious creator, *monism* or *unitism*, considering the real causes, finds in these evolutive phases only the necessary effects of natural, eternal, and insurmountable laws.... Monism is the only theory which explains the origin of species in a rational manner. If we reject it, all that remains is the irrational hypothesis of a miracle, of a supernatural creation."[1]

64. HAECKEL'S MONISTIC RELIGION.—Thus Haeckel pretends to build up both a philosophical and a scientific system. Nay, more, he has the ambition of founding a new religion, a monistic religion, which, according to him, will be the religion of the future. Listen to his own words:

"The monistic religion of nature, which we must regard as the only true religion of the future, is not, like the religions of the Churches, self-contradictory, but in harmony with our rational knowledge of nature. Whilst the former have no other source than illusions and superstitions, the latter rests on both truth and science. The simple natural religion, based upon a perfect knowledge of nature and upon the inexhaustible treasures of its revelations, will in the future imprint on human evolution a seal of nobility which the religious dogmas of the different peoples were incapable of bestowing on mankind; for all these dogmas rest upon a blind faith in obscure mysteries and mythological revelations formulated by the sacerdotal caste. Our epoch, which will have the glory of establishing scientifically the most brilliant results of human knowledge, the doctrine of descent, will be celebrated by the coming centuries as having inaugurated for the progress of humanity a new and fruitful era, characterized by the triumph of free

[1] Haeckel, "Schöpfungsgeschichte," p. 36.

research over the domination of authority, by the noble and powerful influence of the monistic philosophy."[1]

Thus Haeckel is not only a Darwinist, but also a transformist in the widest sense of the word; he is a reformer of both philosophy and religion, and a savant at the same time. His doctrine admits the theory of descent with all its consequences; that is, the eternity of matter, spontaneous generation, the primitive existence of eternal atoms from which everything descends through a series of developments and evolutions.

65. THE "MONERON" THE ORIGIN OF ALL THINGS.—From the preceding chapter we know that Haeckel places at the beginning of all things the so-called moneron; hence his system is called monism to indicate that it is derived from the most simple primitive being, unique in its nature and without any composing parts. From the moneron, which constitutes the first link in the organic chain, the amœba developed; this is a simple protoplasmic cell, containing a nucleus, but already endowed with sensibility and will.[2] Afterwards, several of these cells associating together begin to form what Haeckel calls synamœbæ.[3] This is the third link of the series. In their turn, these synamœbæ, which have no longer any representative in nature, became successively ciliated larvæ, shapeless worms, lampreys, salamanders, inferior monkeys, anthropoids, and, finally, men. According to Haeckel, there are twenty-two links which separate man from his primitive ancestor—the moneron.

66. MONISM IS INCAPABLE OF ESTABLISHING THE FILIATION OF SPECIES.—As monism is incapable of explaining the origin of the world and of life, it is still less able to establish the filiation of species and the ori-

---

[1] Haeckel, "Schöpfungsgeschichte."
[2] Haeckel, "Anthropogenie," p. 87.
[3] *Ibid.*, p. 338.

gin of man; the last point we shall prove in another chapter. In our criticism of Darwin's system we saw that it is not at all scientifically proved that a single species descends from another species by way of generation and evolution. According to transformism, one species arises from another by the gradual and insensible transformation of the type, by the accumulation of variations at first extremely slight and almost imperceptible, which finally constitute quite different beings, and, in the course of centuries, evolve from the primitive moneron man as we see him with his different races. But Haeckel and his adherents do not bring forward one single positive and direct proof in support of their assertions. They simply pile hypothesis upon hypothesis. They erect an imaginary scaffolding without giving to it a basis in fact. Their theory of the evolution of species by descent is supported by no proof. Albert Gaudry, Professor of Paleontology at the Museum in Paris, who believes in evolution and in the slow and progressive development of species, acknowledges this. He says:

"To tell the whole truth, we have to add that the actual state of science hardly allows us to go any further; it does not allow us to pierce the mystery which surrounds the primitive development of the great classes of the animal world. No man knows how were formed the primitive individuals of the foraminifera, echini, cephalopods, trilobites, insects, etc. . . . The primary fossils have not yet furnished us positive proof of the passing of animals from one class to another class. I acknowledge that when I commenced to study the reptiles of the Permian age, which in certain regards present characters of inferiority, I expected to find them related to fishes; but I have established just the contrary."[1]

[1] A. Gaudry, "Fossiles Primaires," Paris, 1883, p. 292.

Other eminent paleontologists tell us the same fact: "For twenty-five years I have followed the fossiliferous discoveries in the Belgian plain, isolating them carefully one from the other. . . . I have not yet found the transition of two well-determined types, either in time or in form" (Gosselet). "One thing is certain, that all the testimonies from the fossil flora are opposed to the doctrine of development due to evolution by filiation" (Carruthers). "On the one hand, all the facts are in favor of independent creation; on the other, they are equally contrary to transmutation" (Grand Eury).[1]

67. A LAST RAY OF HOPE.—However, another ray of hope is left to transformists. The adherents of transformism are pleased to insist upon recent discoveries in paleontology and the numerous gaps which they have filled up in the scale of beings. They live in hopes that the day will arrive when no void will be left, when each species will closely follow the preceding one, without the least abrupt transition, insensibly and by degrees, so that they will form a continued chain without any break.

Conteyeau, a freethinker who denies God and miracles, says: "These brilliant views are pure illusions. If this chain of beings is to have a questionable existence, the difficulty of which has been lost sight of too often, it would be necessary first to prove the transition of one species into another, and to make known the forms which connected them together. With a little attention we will soon be convinced that the intermediate links between classes, orders, genera, and even species, have no significance, because they allow numerous gaps to subsist. The continual discoveries of paleontology only prove that the frames of the organic world, considered as a whole, are infinitely more complete than those of living

[1] Cf. "Revue Scientifique," April, 1879.

nature. Fossil families, genera, species, insert themselves between other families, other kinds, other species, without the distance which separates the specific types diminishing in the least on this account. We can compare species to the soldiers of a company which continually receives new recruits; the ranks fill up, but the men are not distinguished from one another on this account. Hence it is between the species that we should discover links; but these links do not exist. Unless we suppose that species are formed, not gradually, but by abrupt leaps, and without links (which would be contrary to the transformist doctrine [1]), we must admit that the intermediate forms that ought to mark the transformation of two specifically related types must be represented by particular forms which we ought to find in the fossil state. But if we admit such forms, then these transitional forms would be infinitely more numerous than the known species; besides—and I cannot insist too strongly upon this point—the specific types lost in this multitude of intermediate forms could not be distinguished from one another, or, in other terms, could not exist. Now, what took place is just the contrary."

To escape this difficulty, the transformists have devised the theory of migrations. When, for instance, they are told that no intermediate form between the hipparion [2] and the horse of to-day is known, the answer is: That is not astonishing; the being you seek is found only in a region remote from where these animals used to live; otherwise it could not have transformed itself.

[1] We must remember that, according to the transformists, one species arises from another by the gradual and insensible transformation of the type, by an accumulation of variations, at first extremely small and almost imperceptible, which finally give rise to quite different beings.

[2] The hipparion is a genus of miocene or pliocene horse.

It is in a strange country (perhaps in Lemuria, where our anthropoids used to live) and under a different climate that you may meet the middle term in question.

Certainly, such a theory is very convenient, in the sense that it permits the transformists to answer all difficulties drawn from paleontology; but it is gratuitous, arbitrary, and presents, to say the least, a high degree of improbability, for which reason it was rejected even by most Darwinists. Indeed, great effort is needed to imagine a long voyage to and fro, in order to explain the formation of each species; moreover, species are counted by thousands in the different strata and in the various epochs. It seems, therefore, impossible that they should not have left, here and there, a little bone, some traces of the intermediate links.

The forms of transition, the intermediate species claimed by the theory of Haeckel, are absolutely wanting, whilst they should be infinitely more numerous than the species. Traces of an unfinished being have never been found, of a being imperfect in its kind, while becoming "provided with new organs," in the process of formation, and really transitional. The absence of these essential proofs is a fact; it is childish in Haeckel to hide himself behind a heap of hypotheses without an iota of proof, and to draw premature conclusions in favor of an unsupported system, which he hands down to posterity in the hope of its being received and established by discoveries which time may bring to light. On the other hand, it is well to remark that if it be true that thus far only a part of the organisms of each country is known, it is also true that we possess such remains from the greatest part of the earth's surface. Now, everywhere the organic products are the same; we meet the same abrupt appearances, the same absence of transitional forms. Finally, besides the intermediate types which have already been discovered or which, it is likely, will be discovered, there are and there will be abnormal types, whose origin is completely inexplicable, and among the intermediate types themselves there are such as are links as regards form, but not as regards the time of their appearance; for example, the type gyroceras, intermediate between the nautilus and lituiter, appeared long after both of these.

The inequality in the evolutionary types during the primary period is evident, and does not confirm the theory of a struggle for life. Paleontology suggests the contrary; some of the strongest animals passed away, while the smallest survived. The superior vital force of inferior beings sometimes is found to consist in their weakness (Gaudry).

68. CONSOLATION OF THE CHRISTIAN.—It is the consolation of the defenders of Christian doctrine that error passes and truth survives. The light of the sun can be obscured for a moment by thick clouds, but it dispels them finally. Transformism makes continual appeals to the unknown future in order not to be found flagrantly guilty of falsehood; it does not affirm what it cannot prove in its own way, but it invokes now the possible, now the past or the future, which cannot be called to account. Such is its answer to the objections which are made against it. All experience is contrary to spontaneous generation, which serves as its starting-point. After resorting to all kinds of scientific quibbles and to verbal sophistry, the final answer is: Some day we will be able to establish the existence of spontaneous generation! Nowhere have the links been met which genealogically bind one species to another. Transformism answers: they will be met with later on. The learned have looked in vain for man's ancestor, even the pithecoid monkey. Transformism answers: the pithecoid is

buried in the ancient continents, submerged to-day by the waters.

But a time will come when reason will assert its power over the human mind, when those who are misled by the materialistic mirage will perceive the illusion and see clearly that all these pretended answers and quibbles have no foundation in fact, are not reasonable deductions from the laws of nature, are not consistent with the experiments of science. Then they will recognize that reason in harmony with faith demands a Creator, in order to account for the origin of the universe and of ourselves; then they will admit that what Christians believe is the truth, and that the best, the only explanation of the order of the world and the hierarchy of species is the explanation of Genesis. The existence of a plan in creation which has inspired such beautiful pages from Fénélon and many other illustrious and shining lights of Christianity, will always remain true.

CHAPTER III.

ORIGIN OF MAN.

What is man?—Whence does he come?—Different methods followed to arrive at the knowledge of man.—Man's origin and nature.—Teachings of faith.—Scientific certainties.—Harmony between faith and true science.—Pseudo-scientific systems.—Man's immediate ancestor.—Professor Mivart's theory.—Can it be maintained?—Conclusion.

THE development of life in nature reaches its highest perfection and crown in man. Despite evolution and materialistic theories, man must have a distinct place in the plan and order of creation—a place becoming his rank, intelligence, and power over all created beings.

69. WHAT IS MAN AND WHENCE DOES HE COME?—Man is so differently viewed by different thinkers that it is not surprising to hear him styled—son of God, king of creation, microcosm, glory and wonder of the universe (Darwin), thinking reed, an animal which knows how to make tools, an animal which can laugh, the last product of the creative soil, a perfected monkey, the first of the primates, etc.

What is man? Is he formed of one substance only? Is he only a little organized matter, endowed with some movement for a very short time, an invisible atom in the great whirlpool of life, in the immensity of the worlds? Or is he, on the contrary, a composition of two substances essentially distinct and united in one person, of a body and a soul, according to the traditional belief of centuries?

Whence does man come? Did he always inhabit this

terrestrial globe upon which he reigns as master? How did he appear for the first time? At what time, in what place? Is he simply the highest step in the ascending scale of the animal series, or has he the right to a distinct place in nature? Must he maintain his place as the highest embodiment of corporal and spiritual existence, apart from all the rest of visible creation?

What is the destiny of man's body, which can see and touch itself, which forms a part of the Ego, which moves, lives, palpitates, grows, declines, and dies? What becomes of it after the grave—after the disintegration of the elements of which it is composed? And the soul?—the "unknown cause of exclusively human phenomena" (Quatrefages), which we call the Ego. Can it exist separated from the body—isolated from all matter? Will it really exist in a future life? Will it be completed anew—furnished with organs? And then! Where will it be? Will the worlds which surround us—the infinite worlds—will they be of its domain?

Is this thirst for life, light, love, and happiness—this insatiable thirst which devours us—a snare, a cruel enemy, or an intuitive foretaste, an infallible presentiment, a Divine promise? And this word which ravishes and terrifies at the same time—*immortality?* this word which is not the infinite, but almost as crushing for the human thought as the infinite—immortality, eternity; will eternity be my dwelling-place, will I be a guest of eternity?

It would be difficult to conceive a series of scientific or philosophical questions which are more important and more absorbing, for to answer them is to know what we are to-day and what we shall be to-morrow.

70. MAN'S ORIGIN AND NATURE; TEACHING OF FAITH. — What does faith teach us concerning the origin and nature of man? It teaches us that God is the

origin and end of man; it teaches us the personal union of a material body and of a spiritual, free, responsible and, consequently, immortal soul.

The creation of Adam and Eve is related in clear terms at the beginning of our Sacred Books; the narrative there found excludes any doubt of the direct intervention of the Creator.

All men who have existed since Adam and Eve, who exist to-day, who form or will form part of the human family, descend from this primitive and only pair. Let us ask now what science teaches.

71. MAN'S ORIGIN AND NATURE; SCIENTIFIC CERTAINTIES.—What are the teachings of science with regard to the origin of mankind? One of its best-informed representatives to-day is Quatrefages, who answers our question as follows: "Some men, eminent in science and rich in imagination, have thought that they could dispense with observation and experience. Others have resisted the impulse of the time and remained faithful to method, the mother of modern science. . . . As warmly as the most fiery partisans of the so-called advanced theories, they have applauded all true progress; they have welcomed as enthusiastically every new idea, on condition of exposing it to the tests of experiment and observation. But when they met with questions which cannot be solved now, and which perhaps will never be solved, they did not hesitate to answer: *We do not know.* I venture to say that I have always remained in the ranks of this phalanx, to which the future certainly belongs. For this reason, to those who question me on the problem of our origin, I do not hesitate to answer in the name of science: *I do not know.*"[1]

72. SCIENTIFIC CERTAINTIES ABOUT MAN.—In these lines, written yesterday, there is nothing to be changed

[1] Quatrefages, "L'Espèce Humaine," vol. ii. ch. xi.

to-day. Every anthropologist faithful to the principles of scientific method agrees with Quatrefages. But alongside of these, sciolists who have often displayed shallow views touching certain truths of scientific certainties on the origin of man have made their appearance. These truths are: man did not always exist on earth; long geological periods passed before his appearance. His existence is scientifically established only at the epoch called quaternary—the last of all. Tertiary man is undoubtedly a myth; but even if he were proved, the conclusions would be the same. The origin of the human species is relatively recent.

By his nature, by his physical, physiological, intellectual and moral characters, man occupies the highest place in the animal kingdom; his royalty in creation is universally conceded and beyond question; it is acknowledged as a royalty *de facto*, if not by divine right, by all anthropologists, even by the most obstinate defenders of transformism and materialistic doctrines.

"All men are of the same species. . . . There exists only one human species. The facts so far collated authorize us to look upon the plain of Central Asia as the cradle of the human species."[1] The teaching contained in these propositions is not given with the same unanimity, but it possesses all the characters of real certainty. On account of the number and the nature of the facts on which it is based, on account of the number and authority of the savants who maintain it, it can be regarded as the teaching of anthropological science at the present hour.

73. HARMONY BETWEEN FAITH AND TRUE SCIENCE.—Here, as upon many other points, we find that the teaching of the Bible and of faith agrees with the answers to the gravest problems solved by science.

[1] Quatrefages, "L'Espèce Humaine," vol. ii., ch. xi.

On man's origin, the Bible affirms, faith defines, positive science affirms nothing; it "does not know." Hence there is and can not be any conflict with regard to this point.

On the question of the date of man's origin, of the appearance of man in the series of living beings, the Bible and nature, faith and science, each following the principles and method which are proper to it, arrive at the same conclusion: man is the last term of creation.

As to the question of the rank man holds in nature, the methods of science and faith are different, but the conclusion is still the same: Man is the highest term of creation.

On the question of descent, faith teaches the unity of the human species; the immense majority of savants affirms and demonstrates monogenism; positive anthropology is monogenistic. The Bible and science agree in assigning to mankind the same cradle, in the centre of the same continent.

In this harmony of faith and science there is nothing forced; no violence is done to the doctrine, to the text of Scripture, to the scientifically manifest laws of nature. Before the discoveries of geology and paleontology, without revelation nobody could even have surmised that man had appeared last, at the end of numerous geological transformations, after long periods of purely animal life. The Bible has taught for thirty centuries what science could establish only with difficulty since yesterday.

Huxley, borrowing from the inspired Book, which he rejects, one of its most striking figures, seems to pity those who "waste their lives in attempting to put the new and generous wine of science into the old utricles of Judaism." The new wine of science, generous as it may be, will be preserved in the old utricles of Judaism, which have become, by a Testament in good and due form, the utricles of Christianity, as the not less tumultuous waters of the ocean are kept in the old bed which the hand of God has dug for them.'

74. PSEUDO-SCIENTIFIC SYSTEMS: THE NATURAL ORIGIN OF MANKIND, OR THE ANIMAL DESCENT OF MAN.—Unfortunately, not all anthropologists have either the frankness or the reserve of Quatrefages when there is question of the origin of man. There is a young school too much infatuated with itself to humbly confess its inability to solve a problem of such importance, and as its principle and its end are to exclude the supernatural, it does not hesitate to affirm the animal origin of man, though neglecting to bring the proof for its assertion. Its principal representatives are mainly in Europe: in France, M. Mortillet, the legislator of pre-historic science; in England, Darwin, who has given his name to the transformist system most in vogue; in Germany, Haeckel, the best known and the cleverest of his adherents; in Switzerland, Karl Vogt, who has the doubtful honor of not being surpassed by anybody in impiety, not even by our American Ingersoll, whom we may consider as the representative of the above school in our country.

For the men of the above school man is nothing else than a mammifer, whose organization, needs, sicknesses are the most complicated, whose brain and admirable functions have attained the highest degree of development. As such he is subject to the same laws as the rest of animals; as such he shares their origin and their end.

Professions of faith of this kind can no longer be counted. Some years ago the *Revue des Deux Mondes* published an article by Ch. Richet, Director of the *Revue*

¹ Duihlé, "Apologie Scientifique," ch. xvi.

Ecclesiastique, on the "King of Animals." The importance and publicity of this document gave a particular significance to the conclusions of the author, who says:

"All organic beings form one chain of life, which appears interrupted only in consequence of our ignorance of forms that are extinct or have disappeared. In this hierarchy of beings man is found in the first rank. It is not only by descent or by birth that man is one and the same with the animal, but also, perhaps, by his death and destinies.

"The same organs, the same appearance, the same functions; the same birth, the same life, the same death. . . . There are no longer two ways of dying, one for the demi-god man, the other for the simple animal; both perish in the same manner. The heart ceases to beat, the respiration stops, the nervous system loses its properties; afterwards, the chemical atoms which constitute the body separate and go to form other combinations. The carbon and oxygen of man's body are not of a different nature from the carbon and oxygen of the body of other animals. . . . Therefore, it may be considered as proved that there is no impassable abyss between man and the animal."

This is what is asserted in the name of physiology and psychology.[1] Poetry even takes its turn.

"My dog is sitting before me and looks straight into my eyes, and I, too, am looking into his. . . . I understand there is no difference between us. We are the same; in each of us oscillates the same little trembling flame. Death will befall us both, and strike us with its large, cold wing. Who will recognize afterwards the difference between the little flames which were in him and in me?"[2]

[1] "Revue des Deux Mondes," Feb. 15, 1883, pp. 819-821.
[2] Tourgenief, "Petits Poèmes en Prose."

"Man, both in his corporal and his spiritual being, is a mere chemical product of matter."[1] "His being is the sum of the combined actions of the atoms of his body and the exterior world; a pure product of the corporal change of matter, which judiciously puts itself into motion and continually moves until its dissolution. It is nonsense to believe that a higher power breathes a spirit and soul into the fœtus."[2] "The moneron which digs for phosphate of lime seeks more than gold; it digs for wheat for man. It raises the treasure of the spirit (for without phosphorus, no thought), which the farmer puts into circulation, reserving for the wheel of time its own force."[3]

Such is the doctrine of materialism on the nature of man. Let us listen to its doctrine about his origin.

"The organic beings that people the earth owe their origin and propagation only to a combination of the natural forces and materials that are in them. These are the germs of everything living, endowed with the idea[4] of genus from all eternity, and waiting for the action of certain external circumstances in the formless atmospheric mass, out of which the earth was gradually formed. These germs were present in space, and after their formation and cooling settled upon the earth, but were hatched and developed only by chance, in some cases when both the unity and generality of external conditions were present."[5]

The proceeding in detail was the following: "Man developed from the primordial slime of eternal matter partly owing to accident, partly of necessity, by the throwing and mixing together" (says Vogt; Büchner

---
[1] Büchner, "Kraft und Stoff," p. 286.   [2] *Ibid.*, p. 159.
[3] Moleschott, "Kreislauf des Lebens."
[4] These germs, according to Büchner, were a box of Pandora.
[5] Büchner, *op. cit.*, pp. 78, 91.

calls it combination) "of the materials of the first organic cells. From this original genesis arose at first the vegetable, then the animal forms, which, through infinite changes (metamorphoses), finally developed into the ape. The first man sprung from the ape; at the breast of the she-monkey he sucked his mother's milk."

Haeckel is more exact about the matter. According to Darwin, man descends from a monkey, but Haeckel wants to know the pedigree of the monkey. He is right, and he also succeeded in finding it in the moneron which "is neither plant nor animal, and is in fact without organism; a shapeless, simple, homogeneous protoplasm, a lump of jelly, in which the thing itself, not larger than a pin's head, was enveloped." Now we know our ancestor. Of course, this moneron obtained its living organic form through spontaneous generation, so Haeckel tells us, using a brand-new word—*autogony*. Hence no Creator is needed any longer, and according to Haeckel and his adherents, He was never needed.

75. NO PERSONAL CREATOR NEEDED ANY LONGER.—Darwin made a mistake in still accepting a Creator for a few primitive species, or at least for one. His more advanced followers do not need a Creator at all; they can explain things without Him. Bronn, the translator of Darwin's book on the "Origin of Species," adds: "If a personal creative act is necessary, then it is quite indifferent to us whether the first creative act dealt with only one or with ten or with one hundred thousand species, or whether it did this once and for all times to come, or whether it repeated this from time to time. The question is not, how many species of organisms it called into existence, but whether it was necessary at all to meddle with the wonderful workings of nature and to assist its creative laws? When Darwin attacks

creation in general, then, according to our conviction, he must renounce creation for the first alga."¹ The words of T. V. Bischoff have a similar sound. He sees in creation a very critical and dangerous restraint of our inquiries. But Vogt's literal expression is the climax of all: "The Creator must be put out of doors unceremoniously, and we cannot allow the least room for the operations of such a being."²

However, Haeckel's moneron, our great-grandsire, like the rest of the human beings had its weak points when brought before the light of reason and sober judgment. Let us examine it.

76. THE PRECURSOR OF MAN NO LONGER FOUND AMONG THE LIVING. — When anthropologic monism attempted to support its *a priori* doctrine of the animal descent and the purely natural origin of man by facts, when it attempted to pass from theoretic fancy to positive science, the first difficulty which presented itself was to determine what is the last term of animal evolution, the immediate ancestor of man.³ None of the actual anthropoid monkeys can pretend to that honor; the warmest adherents of the animal descent of man are agreed on this point. The ancestor of man no longer exists among the living; he cannot be found even among the dead; not even the least fragment of his skeleton is left to us. On this second point also the agreement is unanimous.

77. THE GODFATHERS NOT HAPPILY INSPIRED. — Although there was no certainty at all about the matter, nevertheless some believed they had found the fossil remains of man's ancestor, and immediately proceeded to

---

[1] "Ueber die Verschiedenheit der Schädelbildung des Gorilla," pp. 79, 81.

[2] Vogt, "Vorlesungen über den Menschen," p. 133.

[3] Tourgenief, "Petits Poèmes en Prose."

give him a name. The eozoon[1] and bathybius also had been baptized prematurely. But on this occasion the godfathers were less happily inspired, for they selected a name that is less poetic and harmonious. Our simian ancestor will, if ever discovered, be called *Pithecanthropus* or *Anthropopithecus*, according as he will appear to be more nearly related to monkeys or, to man; or perhaps the name of *Homo alalus* will be given him as the name nearest to the *Homo sapiens* of Linnæus; for it is a settled fact with these gentlemen that the immediate ancestor of man and woman was dumb; the monkey theorists wish it so.

From the scientific label to the learned and detailed description the distance is not great. The road is the more pleasing the less one needs to fear refutation by facts. Charles Darwin, however, did not abuse the situation; he shows himself more modest, even a little vague. He says:

78. MAN'S ANCESTORS.—"Man is descended from a hairy, tailed quadruped, probably arboreal in its habits, and an inhabitant of the Old World. This creature, if its whole structure had been examined by a naturalist, would have been classed amongst the quadrumana as surely as the still more ancient progenitor of the Old and New World monkeys. The quadrumana and all the higher mammals are probably derived from an ancient marsupial animal, and this through a long line of diversified forms from some amphibian-like creature, and this again from some fish-like animal. In the dim obscurity of the past we can see that the early progenitor

[1] A supposed fossil animal discovered some years ago in Canada in the Laurentian rock; hence it is called *Eozoon Canadense*. The discovery caused a great noise at the time. However, to-day most geologists and naturalists doubt, and not without reason, whether the Eozoon Canadense was really an organic being at all.

of all the vertebrata must have been an aquatic animal, provided with branchiæ, with the two sexes united in the same individual, and with the most important organs of the body (such as the brain and heart) imperfectly or not at all developed. This animal seems to have been more like the larvæ of the existing marine ascidians than any other known form."[1]

Thus, according to Darwin, man's immediate ancestor was some kind of a monkey with "pointed ears"; he does not tell us whether he could move his ears at pleasure or not. If he could, then surely the human species seems to be degenerating.

79. MAN'S ANCESTORS ARE TWENTY-TWO.—While Darwin is somewhat vague and uncertain about man's lineage, Haeckel is more precise. The latter also succeeded in discovering our progenitor in the famous moneron, *Bathybius Haeckelii*, in the depths of the ocean. The sole survivor of man's prehistoric ancestors is the lancelet (amphioxus), which we must therefore regard with special veneration as the only animal now existing which can enable us to form an approximate conception of our silurian vertebrate ancestor.[2]

It was Huxley who, in 1863, in his book "Man's Place in Nature," was the first to teach that our species descends from an ape. The German transformist accepted this opinion, and has since defended it with the ardor which is so characteristic of him:

"The catarrhinian monkeys, provided with a tail, sprang from prosimians by the transformation of their set of teeth and the change of the claws into nails; this

---

[1] Darwin, "The Descent of Man," p. 609.
[2] Haeckel defends this view in his "Anthropogenie," p. 337, and there repeats that the amphioxus is "flesh of our flesh and blood of our blood." This, he assures us twice over, "is the most interesting of the vertebrate animals after man."

probably happened since the tertiary age. The anthropoids descended from the catarrhinians. . . . For this reason the latter had to lose their tail and partly their hair also; besides the cerebral skull predominated over the facial skull. . . . These ancestors belonged to the miocene period. . . . The man-monkey very probably lived towards the end of the tertiary age. From the anthropoids, owing to improved habits and more complete differentiation of the two pairs of extremities, he derives his erect position. The anterior extremities became the hands of man, the posterior the feet. Although these men-monkeys were not only by their exterior conformation, but also by the development of their intellectual faculties, nearer to the true man than the anthropoids, nevertheless they were wanting in the peculiarity really characteristic of man—articulate language, with the development of intelligence and of consciousness which is inseparable therefrom. The existence of primitive men deprived of speech is a fact of which every serious mind can find the proof in comparative linguistics, or the comparative science of language, and especially in the history of the evolution of language in the child and in every people. . . . True, man proceeds from the anthropoids by the gradual transformation of animal cries into articulate sounds. The development of the faculty of speech naturally caused that of the organs which corresponded thereto, that is of the larynx and of the brain. . . . The transition of the man-monkey deprived of speech into the perfect man endowed with language took place by degrees."[1]

According to Haeckel, the genealogy of man is a very long one. Twenty-two animal forms mark the line of development, and are the principal halting-places in nature's progression from the moneron to

[1] Haeckel, "Geschichte der Schöpfung," pp. 580, 581.

man. Let us give the main outlines of this long and mysterious genealogy, which is enough to provoke a smile or draw a tear of compassion for one who is so deluded as to believe that the noblest work of God is, after all, only an animal developed from a lump of jelly, a cone-shaped worm, a dog-fish, a kangaroo, an orang-outang, etc. According to Haeckel, our ancestors, after having been at first mere inorganic matter, were endowed with life through spontaneous generation; man by degrees crept along the ascending scale from a moneron, an amœba, a synamœba (morula), a ciliated larva (planula), a gasteropod, an acœlomate (turbinated) worm, a scolopendrous worm, a sacciform worm (ascidia), an acranian (amphioxus), the most ancient of the vertebrates, a monorrhine (lamprey), a dog-fish (fish of the shark species), a mud-fish (vertebrate standing between fish and amphibia), an amphibian like the celebrated *Proteus anguineus*, which inhabits the grotto of Adelsberg, a tailed batrachian (resembling the present salamanders and newts); then, in the secondary period, a beaked animal (ornithostoma), resembling the ornithorhynchus of Australia and Tasmania (*Ornithorhynchus paradoxus* and *Echidna hystrix*), a marsupial (resembling the kangaroos); in the beginning of the tertiary period, a semi-ape (prosimia), a tailed ape, catarrhinus, with a narrow nose, a cheek pouch and tail, an anthropoid (without a tail, resembling the orang, gibbon, gorilla, and chimpanzee), the pithecanthropus or man-monkey, and finally the real man.[1]

Of course, Haeckel does not consider himself obliged to furnish the proof of all he advances. His whole argumentation is based on theoretical considerations, as he

[1] See the genealogical tree of man in the "Anthropogeny," pl. xi. The first twenty-two are described in the "Geschichte der Schöpfung," pp. 500, 515.

is obliged to confess himself, on a simple reasoning of fitness; he must escape the miracle of creation. This is what is presented to us as experimental science.

80. HAECKEL SEVERELY CRITICISED.—However, in order to be just towards his party, we must not omit to inform our readers that Haeckel was severely criticised for this by his own adherents. Vogt, one of the most zealous, giving an account of what he calls his "large book," the Anthropology, qualifies his Darwinism as exaggerated, and he adds: "If M. De Quatrefages is too modest when he says, *I do not know*, M. Haeckel, on the contrary, knows everything. For him there is nothing obscure; everything is proved to evidence. From the amorphous moneron up to speech-endowed man, all the stages are determined by induction, their number fixed at twenty or twenty-two, and all these phases are placed in the corresponding geological ages. Nothing is wanting. Unfortunately, this complete and this well-managed genealogical tree, like Roland's horse, shows one single small defect. As life was wanting to the paladin's horse, so reality is lacking to Haeckel's pedigree. Every step is traced by means of imaginary beings, of the existence of which nobody ever found any proof, but which nevertheless must be looked upon as entirely real beings. If they have not been found as yet, they will be later on, or their constitution was such that they were not preserved in geological strata."

These are wise words, but is the system of Vogt any better than that which he criticises so severely? According to him, man descends from the annelides or worms, and did not pass through the ascidians and amphioxus, as the Jena Professor pretends. Vogt goes further, and in a memoir crowned by the Society for Anthropology, Paris, he denies that any species of the now existing monkeys can be looked upon as representing one of the phases through which mankind passed in the course of development. According to him, we have to go further back in order to find the common ancestor of the primates, the family in which he places man.

This categorical avowal does not hinder the Geneva Professor from proclaiming occasionally the simian origin of man, and, what is more, to pride himself on it, because, as he says: "It is better to be a perfected ape than a degenerated Adam."[1] Being a polygenist as well as an adherent of the evolutionary system, he asks himself whether we could not derive the American Indian from American monkeys; the negroes from African monkeys, and the negroids from the monkeys of Asia. Vogt often contradicts himself; for in one place he denies our descent from the existing monkeys, in another, as a transformist, he pushes this doctrine to such extremes that he denies the possibility of determining the transition of one race of men to the next. But the advantage of opposing orthodox doctrine on all these points justifies, it appears, all his contradictions.

Such is the evolutionary and materialistic doctrine on the origin of man; such are the hypotheses, the affirmations, the fantastic amplifications to which it has given rise.

81. MIVART'S VIEW ABOUT MAN'S BODILY ORIGIN.—The most important question connected with this subject is the relation of faith to the theory of development. We have seen before what faith teaches us with regard to the origin of man—God is the origin and end of man. His person is made up of a material body and a spiritual, free, responsible, and consequently immortal, soul. Just as the soul of the first man was created immediately by God, so also the soul of every man is created by Him. These are propositions from which we are not allowed

[1] "Leçons sur l'Homme," 1878.

to deviate, and all the faithful are bound to accept them without any misgiving or doubt. There cannot be any question as to the development of the human soul, as to its origin and nature. Matter by itself can never produce spirit; every true philosophical thinker has to admit this, and faith does not leave any doubt upon this subject.

But what of man's body? Here we come to speak of a view which has already caused a good deal of comment, surprise, and quarrelling among European Catholics, and also to some extent among the highly educated Catholics of America. There is no question here of the theories of man's descent as set forth by Darwin, Haeckel, and their followers; we are now examining the hypothesis of Professor Mivart, according to which the theory of descent should find its application in the formation of the body of the first man. Professor Mivart asserts in all earnestness the spirituality and immortality of the soul and its immediate creation by God. This is understood as a matter of course, as he is one of the most respected Catholics in England, and was professor in the Catholic College at South Kensington. However, he believes that he has a right to hold on the origin of man's body opinions very different from those usually accepted heretofore. He thinks it possible to maintain, without opposing any doctrine of faith, that the body of man originated like that of every other animal, that is to say, by descent, and that God then breathed the reasonable soul into this body, which was derived from an animal organism. Thus, the body of Adam was similar to that of a man-like monkey, and we should have to admit that the development of this animal's body was guided and protected during its development with particular care, in view of receiving in the future a reasonable soul. After this animal had lived through a series of years, and after the removal of the animal soul, God created in the full-grown body a reasonable soul as the only principle of life, and thus, says Mivart, arose the first man. Hence the body of man arose under the guidance and superintendence of Providence; but this development took place in harmony with nature's law. To prove that this is man's origin, Mivart argues that the human body, from the point of view of anatomy, is only the animal organism further developed and perfected.

Man, he continues his argument, is a rational animal (*animal rationale*). It is certainly natural and fitting that, if a being (animal) of the class of the mammalia should be formed and endowed with reason, it should also be formed in accordance with the general laws of its class, and this not only as regards the shape of the full-grown body, but also in its development to its present state as regards kind and manner. Professor Mivart bases this supposition on its possibility, and because man is a being endowed with sense (animal), he believes that this kind of explanation is reconcilable with the teaching of the Church, though he admits that some do not agree with his views on account of the teachings of faith.[1] The *Augsburger Allg. Zeitung* lately said that A. R. Wallace ascribed the great spread of Darwinism in England largely to the views of Professor Mivart, "who is as good a Catholic as he is an anatomist, accepts unconditionally the descent of man, as regards the body, and who is only in doubt whether the entire intellectual and moral nature of man does not also come from the same source and through an analogous development."[2]

---

[1] Cf. "Genesis of Species," p. 277; "Lessons from Nature," 1876, p. 177; Dublin Review, January, 1872.

[2] Augsburger Allg. Zeitung, 1877; Beil. Nr. 17; cf. "Theol. Quartalschrift," Tübingen, 187", p. 171.

82. CAN MIVART'S HYPOTHESIS BE MAINTAINED?—
According to our plan, let us now examine the question
of the corporal origin of man on the basis of the sources
of faith, and particularly of the account of Holy Scripture. There is question here of the origin of the first man.
"But," says the Jesuit Knabenbauer,[1] "Adam, just because he was the first man, could not enter the world like
all men after him, who are generated and born. All will
agree in this. Now, how did he come into the world?
Various suppositions are imaginable and possible. God
could, if He wished, create him according to the body
out of nothing, just as well as He created the fundamental
matter of all things and the human soul out of nothing.
He could, as the human body was to be material, use
already existing matter for its formation. He could also
allow a man-like body to develop itself through a natural
process, according to the hypothesis of Professor Mivart.
The question now is, Which of these possible ways did
God in fact employ, and have we the means to learn this
as a matter of fact? In many cases we have two sources
of knowledge; on the one hand, the nature of things which
our reason comprehends and understands, and from which
it draws conclusions; on the other, supernatural Scripture and tradition. These are at our command in this
case, and we have to consult both if we wish to form a
correct opinion on this question.

"When we consider our question according to the first
source, we may view man's corporal likeness to other animals, his sensitive activity and everything that is proper
to man as we view animals; but we must not forget,
even when investigating from this point of view, that the
reasonable soul, the influence of which cannot be weighed,
because it cannot be compared, surpasses every purely
sensible principle of life; that therefore the reasonable

[1] "Stimmen aus Maria-Laach," 1877, vol. ii., pp. 123, 125.

soul must find instruments in the body for activities, for which no analogy is possible in the domain of the purely sensible expressions of life. The *dignity* of the soul in itself and the *peculiarity* of its functions, whose instrument the body should be, raise the question whether the corporal descent of man from an animal body is conceivable at all, or whether it really corresponds to the nature of things. It seems equally proper to consider whether God, when He wished to make man the lord and master of the visible world (to speak from quite a human standpoint), might not have good reason to introduce him into the world in a striking manner, even as regards his corporal part. This and much more one might weigh when considering our question from a natural point of view in order to solve the question of man's corporal origin with more or less probability. But evidently we must refer here to our second source of information, to revelation, and inquire whether this enlightens us on the way which, as a matter of fact, God followed in creating man's body. Absolutely speaking, could God have given existence to man's body in different ways? Do we find indicated in the Sacred Books with sufficient clearness the way He chose? If that be the case, then the question is settled. It appears to us that Holy Scripture instructs us clearly and distinctly on the origin of the human body,"[1] and indeed in such a way as to exclude Mivart's hypothesis.

83. WHAT DOES SCRIPTURE TELL US ABOUT MAN'S BODILY ORIGIN?—What does Holy Scripture tell us about the origin of the first man? God created all other things simply by an act of His will: *Let there be*. But He created man by an especial act. Although he appeared on the earth during the same period as some animals, that is to say, on the sixth day, he does not receive

[1] Gen. i. 26.

his existence like the rest of creatures by a simple command, but after a solemn consultation: " Let us make man to our image and likeness," says the Lord; thus He Himself with His own hands formed man of the slime of the earth and breathed into his face the breath of life, and man became a living soul. This is the short and simple account which Revelation gives of man's creation: Thus, according to God's word, the first man was formed of the earth, and neither exegesis nor natural science can interpret the sacred words in any other sense. Baer, a naturalist and savant, says of the creation of man: " If we understand by 'the slime of the earth,' from which man was formed, the terrestrial elements which have received life, the natural sciences cannot go beyond this truth."[1]

On the hypothesis "that it is not irreconcilable with faith that man's body arose in the same manner as every other animal body, through descent," this supposition might be brought into agreement with the above words of the sacred text, if we had nothing in Holy Scripture to guide us except the simple indications of that line. For even on this supposition, considering the matter on the whole, we might yet do justice to the sacred text.[2] But we read in Holy Scripture the words: " Let the earth bring forth the living creatures," and "God formed out of the ground all the beasts of the earth,"—expressions which tell us that the necessary matter and the compounds (albumen, hydrate of carbon, inorganic salts, water) necessary for the formation of animal bodies were taken from matter already existing and chemical combinations. The mass of matter already existing, which here furnished the material, Holy Scripture simply designates by the word "earth," because this

[1] Gen. ii. 7.
[2] Knabenbauer," Stimmen aus Maria-Laach," 1877, vol. ii., p. 125.

material was indeed in and upon the earth and formed part of terrestrial bodies. Or how could the idea of formation from pre-existing material be expressed otherwise in a popular manner? Nobody will look for chemical formulas in Holy Scripture! Now if the human body was really formed from the organism of a monkey, then it might yet be described as "formed of the earth." Of course, not in itself and immediately, but in a remote way, in its root and first cause, so to say,—it would, although mediately, descend "from the earth" in the true sense. Thus our question comes to this: Does Holy Scripture exclude such a mediate formation of the first man's body from the earth and teach its immediate formation therefrom? It seems to us that there cannot be any doubt that the former view is against all Scriptural exegesis, and that we have to accept the latter, that is, that the body of the first man was immediately formed by God from the slime of the earth, as Genesis tells us.[1] According to some theologians, the immediate creation of the body of the first man is an article of faith, not indeed defined by the Church, but evidently taught by the Bible and tradition.[2]

Other passages in Holy Scripture confirm our view. The sentence of God pronounced on fallen man reads as follows: "In the sweat of thy face shalt thou eat bread, till thou return to the earth, out of which thou wast taken." But these words, clear in themselves, are followed by an explanatory clause: "For dust thou art, and unto dust thou shalt return."[3] This certainly means, Just as thou wast formed out of dust, as far as thy body is concerned, so also thy body shall return to dust. Compare also what Ecclesiasticus says: "God created man of the earth, and He turned him into it again,"[4] and

---

[1] Knabenbauer, "Stimmen aus Maria-Laach," 1877, vol. ii., p. 133.
[2] Cf. "Mazella," etc.   [3] Gen. iii. 19.   [4] Ecclus. xvii. 1, 2.

what Ecclesiastes teaches: "And the dust return into its earth, from whence it was, and the spirit return to God, who gave it."[1] The bosom of the earth takes up the dead body, the spirit returns to God, who created it directly, as the body is derived from the earth. Is not the immediate formation of the body of the first man from the earth supposed throughout all these passages?[2]

To conclude this subject, we must admit that the description which Moses gives of the creation of man shows at once that man is an essentially different creature from any of those which he describes before man's creation. This essential difference and his higher nature are implied in the fact that God announces His resolution of creating man before He does so: "And God said, Let us make man to our image and likeness; and let him have dominion over the fishes of the sea, and the fowls of the air, and the beasts, and the whole earth, and every creeping creature that moveth upon the earth. And God created man to His own image; to the image of God He created him; male and female He created them."[3] "The world and its parts," says St. Gregory of Nyssa, "are as it were at once created by the divine power, inasmuch as they came into existence by the mere command of God: 'Let there be'; but the creation of man is preceded by reflection; the Creator describes in words what is to exist. The divine words decide how man shall exist, to what end he shall be made, what he shall do after he has been made, what he shall govern, so that man partakes of his high honors even before his creation, and before he has come into being he has obtained the dominion of the world."[4]

The questions, wherein man's image and likeness of

---

[1] Eccles. xii. 7; cf. also Wisdom vii. 1; Ecclus. xxxiii. 3.
[2] Knabenbauer, *op. cit.*, p. 134.
[3] Gen. i. 26, 27.   [4] "De opif. hom.," c. 3.

God consists, and how far we are to distinguish between the image of God and the likeness to God, have been differently answered by theologians. If we overlook the dogmatic side of the question, which does not concern us here, we must from the exegetical point of view say, firstly, that man's likeness to God certainly consists in the sovereign authority which has been given to him. St. Chrysostom observes strikingly, that "God does not only say: Let us make man to our image, but He shows in the words which immediately follow in what sense the word image is used. He says: Let them have dominion, etc. Therefore, He speaks of the image with reference to the dominion, and to nothing else."[1] But the dominion of man involves the possession of an immortal, reasonable, and free soul, so that the other fathers and theologians are also right when they name this point as the one in which man's likeness consists.

After having learned what faith, positive science, and materialism teach about man's origin and nature, let us consider the proofs which pseudo-science brings forward for the theory of man's descent from the animals. This we shall do in the three following chapters.

[1] Hom. 8, in Gen.

CHAPTER IV.

MAN AND BEAST.

Is man merely a perfected animal?—Darwin's "struggle for life."—How does it correspond with the wisdom, order, and omnipotent power of God?—The assumed change of inferior species into superior ones, by the struggle for life, does not explain their origin.—It is impossible to explain the origin of man from an ape by the struggle for life.—How did the last monkey acquire the faculty of thinking, speaking, walking on two legs, etc.?—No trace of a higher development is found in any animal species.—If species changed in former times, why does this not happen in historical times? — Darwin's "struggle for life" is purely imaginary.

84. CONSOLATION IN HAVING AN ANTHROPOID MONKEY FOR ANCESTOR.—As we saw in the preceding chapter, the naturalists of the materialistic school are all agreed in looking upon some anthropoid monkey as our immediate ancestor. Most of those who defend the theory of man's relationship to the apes think it well to begin or to end their argument by assuring us that there is nothing lowering or disgraceful to man in their theory. Haeckel says that it will "even have an enlightening and ennobling effect, and thus will lead men more and more towards their eternal goal through the light of truth to the joy of liberty."[1] "There is one thought," says another apostle of this doctrine,[2] "which reconciles us to the conclusions of science so startling to human

[1] "Entstehung," pp. 35, 36.
[2] Schaafhausen, in the "Archiv für Anthropologie," vol. ii., p. 336.

feeling; man is not descended from the ape. This form is the last he broke through, the last veil he threw off, the envelope beneath which the finer form developed, as a butterfly from its chrysalis, which came from the caterpillar, as did the caterpillar from the egg. Thus everything in nature becomes a parable, because one law governs the whole. Natural science places man just as high as do the philosopher and the poet; but natural science alone can trace the way by which he has attained to this height. When we see a man who was born in a poor cottage, and has attained to power and happiness through his own efforts, at the height of his fame, do we not admire him much more than the man who boasts of his inherited riches? So it is with our race. For this reason we are not ashamed to look back into the past; it is our surest proof of a better future. We have ideals beyond our own nature, but we try to reach them, and we can in reality approach them. Is not the golden age which our poets sing of as a lost good, as a past splendor, and also as an undeserved happiness,—is not that golden age more beautiful if it lies before instead of behind us, if we must gain what we have never possessed?"

No Christian will be able to be quieted by such edifying thoughts, and if it were as true as it is false that man's descent from the beast is "a scientific conclusion," with this would vanish, as Frohschammer[1] and others have well said, not only the poets' descriptions of the golden age, but also the Christian doctrines of the creation and the original state of man. Christian anthropologists, therefore, have every reason not to "become enthusiastic over the results of natural science," but to try to prove scientifically that the theory of the genealogical connection between man and beast is not a "scientific conclusion." Therefore, let us now consider

[1] "Das Christenthum," p. 126.

the proofs for the doctrine of man's descent from the animals.

85. Proofs in Support of Man's Descent from an Ape.—Millions of years ago, we are told, there existed only elementary substances, "atoms;" from these the monera were developed. Through continual transformation nobler organisms arose. Then came the "struggle for life;" inferior beings had to perish, only the fittest survived, and from the latter man finally went forth. The orang-outang, chimpanzee, or gorilla are generally looked upon as the last stage of transformation before the appearance of man, as he exists.

One of these anthropoid apes, it is asserted, gave up the habit of creeping on all fours, of climbing trees, and thus it gradually accustomed itself to walk on its hind legs. In this way it gradually took the shape of man. Its tail grew shorter owing to disuse, and finally was lost altogether; it gave up the habit of eating fruit, and its features took quite a different form; the snout became smaller and the countenance perpendicular. In the course of its further development, the grin of the monkey turned into man's pleasant smile, and from his monotonous cries articulate language arose. Afterwards man began to think, his brain became larger, and fathers begot children endowed with yet larger brains. It was thus that man gradually rose to his present perfection, in order perhaps to transform himself again after some millions of years by further development. This, in substance, is the theory of Darwin with regard to man's position and his origin.

86. Criticism of the Pithecoid Theory.—Now in the name of common sense and positive science, in the name of our Christian faith and human dignity, we protest against so debasing and pernicious a doctrine; and we do so on the following grounds: (1) Darwin's theory of man's descent is ridiculously absurd and impossible. This we intend to prove in the present chapter. (2) There is a vast difference between man and an animal—monkey—both in body and soul. This will form the subject of our next chapter; after that we shall weigh the objections of the Darwinists against the Christian doctrine of man's origin and nature.

A man's origin based on the theory of ånything except revelation is pure imagination, a delusion and a snare. Now, when this hypothesis is based on such a silly and delusive foundation as that just before set forth, it must be considered by every sensible person as the sheerest nonsense.

87. DARWIN'S VIEW OF MAN'S DESCENT IS ABSURD AND IMPOSSIBLE.—(1) We said the Darwinian view of our origin is absurd and impossible. Let us make this clear. When we reject God as the Creator of man and accept man as the result of a natural process, we must repeat the question: Whence comes the "moneron" from which all forms of life up to man are derived? Does it exist from all eternity, or did it arise by chance? The first cannot be true, for what is eternal does not admit development into higher forms. That something should arise by chance, and that higher forms of existence should again develop by chance from this something, only an idiot can believe. Every sensible man knows that nothing arises by haphazard, much less a settled order of organic beings. The adherents of this doctrine must either be atheists or they must at least admit that the primitive forms of life from which the more perfect ones were developed came from the hand of God. But if we accept a God, then we believe it is more rational, more just, and more in harmony with the wisdom of the Almighty, to create the species of plants and animals by separate acts rather than by the "struggle for existence."

What is this struggle for life? In brief, it is a war of all against all; the killing and annihilation of the weaker by the stronger. This incessant struggle is always going on until only the stronger and more perfect forms remain.[1] This results from natural selection. Nature calls forth and pushes the power of variation by the fearful struggle for existence, that widespread and remorseless conflict, under the steady pressure of which each living form is forced to develop to the utmost to retain and augment every advantage—a conflict that issues in the "survival of the fittest."

How does this constant struggle, this remorseless conflict of all forms of life for existence harmonize with the wisdom, the order, and the omnipotent power of God? Does it appear reasonable to make this struggle for life the principle of His creation, and to ordain beforehand the killing and annihilation of the weaker beings as the occasion and source of its various species? It is a mystery to us how the perfect forms and organizations of the surviving species cause variation, when experience goes to prove that the weak and deformed are more likely to transmit peculiarities and abnormities than the strong and well-made.

We have quite a different conception of God and His creative power. Since our reason forces us to adore Him as the Creator of heaven and earth, we prefer to believe that He has made His creatures, be they many or be they few, according to their different kinds and species, by His almighty will, rather than admit that they arose by an endless conflict. The disposition on the part of many Darwinists, not only to insist on natural selection, under the conditions imposed by the fearful and protracted struggle for existence, as indicating the method by which the creative intelligence produced the multitud-

[1] Darwin, "Origin of Species."

inous forms of present life, but also to deny creative intelligence altogether, or to base it on natural selection, acting in a blind and unconscious way, confirms us in this view.

88. "The Struggle for Life" does not Explain the Origin of Species.—(2) But let us go further. The supposed change of lower species into higher ones by the struggle for life does not explain their origin. Haeckel posits one progenitor—the moneron; Darwin eight or ten, from which the three hundred and seventy thousand species of plants and animals have sprung. Now the question arises: Who created the one or the ten primordial forms? Did the moneron or the other primordial forms fight and struggle for existence? Did the moneron struggle single-handed? Who gave these primitive forms of life the natural instinct of unceasing warfare, that they might beget and perpetuate a higher and a more varied form?

Let us imagine a great number of creatures of lower forms purposely wrestling and struggling against one another for existence; what would be the result? The consequence of such perpetual conflict would be to strengthen and develop the organs for combat, but not their noble qualities nor their intelligence. When animals of the same genus fight among themselves for mastery, their jaws, teeth, claws, nails, muscle, activity, courage, endurance, or other natural means of defence, may increase and develop. But are they by this conflict changed into another genus, and do they assume their defensive and aggressive organs, as well as their type, organization, and habit? It would be nonsense to believe that the more beautiful and perfect species of animals, and, above all, that man, is the result of such a struggle. On the contrary, war renders the combatants more savage; it never civilizes nor develops the finer and more exalted qualities.

89. ABSURDITY OF EXPLAINING MAN'S DESCENT BY "THE STRUGGLE FOR LIFE."—(3) It is absurd to explain the origin of man from the monkey by "the struggle for life." In this struggle it is supposed that the most intelligent monkey abandoned the habit of creeping on all fours, of climbing trees, and using its tail. In this struggle it is supposed to have lost its hair and become more handsome. We should believe that the contrary took place. The struggle for life might have changed men into very formidable monkeys, but not monkeys into men. The monkey's physique is better adapted for this struggle against the elements and other hostile influences than man's delicate body. In the struggle for life the monkey, with its four arms, which enable it to move at pleasure on the earth and amidst the branches of trees, with its hairy skin and its tail, which helps its legs, is certainly better fitted for this struggle for existence than man. We cannot understand how the struggle for life could transform an ape's body into a human body. Hence, if the struggle for life is the law of life, we ought again to become monkeys.

90. HOW DID THE LAST MONKEY BECOME A MAN?—(4) We next ask: How did the monkey which became the first man begin to think, reason, talk, walk, smile, laugh, blush, and sing? How did its skull increase by at least eleven cubic inches in cranial capacity? And its hand? The difference may seem small when placed alongside of man's on the dissecting table, but in that difference, whatever it be, lies the whole difference between an organ limited to the climbing of trees or the plucking of fruit and an organ which is so correlated with man's inventive genius that by its aid the earth is weighed and the distance of the sun is measured. In

reply to the first question, Vogt answers: "This happened through the increase of the brain." When we ask: How did the brain increase so largely and so rapidly? he again answers: "Through its activity in thinking."

It is evident to every sensible and rational man that Vogt's answer will not stand the test of experience and practical observation. For we must infer from what he says of the increased brain capacity of the monkey as it changes from brute to man, that the brain augments in proportion to the faculty of thinking. If it were so, then the heads of the men of enlightenment now living—men whose brains have been developed by the thinking process of thousands of years, would be so big and heavy that they could hardly carry their skulls erect upon their shoulders. But both paleontology and archæology prove that the primitive men of Europe and Egypt, for instance, had skulls of the same size as we have to-day. Therefore it is false to assert that the irrational is capable of producing the rational spirit of man; the higher will not develop itself from the lower, because no being can bequeath more than it possesses itself.

91. NO TRACE FOUND OF DEVELOPMENT IN ANY SPECIES.—(5) All the observations of the past, as we proved at length in our chapter on Darwinism, fail to find the least trace of development in any animal species. Birds build their nests, beavers their dams and dwellings, bees make their cells, as their ancestors did long ago; dogs are no more docile, nor foxes more cunning than of old. Though the unceasing struggle for existence goes on, still we do not notice any progress nor the changing of one species into another. The different species and varieties of monkeys are still monkeys; none walk erect, speak, laugh, sing, or make

tools and implements. The most "developed" among them would sit by a fire and see it go out without having enough of reason to feed it, though the fuel be before its eyes. What we observe in the animal kingdom we find also in the vegetable. Not the least development is visible. Certain species may have grown larger or smaller, more symmetrical in type and more uniform in their organs, but they still belong to their respective species and races.

If there be question of mere theory, if we reason on pure possibilities and not on facts, it is certain (always excepting the spontaneous generation of the first being, which is an impossibility) that God could have created the world according to the transformists' system—that is to say, He could create only one being, capable of developing itself gradually, and of producing the different organisms of all actually existing beings. But this is not the question; we are not inquiring what could have been, but what are the facts. Now the facts contradict the doctrine of Darwin and Haeckel; they afford no direct proof of the transformation of the species; they show that there exists many a break between species and species. Still the passage from one to the other should be by insensible and imperceptible degrees. Such a transition has not been proved. Darwin and Haeckel affirm as real that which is only possible, although *a posse ad actum non valet consecutio.*

92. WHY ARE MONKEYS NO LONGER TRANSFORMED?—(6) Finally, we ask: If in prehistoric times animals have been changed into men, why did this not take place during historical times, seeing that the same struggle for existence is still going on? What has happened once, can be repeated, unless some sufficient cause intervenes. No naturalist has yet discovered a monkey on the point of assuming the form,

features, functions, and intelligence of man, nor has any one dug up a fossil that showed this transforming process, so that even Vogt despairingly admits that there is no hope of ever discovering the "missing link" which connects man with the monkey.

93. CRITICISM OF DARWINISM BY VIRCHOW AND DAWSON.—Virchow, a rationalistic naturalist, says: "When we study the quaternary fossil man, who certainly should resemble our original ancestors more than we do, . . . we always find a man like ourselves. It is a little over ten years ago that skulls were found on the turf, in the lacustrine deposits, or in the ancient caves. Scientists thought they saw in them singular characters pointing towards a savage state, incompletely developed. They were on the point of pronouncing them very like apes' skulls. But all such notions are vanishing. The ancient troglodytes, the cave-dwellers, the men of the turf, prove to be quite a respectable society. They have heads of such proportions that many individuals now living would think themselves happy if they had heads as large. In short, we must acknowledge that no fossil types present marked characteristics of inferior development. And when we compare the whole of the fossil remains known until now with the present state of things, we may boldly say that among the men now living there exists a much greater number of individuals relatively inferior, than among the fossils in question. . . . No skull of a monkey or of a man-monkey has been found that had really belonged to a man."[1]

Despairing of their cause, the adherents of the monkey theory pretend that somewhere in Asia or Africa, they cannot exactly tell where, now submerged under the sea, the monkey ancestors of man would be found, if one

[1] Virchow, "Discours au Congrès des Anthropologistes* de Munich," September, 1877.

could dig up its depths. When men are obliged to have recourse to such arguments to bolster up their theories, we have reason to believe that they defend a weak and bad cause.

In conclusion, listen to what J. W. Dawson, an American author, has to say on this subject:

"If we gather the bones of man and his implements from the ancient gravel-beds and cave-earths, we do not find them associated with any creature in these rich tertiary beds, which have yielded so great a harvest of mammalian bones. In the modern world we find nothing nearer to him than such anthropoid apes as the gorilla and orangs. But the apes, however nearly allied, cannot be the ancestors of man. If at all allied to him by descent, they are his brethren and cousins, not his parents, for they must, on the evolutionist hypothesis, be themselves the terminal ends of distinctive lines of derivation from previous forms.

"This difficulty is not removed by an appeal to the imperfection of the geological record. So many animals contemporary with man are known, both at the beginning of his geological history and in the present world, that it would be more than marvellous if no very near relative had ere this time been discovered at one extreme or the other, or at some portion of the intervening ages. Further, all the animals contemporary with man in the post glacial period, so far as is known, are in the same case. Discoveries of this kind may, however, still be made, and we may give the evolutionist the benefit of the possibility. We may affirm, however, that in order to gain a substratum of fact for his doctrine, he must find somewhere in the later tertiary period animals much nearer to man than are the present anthropoid apes.

"This demand I make advisedly; first, because the

animals in question must precede man in geological time, and, secondly, because the apes, even if they preceded man, instead of being contemporary with him, are not near enough to fulfil the required conditions. What is the actual fact with regard to these animals, so confidently affirmed to resemble some not very remote ancestors of ours? Zoölogically they are not varieties of the same species with man; they are not species of the same genus, nor do they belong to the genera of the same family, or even to the families of the same order. These animals are, at least, ordinarily distinct from us in those grades of groups in which naturalists arrange animals. I am well aware that an attempt has been made to group man, apes, lemurs in one order of 'primates,' and thus reduce their difference to the grade of the family; but, as put by its latest and perhaps most able advocates, the attempt is a decided failure. One has only to read the concluding chapter of Huxley's new book on the anatomy of the vertebrates to be persuaded of this, more especially if we can take into consideration, in addition to the many differences indicated, others which exist, but are not mentioned by the author. Ordinal distinctions among the animals are mainly dependent on grade or rank, and are not to be broken down by obscure resemblances of internal anatomy, having no relation to this point, but to physiological features of very secondary importance. Man must on all grounds rank much higher above the apes than they can do above any other order of mammals. Even if we refuse to recognize all higher grounds of classification, and condescend, with some great zoölogists of our time, to regard nature with the eyes of mere anatomists, or in the same way that a bricklayer's apprentice may be supposed to regard the distinction of architectural styles, we arrive at no other conclusions. Let us imagine an anatomist, himself neither a man nor a monkey, but a being of some other grade, and altogether ignorant of the higher ends and powers of our species, studying the skeleton of a man and that of an ape; he must infer that they belong to different orders on account of the correlations and modifications of structure implied in the erect position. It would be sufficient for the purpose to consider the balancing of the skull on the neck, or the structure of the foot, and the consequences fairly deducible from either of these features. Nay, were this imaginary anatomist a derivationist, and ignorant of the geological date of his specimens, and as careless of the differences in respect to brain as some of his human *confrères*, he might, referring to the less specialized condition of man's teeth and foot, conclude not that man is an improved ape, but that the ape is a specialized and improved man. He would be obliged, however, even on this hypothesis, to admit that there must be a host of missing links; nor would these be supplied by the study of the living races of men, because these want even specific distinctions, and differ from the apes essentially in those points on which an ordinal distinction can be fairly based. . . .

"I do not attach any importance whatever in this connection to the likeness in type or plan between man and other mammals. Evolutionists are in the habit of taking for granted that this implies derivation, and of reasoning as if the fact that the human skeleton is constructed on the same principles as that of an ape or a dog must have some connection with a common ancestry of these animals. This is begging the question, however; creation as well as evolution admits of a similarity of plan. . . . But while a man is related in his structure to the higher animals, his contemporaries, it is undeniable that there are certain points in which he constitutes a new type; and if this consideration were properly weighed, I believe it would induce zoölogists, notwithstanding the proverbial humility of the true man of science, to consider themselves much more widely separated from the brutes than even by the ordinal distinction above referred to. I would state this view of the matter thus: It is a law in the lower animals that the bodily frame is provided with all necessary means of defence and attack, and with all necessary protection against external influence and assailants. In a very few cases we have exceptions to this. A hermit crab, for instance, has the hinder part of its body unprotected, and has, instead of armor, the instinct of using the cast-off shells of mollusks; yet even this animal has the usual strong claws of a crustacean for defence in front. There are only a very few animals in which instinct takes the place of physical contrivances for defence or attack, and in these we find merely the usual unvarying instincts of the irrational animal. But what is the rare exception in all other animals becomes in man the rule. He has no means of escape from danger compared with those enjoyed by other animals; no defensive armor, no natural protection from cold or heat, no effective weapons for attacking other animals. These disabilities would make him the most helpless of creatures, especially when taken in connection with his slow growth and long immaturity. His safety and dominion over other animals are secured by entirely new means, constituting a 'new departure' in creation; contrivance and inventive power, enabling him to utilize the objects and forces of nature, replace in him the material powers bestowed on lower animals. Obviously the structure of the human being is related to this, and so related as to place man in a different category from any other animal."[1]

From what has been said it is plain that the so-called "struggle for life" is a figment of the imagination. It is impossible to explain by its means either the existence of organic beings, or their development into man. However, in order to solve the question more completely, we shall now examine the special differences which exist between man and animals.

[1] J. W. Dawson, "The Story of the Earth and Man," New York, 1887, pp. 360-365.

CHAPTER V.

MAN AND BEAST.—Continued.

The structure of man and that of the ape.—Two kinds of distinctive characters. — Physical characters. — The head.—The brain.—The foot and the hand.—Bodily development.—Rudimentary formations. — Embryological development.—Universality.—Senses. —Psychological characters. — Reason.—Liberty.—Language.—Results of language.—Genius.—The Tasmanians.—Sense of shame.—Conclusion.

WHEN the Church teaches that man is a reasonable being, composed of a body and a soul made to the image of God, and therefore free, responsible, and immortal, science does not oppose this teaching; on the contrary, she supports it when, in her turn, she states that man appeared upon the earth after all other creatures, and that he is the most perfect of organic beings. But when there is question of determining exactly the measure of man's superiority, materialistic science holds views in bitter conflict with the teaching of theology. Until at present, it was generally admitted that man alone is free and responsible, that he occupies a place apart in nature, and that an impassable gulf separates him from the animal placed next in the zoölogical series. Man's nature, said Buffon, is "so superior to that of beasts that one must be blind to confound him with the latter."

However, the anthropologists of the materialistic school have changed all this, and for them there exists between man and the beast only a difference of degree. For them, man is *primus inter pares*, constituting always, it is true, a separate genus, but at bottom he is less distant from the anthropoid monkeys—the gorilla, for instance—than the gorilla is from the inferior apes.

94. THE CATARRHINE MONKEYS OUR IMMEDIATE ANCESTORS.—All transformists are agreed that we must look upon the catarrhine monkeys (in contra-distinction to the platyrhine) as our great-grandfathers. The reason for the distinction of these two species lies in the formation of the nose. In the platyrhine, the American monkeys, the nose is pressed flat and the nostrils dilated and extended outwardly. The monkeys of the ancient world, on the other hand, have a septum in the nose, and the nostrils point downward. Again, the number of teeth in the small-nosed species corresponds to that of man, whilst, on the contrary, the flat-nosed species has four molar teeth more.

It is Haeckel again who tells us all this when he says: "This perfect harmony of all small-nosed men in regard to the characteristic formation of the nose and the set of teeth, proves distinctly that they have a common origin and have developed from one common root." A few lines further on he confesses "that the establishment of the human genealogical tree at present presents great difficulties, and we can only assert that it must have been tailless catarrhini, so-called monkey-men, or anthropoids, which probably in the pliocene or miocene period, perhaps only at the beginning of the diluvian period, developed through natural selection into the ancestors of mankind."[1]

But it was Darwin who made every effort to bridge the gulf between man and animals and to account for the difference between them, and he concludes that man is a perfected animal. The manner in which he

[1] "Natürliche Schöpfungsgeschichte," p. 574; "Anthropogenie," p. 487.

accounts for this gradual development is so peculiar that in contradistinction to all his rivals we may aptly style him the "man-breeder" of the nineteenth century.

"What will lead me to my goal?" he asks himself, and when he has recognized the means, he skilfully and carefully uses every point in steering around every abyss, cliff, and promontory, so as to reach it. Naturally he looked first for similarity in bodily structure, and like all man-monkey theorists, he dwelt especially on similarity of anatomical structure.

Let us ascertain whether the resemblance between the structure of man and that of the highest class of monkeys now existing is sufficiently great to make it necessary to assume scientifically that both are descended from the same common stock of ancestors.

95. THE CHARACTERS DISTINGUISHING MAN FROM THE ANIMAL.—The characters which distinguish man from the animal have been divided into two groups: *physical characters*, determined by physiology and comparative anatomy, and *psychological characters*, that is, intellectual and moral ones. The first have been minutely and learnedly studied and described; they have inspired many beautiful pages, where science, philosophy, and poetry vie in showing in the organization of man's body an incontestable superiority. As we cannot enter into detail on all these characters, we must content ourselves with considering the principal ones.

96. PHYSICAL CHARACTERS.—In the first place, let us consider man's principal physical characters. Even the corporal difference between man and the most highly organized animal is an immense one. Take a monkey, which is looked upon as the nearest to man in appearance, and place it alongside of man. How proudly and erectly does man carry his head! He shows by his car-

riage[1] that this is his natural position, and that even in his body he is the king of creation and no animal. Everything in him bespeaks dignity and nobility. His skeleton proves that he never walked on "all fours;" his head, hands, and feet do not fit the quadrumana. How beast-like stands the highest animal alongside of man! How great is the difference in the monkey, with its tail, and its hairy body, which never exceeds three to four feet in height; which indeed makes efforts to raise itself on two legs, but always falls back to its normal position on "all fours."

His vertical attitude is a character proper to man, although Linnæus and Buffon doubted this. Indeed, in their day it was believed that certain anthropomorphous apes walked erect like man. It is true that this is the case with domesticated orang-outangs, the only ones known then; but since these animals have been studied in the forests where they live, it has been found that this is not their normal posture. In reality their position, in consequence of the excessive length of the anterior arms, is neither a horizontal nor a vertical one; it is oblique. The anthropoid monkeys, whether orangs, gorillas, chimpanzees, or gibbons, are built to climb and not to walk. This is so true that even in the domesticated state they need a stick to hold themselves erect. On the contrary, man is built for the vertical posture. The manner the head is articulated at the vertebral column and the form of the foot are evident

---

[1] According to Quinet, the vertical position of man is explained quite naturally. "Man must have arisen on a table-land, where he perceived above himself a mountainous country, which constrained him to raise his head until he saw the firmament. . . . While scaling steep rocks he naturally held himself erect, and it was thus that he disengaged himself from the habits of the quadrumana."—" La Création."

proofs of this. But let us inquire more minutely about these physical characters.

97. (1) THE HEAD.—Even Huxley admits that the differences between a gorilla's skull and a man's are truly immense. Man's skull in the frontal region presents an elevated and round contour, very different from what we find in the ape generally, and notably in the higher families of apes. It is in the American forms of monkeys—especially in the callithrix and pithecia—that we find the greatest resemblance to man in this respect. In the gorilla great bony crests (for muscular attachment)—like those in the carnivorous animals—attain their maximum of development.

The relation of the face to the brain envelope is shown by what is called the cranio-facial angle. This angle is estimated by comparing the direction of a line drawn parallel to the base of the skull with that of another line drawn from the front end of that base to the middle of the lower margin of the upper jaw. Stress has been laid on the difference existing between man and the gorilla as regards this angle. But it does not appear to be a really important character in forms admitted by all to be closely related, such as the two baboons, the mandrill, and the chacma.

There is one cranial character, however, in which the gorilla approaches man more nearly than does any other primate. This is the existence of a certain ridge (termed vaginal) on the under surface of the bone which encloses the internal ear. Another process of the same bone (called styloid) is, however, sometimes developed more like the same bone in man in one of the baboons than in any other primate; while of the latisternal apes it is not the gorilla, but the orang which in this matter is the most man-like.

The gibbons resemble man more than the orang, chimpanzee, or gorilla, in the preponderance of their skull over the bones of the face. But the smaller American monkeys surpass the gibbons in this respect, while the squirrel monkey exceeds even man himself.

A striking feature in the human skull is the prominence of the inferior margin of the lower jaw in front, *i.e.*, the presence of a "chin." This feature is quite wanting in the gorilla, in the orang, and the chimpanzee; a more or less developed "chin," however, exists in the siamang, although no other species of gibbons, and indeed no other ape or lemuroid, shows a similar structure.

Another marked character of man's skull is the projection and the transverse convexity of the bones of the nose. This convexity is quite absent in the chimpanzee and in most gibbons. In the orang these bones are exceedingly small and flat, often even uniting into one bone, or with the adjoining jaw-bones, if indeed they are not altogether absent.

In the gorilla, on the other hand, they are slightly convex transversely at their upper part, so that here we seem to have evidence of the predominant affinity of the gorilla to man. Further examination, however, shows that the character can have no such meaning, since a still more decided convexity is found to exist in some semnopitheci, and even in the lower baboons. Moreover, in the baboons the nasal bones become convex only towards maturity, being at first flat. This character, therefore, can hardly have been at one time a general one, now preserved only in a few scattered forms.[1]

98. (2) THE BRAIN.—Man's brain no doubt is not absolutely the largest, for the brains of the elephant, the whale, and narwhal are far larger. But, as Huxley says, it must not be overlooked that there is a very striking difference in absolute mass and weight between the low-

[1] Huxley, "Evidences," p. 102.

est human brain and that of the highest ape—a difference which is all the more remarkable, when we recollect that the full-grown gorilla is pretty nearly twice as heavy as a Bushman or as many European women. It may be doubted whether a healthy human brain ever weighed less than 31 or 32 ounces, or whether the heaviest gorilla brain has exceeded 20 ounces. The rule that man's brain is the largest in proportion to the weight of his body is not, however, without exception, for some of the smaller birds probably possess a brain which is relatively larger.[1] But still there is no doubt that the human brain differs very remarkably from the animal brain—a conclusion which has been arrived at by many anatomists, however widely they may differ as to details.

According to the account given by Quatrefages[2] on the progress of anthropology in France, the eminent physiologist Gratiolet speaks in the same way of microcephalism as the German savants. According to this account the doctrine of man's relationship to the ape finds much less support among French anthropologists than it does in Germany.

Anthropologists who are disagreed on many other points are at one on this point, and have arrived at the same conclusion, namely, that nothing warrants the assertion that the brain of the ape is a human brain arrested in its development, and that man's brain is a better developed ape's brain (Gratiolet); that an examination of the organism in general, and of the extremities in particular, shows us that combined with a common plan there exist differences of form and structure which are incompatible with the idea of a common descent for man and the ape (Gratiolet); that apes

---

[1] Tiedemann, "Das Hirn des Negers," p. 14.
[2] "Correspondenzblatt für Anthropologie," Sept. 9, 1877, pp. 131, 135.

do not approach man by being perfected, and the human type does not approach the ape by degradation (Bert); that there exists no possible bridge between man and the ape, unless we turn the laws of development upside down (Pruner-Bey).

At the session of the Society of Anthropology, November 18, 1869,[1] Pruner-Bey declared:

"The differences are striking. The ape is covered with hair, which man lacks; an anatomical character whose functional results are immense, as man is forced to supply by his industry what nature has refused him.[2] The ape has canines which serve him as weapons; man is deprived of these, and has to supply the defect by inventing improved arms. Whilst everything in the structure of the bones of the monkey is so disposed as to make a quadruped and a climber of him, in man, on the contrary, everything reveals a biped and a walker. The muscular system in man and monkey offers contrasts, and Gratiolet has demonstrated that, as regards the circulation, man compared with the monkey is an arterial being. In some apes—the gorilla and the chimpanzee, for instance—the viscera reveal every characteristic of a herbivorous animal. The study of the skulls also is conclusive. All the apes have similar faces, and all equally unlike man's; in contrast to man's skull the skull of the hairless ape is so built as to reduce its cavity to a minimum. In the monkey everything is constructed so as to enlarge his face. The skull is a simple appendix of the face. Its contents are

---

[1] "Bulletin de la Société d'Anthropologie," vol. iv., ser. ii.
[2] Pliny said: "While nature has placed the animals upon earth provided with everything necessary to them, that is to say, clothed, armed, and guided by a sure instinct, like a stepmother, rather than a mother, she has placed man *nudus in nuda humo.*"

in proportion to the cover. Whilst in man the outer ear rises above the occiput, the inverted order is found in the ape. The dental system of the ape reveals a herbivorous array for his defence. Man has no intermaxillary bones; they are found in the quadrumana."

With regard to the development of the brain, Th. Bischoff gives us the following as the result of his observations:

"The brains of man, of the orang, the chimpanzee, and the gorilla are nearly related, in spite of the great differences between them. But if we compare the human brain with that of an orang, the brain of the latter with that of a chimpanzee, and so on through the hylobates, semnopithecus, etc., we shall nowhere find a larger, or nearly so large a gulf, in the brain development of two of the series, as we find between the brain of man and that of the orang or chimpanzee. The gulf which separates the convolutions of a man's brain from the convolutions in the brain of an orang or chimpanzee cannot be bridged over by pointing to the gulf which separates the orang or chimpanzee from the lemur. The latter is filled up by the different intermediate kinds of apes; the forms to fill up the former must still be found."[1]

99. (3) FOOT AND HAND.—The apes and half apes agree together, and differ from man in having the great toe, or the hallux, as it is called in anatomy, so constructed that it can be opposed to the other toes (much as our thumb can be opposed to the fingers), instead of being parallel with the other toes and exclusively adapted to support the body on the ground. The prehensile character of the hallux is fully maintained even in the monkeys which, like the baboons, are terrestrial rather than arboreal in their habits, and which are quite quadruped

[1] Th. Bischoff, "Die Grosshirnwendungen," p. 102.

in their mode of progression. It was this circumstance that led Cuvier to give to the separate order in which he places man alone the name *bimana*, while to the order of apes and lemurs he gave the name of *quadrumana*.[1] If, with Professor Owen, we define the word "foot" as an extremity in which the hallux forms the fulcrum in standing or walking, then man alone has a pair of feet. But anatomically the foot of the ape agrees rather with man's foot than with his hand, and similarly the ape's hand resembles man's hand, and differs from his foot. Even judged physiologically, or according to use, the hand throughout the whole order of quadrumana remains the prehensile organ *par excellence*, while the predominant function of the foot, however prehensile it be, is constantly locomotive. Therefore the term quadrumana is apt to be misleading, since, anatomically as well as physiologically, both apes and man have two hands and a pair of feet. The thumb (in anatomy the pollux) shows no similar uniformity and condition. In the most man-like apes it is relatively much smaller than in man, and the lemurs are more man-like than the apes in the development of this member.[2]

A. Ecker, the anatomist, says: "I have shown that the special characteristics of the hand are the opposable thumbs, the long, prehensile fingers for grasping, and the general mobility of the whole; while those of the foot are the arched shape, the short and unprehensile toes, and the impossibility of stretching the bone of the great toe far from the others. The reader will therefore see clearly that the foot in no way resembles the hinder extremity of the ape; but the latter is much more like a hand, and therefore should be called a hind hand. It is only in man that the foot is exclusively a means of

---

[1] Cf. "Philosophical Transactions," 1867, p. 362.
[2] Mivart, "Man and Apes," pp. 87-89.

support, and the hand exclusively a prehensile organ. Man alone has hands and feet."[1]

100. (4) BODILY DEVELOPMENT.—In addition to the above anatomical differences there is a still greater difference with respect to bodily development.

"Apes have generally a short life and a rapid development; they are born in a condition of bodily and mental maturity, which occurs in animals, but never in man. Their further development takes place in a few years, and an early death brings their life to a close. Although we are not fully informed as to the absolute duration of life among the anthropoid apes, it is questionable whether any of them attains to the age at which the growth of man ceases; at any rate it is certain that even the highest apes have reached their full development when man is still in early youth. They arrive at sexual maturity at an age when man has not outgrown childhood. Still greater is the difference as to the time when the various parts of the body develop. The brain of the ape grows less than any other part of his body; it is usually complete before the change of teeth takes place, whereas in man the real development only begins then. In the ape, directly after the change of teeth the quick growth of the jaws and facial bones begins, and the enormous increase in the outer parts of the skull, which are the distinguishing marks of the bestial character."[2]

Professor Ranke, speaking before a meeting of the German Anthropological Society, at Berlin,[3] August, 1880, gave an account of the scientific work lately done by Th. Bischoff, A. Ecker, and R. Virchow. In the course of his remarks he said: "The popular writings

[1] "Correspondenzblatt für Anthropologie," 1881, p. 9.
[2] Virchow, "Menschen- und Affenschädel," p. 25.
[3] The account may be found in the 13th volume of the "Archiv für Anthropologie."

of the present day would almost lead us to suppose that the differences between man and the anthropoid apes are so slight that if the latter were committed to the care of a German schoolmaster for a few generations they would develop into man. This view is decidedly controverted by comparative pathological anatomy, and by the history of development. The savants I have named are distinctly opposed to that popular philosophical tendency in natural science which falsely seeks to entrench itself behind the name of a great English savant. The most eminent biologists are distinctly and openly opposed to the way in which scientific conclusions are now made use of to establish assertions in natural philosophy."

101. (5) RUDIMENTARY FORMATIONS.—Judging by the importance which Darwin attaches to rudimentary formations in the theory of descent, it was to be expected that they would play an important part in the descent of man. Indeed, he tells us that several muscles, the *plica semilunaris* of the eye, the hairs of the eyebrow, the wisdom tooth, the supra-condyloid hole on the upper arm of man, etc., find a scientific explanation only as reminders of corresponding formations in the primordial animal man. We regret that, for want of space, we cannot go into details and follow up these reduced inheritances of Darwin's progenitors, as it would take up too much space to speak at length on the rudimentary muscles of the skin and ear, as well as on the lengthened hair in the eyebrows of some persons, which evidently represent the feelers that are used by many lower animals as organs of feeling,[1] or on the rudimentary sense of smell in man—in a word, on all the arrested organs of the human body. We shall notice only one of these inter-

[1] Darwin, "Descent of Man," vol. i., p. 24.

esting rudiments, on account of the prominence which it holds in the theory of descent.

The famous sculptor Woolner is at work on his "Puck." He intends to give it pointed ears, and therefore studies with the greatest care the ears of men and monkeys; and lo! he discovers in the exterior of the ear of many men and women a small peculiarity, an "evident proof" that these pointed ears descend from Darwin's primogenitor. Examine the interior rim of the ear-shell, a little above the middle, and you may discover this "proof" that your ancestors had pointed ears. It may be recognized as a small prominent point that not only projects inwards, but also often outwards; in the latter case it becomes visible when we look at the head either from the front or from behind.

Let us now follow Darwin in his study of monkey ears. We remark in many monkeys—for instance, in the baboon, and some macaci—a slight pointing of the upper half of the ear, but we do not perceive any folding of the margin towards the inside. If, however, we imagine this folding carried out, then a slight point would project inwards towards the centre, and probably a little outwards from the centre. Hence, what can be "scientifically" more certain than the assumption that man's ear was once pointed like the baboon's, and that after the folding was accomplished the projecting point was formed?

Great as is our satisfaction with this more than evident "proof" of our simian descent, we should like to have a little clearer explanation on one point. Darwin, when speaking of man's pointed ear, impresses on us that every mark, however insignificant it may be, must be the result of a definite cause. Now what is the cause of the folding of the ear in the baboon, man's ancestor? Of what use was it? "It appears," says Darwin, "to be in some manner connected with the entire exterior ear being permanently pressed backwards."[1] Is that a cause in the scientific sense? And why is the entire exterior ear pressed backwards? Would it not have been more advantageous if the ears of our primitive ancestors had retained the mobility which we often admire in the horse or mule?

102. (6) EMBRYOLOGICAL DEVELOPMENT.—We have in a former chapter commented on the embryonic development of animals as set forth by the advocates of materialistic science. Man develops from a seed the one hundred and twenty-fifth part of an inch in diameter, which does not differ in any manner from the seed of other animals.[2] The human embryo in its early stages can hardly be distinguished from that of other members of the vertebrate kingdom. "The origin and the early steps in the development of man are identical with those in the forms immediately below him in the animal kingdom. Without doubt, he (man) is nearer to the ape in this regard than the apes are to the dog."[3] Haeckel, in his latest work on anthropology, lays particular stress on this "original relation between ontogeny and phylogeny."

Before Darwin, Haeckel had tried to support his thesis by appealing to the process of embryonic development.[4] He asserted that the homology between the human embryo and that of the dog can be explained only on the hypothesis that man is descended from some lower mammal, and that this is the reason why man at the

[1] "Descent of Man," vol. i., p. 22; Cf. "Stimmen aus Maria-Laach," 1875, vol. i., p. 80.
[2] Embryology teaches that all life begins in an egg, and that all have the same chemical composition. However, they are not of one type, there being at least four embryonic forms.—Agassiz, "Atlantic Monthly," Jan., 1874, p. 93.
[3] Cf. Huxley, "Position of Man in Nature," p. 81.
[4] Haeckel, "Natürliche Schöpfungsgeschichte," p. 353.

beginning of his development sinks to the plane of his lowest ancestors by a kind of reversion—"atavism." But what is to be proved in this argument is used as a proof—in other words, Haeckel argues in a circle. Listen to Dr. Hettinger:

"Were the descent of man from an animal proved, it could be used as an explanation for his embryonic development; but this is not the case. Besides, the parallelism in the development is neither as complete nor as general as is asserted; only the embryos of vertebrate animals show it, and these only within their class; no vertebrate appears as a membranous animal or mollusk. In the lower classes of animals even retrograding metamorphoses appear. Besides the major proposition that the seed of man does not differ from that of other animals is false. Darwin and Haeckel, if they wish to speak correctly, must say: The seed of man, at present and according to appearances, cannot be distinguished from that of other animals. But that there is a difference the development itself proves, because in the one it brings forth a man and in the other a dog; every being produces young according to its own kind; hence the embryos in the different living beings—man included—are not alike, but are different in kind and species, although physico-chemical examination is unable to establish this difference. Life does not allow itself to be examined with the probe, and we cannot subject it to alembics and retorts. Therefore this fact truly proves the existence of another force for the bringing forth of living beings than merely physico-chemical powers. Again, the development of the individual until the genus and species are completed cannot be brought into parallelism with the asserted development of the genera and species into new higher genera and species. For the embryo is not a full-grown individual, and instead of tending towards a new form, always tends to homogeneousness with its parents. If a man should spring from the embryo of a dog, or if a dog should spring from the seed of a man, then the comparison would be justified. Finally, the fact of embryonal development in man militates against Darwin and Haeckel. For, during his development in the womb, man morphologically passes through the various stages of the lower organisms until he reaches the highest—*i. e.*, the human form, without being influenced from without; so that neither "natural selection," nor the "struggle for life" determines this development. Therefore, there is in the germ of the human being a principle for its development which acts according to immanent laws, and builds up the human organism."[1]

103. (7) UNIVERSALITY.—Man's body can live under all the climatic conditions found on the earth—a quality we do not discover in animals. Every animal has its appointed land and climate, and its existence is endangered if removed thence. Man can live under all climatic relations, accustom himself to the hot sun of Africa or Asia, or to the eternal snows and cold of the northern regions. His body is adapted for every kind of nourishment—flesh, fish, roots, vegetables, fruit, farina, etc.—and he can support himself in every country without much difficulty.

In the body of animals we perceive at the first glance the end for which they were created or designed. We can see that the organs of each species are adapted to their natural pursuits of life. In one, they are arranged for flying; in another, for swimming; in some for creeping; in others, for running, etc. If they were taken from their habitat and natural sphere of life and habits, they would perish. But man can accustom himself

[1] Hettinger, "Apologie," vol. i. 1, pp. 424, 425.

to all pursuits of life, to every change of climate and food. All his organs are wonderfully harmonized for a cosmopolitan life; the symmetry, harmony, and adaptability of each show that his corporal life is not its own end, but that each organ is destined to serve as an instrument to the higher activity of his soul.

We must add, however, that man does not seem to be the only cosmopolitan being. Hitherto it was held as a rule that certain kinds of animals could not live in certain regions. This rule, however, seems to admit of exceptions. Only lately, for instance, Milne-Edwards has proved that the common mole extends from western Europe to Japan. Dobson observed the bat of western Europe at Nikko, Japan; the late-flying bat (*Vespertilio serotinus*) is found not only in Europe, but also in Central America and California, from the west of Europe to China, in fact over the whole earth. Whales are found in both hemispheres; the famous dolphin, formerly considered as peculiar to the Mediterranean Sea, has been caught on the shores of Tasmania.

The albatross is travelling continually, and moves all over the earth; a sea-swallow which does not differ from the *Sterna Caspia* of the European and Asiatic seas is found frequently near New Zealand, and appears to be spread all over the globe, for it is found also in Australia, Cochin-China, Madagascar, on the shores of the Red Sea, and in North America.

The reptiles are, as a rule, no great lovers of long voyages; and nevertheless some large sea-crocodiles are found in nearly all the tropical and moderate zones—nay, one kind of sea-crocodile must be considered a perfect cosmopolite. It is said that the Venus shell has been observed on the Antilles, in the west of Europe, in Senegal, on the Canary Islands, in the Mediterranean and ·Red seas, at the Cape of Good Hope, and in Australia.

Many spiders make great voyages against their will, and spread their kind over different parts of the earth. The wandering locust (*Pachytelus migratorius*) embraces a domain which extends from Madeira, in the west, to the Fiji Islands, and in latitude from the 50th degree north to the 40th degree south. Its home seems to be in the swamps and marshes of southeastern Europe, in Hungary, and southern Russia.

104. (8) THE SENSES.—The senses of animals as a rule surpass the senses of man. Their sight, hearing, and smell are stronger and keener. The eagle can bear the glare of the sun while he wings his way through the bracing air; the falcon can see his prey while coursing in aerial space; the hare can detect the faintest sound near by; the dog can scent his prey or the footsteps of his master anywhere; the pigeon can return to its cote, though liberated at sea, hundreds of miles away. Man, if he were obliged to depend on his sight and hearing, would perhaps equal some animals; this is proved by our American Indians and other savage races, whose hearing, sight, and running powers are marvellous. However, there is only one sense very prominent in the animal—the sense most usually exercised in procuring subsistence, in self-defence, or in attack. No animal has all the senses as perfect as man, and none has them so completely and judiciously under control for every necessary occasion.

It needs but little philosophy to learn and prove that the animal body has not the same end as that of man. The animal, in make-up, organization, manner of living, characteristic traits and activity is fitted only for a material life. Man, on the contrary, by his organization

[1] "Jahrbuch der Naturwissenschaften," 1886-1887, p. 284.

and intelligence shows a higher origin and end. * He shows he is possessed of higher attributes, higher ideals, and higher aspirations; that the destination of his body is something higher than earth; that it is during life the tenement of a God-given soul, immortal and imperishable.

105. RECAPITULATION.—To recapitulate what we have said. Even supposing the theory of descent to be true, its application to man is arbitrary, because man differs more conspicuously from the highest ape than any two kinds of animals differ from each other; because there are no intermediate forms that bridge over the wide gulf between rational man and the irrational brute, and the chasm is too wide and deep between man and monkey to be bridged over by assumptions. It has been proved that microcephalous idiots are by no means such intermediate forms. Only one possibility remains; such intermediate forms may have existed in the dim past, and become extinct like other species or organic forms. Have we any proof that beings more man-like than the gorilla or more ape-like than the negro have ever existed? Huxley has exhaustively discussed this question, and all know he is not likely to favor our views. He ends his discussion with the confession that the question must be answered in the negative, and that we must rest content with the hope that perhaps in still older strata the fossilized bones of an ape more anthropoid, or of a man more pithecoid than any yet known await the researches of some great and unborn paleontologist.

From the foregoing it follows that between the bodily conformation of man and the animal there is some similarity; but that there is an absolute identity in physical structure between man and any other animal we have to deny. If there are points of resemblance between the two there are also points of divergence. Besides, whatever similarity exists proves nothing, as Dr. Hettinger says: "However, supposing that man's structure is in every respect homogeneous (which is not the case) with that of an animal—of an ape, for instance—what would this prove? That man therefore descends from an ape? Not at all, it would only establish that his body is like it, but not that the likeness results from descent from an animal, that is, a monkey, in the manner accepted by Darwin and others. . . . Why should man not be like an animal in body? No doubt man is an animal, but a rational animal, that is, an animal endowed with reason, which makes him a being of quite a different kind."[1]

106. CHARACTERS OF THE PSYCHICAL ORDER.—The proper difference between man and animal lies in man's soul. Two faculties, reason and intelligence, constitute between man and animal an essential difference, a barrier absolutely insurmountable by way of progressive transformation or evolution; in short, an abyss. The existence, the properties, the nature of these faculties proper to man are demonstrated by a series of facts, established by observation, rigorously determined after a method and with a certainty which does not yield in anything to scientific method and to scientific certainty. Every phenomenon requires a proportionate cause; the nature of the phenomenon infallibly reveals the nature of the force that produces it. Such is the double principle, absolutely indisputable, which will serve as basis for our demonstration, as it will serve as basis for scientific determination.[2]

In order to avoid all confusion of language, let us first distinguish intelligence from reason. Intelligence is the general faculty of understanding, and comprehends the

[1] Hettinger, "Apologie," vol. i. 1, p. 392.
[2] Cf. Duilhe, de St. Project, "Apologie Scientifique," ch. xvii.

different kinds of knowledge; both sensible and reflective, or rational knowledge. Using intelligence in this sense, we may admit the expression, otherwise a little hard and too commonly employed—"the intelligence of the animals."[1] There are phenomena of sensible knowledge in the animal, which offer the appearance, but only the appearance, of superior knowledge.

107. (1) REASON is the power to abstract, generalize, and invent, the power to seize principles, first and necessary truths, immaterial realities, the conceptions of being, substance, cause, simplicity, unity, plurality, of the true, good, and beautiful, of time, space, of the infinite and absolute. Reason is an element, an essential condition of liberty, responsibility, spirituality and immortality; it cannot be reduced by analysis to other faculties; it cannot be conceived as a synthesis or as one resulting from inferior powers, much less as a function of purely material organs. Such is reason, the principle of intellectual knowledge proper to man.

The sensible knowledge common to man and the animal has for object the particular, the singular, the concrete; this individual, this pleasure, this need, this pain. It comprehends the remembrance of visible things, the faculty to retain, to recall, to associate entire impressions; it is sufficient to explain all the facts attributed to what is called the intelligence of animals.

Montaigne said that there is more difference between man and man than between animal and animal. Bossuet cannot refrain from pitying so eminent a mind;

---

[1] The word "intelligence" in the etymological and rigorous sense does not differ from reason; it is the acting or active intellect of the scholastics; the faculty to discern and comprehend the species, the intellectual, the universal, from the material images furnished through the senses; the power to abstract the essence from the things that are gross, and to render them intelligible.

it may be that he is serious in saying some ridiculous things; that he jests and trifles with serious matters. Transformist anthropology has taken hold of Montaigne's words and treasures them up for every occasion. It takes the fossil man of early quaternary times, such as he is supposed to have been, and the savage man such as he is believed to be, and compares these with the animals that appear most intelligent, and concludes, dogmatically, that even from the standpoint of reason and of the power of reflection there is a greater difference between the man of genius and the savage than between the savage and the gorilla or chimpanzee.

In dealing with this question two things are often forgotten or overlooked: one, that all men having the same nature, the perfection of the soul must be examined with regard to all its powers wherever the human species can develop itself; the other, that the most stupid men —as we shall show further on—have faculties superior to the most perfect animals. But let us admit that there exist savage men so degraded that not the least trace of reason can be found in them. This would be a purely accidental state, and would not at all affect their nature as men. Reason in them is irredeemably atrophied, annihilated for want of culture or use, but as a faculty it is unimpaired. What proves this is that the descendant of savages may be a civilized man, a man of genius. But the animal and its descendants, in spite of all culture, cannot pass beyond the limits of their natural intelligence. With the hide of a rhinoceros, the wool of a sheep, or the shaggy coat of a bear, are never associated the feelings of the human heart, nor the intellectual sensibility of the cultivated mind. Reason, which reflects, generalizes, invents, adapts, and progresses, is always and essentially absent in the animal; all these faculties are proper only to man. Hence, between man, whoever he may be, and the beast, whatever it may be, there is an insuperable abyss.

108. (2) LIBERTY.—The second faculty which establishes between man and the animal a specific difference is liberty. "From the principle of reflection which acts in us," says Bossuet, "springs a new principle, namely, liberty. The soul elevated through reason above corporal objects is not carried away by the impressions of these objects and of itself. Thus it attaches itself to whatever it pleases, and considers whatever it wishes, in order to make use thereof and to obtain what it proposes to itself."[1]

The philosophical thesis of liberty, so falsely interpreted and so unfortunately perverted in our day, even by the most distinguished minds, cannot enter into our programme. Here as elsewhere we keep as near as possible to the methods of experimental physiology and psychology—or, in other words, to psycho-physical methods. Therefore, let us examine attentively the play of "reflex action," that is, a reaction proportionate to the direct action. Man alone, endowed with free will, has the power to interrupt, modify, or turn aside the reflex transmission of an impressional movement, the natural effect of a cerebral vibration. He is not, like the atom, subject to mechanical action, nor like the animal, to physiological and necessary involuntary action. True, he does not annihilate the force put into play, but he directs it; he averts and restricts it; he can even transform and reverse it, as the engineer reverses the motive power of his engine. To a cerebral vibration naturally destined to provoke pain or anger, he can answer, and in fact does answer sometimes, by a contrary expression—scorn, indifference, joy, sorrow, or a smile. The testimony of facts here supports the testimony of conscious-

[1] "De la Connaissance de Dieu et de Soi-même," ch. v., 9.

ness. Under the knife of the vivisector the animal cannot help manifesting outwardly the suffering which it endures; man, even the most degraded, may endure being scalped, shot, or hung without showing pain or fear. Indeed, to evince signs of pain or fear under the most trying circumstances is deemed a lasting disgrace among the American Indians.

The wonderful expressiveness of the human face is another physical peculiarity which removes man far away from the animal. Animals are capable only of the rudest expressions of anger, fear, and attachment. Man alone weeps, and weeps as early as the fourth month of his infant life. Man alone laughs, alone has the muscles by which the corners of the mouth contract in a smile, and that smile plays on his features as early as the forty-fifth day of his infant existence. Man alone blushes, and the blush, even Darwin admits, is a most peculiar and human expression. It is involuntary but universal among men. The blind blush, as well as the most barbarous races — the Malays, Polynesians, Fuegeans.[1] Again, the expression of anxiety, despair, contempt, reflection, pride, horror, etc., is peculiar to the human face. Animals are incapable thereof, because the transmission of nervous and cerebral movements is beyond their control. Man, who is reasonable and free, can do what the animal cannot. His reason and liberty are here manifest; they explain the faculty, which he alone possesses, to create language, language in which there is no natural relation between the sign and the thing signified.[2]

109. (3) CONVENTIONAL LANGUAGE.—The two qualities characteristic of the human soul—reason and liberty—are made more manifest by an ensemble of facts, of internal and external operations, directly and universally ob-

[1] Behrens, "Lecture on Charles Darwin."
[2] Cf. J. Rambasson, "Phenomènes Nerveux," etc.

served, which result from these qualities and lead to the scientific determination of man.

This ensemble of phenomena comprises conventional language, whether verbal, written, or by signs; the power to invent, to progress—perfectibility; the perception of moral good and evil—the moral conscience; the perception of the beautiful—the æsthetic faculty; the perception of the divine, the idea of God and of what relates to this idea. Here we shall speak only of language and perfectibility, because they are most easily reached by observation.

What enables man to live in community and intercourse with his fellow-men, for the purposes of defence and attack, for his own well-being and pleasure, is the faculty of language, the possession of which man alone enjoys. Thanks especially to this incomparable instrument, he can develop his intelligence by fixing his ideas, by receiving ideas from his kindred, and by communicating them in turn. "*Quel est ton sort, dis-moi? D'être homme et de parler,*" says Sosie in Molière. Articulate language is exclusively the portion of man, and he makes use of very different sounds in various countries, in different latitudes, and under different conditions of life, to express the same ideas. The foundation of language, in spite of this variety of arbitrary sounds, is identical everywhere, composed of the same elements and governed by the same fundamental laws. It is a long time since Quintilian said: "When the Creator distinguished us from the animals, it was especially by the gift of language. They surpass us in strength, in patience, in size of body, in longevity, in quickness, in a thousand other qualities, and especially in dispensing with all assistance from without Guided only by nature, they learn very soon and by themselves to walk, to nourish themselves, to swim. They are provided with something to protect them against the cold; they have weapons which are natural to them; they find their nourishment wherever they go. Man—with what effort does he procure all these things! Reason is our portion, and seems to associate us with the immortals; but how weak would reason be without the faculty to express our thoughts by words, which faithfully interpret them! This the animals want, and this is worth more than the intelligence of which, we must say, they are absolutely deprived."[1]

The physiological differences then reveal their high importance in their uses, as correlated to the mental differences which, by common confession, are "enormous." A gauge for these may be found in language, the power of articulate and intelligible expression, the vehicle of civilization, the creator and conservator of literature. It is language that, in Huxley's own phrase, "constitutes and makes man what he is." Philology, therefore, as well as comparative anatomy, must be consulted on the question of man's origin. This claim Professor Whitney emphatically enforces.[2] And Max Müller, an acknowledged master in this department, declares: "Man means the thinker, and the first manifestation of thought is speech."

110. (4) WHAT WE OWE TO LANGUAGE, REASON, AND LIBERTY.—Thanks to language, man can transmit to his posterity what he has accomplished. Living speech and the written word, of which the latter gives a kind of an eternity to the former, allow us to gather treasures of experience heaped up by those who have lived before us, and to leave them as our most precious heritage to those who will come after us. While the instinct of the animal is unchangeable, the reason of man is essentially progressive. The swallow builds its nest as it did in the dawn of its creation; the bee

[1] Quintilian, translated by La Harpe, Dijon, 1820.
[2] "Language and the Study of Language," pp. 8, 46, 53, 381.

gathers honey from the blossoms of the field and constructs its honeycombs as in days of old; but the man of our days, although physically the same as our first ancestors, has accomplished great things since then. No longer does he dress in the skins of wild beasts nor cover himself with leaves; he does not shield himself against sun and weather by the shade of trees, nor make his dwelling-place in caves; he knows how to weave and sew wool, cotton, silk, and other textile fabrics; he knows how to build houses, construct ships and railroads; he has invented steam and electricity for motive power, for the transmission of his ideas, for the generation of heat and light, and for other purposes; he knows how to make works of artistic and useful design, to adorn and add comfort to life. While some savage tribes still appear in a semi-nude state and live in miserable huts, it is only necessary that they should be transplanted to cities, to enjoy the comforts and benefits of civilization, and all the intellectual and artistic treasures of former generations.

Thanks to reason and free will, even the most degenerate races have their own forms of industry. If there be differences between races in this and other points, they do not consist in the faculty itself, but rather in the progress and needs of life. Everywhere man knows how to make fire,[1] cut wood, cook food, invent and make instruments for hunting and fishing, prepare skins and other material for covering, construct canoes, rafts, or devices for going on water. His wants and mode of life tend to industry. Franklin, being struck with admiration by this gift of the Creator, defined man "a tool-making animal."[2] This definition can indeed serve to

[1] Cf. M. Jolly, "L'Origine du Feu," in "Nature," 1879, vol. ii., pp. 144, 145.
[2] L. Noiré, "Das Werkzeug," Mainz, 1880, p. 24.

distinguish us from the animals, because we are the only creatures that know how to invent and make tools and make use of them.

Man alone is possessed of inventive genius, and the hand is trained to do the bidding of this and other faculties; so wondrous is its structure, so manifold are its uses, that it has been called "the chief and distinguishing feature of the human frame." Without it, as Galen said centuries ago, man "would no longer work as an artificer, nor protect himself with a breast-plate, nor fashion a sword or spear, nor invent a bridle to mount the horse and hunt the lion. Neither could he follow the arts of peace, fashion the pipe and lyre, build houses, erect altars, inscribe them, and by means of letters hold communion with the wisdom of antiquity." By its means we can supply all our wants rapidly, overleap rivers and mountains, span distances, connect the world by commerce and instantaneous conversation, fly through the air, pass over land with the rapidity of a bird, dig in the bowels of earth, and make its treasures minister to our wants and enterprise; in a word, subdue the forces of nature.

111. THE TASMANIANS.—For a long time it was generally believed that the Tasmanians had no instrument for fishing, but only a straight pole sharpened at the end. According to Sir John Lubbock, they did not know how to rekindle a fire when it was extinguished. But M. Jolly proves that Lubbock was mistaken; they see that the sharpened and polished assagais nourish and keep up fire, and this would in itself be sufficient to reveal the secret to man. Quatrefages collected among the poor inhabitants of Van Diemen's Land many proofs of much more advanced industry than is generally credited to them. The Tasmanians, in order to dislodge the sarigues (opossums), which often hide themselves very high up in the branches of trees, used a thick rope which sup-

ported the climbers, while with a stone hatchet they cut the notches or steps in the bark, which excited the wonder of early travellers.'

We thus behold a people whom Dove considered hardly endowed with intelligence, following a very rational and ingenious method of climbing very large trees—a method which is often practised among peoples who are rated quite high in industrial civilization. We may even learn some things from these unfortunate islanders—one thing in particular, which is a highly characteristic trait, and which may put to blush our boasted refinement:

112. THE SENSE OF SHAME.—Among the phenomena and manifestations of the intellectual order which prove the essential difference between man and the beast is the sense of shame. "A spider's web," says Joubert, "made of silk and light would not be more difficult to execute than the answer to this question: What is the sense of shame?" Hence we shall not try to define it, and will only say that it is derived from both our moral and our æsthetic sense; that it is a manifestation both of the good and beautiful, and a discrimination between moral and immoral conduct. Quatrefages tells us of the Tasmanians, whom he studied so carefully, and who are represented as the lowest savages: "Their daily habits show a profound sentiment of decency and sense of shame. The boys who had passed beyond childhood had their fires and quarters apart in the camp. In the morning they went away early, in order not to be present at the awakening of the tribe. The young men never ran around in the woods with the women, and when they met a group of the other sex, they had to go off in another direction."²

---

¹ Quatrefages, "Hommes Fossiles et Hommes Sauvages," 1884, p. 330.   ² Quatrefages, *op. cit.*

To pretend to find and recognize in the animal, even the most intelligent and best domesticated, even a trace of the sense of shame is ridiculously absurd and nonsensical. Not even the most enthusiastic transformist would have the hardihood to venture such an assertion, and, as far as we know, no one has dared to do so. Hence we can reiterate our statement, that between man and the beast there is a great difference, a wide gulf which no one can bridge over.

In the last chapter of his "Prehistoric Times,"[1] entitled "Concluding Remarks," one of the patriarchs of prehistoric and archeologico-ethnological science, whom we have quoted before, Sir John Lubbock, condenses his theory in an argument of the most striking interest, which allows him to pass softly and smoothly from the ape to man.

We know that apes use round stones to break nuts;[2] from this to making use of a sharp stone in order to cut is surely not so far; from this to sharpening stones by chance, if not by reflection, there is only one step; the stone roughly cut and the polished stone touch each other; when we polish a stone we cannot fail to notice that it grows warm; next the fire is invented.

Here we have a direct and rapid way to reach civilization. However, it seems to us that with the same system, by forcing the steam a little higher, the grand triumph of motive power might be achieved. It is too bad that Sir John stopped short on so fascinating and promising an advance for his ape, and did not pursue his fecund reasoning. Any animal, if not blind like the mole, can see an apple fall. From the fall of an apple to the hypothesis of universal attraction is surely not so far; Newton has

[1] "L'Homme avant l'Histoire," ch. xiv.
[2] We shall meet this statement, as well as some others, in the next chapter.

proved it. From the hypothesis of attraction to the explanation of celestial mechanism there is only a step; Laplace has proved it.

Without reflective reason and free will it is just as impossible to invent and make the stone hatchet, or the needle with its eye, as to invent the compass, the printing press, or the steam locomotive. These inventions suppose intellectual operations which may differ in degree, but which are the same in kind, and presuppose the activity of the same faculties.

M. Fabre, who, we regret, cannot be quoted at length, shows by facts and by various profound observations the inertness of instinct; that is to say, the extreme stupidity of animals alongside of their extreme cleverness. So long as they follow the straight line which has been primitively traced for them, they work prodigies of cleverness; but as soon as they branch off from this line their doings are prodigies of stupidity. "The animals which we behold achieving the most beautiful works," says Bossuet, "are those which appear to have the least sense."

113. CONCLUSION.—We have shown the extreme and essential difference which exists between man and the beast by adducing two orders of facts or phenomena—the phenomena of artificial language and the phenomena of invention, of industrial civilization.¹ We cannot discuss this subject in all its bearings; but we trust what we have said and what we are going to say is sufficient for the attentive reader to understand that there is a vast difference between man and animals, not only in body but especially in his soul—not only in degree but also in kind. We purpose in the next chapter to meet some of the objections brought up by those who pretend to be-

¹Cf. F. Duilhe, de St. Project, "Apologie Scientifique," ch. xviii.

lieve that man descends from an animal, and that there is between them only a difference of degree.

Some one has facetiously said that he did not care whence he came, if he only knew whither he was going. The question of our material and historical origin may throw light on our destiny; but, after all, human destiny is the great practical problem of human life. And a creature's destiny depends upon its organization. It matters comparatively little how we came into existence. Here we are; what *are* we, and what is to *become* of us? The reply to the first question gives us a clue to the answer to the second. Let every man take counsel with himself, and I am sure that the deepest voice within us, heard in our profoundest convictions, in our loftiest aspirations, in our ineffable yearnings, in the spirit's daring ambition for the infinite, in its passion to possess God and to be possessed by Him, will proclaim to our expectant souls that, however linked to the earthly and perishable, we are none other than the offspring of the living God.'

[1] Behrens, "Lecture on Charles Darwin," p. 24.

CHAPTER VI.

MAN AND BEAST.—Concluded.

Instinct and intelligence.— Difference between the intelligence of man and that of the animal.— Objections and answers.— The animal has passions and affections like man.— Man is not the only animal that can speak.— Self-consciousness.— Individuality.— Abstraction.— Belief in God.— Sense of beauty.—Moral sentiment.—Destructive criticism of Darwinism by Professor Virchow.

114. THE MENTAL FACULTIES OF MAN AND OF ANIMALS ACCORDING TO DARWIN.—Indefatigable Darwin! He not only occupied himself with the corporal structure of animals, comparing it with that of man, but also extended his labors to their mental faculties, and he did this with a dexterity that is indicative of the genius of paradox. Listen to the conclusion at which he arrived: "There is no essential difference between man and the highest mammalia as regards the mental faculties."

Thus, according to Darwin, man and beast, from the intellectual point of view, are one and the same being. Let us note this. However, before discussing the views of Darwin, let us try to understand well what is meant by these so-called "mental faculties."

115. INSTINCT AND INTELLIGENCE.—By mental faculties we understand two primary attributes—instinct and intelligence. But primary as they are, there is a marked contrast between them. In instinct, everything is blind, necessary, invariable. In intelligence, everything is elective, conditional, modifiable. In instinct, every-

thing is innate and fatal; in intelligence, everything results from experience and instruction, everything is free. Finally, in instinct, everything is personal and limited; whilst in intelligence everything is general and perfectible.

When we ask what faculties are included in the generic term "instinct," we may say that it comprises all those mental faculties which lead to the performance of actions that are adaptive in character, but pursued without the knowledge of the relation between the means employed and the ends attained.

116. WHAT IS INSTINCT? EXAMPLES.—We cannot deny that most animals, by a kind of natural intuition, or, if you please, by instinct and intelligence, are informed of their present needs and their future necessities. Who does not know that young ducks, hardly out of the egg, rush toward the water, this being their element, and the young colt, hardly born, goes and seizes the teat of its mother?

The larvæ of a great number of hymenopterous insects are carnivorous. Their prey must be both living and immovable, for the least movement would, in the first place, endanger their eggs, and afterward the small worms, both of which are very delicate. The animal solves the problem by paralyzing its victim; it destroys its movement and leaves organic vitality intact. Let us take, for instance, the ammophila (a kind of hornet). This animal feeds its larvæ with a very lively caterpillar, which must be stored up in the same cell with the egg, but only after having lost all power of motion. Now, in this caterpillar the nervous centres are scattered in the rings of which its body is formed. One ring rendered motionless would not cause the insensibility of the next ring. They all have to be paralyzed. What the most expert physiologist would suggest the ammophila carries out; its sting pierces one ring after the other (nine in all), until the animal is completely paralyzed. The victim, still alive, but incapable of movement, is then seized by the nape of the neck and dragged into the nest.

The necrophori, when they have laid their eggs, go and seek dead meat and lay it alongside of the eggs, in order that the young ones, hardly hatched, may find their nourishment quite ready; sometimes they even lay their eggs into the dead meat itself. Who could have taught the ammophilæ that their larvæ are in need of live meat and the necrophori that the proper nourishment for their offspring is rotten meat? The pompilæ offer even a more wonderful instance of foresight. They are wholly carnivorous, but they know—how do they know?—that their young at birth are herbivorous. Hence before dying (for it is not given them ever to see their young) they place a lot of vegetable provisions at their disposal.

Let us pass to another order of animals. These, endowed perhaps with less refined foresight, are distinguished by the difficulty and perfection of their instinctive acts.

The bird divines that it is in need of a nest, and this nest is a wonder, on account of the choice and combination of the materials used for its construction. The beaver knows beforehand that he will be in need of a hut, and this hut is a wonder, on account of the profound knowledge of architecture which the animal displays in its construction.[1] Finally, the spider knows that it is in

[1] Flourens relates the history of a young beaver which, taken on the banks of the Rhone, was brought up in the "Jardin des Plantes." It had been put in a cage, consequently had no need of a hut. However, as soon as it could procure the required material, it began to build one as perfect as that of the most skilful beaver.

need of a net, and this net is equally a wonder, both on account of its weaving and the success with which it serves as a snare. Here are faculties which reveal a great amount of intelligence, and, nevertheless, we call this intelligence "instinct." Why? Because however perfect the acts may be, which are its expression, the animal has neither learned, nor calculated, nor foreseen them. It possessed the germ thereof from its birth as well as it possessed the germ of its physical development; afterwards it executed them like a machine. The proof is the bird, which does not know how to make anything else but its nest; the spider, which can build nothing but its net. So fate has ordained. We may, therefore, compare the animals that perform these instinctive acts with a watch that unwinds its chain quite regularly, but the springs of which a powerful and intelligent hand arranged long before.

Another observation. Instinct not only constitutes an innate propensity to do certain things, always in the same manner; it is also, sometimes, an intermittent force which the animal obeys at certain moments.

Watch the swallow in captivity. You may hide it in the interior of an apartment, consequently far from its companions and from the atmospheric variations of the open air, in fact, from everything which may give it information; nevertheless when the time comes for migration it shows quite a fever-like agitation; it struggles in its cage, seeks an exit, and, not finding any, it throws itself against the bars with such violence that it tears out its feathers and rends its little breast, so as to be quite bloody.

We may observe the same phenomenon, more or less clearly, in all other migrating birds and animals. Such is instinct. Let us now consider briefly "animal intelligence."

117. **INTELLIGENCE MAY BE UNITED WITH INSTINCT.**—
Intelligence, we said, differs from instinct inasmuch as it is a reflective faculty. It may happen that it only combines with an act which, in principle, is the product of instinct. Thus, we come to speak of the spider, "whose net," to use the words of Reimars, "is on the pattern of rays diverging from a centre." If I tear this net the spider repairs it; but it repairs it only in the torn spot, and does not touch the rest. In the spider, therefore, there is a machine-like instinct which makes the net; afterwards intelligence intervenes, which informs it of the spot to be repaired and also of the nature of the mending to be done.

But animal intelligence can be exercised in a manner completely independent of instinct. It is applied to such spontaneous acts as indicate in the animal an impressibility similar to that of man—acts in which we sometimes find traces of human sentiment and even of human passion, as we shall very soon see.

It is especially in the state of domestication, that is, of cohabitation with man, that the animal attains the highest development, something that we might call heart and mind. Take the pointer, for instance. He has found the scent of the game; he hesitates, slackens his pace, looks anxiously around, rather creeps than walks, finally shoots towards his prey with an immovable and piercing eye, which has something fascinating in it. Sometimes he even turns his head slightly toward his master, as if to ask him: "It is this way?"

Take the shepherd dog. What solicitude, and, at the same time, what skill does he not display in watching the flock intrusted to his care! Always on the lookout, he keeps it in place and is unmerciful in driving it from forbidden pastures; and he does this with so sure an eye that he never makes a mistake.

How can we pass over the blind man's dog? Examine his walk. It is slow, measured, interrupted by short stops, in order that the unfortunate, whose protector he has become, may find his position and take breath. See the care he takes to avoid the least obstacles on the road, even the smallest unevenness of the ground! See his caution in crossing streets and public places! He is careful to prevent every sudden shock, every false step, every collision. With a suppliant expression of look he appeals to passers-by to drop a small coin in the dish he so humbly holds up. But this is not all. If his master should die he hardly has the courage to survive him. This is animal intelligence.

Among domestic animals, it is especially the dog which shares to a certain degree our intelligence. There are some other animals, the horse and the elephant, for instance, whose intelligence deserves to be described; but let us pass to human instinct and intelligence.

118. MAN ALSO HAS INSTINCT. — Man also has instinct, but in a less degree than the animal. The first act of the new-born child is an instinctive act. It lengthens or spreads out its lips instinctively, in order to take hold of the nipple which is to nourish it, and even makes slight movements of suction. Later on, man reveals other instincts. That which overrules all others in our days is the instinct of popularity; the poet will abandon the muse, the lawyer the court, the doctor his patient, in order to crave the favors of the crowd.

119. MAN'S INTELLIGENCE: EXAMPLES.— But it is by his intelligence that man is distinguished from the animals. We have already referred to this point; hence we shall be brief. In this respect there is such a sharp and deep line of demarcation between man and beast that some hesitate to apply the word "intelligence" to animals, through fear that it might be looked

upon as a concession to materialistic opinions! However, these scruples are exaggerated. In fact, nothing proves more conclusively the immense superiority of man over the animal than a comparison of the two while performing certain actions which are common to them, and a study of the manner in which man supplies by his intelligence his lack of some of the means with which other creatures are endowed.

Let us take the matter of food, for instance. Animals find their own support. The herbivora will browse on the first grass they find in the fields; the carnivora will devour the first animal they can seize; afterward, both will quench their thirst at some spring or brook, water being their only drink.

And man? Although he is both herbivorous and carnivorous, he must undoubtedly die of hunger were he limited to the expedients of these animals. He cannot, like the herbivora, live on the grass he finds; he cannot, like the carnivora, eat meat raw; both must be prepared for him by the action of fire. But where and how procure this fire? Here intelligence comes to his assistance. Fire once obtained, man's intelligence will teach him the various ways of preparing the nourishment best fitted to his needs and tastes. It will teach him to grind wheat, extract the flour and make bread thereof. It will teach him to obtain from the grape, apple, barley, and other fermentable substances, drinks more agreeable than water and often more useful to his organism.

Shelter? Most animals are in no need of shelter. Those that need it find it in the trunks of trees, underbrush, caves, or they instinctively dig for shelter.

Nothing of the kind meets man's wants. True, our ancestors also dwelt in caves (hence the name, troglodytes), but their intelligence taught them to air them sufficiently, to close them securely, and to furnish them adequately for the needs of subsistence.

The animal is just as comfortable in the most pestilential marshes as in the most wholesome woods and plains. Man, on the contrary, has everything to dread from the deadly exhalations of swamps. If he does not fall a victim to them, it is because his intelligence has taught him to fly from the localities where malaria reigns, or, if he is obliged to live there, the same intelligence again makes him acquainted with the medical properties of the plant fitted to combat the disease.

Suppose that a man or an animal is wounded, that a vein is cut. The animal will stop bleeding naturally; man will continue to bleed freely. What is the cause of this difference? The blood of the animal is more coagulable than man's blood, and consequently more apt to form the clot of blood needed to act as an obturator. Man would die of hemorrhage if his intelligence did not inform him of the means needed to stop the flowing of the blood.

But enough of comparisons. We have said sufficient to show that there is an abyss between the faculties of man and those of the animal. While God has granted a certain kind of intelligence only to a small number of animals, and while on all of them He has lavished instinct, man has received few instincts; but, on the other hand, he has received all the gifts of intelligence, or, rather, he has been endowed with intelligence in the most sublime sense of the word.

After these preliminary remarks, we shall consider the main objections which Darwin and his adherents bring against our view, which holds that there is not only an essential difference, but also a difference of degree, between the intellect of man and that of the animal.

120. OBJECTION: THE ANIMAL ALSO HAS PASSIONS AND AFFECTIONS.[1]—The animal has passions and affections like man. It allows itself to be carried away by anger and jealousy. The feeling of love in the superior animals is no less warm than in man. The fidelity and devotion of the dog, the maternal love of the lioness, the conjugal love and connubial fidelity of doves and love-birds are proverbial.

ANSWER.—All this we do not deny; but we say that the causes and motives which produce these effects in man are essentially different. In animals they seem similar to a certain degree outwardly, but they proceed from quite a different source. Man has passions, because he has a soul which allows itself to be guided and led away by its thoughts and feelings as well as by the sensitive movements of the body. Our passions arise from thoughts and considerations in our mind, but we can command, rule, and control them. We can also, if we wish, not be passionate, not be affectionate. But the animal must be passionate and affectionate; it cannot act differently. It must love its master and obey him, and it must be grateful to him, just as necessarily as it must hate its enemy and persecutor. The animal is passionate and affectionate because it is subject to the impressions of its senses, and is unable to resist them.

121. OBJECTION: THE ANIMAL ALSO HAS INTELLIGENCE.—Again, we are told that the animal also has intelligence—that it reflects, resolves, etc. Young animals are more easily caught than older ones; our hunting dogs, for instance, have made progress in certain moral qualities, and also, probably, in intelligence. . . . Again, animals use instruments; the chimpanzee cracks with a stone a wild fruit similar to our walnut. Another

---

[1] For many of these objections cf. Darwin's "Descent of Man," vol. i., pp. 42, 52, 62, 76, 78, 79, etc.

monkey was taught to raise the cover of a large chest with a stick. Monkeys also use stones and canes as weapons. It is known that the orang covers himself with the leaves of a palm-tree at night; monkeys build huts for themselves in the branches of trees. Brehm tells us that one of his baboons protected himself against the heat of the sun by throwing a straw mat over his head. Here we see the beginnings of clothing and architecture.

ANSWER.—All these alleged examples as proofs of active animal intelligence and reflection, of a conscious pursuit of an end, and therefore of the choice of the proper means, do not prove what they aim to prove, but simply illustrate the instinct of the monkey and the hunting dog. Instinct drives the monkey to open eggs, because it was taught by previous experience that it contained something eatable, just as the fitchew and the weasel suck eggs, and even break a small hole in the opposite side, as if they understood the laws of atmospheric pressure. When the hunting dog does not allow game to escape, as the untrained dog does, but bites it to death, this only proves his instinct. Nobody has denied that, in a certain sense, animals are capable of development, in the sphere of their instinctive impulses, especially that of self-preservation. An old hare is more watchful than a young one. And why should animals be incapable of development to a certain degree? Have they not the capacity of receiving sensible impressions and thus gathering experience in a certain way? But who would compare this application of instinct, which is always confined to self-preservation, nourishment, and propagation, with man's power of development, which is universal and unlimited, like the dominion of his spirit? What sensible person ever spoke about progress in bees or ants? But when Darwin directs our attention to "the moral qualities of the dog," we reply that the domestic dog has become what he is only by the guidance of man. The peculiar instincts of an animal suggest to thinking man the possibility of making use of them for his ends, *e.g.*, by training the dog to hunt and watch, the blackbird and the bullfinch to whistle certain melodies, the starling and the parrot to speak words. In this sense, certainly, we can speak of training, but not of development in the proper sense of the word; wherever innate instinct is wanting all training will be useless. The wolf will never become the companion of man, as the dog or sparrow will never whistle songs.

When the monkey is taught to raise with a stick the cover of a large chest, then, because of his peculiar imitative instinct, he only apes what he saw man do. But how can such an act be used as an argument proving that there is in him an active intelligence similar to man's, who works for a purpose and uses instruments to achieve his ends? As regards the building of huts by the anthropoids, Darwin himself declares that they are "probably guided by instinct;" but when he says: "This may easily pass into a wilfully conscious act," we find his conclusion altogether illogical. The building of huts by monkeys does not even show as much mechanical instinct as the building of nests by birds, etc. Again, the dog seeks the shade; why should not the baboon seek protection under a straw mat against the heat of the sun? And when the chimpanzee breaks walnuts with a stone it apes what he saw a man doing. But why does not the chimpanzee form the stone into an instrument and perfect it? The monkey sees a fire and warms himself; but why did it never think of lighting a fire or keeping it up by piling wood thereon, as the lowest savage does?

If the animal had intelligence, properly speaking, it

would also have general ideas, a conscious aim and choice of means; but it has only instinct, animal intelligence, that is, a judicious activity without consciousness of aim. "The dog can distinguish dogs the one from the other," Darwin tells us, "a dog from a man and both from a horse." But what does this prove? That the dog perceives man as one particular species of beings, the horse as another species, and both as species of different genera? Not at all. The dog distinguishes a horse, a man, and a dog as three different individual beings, but not as three different species. Undoubtedly, the dog sees clearly that man and man are more like to each other than man and horse; but it does not determine the degrees of similarity according to species, it does not conceive as species the similarities existing within described limits. The dog distinguishes the dog from the bitch; but does it also consciously distinguish the male and female sexes? Will it combine the bitch, the cow, and woman under the general conception of female? the dog, the bull, and man under the general idea of male? Does the bitch know that it is made to be impregnated and to bring forth young ones, which it is to suckle? Does it know the causal connection of these events, and their temporal succession? Nobody would dare to assert it. The bitch follows the unconscious instinct of coition, and knows nothing about the sexes. If animals had an intelligent soul like man, which could be trained, then certainly well-trained dogs would have begun to give instructions to their young.

122. OBJECTION: THERE IS ONLY A DIFFERENCE OF DEGREE BETWEEN THE INTELLIGENCE OF MAN AND OF THE ANIMAL.—As regards speech, the supporters of the pithecoid theory will acknowledge only a difference of degree between animals and men, not an essential difference. Darwin mentions the case of an ape in Par-

aguay who, when excited, utters at least six distinct sounds, which excite corresponding emotions in other apes; and also the still more remarkable fact "that the dog, since being domesticated, has learnt to bark in at least four or five distinct tones. . . . We have the bark of eagerness, as in the chase, that of anger, as well as growling; the yelp or howl of despair, as when shut up; the baying at night; the bark of joy, as when starting on a walk with his master; and the very distinct one of demand or supplication, as when wishing for a door or a window to be opened." Darwin further says that only *articulate* language is peculiar to man, but he adds that "it is not the mere articulation which is man's distinguishing character, for parrots and other birds have this power. The lower animals differ from man solely in his almost infinitely larger power of associating together the most diversified sounds and ideas, sounds with definite ideas; and this obviously depends on the high development of his mental powers. . . . The fact of the higher apes not using their vocal organs for speech no doubt depends on their intelligence not having been sufficiently advanced. The possession by them of organs which with long continued practice might have been used for speech, although not thus used, is paralleled by the case of many birds, which possess organs fitted for singing, though they never sing."[1]

ANSWER.—That the language of man is essentially different from merely emotional sounds (animal language) does not need any proof. Just as little as sensations rise to ideas, so little do interjections become the expressions of ideas if no higher faculty than sensation and sensible perception exists. "The kingdom of speech," says Horne Tooke, "is founded on the fall and

[1] Darwin, "Descent of Man," vol. i., p. 54.

destruction of the interjection."[1] Max Müller says: "Language begins where interjections cease. There are no structural hinderances which forbid animals to speak. But the animal will learn to speak only if it can become a thinking being. Man speaks, but no animal ever gave forth a word. Language is man's Rubicon, which no animal will ever dare to cross. This is the answer, based upon facts, which we give to those who speak about development, who believe that they discover in monkeys at least the beginnings of human activity, and who would uphold the possibility that man is nothing but a more favored animal, the triumphant victor in the struggle for life. Language is something more tangible than a fold in the brain or a formation of the skull. It does not admit subtilities, and no process of 'natural selection' will ever be able to find significant words in the songs of birds or in the cries of animals."[2]

Frohschammer speaks in the same terms: "Animals do not speak, because they are mentally incapable of speech, because they are not really capable of thinking. Man's power of thought is the cause of his power of speech, and not his power of speech the cause of his power of thought, as has been asserted, although, of course, the power of thought is stimulated and developed by speech. For this reason a being incapable of thought can never be taught really to speak, although, parrot-like, it may imitate words; on the other hand, a being possessing real power of thought, if it fulfils even to a slight degree the primary conditions of the development of its spiritual powers, will form for itself some signs by which it can impart thought, even

[1] Cf. Hettinger, "Christenthum," 6th ed., vol. i. 1, p. 433, from whom we translate.
[2] Cf. Hettinger, *op. cit.*.

though, like the deaf and dumb, it cannot hear a human sound."[1]

But Haeckel, in his "Generelle Morphologie," retorts, saying:

"Birds with highly differentiated gullets and tongues, such as parrots, can learn to speak; that is, they have the power of making articulate sounds just as perfectly as man. The most important step in the development of real men from real apes is the differentiation of the gullet, and to this man owes the power of speech and historical tradition."

"It would be an interesting task," says Dr. Reusch, "for a historian to collect the historical traditions of their race from the parrots, who, as Haeckel assures us, can learn our language as perfectly as a Frenchman can learn German."[2]

When Haeckel in his "History of Creation" says, "Very many wild tribes can count no further than ten or twenty, whereas some clever dogs have been made to count up to forty and even beyond sixty, and yet the faculty of appreciating number is the beginning of mathematics," we suppose he means to imply that dogs will probably be able at some time or other to do fractions and the rule of three.

123. OBJECTION: THE ANIMAL ALSO HAS SELF-CONSCIOUSNESS, ETC.— Consciousness, individuality, abstraction, general ideas, belong to man. But can we feel sure that an old dog with an excellent memory and some power of imagination, as shown by his dreams, never reflects on his past pleasures in the chase? This would be a form of consciousness. Dogs certainly possess something very like conscience, and this does not appear to be wholly the result of fear. A dog, for

[1] "Quarterly Review," vol. cxxxvii. (July, 1874), p. 43.
[2] Reusch, "Bibel und Natur," p. 139.

instance, will refrain from stealing in the absence of his master. What a strong feeling of inward satisfaction must compel a bird, so full of activity, to brood on its eggs day after day. . . . The worn-out wife of an Australian savage, says Büchner,[1] can hardly make any use of abstract words, and is incapable of counting beyond four. How little can such a woman prove her consciousness or reflect on the nature of her existence? When my voice awakened a series of old associations in the soul of the above-mentioned dog, he must have preserved his spiritual individuality, although every atom of his brain had changed probably more than once in the course of five years.

ANSWER.—When we look more closely at Darwin's argument, we see that he did not make a direct attempt to ascribe the above qualities to the animal. Everything we have said thus far speaks against this. That a dog has mental pictures of the chase after the "pleasures of the chase are past" nobody will deny; but that he should make "reflections" on them, like a hunter, who likes to tell his hunting stories, Darwin himself would not have dared to assert in earnest. Indeed, the dog is the same after five years; but he does not know that he is the same. Lastly, if "an Alexander von Humboldt is far superior to the worn-out wife of an Australian savage," this only proves the educational adaptability of human nature on account of its spiritual disposition; but this worn-out woman, when speaking at the point of death of a continued existence in another world, is separated from the highest animal by a gulf which cannot be bridged.

124. OBJECTION: THE ANIMAL HAS THE ÆSTHETIC SENSE.—The sense of beauty does not belong exclusively to man. Male birds exhibit their plumage and magnifi-

[1] "Kraft und Stoff," p. 230.

cent feathers before the females, while other birds not so adorned do nothing of the kind. As women all over the world adorn themselves with feathers, the beauty of such ornaments is indisputable; the same is true of the charming sounds males utter, which are certainly admired by the females.

ANSWER.—What do the facts alleged above prove? The bird only admires the feathers and the singing of the males of its kind, and, besides, all this belongs to the sphere of the sexual instinct. Darwin's entire hypothesis of sexual selection—that is, that the female always seeks the more beautiful and stronger male—is without foundation. Darwin himself cannot deny this. What foundation has such a comparison with the sense of beauty in man, who looks not only on what is beautiful to the sense, but rises to the domain of ideal beauty?

125. OBJECTION: THE ANIMAL ALSO HAS RELIGIOUS IDEAS.—We have no proofs of man's aboriginal belief in a God. Numerous races have neither the idea of God nor a word to express it. Religion and belief in invisible powers arose at first from dreams, which the savage could not distinguish from real events, and thus he came to believe in the existence of gods. "The most courageous dog," says Vogt, "will show senseless fear in the presence of strange appearances, of which his nose can give him no warning: the dog is evidently afraid of ghosts. Fear of the supernatural, of the unknown, the germ of religious ideas, is found developed in a high degree in our intelligent domestic animals, the dog and the horse; men only developed these farther, and formed them into a system of faith."

ANSWER.—Law-givers and priests did not invent the belief in a God. Had the belief in a Supreme Being, and the desire to know more about Him, not dwelt in man, neither law-givers nor priests could have spoken at all about a God; and if they had done so, nobody would have understood them. No nation or tribe has yet been found that had not some idea of a Supreme Being. Even the poor Andaman Islanders, who were once considered the missing link between man and the ape, have ideas about a God which are superior to those held by the Romans. Belief in a God arisen from dreams! But cats and dogs also dream without converting themselves or getting religion. If a man does not know or hear anything about God in a wakeful state, how can he dream of Him? For dreams will represent to the soul only the sensitive impressions of the day. Is it by dreaming that man has arrived at the ideas of ghosts and gods? Indeed, only a dreamer can make such an assertion.

126. OBJECTION: THE ANIMAL ALSO HAS MORAL SENTIMENTS. — The moral sense does not prove an essential difference between man and the animal. Hear what Vogt has to say: "The cuffs which the old bears give to the younger ones show distinctly that animals are not devoid of the ideas of parental authority and filial obedience, that is, of the fundamental notions of human and Christian morality." "Animals," says Darwin. "manifestly feel emulation. They love approbation or praise; and a dog carrying a basket for his master exhibits in a high degree self-complacency and pride. There can, I think, be no doubt that a dog feels shame, as distinct from fear, and something very like modesty when begging too often for food. A great dog scorns the snarling of a little dog, and this may be called magnanimity. Monkeys certainly dislike being laughed at, and they sometimes invent imaginary offences. . . . The idea of property is common to every dog with a bone, and to most or all birds with their nests. The social instinct allows the animal to find pleasure in

society. . . . It seems to me very probable that every animal, if it were only endowed with sharply expressed social instincts, would surely obtain a moral sentiment, or conscience, as soon as intellectual faculties, like, or nearly like, those of man, would have developed themselves."[1]

ANSWER.—Vogt's argument is too ridiculous to deserve an answer. Darwin's arguments are not quite clearly stated. We can see that this author is not quite sure of the presence of the moral sense in animals. Certainly if intellectual faculties "like, or nearly like, those of man" could be developed in animals, then animals would possess a moral sentiment. But then animals would be men and no longer animals. But it may be asked: Is it possible to speak of morality, when man is nothing but a perfected animal? Morality rests on the idea of duty; this presupposes liberty and intelligence. The animal is wanting in both. Instead of this, according to Darwin, all morality rests on the "social instinct," which rules as public opinion through the gradual development of language. The social instinct in certain animals falls in the same category as their instinct of self-preservation and propagation. How a moral life, conscience, and the sense of duty can develop from this is as little conceivable as how love of parents in the monkey, economy in the marmot, monogamy in storks and deers, etc., can be looked upon as moral, and not as merely instinctive actions.[2]

127. WHAT SAVANTS SAY ABOUT DARWINISM. — In conclusion we say, with Dr. Reusch, that it has only been with some repugnance that we have discussed the theory

[1] Cf. "Vorlesungen," vol. i., p. 393.
[2] For a fuller development of all these objections, see Hettinger, "Apologie," vol. i. 1, pp. 416-440; Reusch, "Bibel und Natur." pp. 356-385.

of our relationship to the monkey in detail. It is certainly depressing to find that such a question can come up for discussion towards the end of the nineteenth century; but we could not avoid such a discussion. These theories are brought forward in popular and superficial books and pamphlets, and even newspapers, from which the so-called educated people learn their wisdom. The poor readers are persuaded, very often to their great dismay, that they are dealing with the results of the most careful, conscientious, and exhaustive observations and investigations. They believe that natural science, which is admitted to be accurate science, resting on observations and inductions, is carried on in our time with a thoroughness not even dreamed of formerly. It has consequently reached the greatest results. They believe that this science necessarily leads to these conclusions, and that the reader must therefore either ignore science or give up the old belief that God on the sixth day of the Creation finished the creation of the animals, including the monkeys, and then made man to His image and likeness. There is no way by which we can answer such misconceptions, and save the honor both of the Bible and of science, except by showing what science has really discovered and can discover; what is the result of sober, conscientious investigation, and what, on the other hand, belongs to the realm of airy hypotheses and fantastic speculations, which the student will mingle with his scientific conclusions only if his fancy runs away with his understanding, or if he mixes up his philosophical or theological views with his scientific opinions. Neither of these is very likely to happen to the leaders in science, whether they believe in the Bible or not. But the great mass of amateurs, those who have a smattering of science, believe in a hodge-podge of the true and false, of certain and uncertain scientific statements, of rash hypotheses and philosophical and theological opinions. The same mixture of fancy and science is found in authors who, like Vogt, Darwin, and Haeckel, propagate their atheistic opinions with the zeal of missionaries, and, as has been justly said of Haeckel, "use scientific facts only as mortar for the stones supplied by fancy or by philosophical unbelief."[1]

Other earnest men of science protest quite as strongly as could any theologian against such misuse of science. Thus Aeby says:

"It is very pleasant to read how the three anthropomorphous apes attained the human form; how the wild ancestors of our race stood tribe against tribe, kind against kind; how gradually with increasing civilization they recognized that they were brothers, intermingled, intercrossed, removed the original difference by hybrid forms, and so were slowly but surely brought to final unity. But we look in vain for any foundation of fact for all this. We know the human type as a solitary island, from which no bridge leads to the neighboring land of the mammals. At present there is no scientific document, but only the speculations of the human spirit, to tell us whether it was torn off from that land ages ago, or whether it rose independently from the ocean of creation."[2]

Oscar Traas speaks still more strongly: "The idea that the human race came from one of these kinds of apes is the most insane ever conceived by man about the history of man; it is worthy to be preserved in a new edition of the 'History of Human Folly;' besides there is no pretence that this absurd idea is founded on fact. We may therefore calmly leave the

[1] Reusch, "Bibel und Natur," pp. 280, 281.
[2] Aeby, "Die Schädelformen," p. 90.

gorilla in the tropical swamps of Lower Guinea, the only place on this planet where he is found. The proof of man's relationship to this monster has still to be discovered."[1]

Quatrefages speaks in the same strain. "The idea that the apes are our ancestors has caused great sensation, because it has been defended in the name of philosophy and controverted in the name of theology, and has therefore been connected with the controversies which have only drawn scientists beyond the boundaries of a province they ought never to have left. We do not pretend to be either theologians or philosophers; we are purely men of science, and, therefore, care only for scientific truth. In the name of this truth I must acknowledge that natural science knows nothing as yet about the origin of man; but in the name of the same truth, I can assert that neither a gorilla, nor an orangoutang, nor a chimpanzee, nor a sea-cow, nor a fish, nor any other animal, was our ancestor."

128. DAWNING OF HEALTHIER VIEWS. — But, thanks to a calmer examination of the subject, the day begins to dawn when men who were formerly the champions of this foolish and infidel doctrine will hold quite different views. Only very recently the father of modern rationalistic anthropology, Professor Virchow of Berlin, made the following annihilating criticism of Darwinism at the "Congress of Anthropology," held in Vienna in 1889. He says: "When we were together at Innsbruck, twenty years ago, it was just at the time when Darwinism held its first victorious progress through the world, and when my friend Vogt jumped at once with great animation into the ranks of the champions of this doctrine. In vain were we hunting for these missing links which ought to connect man directly

[1] O. Traas, "Vor der Sündfluth," p. 399.

with the monkey; the primitive man, the proper pro-anthropos, has not yet been found. The pro-anthropos is generally no subject of discussion for anthropologists. The anthropologist may perhaps behold the pro-anthropos in a dream, but whilst awake he certainly will not assert that he approached him very closely. At the time in Innsbruck it looked as if it were possible to establish the course of descent from monkey to man without any difficulty whatsoever. But at present we are unable to establish even the descent of the particular races from one another. At the present moment we can say that among the peoples of ancient times none was any nearer to the ape than we are. In our days we can say that upon this globe there is not a tribe in the human family which is absolutely unknown to us. The least known are the nations of the central mountains of Malacca; but we know the Fuegeans as well as the Esquimaux, the Bushmen, the Polynesians, and the Lapps. Yes, we know more of some of these tribes than of some of the peoples of Europe. I need only remind you of the Albanians. Every existing race is human; none has yet been found to which we could point as wholly or partly akin to the ape. Even though some show characteristics or forms peculiar to the ape—as, for instance, forms of the skull more or less analogous to those of the apes—we cannot assert positively and truthfully that on this account these men look like monkeys. As regards the ancient lake-dwellers, I have been able to subject almost all the skulls found to a comparative inquiry, and it is now certain that we meet differences between various tribes, but that there is not a single one among them which lies outside of the framework of the races now existing. It can be shown most clearly that in the course of 5000 years no change of types worth mentioning has taken place. If you ask me to-day, Was the first man black or white? I must tell you, I do not know."

After this the speaker sums up the results of anthropological science during the last twenty years, inquiring whether retrogression, as many assert, or progress can be noted: "Twenty years ago the representatives of our science claimed to know a good deal that they did in fact not know. To-day we know what we know. The only report I can give is to say: We have not made any debts, that is, we have not borrowed from hypothesis, we need not to go around fearing that what we know may be overthrown. We have prepared the ground so that the generation coming after us can make full use of the material presented. The recognition of the government, the sympathy of the people, give us the assurance that we shall not want material. To settle the anthropology of the races of Europe appears to us an end attainable during the next twenty years."

The above words from the mouth of one whose words re-echo in the ears of every rationalist of Europe, yea, of the whole world, was the death-blow to Darwin's views on the descent of man.

"Man when he was in honor did not understand: he hath been compared to senseless beasts and made like to them."[1] These words of Holy Scripture we hold up to all those who still look upon some animal species as their origin and ancestors. Every one may hunt for his origin wherever he pleases. We know that our origin is from God and in God. This descent is worthy of our soul, which is created after God's image and likeness.

[1] Ps. xlviii. 21.

CHAPTER VII.

THE STATE OF PRIMITIVE MAN.

Infidelity and the state of primitive man.—Man's primitive state was not a state of savagery.—His state is one of degradation and degeneration.—Savages in Europe during the last century.—The Fuegeans.—The Veddahs of Ceylon.—Andamans.—Hottentots.—Bushmen.—Shameless exaggerations.—A people in the mere natural state discovered nowhere.—The paradisiac state and original happiness mentioned in the myths of all nations.—Civilization in Asia when barbarism prevailed over Europe.—Really progressive development possible only through Christianity.—Man could not rise by his own powers from the state of savagery or from that of a helpless child to higher perfection.—It were unworthy of God to place man in the world a savage or a harmless child.—Only materialists believe this.

WE know the nature and origin of man; we know he is the immediate creature of God, and know he is composed of a body and a soul. The soul is a substantial, reasonable, and free principle, essentially distinct from the body, independent of matter in its functions; it cannot be the result of a simple biological evolution from an animal.

Man, by virtue of his special creation, holds a distinct position in the visible world, because he is a reasonable and free being, able to reflect, conceive, devise, and create modes of thought, speech, and language; able to pursue, improve, and achieve triumphs in every art, in every science, and in every pursuit of life; because he is the only being who knows the principle and essence of things: the true, the beautiful, the universal, and the absolute. Such, in substance, are the attributes of man, such are the gifts of his Creator, and such is the inheritance of the human race, individually and collectively, as we have shown in the preceding chapters.

Having proved these propositions, having outlined man's inherited and acquired attributes, it now remains for us to seek and determine the conditions under which man first appeared on the world's stage; the teachings of faith and science—the truths of one and the speculations of the other on the history of primitive man and of the primitive races.

129. INFIDELITY AND THE STATE OF PRIMITIVE MAN.—Infidelity makes three assertions which contradict divine revelation on these subjects. The first two concern the age and education of man, and the third bears on the descent of the human family from a single pair. Revelation teaches us that the first man was created in a *preternatural* state, that is, with privileges above the strict requirements of his nature. These gratuitous gifts comprised—with original justice—immortality, the knowledge of all he should know to fulfil his high calling, exemption from physical (pain, etc.) and moral evil or disorder (concupiscence). After a time of faithfully fulfilled probation, man was to enter the realms of the blessed and enjoy the beatific vision of God.

We learn that man abused his moral liberty, revolted against his Creator, and that spiritual death was the consequence of his fall. Natural death and all that precedes or accompanies it—labor, suffering, struggle for life, etc.—were the punishments of man's disobedience. Man, in his material life, becomes, thenceforth, similar to the other animals. From the preternatural and exceptional state to which he had been raised, he fell to the condition of other living beings. Great was his fall, and it might well cause him to sink rapidly to the most wretched savagery.

Those who hold that man is descended from an animal teach, as a necessary consequence of their doctrine, that man originally lived in a barbarous condition, similar to that of the so-called savage races. They say it is untrue that the first man and woman were created by God in a state of perfection, but declare that at the beginning they lived in a state of savagery like animals, and only after thousands of years their descendants raised themselves to their present knowledge, place, and power. According to this view, primitive tribes and races wandered over forests and plains, hunting and fishing to supply the common necessaries of life. Their habits and ways of living were not much above those of animals. Gradually they grouped themselves into families and tribes for better security; again they formed communities for barter, exchange, and trade; gave themselves to a more peaceful, staple, and industrious life; tilled the ground, domesticated useful animals; learned trades and industries; engaged in commerce, and, finally, acquired the arts and sciences.

The same view of primitive man is often brought forward in a more sentimental way. Writers speak of the primitive men as simple and untutored children of nature, who dwelt on the earth in a state of childlike simplicity. Only gradually their passions awoke, and through their passions every evil in the world arose. But by their own activity, especially by progressive education, they raised themselves to a higher state, which unfortunately troubled their happiness more and more as they progressed, and gained new ideas and wants, new tastes and luxuries, in their progress to civilization. Such is Jean J. Rousseau's imaginary picture, and he has made great efforts to set it forth in his work, "The Ideal Man of Nature."

This opinion is held and believed in by many who have not given the subject careful consideration. All who accept it, though they reject the descent of man from an ape and also the materialistic doctrine of his origin, have not grasped the Christian teaching on man's creation, or have not the courage to acknowledge it. We deplore the state of modern society, which so readily accepts so fanciful a hypothesis, with its pernicious principles. It is taught in the public schools, and it is so flattering to the vanity of an egotistical people with unchristian ideas, that it is believed the true and correct view of the original state of the human family—the "children of nature." Man, they say, must return to "mother nature," and was weaned from it by the process of education.

130. MAN'S PRIMITIVE STATE WAS NOT A STATE OF SAVAGERY OR CHILDISH INNOCENCE.—The hypothesis of man's gradual development from a rude state of nature contradicts the doctrine of Holy Scripture, which teaches us that the first man was created in a state of perfection, in the image of God, and that he degenerated only through sin.

A number of reasons are at our command which show that man did not raise himself to his present perfection from a state of savagery or childish innocence and simplicity.

131. (1) IT IS HISTORICALLY FALSE.—To refute this error it is necessary to observe that the word savagery has been badly defined. Undoubtedly if we accept the word savage in its etymological sense of "dweller in the woods" (*silvaticus*), primitive men may have been savages; for no city existed as yet; they built them later on. Again, if we give to this term the meaning of "not

civilized," it is true our first parents and their immediate offspring knew neither the benefits nor the inconveniences of what we call civilization in our days, because civilization is the result of experiences accumulated during centuries; they knew neither how to read nor to write, were ignorant of our sciences; they could not possess them, as they were not known; they knew nothing of refinement, luxuries of life, clothing, comfortable dwellings, modes of travel, etc., which people possess in our days. But if by the word savages we mean men of rudimentary intelligence—rude, dirty, inhuman, like the people we call savages now—then nothing is further from the truth, and nothing rests on a weaker foundation than the assertion that primitive man was a savage.

The vestiges of former civilization in semi-civilized countries to-day are sufficient to show this, and if we study the history of mankind we find that, properly speaking, there was neither a primitive nor a natural man. Man degraded himself by plunging into gross sensuality and living like a brute. When he lost his moral nature, his animal propensities had no check. To eat, drink, propagate his kind, and satisfy his passions, was the result of this double need. Man, when not completely idle, either gives himself up to the excesses of foolish pleasure, or, perhaps, goes howling about, kills and eats with relish his fellow-man. Can such a man be called a natural man? Is not this state, on the contrary, what is most opposed to human nature?

132. (2) THE SAVAGE STATE IS A STATE OF DEGRADATION AND DEGENERATION.—The savage state is really a state of degradation and degeneration—not the state of natural man such as he went forth from the hands of God. The barbarism and fierceness of savage nature are not proofs, as is often asserted, that the character and condition of a savage are those of primi-

tive men. In fact, in the midst of the most civilized nations there are men who are real savages by their instincts, their habits, and their morals. History tells us of a people who, during the last century, was divided into different tribes or families, and was governed by savage chiefs. They occupied themselves with raising herds of cattle, and signalized themselves by stealing, plundering, carrying off men and children in order to sell them as slaves. These cruel barbarians, grossly ignorant, a prey to the darkest superstitions, were hardly acquainted with the first principles of agriculture; they scratched the ground with a piece of bent wood instead of a plough; for harrow, they tied fagots to the tail of an unharnessed horse. Their nourishment, consisting chiefly of oatmeal and milk, was mixed with the blood drawn from a living cow. When they ate more dainty dishes they prepared them in a really disgusting and dirty manner; they boiled the beef with its skin, and roasted the bird with its feathers; and with all this they joined demoralizing habits unknown even to our redskins. These tribes or barbarous clans were no other than the Scotch, leading this life when their aristocracy showed much brilliancy in philosophy, science, and politics.[1]

With regard to cruelty and barbarity, who does not know that during the great French Revolution, the period which contemporaries have called "the reign of monsters," there arose all of a sudden, in different parts of the country, bands of wretches, plunderers, and assassins, who in atrocity did not fall below the most barbarous tribes? The men of Meillard, in the first days of September, 1792, strangled, at Carmes, in the Abbey of La Force, innocent persons who had never done them

[1] Cf. Lecky, "History of England in the Eighteenth Century," 2d ed., London, 1879–1882, vol. ii., p. 36; Max Müller, "The Savage in the Nineteenth Century," 1885, pp. 113, 114.

the least harm, yea, whom they did not even know. This is one example out of thousands of the bloody horrors of the Revolution. Such cool savagery and vile cupidity show plainly that there are savages in the midst of civilized and polished nations and communities. The men to whom materialists applied the name savages are no more the types of primitive men than are the Carriers, Meillards, Robespierres, Lebons, and many others, who committed cruel excesses at the end of the last century. Men of their stamp and views endeavor to deny or palliate these atrocities, but they remain historical facts, and show the utter degradation and cruelty to which some men yield when deprived of the benign influence of morality and religion.

The traditional history of humanity, in the opinion of Dr. Ray Lankaster, furnishes numerous examples of a tendency toward degeneration; states of higher civilization have retrograded to make room for inferior and degenerated states. There was a time when the doctrine which represented the savage human races as degenerated descendants of superior and civilized tribes, was generally admitted. The study of the morals, arts, and religious beliefs of savages has shown how erroneous this too general and hurried generalization was. However, it is undeniable that many savage races now existing descend from ancestors that possessed comparatively a very high and developed civilization. In support of this statement we can quote the American Indians, the modern Egyptians, and even the heirs of the great Oriental monarchies of antiquity. Although the hypothesis of universal degeneration applied to the savage races is liable to objections, nevertheless it is true that degeneration is a great help to us in interpreting the actual state of many barbarous tribes, such as the Fuegeans, the Bushmen, and even the Australians. Ascertained facts tend to prove their descent from ancestors more civilized than they are themselves.[1]

133. THE FUEGEANS.—We see that Mr. Lankaster's opinion of the Fuegeans is decisive. Darwin regarded them as the lowest of mankind. He considered them almost inferior to irrational animals. Those he saw he compares to the devils who appear on the stage in certain operas like the "Freischütz." "At the sight of such men," he says, "one can hardly believe that they are creatures similar to us, and that they inhabit the same world. Their language, according to the idea we have of a language, scarcely deserves the name of articulation. Captain Cook compared it to the noise a man makes when he coughs in order to clear his throat, but certainly no European having trouble with his throat ever produced such harsh, guttural, clicking sounds."[2]

Now it is precisely their language that furnishes proof of the ancient civilization of the Fuegeans. One of their dialects, the Jagan, contains no less than 30,000 words. That is more than the English language could boast of in the sixteenth century; more than Darwin used in all his works. As regards the sound, it is certainly not inferior to our English language. "*Le*

[1] Cf. Ray Lankaster (Darwinist) on Degeneration. See lecture before the British Association at Sheffield. August 22, 1879.

Evidently we must distinguish degrees in degeneration as well as in civilization. We do not wish to maintain that the ancestors of savages had attained a high degree of civilization.

[2] "Journal of Researches into Geology and Natural History," London, vii., 1840.

These assertions of Darwin are greatly exaggerated as regards the physical aspect of the Fuegeans. Darwin publicly mocked the missionaries who undertook the conversion of "these cannibals and plunderers." Some years afterward converted Fuegeans raised over 100,000 francs to assist the shipwrecked. Cf. G. Bove, "Viaggio alla Patagonia ed alla Terra de Fuoco," in the "Nuovo Antologia," Dec., 1882, pp. 778, 801.

parole di quella sono dolci, piacevole, piene di vocale," says Giacomo Bove, who visited them in 1882. Such a language is the wreck of an ancient civilization.

"The state of degeneration in which the Fuegeans are found contrasts singularly with the richness of their language, which proves that we have to attribute to this people an original civilization much higher than their actual condition. The Jagan language is undoubtedly one of the most ancient and purest. It is very complete in its grammar and vocabulary. The latter contains about 30,000 words, which number can even be increased on account of the agglutinative character of the language. The verbs and pronouns are very numerous, and supply in a certain manner the poverty of adverbs and prepositions. The Jagan language differs in a perceptible manner from that of their neighbors, the Alacaluf and the Ona, of which the words are harsh, guttural, and filled with consonants. The richness of the language gives to the Fuegeans a facility of surprising elocution. Hundreds of times in the wigwam have I heard and seen old men discourse for hours without stopping."[1]

The same can be said about the Veddahs of Ceylon, who are now savages of the most debased type. They are believed for good reasons, furnished by their vocabulary, to be degenerate descendants of the tribes who brought Aryan civilization to the plains of Hindostan.[2] "They make themselves understood," says Sir E. Tennent, "by signs, grimaces, and guttural sounds, which

---

[1] G. Bove, *op. cit.*, p. 800.

[2] Rawlinson, "Origin of Nations," p. 5.
The Vedic hymns, which their Sanscrit-speaking forefathers composed, are written in a language far older than the Greek of Homer, and stamps them as a cultivated and progressive race. Andrews, "India and Her Neighbors," p. 4.

have little resemblance to definite words or language in general." Yet Max Müller writes of this very same race: "More than one-half of the words used by them are mere corruptions of Sanscrit. Their very name is the Sanscrit for 'huntsmen.' If at present they are standing very low in the scale of humanity, there was a time when they stood higher. Nay, with regard to language, if not in blood, they may possibly prove to be distant cousins of Plato, Newton, and Goethe."[1]

134. (3) THE RELIGIOUS NOTIONS OF SAVAGE PEOPLES.—The religious notions of certain savage peoples are so lofty that we can hardly suppose that they themselves have invented them. The Andamans, for instance, are a race of the Andaman Islands, hardly known by name even in the last half century, a small people of negro blood, who hunt and fish, live in huts made of stakes or branches. These creatures have been represented as forming the "missing link" between man and the ape, and yet they have a higher conception of the divinity than the polished Greeks and Romans. Mr. Man, who visited them, sums up their belief in Puluga, the good God, in the following manner:

"(1.) Although he resembles the fire, he is nevertheless invisible. (2.) He has never been born, and is immortal. (3.) Through him the world was created; all animate and inanimate objects, except the pleasures of evil. (4.) He is omniscient by day, and even knows the thoughts of the heart. (5.) He becomes angry when one commits certain sins, whilst he is full of pity for those who are in pain and anxiety, and even sometimes deigns himself to assist them. (6.) It is he who judges all the souls after death and passes sentence on them. The hope to escape the torments of Jereg-lar mugo (a

[1] Max Müller, "Chips," vol. iv., p. 360.

kind of purgatory) exercises a great influence on these islanders in the present life."[1]

135. (4) SAVAGE RACES THE VICTIMS OF WARS AND INVASIONS. — The Duke of Argyle observes that most inferior races live on the extremities of continents or at the bottom of sacks; not because they are aboriginal, but because they have been driven there by stronger races than they: they are the victims of wars and invasions. Hence their degraded and miserable character. The Esquimaux have not of their own accord gone to dwell in the northern regions under tents of snow any more than the Fuegeans to Cape Horn; they were constrained to do so by brutal force, which drove them away from more temperate zones, whether we consider them as a detached branch of the great American ethnical tree, or whether they were at first Siberian nomads.[2]

Certainly, only dire necessity could have forced these men to take up their abode in such terrible regions, if the warm and fertile lands of happier climates had been open to them. Indeed, even in the Arctic regions tribal feuds drive the weaker still further north. Thus Admiral Osborne informs us that a tribe wandering along the extreme northern edge of the Siberian coast drove another tribe across the frozen sea to an island lying so far north that only its mountain-tops could be occasionally seen from the Siberian headlands.[3]

"Tierra del Fuego," says Darwin, the man who placed its inhabitants on the lowest step of the human ladder, "is a broken mass of wild rocks, lofty hills, and useless

[1] E. H. Man, "On the Aboriginal Inhabitants of the Andaman Islands," in the "Journal of Anthropology," vol. xii., 1882, p. 157.
[2] "The Unity of Nature," London, 1884, p. 504.
[3] "Times," Dec. 30, 1867; cf. C. Geikie, "Hours with the Bible," vol. i., p. 165.

forests, and these are viewed through mists and endless storms. The habitable land is reduced to the stones of the beach. The people are compelled to wander unceasingly from spot to spot in search for food, and so steep is the coast that they can only move about in their wretched canoes."[1]

"How could tribes," adds Geikie, "in such a land as the uttermost north, amidst eternal ice, be anything but degraded? But it cannot surely be said that they were created at first where we find them, and it is hard to believe that they have not become greatly lower than their ancestors who came from happier lands."[2]

136. THE HOTTENTOTS AND BUSHMEN.—In Africa the most degraded races are the Hottentots and Bushmen. Their general characteristics are described as follows:

"They have a peculiar livid and yellow face, a narrow forehead, projecting cheek bones, a pointed chin, the head covered with crisp, tufted hair, a body of medium height and rather tough and strong, small hands and feet. They are skilled in horsemanship, intelligent and courageous; they are of a mild disposition, but given to lying and stealing, drunkenness and sensuality. Their religious notions are centred in a Supreme Being, which is little else than a deified chieftain. They believe in a future state or life, and fear the return of spirits. As an example of their intellectual capacity may be mentioned the Hottentot Andreas Stoffles, who was master of several languages, and could make a good speech in English. The Hottentot language has four dialects. The Nama dialect is spoken by the Namaquas, northwest of Cape Colony, and also by the Damaras, north

---

[1] Darwin's "Voyage of a Naturalist," p. 216; cf. C. Geikie, *op. cit.*, p. 166.

[2] C. Geikie, "Hours with the Bible," vol. i., p. 166.

of them, but it does not seem to be their original tongue. It is the oldest, purest dialect, but like the speech of all savages, it may be subdivided into several sub-dialects, according to tribes, and even families. The Hottentot language is, generally speaking, of monosyllabic structure. It is rich in diphthongs and remarkably delicate in the use of inflectional final sounds, which contrast strangely with the constantly recurring clicking sounds. The principal occupation of the Hottentots and Bushmen is that of guarding their herds; they live on milk and ignore agriculture. The most important piece of his dress is a sheep's skin, or the skin of a wild kross. The second piece consists of a small skin apron, which he ties around the loins."[1]

The foregoing facts show what exaggerations the human mind can indulge in when there is question of the primitive condition of man, and of coining arguments against revelation and the belief in a Supreme Being. Nott and Gliddon in their "Types of Mankind"[2] assure us that these two races are hardly to be distinguished morally and physically from the orang-outang. "The Hottentots and Bushmen, the latter in particular, they say, are but little removed in both moral and physical characters from the orang-outang. A man must be blind not to be struck by similitudes between some of the lower races of mankind, viewed as connecting links in the animal kingdom; nor can it be rationally affirmed that the orang-outang and chimpanzee are more widely separated from certain African and Oceanic negroes than are the latter from the Teutonic or Pelasgian types."[3]

[1] Cf. Tudall, "Grammar and Vocabulary of the Namaqua Hottentot Language;" Black, "Comparative Grammar of the South African Languages." [2] Philadelphia, 1854.
[3] Max Müller, "The Savage in the Nineteenth Century," pp. 182, 183.

"This," says an unprejudiced author, M. Waitz, "is a shameless exaggeration, which, inspired by the interest of merchants and slaveholders, can find belief only in America."[1] Nott and Gliddon forgot that between the most perfect ape and the most degraded man the faculty of reasoning establishes a great gap. Elisée Reclus has shown that the Andaman, the Khonds of Bengal, and the Nefours of New Guinea have been calumniated and misrepresented.[2] However this may be, the study of savage races has at least had one advantage: it proves that natural man is not the innocent and virtuous creature which J. J. Rousseau had as his ideal, and in which the eighteenth-century rationalists believed; on the contrary, he is usually cruel, wicked, and unnatural. Nor is he a mere animal hardly risen from the depths of bestiality, as evolutionists imagine in our days; he is a man in the full sense of the word. The savage, therefore, is and remains a man from his birth. Savages are not animal men, into whom the man must first be instilled by education, but men who do not till the ground, and live only by what nature produces without their assistance. . . . Although they may not be humane, they are human.[3] But far from rising when abandoned to himself, he gradually sinks deeper and deeper into the abyss of misery and degradation. By bringing civilization to him from the outside, we can insert on this crude plant a graft which will grow, bloom, and bear good fruit.

"Not everything in the savage is savage," says an old missionary.[4] The savage is altogether uncultivated, and

[1] "Anthropologie der Naturvölker," vol. i., p. 105.
[2] "Revue Internationale des Sciences Biologiques," Oct. 20, 1883, Feb., July, 1884. M. Maury states that they have exaggerated the brutishness of the Hottentot race. Cf. "La Terre et l'Homme," p. 411.
[3] J. G. Müller, " Geschichte der Amerikanischen Religionen," p. 333.   [4] W. Schneider, "Die Naturvölker," 1885, vol. i., p. 4.

when he has a little education he shows that he is susceptible of cultivation more or less, and thus becomes similar to us in everything. Our American Indians furnish proof of this statement. The savage is not a primitive man, but a man who has partly retrograded and partly progressed and partly remained stationary. Therefore, as regards the savage man, his condition is degraded and degenerate, but not the condition in which he came forth from the hands of God. He is susceptible of progress, and indeed has progressed immediately under the teaching of civilized races.[1]

137. (5) NOWHERE IS THERE A PEOPLE IN A PURE STATE OF NATURE. — A sentimental enthusiast may imagine primitive man dwelling in virgin forests, free from care and crime, passing his days at ease, and living on fruits and other productions of bountiful nature, eating game at times of feasting and rejoicing. No such men have ever existed, if we consult history; on the contrary, all nations before their conversion to Christianity were more or less degraded and degenerate by habits of indolence, drunkenness, immorality, and kindred vices. They were reduced in power and population, their demoralizing customs preyed on the vitals of their social and industrial resources, and doubtless they would have gradually perished without the blessings of Christianity. Therefore the natural man, as Rousseau and the apostles of materialism picture him, is a phantasm and an illusion without past or present reality.

Of some ancient nations, like the Greeks and Romans, the Chinese and Japanese, we know the history; we can trace their rise and development. The Romans obtained their education from the Greeks, the Greeks from the Phœnicians and Egyptians, the latter, as well as the Chinese and Japanese, from other Oriental peoples.

[1] Vigouroux, "Les Livres Saints," etc., vol. iii., p. 448.

The races found in the so-called state of nature were degenerate, showed their malicious and animal propensities, and every form of immorality and vice, when they came in contact with Europeans.

138. (6) ALL NATIONS SPEAK OF A "GOLDEN AGE."— All nations which have left traces of their existence have also left records of their former greatness or of some past state of prosperity and development, the enjoyment of Elysian pleasures and of intimate relations with the gods. The idea that they have passed from a state of nature to progressive development, is foreign to them all. Backward, not forward, do they turn their eyes. Only one nation looked faithfully and hopefully towards the future— the Jews who hoped for a Messias to come—and inasmuch as this hope was known to Pagan nations, the Pagans shared the belief of the Jews. The longing of the Gentiles was after the "golden age" which formerly reigned upon earth, and they strove to bring it back by penance and reconciliation with their gods. This was the faith of the Greeks, the Romans, the Germans, and the Hindoos.

The Elysian state—the original happy condition of man—is found in the mythology of all ancient nations. According to the Persians, Yima Vivanghvat's son reigned on the earth, which was free from all evil during the golden age. At that time there was no frost or excessive heat, no darkness or death, no wars or discord; fruits, flowers, and the bearded corn were provided by bountiful nature without cultivation; from veins in the valleys flowed milk and nectar, and honey exuded from the pores of the oak; the western winds maintained eternal spring and moisture for vegetation, and the birds made vocal every branch and spray. At Ormuzd's command, Yima built a paradise, in which he placed the germs of all things and select men; here death and corruption never entered, here dwelt eternal life and light, and glorious existence.¹

Hindoo tradition tells of a paradisiac mountain — Meru. It is adorned with beautiful flowers; clear brooks and song of birds are heard in all directions; four large glittering streams, like sheets of silver, flow from it towards the four points of heaven; on its summit is the dwelling of Siva and Indra, with whom the blessed live. There the tree of immortality grows—the tree Pariyata, brought from heaven upon earth by Krishna, with its celestial flowers and sweet fruits — and drives away hunger, thirst, disease, old age, etc.²

According to the religion of Lama or of the Calmucks, men in the first age of the world lived 80,000 years, in a state of happiness and holiness. A plant, fair to view and sweet like honey, sprang up from the ground; a greedy man tasted of it and made others acquainted with its sweetness. A sense of shame arose within them; they saw their nudity, and made for themselves coverings from the leaves of trees. Their age and size decreased; virtue fled and all kinds of vice prevailed.³

The Elysian state of Thibetan mythology was one of perfection and spirituality; but the desire to eat of the sweet herb *schima* put an end to that happy state. Shame seized the fallen ; jealousy, discord, stealing, lying, murder, adultery, and other vices followed. They brought the people to a state of social degradation and moral turpitude.⁴

The paradise of the Chinese is situated in the Kuen-

---

¹ Döllinger, "Heidenthum und Judenthum," p. 368; Lücken, "Mythologie," p. 80; Braun, "Ueber die Paradiessagen," in "Ausland," 1862.
² "Asiatic Journal," vol. i., p. 321; Ritter, "Asia," vol. i., p. 7; cf. Strabo, vol. xv., p. 250; Bohlen, "Das alte Indien," vol. i., p. 12 *seq.*
³ Ständlein, "Archiv für Kirchengeschichte," vol. i., p. 14.
⁴ *Ibid.*, p. 15.

Lun and Thian Shan mountains. In the midst is a garden; there arises the source of immortality; those who drink of its waters will never die; it divides itself into four streams, and from this garden life has gone forth and grown.[1]

The Greek myths are remotely parallel. Herodotus describes the primitive state as one free from toil, sickness, and all kinds of evil; mortals were content with their easily-obtained sustenance, and happy in mind and void of care or crime. But Prometheus deceived Zeus by stealing fire from heaven; the latter, in order to punish him, sent a beautiful woman, Pandora, the first mortal female, according to Hesiod. Her, Prometheus accepted as a gift; she had with her a vessel in which all sorts of misery had been put; out of curiosity she opened the vessel, and out flew all evil in abundance, filling the whole earth; hope alone remained at the bottom.[2]

The garden of the Hesperides was situated in the Atlas. In it was a wonderful tree bearing golden fruit, protected by walls, with a dragon watching its entrance. In it dwell the pious and blessed primitive men—the Atlantiades or Hyperboreans—who, under perpetual sunshine and in a charming climate, know no sickness, sorrow, discord, nor early death; there they pass away their time in peace and pleasure, and are called the long lived.[3]

As regards our primitive ancestors, Plato tells us that God was their keeper. . . . They had plenty of fruit and other productions without cultivation; the earth

---

[1] "Memoires concernant les Chinois," vol. i., p. 106; Windischmann, "Die Philosophie im Fortgange der Weltgeschichte," vol. i., p. 206.

[2] "Opera et Dies," 40–105.

[3] Diodorus, iii., 54; Pliny, "Historia Naturalis," bk. iv., p. 12.

bountifully provided for all their needs. Naked and without tents, they lived under the vaulted heavens; the mildness of the seasons, the soft, velvety grass, afforded them comfort and resting-places day and night. Among the animals none were wild, none devoured one another; no war or discord disturbed their happiness.[1]

Such was the mode of life under Kronos Dikarchos, the peripatetic. These first men who stood nearest to the gods enjoyed the greatest happiness; on that account it was justly called the "golden age."[2] Ovid speaks in the same strain:

> The golden age was first, when man yet new
> No rule but uncorrupted reason knew,
> And with a native bent did good pursue;
> Unforced by punishment, unawed by fear,
> His words were simple and his soul sincere.

We find the same happiness, peace, and virtue reigning among primitive men in Chinese traditions. All over the land everything grew beautifully and spontaneously; animals pastured in large herds on the broad savannas; fruits of all kinds grew without cultivation; man practised virtue, lived in innocence, and for this nothing could harm nor bring death to him.[3]

The Hindoos speak about the four ages of the world. The first was the age of happiness and virtue, but through excesses many fell into vanity; Zeus, hating this state of affairs, destroyed everything and assigned to them a life of pain.[4] According to the Zend doctrine, Ormuzd reigned alone in the first age. The first age he created was an age of pleasantness and abundance.

---

[1] "Politica," p. 217.

[2] Cf. Varro, "De ReRustica," bk. i., 2; Euseb., "Præparatio Evangelica," i., 8; xii., 13.

[3] Lüken, "Die Traditionen des Menschengeschlechts," p. 90.

[4] "Strabo," xv., 8.

There reigned Jemshid, the first king; he and the first man adored Hom (the tree of life), and took therefrom as much as they pleased. Only when Ahriman entered the kingdom of light did he bring death to the first men.[1]

Again, the faith of the Babylonians points to an Elysian state, as is attested by the evidence of recent discoveries. According to their belief, primitive men were pure and beautiful in form.[2] The tree of life is represented on an ancient Babylonian seal; on the obverse side a man and woman are seated, each with hand outstretched to take the tempting fruit. Behind the female figure there rises at full length the form of a serpent in a seductive attitude. This figure is clearly suggestive of the history of the fall of man as related in the book of Genesis. It is frequently found on gems and on the walls of Assyrian palaces and temples.[3]

The Egyptian paradise is both an island and a steep mountain, where Osiris was born. Here were fountains which poured forth their streams towards all parts of the world, and trees with perpetual blossoms and fruits. With Osiris dwell the Makrobians; here he produces wine of rich flavor, and his sister and wife, Isis, wheat.[4]

139. (7) BARBARISM IN EUROPE AND CIVILIZATION IN ASIATIC COUNTRIES.—The fact is that during the ages when extreme barbarism prevailed over Europe civilization existed in Asiatic countries as an inheritance from an earlier period. Past and present archæological discoveries prove this. Among the many grand monuments of early days we need only mention the palace of King Sargon at Khorsabad. There is nothing

---

[1] Plutarch, "De Iside et Osiri," 47; Zend, "Avesta," iii., 68.
[2] George Smith, i., 6.
[3] Delitzch, "Supplement to Smith's Chaldean Genesis," p. 30.
[4] Diodor., i., 14 *seq.* iii., 68; cf. Hettinger, "Apologie," vol. ii., 1, p. 366, *seq.*

like it in the world to-day. A person must read the descriptions which Kaulen and Rawlinson give of it in order to get an idea of its vastness and grandeur. If primitive men were so degraded as to be but little removed from the animal, as Sir John Lubbock and others state, who planned, designed, constructed, and adorned these ancient palaces, temples, and monuments? Surely, some Prometheus must have brought them the divine spark from heaven, or their calumniators must be stricken with blindness.

The Egyptian pyramids existed 3000 years before Christ,[1] that is, 5000 years ago there was a civilization which produced marvels of architecture which excite the admiration of architects and travellers in our progressive age. To illustrate the stupendous works of art which came from the brain and hands of those so-called degraded savages,—to raise a structure like the Great Pyramid, 746 feet square at the base, rising to a height of 450 feet, required the labor of relays of men numbering in all 11,000,000 for thirty years![2] To put it in another way: a structure which covers over twelve square acres, contains 90,000,000 cubic feet of masonry and weighs 6,316,000 tons,[3] implies an earlier civilization, of which it is the crowning triumph. This becomes still more certain when we find it is perfectly square, the sides being equal and the angles right angles; that the four sockets in which the first four stones of the corners rest are exactly on the same level; that the direction of the sides is true to the four cardinal points, and that the vertical height of the pyramid bears the same proportion to its circumference at the base as the radius of a

---

[1] Chabas gives the date of the pyramids at 3300 B.C.; Lepsius and Ebers at 3100 and 3000, respectively.
[2] Herodotus, ii., 124.
[3] "English Cyclopedia," article "Egypt."

circle does to its circumference.[1] Not only are these measures, angles, and levels accurate to the eye, but the best modern instruments can scarcely detect the slightest error. The workmanship of the interior chambers is no less wonderful, for the passages and chambers are lined with huge blocks of granite, polished to the highest degree, and fitted into each other with the greatest accuracy.[2] Such architecture, surely, points back, not to utter degradation, but to a civilization probably older than the Flood.

140. ARCHÆOLOGICAL MONUMENTS IN AMERICA ALSO PROVE A HIGHER CIVILIZATION.—The colossal buildings found in America, especially in Peru, Mexico, on the Mississippi and Ohio rivers, when these countries were discovered by the Europeans, also prove that there existed in America a higher civilization than the present races or the supposed aboriginal Indians can account for by tradition.

"The distinguishing characteristics," says Geikie, "of the corn plants, such as oats, wheat, barley, rice, maize, etc., seem in the same way to point to a very different condition from 'utter degradation,' as that of our first parents. Like the fruit trees and many of the existing animals, they make their appearance on the earth with man, and are entirely unknown in earlier ages. Moreover, while the primitive types of all other esculent plants are still to be found in this or other countries, those of the corn plants are utterly unknown. Corn has never been met with except as a cultivated plant. It is found in the wrappings of the Egyptian mummies, and in the charred remains of the Swiss Lake dwellings, but

[1] Piazzi Smith, "Our Inheritance in the Great Pyramid." Prof. Smith devoted many months to these measurements, etc., using the best instruments.
[2] Birch, "Egypt," i., p. 35; Wallace, "Tropical Nature," p. 299.

never apart from its cultivation by man. It cannot grow spontaneously, and is never, like other plants, self-sown and self-spread. If not cultivated, it soon disappears and grows extinct. It needs human labor to perpetuate it, and seems to have been given us by God, as it is, to stimulate our industry and reward it. . . . Given by God to our first parents, the grain plants secured a transcendant blessing for all their offspring on condition of steady industry in their cultivation, but such a gift implies a condition far removed from Sir John Lubbock's 'utter degradation.'"[1]

141. (8) A DEVELOPMENT TO A HIGHER CULTURE POSSIBLE ONLY THROUGH CHRISTIANITY.—It is foolish and proves a want of reflection to speak of a progressive development of nations through their own efforts. A progressive development of a people to a higher culture is conceivable and possible only through Christianity. Although some countries, like the Chinese and Japanese, for instance, developed great skill in the domain of art and science, still we do not find the least progress in their moral condition. Since thousands of years, these countries have not acquired one new moral or religious truth; still, this alone can be called true progress. They are an immoral and thoroughly corrupt people, as is borne out by the accounts of travellers and missionaries.

"It has been proven again and again that the spirit of man does not naturally carry within itself a tendency towards progress and development. The modern idealistic doctrine, necessary self-development of the human mind from within, is not logical; nay, it is not even a possible opinion; it is a creation of the imagination, which flatters conceited man, while he sneers at the facts of the history of culture. Certainly it is the intelligent activity of man which produces and main-

[1] C. Geikie, "Hours with the Bible," vol. i., p. 168, *seq*.

tains civilization, but this intelligent activity does not spring from itself, does not move forward of itself, is not the function of our mind, but is the activity of individuals living in society, reacting on one another, created through the surroundings in which they are placed, nourished and sustained through the experience of historical events which influence them."[1]

As we know that mechanical motion is by no means a quality of matter, our reason tells us that progress is by no means a quality of the mind. The history of all the nations in antiquity, as well as in modern times, attests this fact very clearly. Those which show apathy to the moral injunctions of Christianity or ignore its teachings altogether, rot and perish, for the Word of God is the life of a people.

142. (9) MAN CREATED IN A STATE OF RELATIVE PERFECTION.—It is inconceivable that the human mind could have raised itself from a savage state, or from that of innocence, to a higher perfection without a certain education. Man must have been created in a state of relative perfection, otherwise he would have perished. When Holy Scripture tells us that the first man went forth from the hands of God perfect and in the height and fulness of life, we must admit that, considering simply his human nature, God could not create man in any other condition, if the preservation and propagation of his species was the will of the Creator. Dr. Dawson and many others maintain that all the evidence we have is in favor of the theory that the first of any species were exceptionally perfect, and that natural selection, acting under the pressure of a fearful struggle for existence, has produced deterioration and not development.

A created being is continually in need of being upheld in existence by the Creator. Place a child in the

[1] Waitz, "Anthropologie der Naturvölker," p. 474.

woods, or several together, and see what will become of them. Man is born more helpless than is the young of any animal. When an animal is placed on the earth it possesses the instinct of its species. Instinct in its sphere is far more perfect and unerring than human intelligence; it makes no mistakes, because determined by structure. Intelligent conduct is self-determined, and becomes wise by individual experience; instinctive conduct is predetermined in wisdom by brain structure. A child will be unable to preserve its life without a mother's care. Ought we to believe that men raised themselves from a state of childhood to a high degree of perfection? We may imagine such a thing, but a mere glance at our nature must dispel such an idea. The first man could not have entered life in a rude and savage state of nature, as it would be contrary to the will, intelligence, and wisdom of the Creator; neither could he enter life as a child, because animal instincts were not given him for self-preservation. He must be created perfect in corporal and spiritual life, organism, intelligence, and functions; endowed with the faculties of comprehending, perceiving, and enjoying the true and the beautiful; knowing God as his Creator; seeing Him and hearkening to His loving words at the moment of his creation. In a word, man must "have sprung fully armed, like Athene, from the head of Zeus."

143. (10) TO CREATE MAN AS A SAVAGE WAS UNWORTHY OF GOD.—To all these reasons we may add one more, namely: that it would not be in accord with God's love, wisdom, and solicitude for man, to place him in this world like a savage, an orphan, or a defenceless child. He could create man for every possible state, and through His almighty power preserve him in every one. But is it not more in harmony with His paternal and infinite love and wisdom, and with the purpose and

arrangements of creation, to create man in the plenitude of spiritual and physical power; man, who, according to his spirit, is God's own image and likeness? Is not this a view more beautiful and satisfactory to our reason than that which asks us to assume that our primitive parents were like fishes lying on the sand of the shore, like jelly on the rocks of the ocean, like tadpoles in stagnant ponds, or like wild animals roving the forests and awaiting culture and development? Away with such a horrid and debasing doctrine! None but materialists can believe such a thing!

CHAPTER VIII.

THE ANTIQUITY OF MAN AND BIBLICAL CHRONOLOGY.

The antiquity of man and modern chronologists.—Are their calculations reconcilable with the accounts given by Genesis?—The genealogical tables.—Three lessons.—Consequences resulting from Biblical chronology.—Impossibility of fixing the date of man's creation.—Mankind very probably over 8000 years old.—New difficulty.—Supposed omissions in the genealogical tables.—Proofs of this supposition.—Admitting such omissions, mankind dates back more than 8000 years.—The ten Chaldean antediluvian kings.—The value of the Chaldean Sar.—Tabular view.—Theory of P. Bourdais.—Conclusion.

MODERN science within its legitimate sphere has largely benefited the human race. It has done much to cultivate and elevate the present generation in mechanics, commerce, and industry. It has dispelled many illusions, superstitions, and false ideas of natural laws; but scientists have also done much to create and foster irreligious views, indifferentism, latitudinarianism, and scepticism, by encroaching on the domain of theology and attacking the fundamental truths of Christianity. True science is the handmaid of revelation; rationalistic science is the Lethe of moral depravity. It is a matter for regret that only too many scientists, to say nothing of their crudeness in theological knowledge, are children in philosophy, bad metaphysicians in their own science. Such sciolists and charlatans ridicule and deny revelation and set up science as judge and standard of sacred as well as profane things.

144. IN WHAT GEOLOGISTS AND CHRONOLOGISTS AGREE AS REGARDS THE AGE OF MANKIND.—Modern geologists and chronologists are unanimous in the belief that man is of more recent origin than the earth we inhabit; the majority are also in accord regarding his age, and attribute to him a longer period on earth than the interpreters of the Bible are willing to concede; while many, as Lyell, for instance, acknowledge and confirm the Biblical account that our ancestors appeared upon earth after the creation of plants and animals; evolutionists and infidels, rather than pay homage to the Sacred Text on this point, fix his origin thousands of years prior to sacred and profane chronology.

Haeckel and those of his school who maintain that man is descended from an anthropoid monkey, assume many centuries, in order to explain the transition of man from an irrational and bestial state to a rational and highly cultivated human condition. "More than one hundred thousand years," says the Jena professor, "perhaps hundreds of thousands, have passed since the origin of man."[1]

These gentlemen without hesitation assume thousands of years; many throw in millions to balance their wild and reckless speculations with geology and the long periods of organic and atomic formation that culminated in the formation of man. Dr. Draper attributes to man in Europe an antiquity of 250,000 years. Burmeister places the appearance of man in Egypt at 72,000 years ago, and Dupuis gives him an existence of between 14,000 and 15,000 years. Some geologists are disposed to believe that the human species is about 100,000 years old, while others, like Mortillet, demand from 200,000 to 250,000 years.

[1] Haeckel, "Schöpfungsgeschichte," p. 509.

Certain naturalists, however, who do not belong to the materialistic school, theorize in an analogous manner. M. Saporta, for instance, puts the appearance of man upon earth at least 200,000 years ago. Calculations based on the bones of animals, flints, stone hatchets, lake dwellings, cave deposits, pottery, etc., have no satisfactory foundation.

145. ARE THEIR CALCULATIONS RECONCILABLE WITH THE ACCOUNTS OF GENESIS?—Are these and similar calculations reconcilable with the accounts given by Genesis? In order to answer this question intelligently, we must inquire into the speculations of science and the generally received chronology of the Bible and sift the true from the false as far as possible.

The patriarchal age, which furnishes the elements of Biblical chronology, extends in sacred history from the first man Adam to the exodus of the Israelites. From the chronological point of view, the latter part of this age, which begins with the vocation or birth of Abraham, ought to be examined and studied apart, because no serious apologetic question is raised in regard to it. Both historians and critics agree in placing the life of the "Father of the faithful" about twenty centuries before the Christian era. Hence there is question here only of the period anterior to Abraham.

146. THE GENEALOGICAL TABLES OF GENESIS.—The sacred documents which we have to consult in regard to this subject are not numerous, and may be reduced to two: the tables of Genesis v., 1–32, and xi., 10–26. However, we do not find in these chapters an established chronology, but only the elements from which to construct a scientific system of Biblical chronology. It is very important to make this remark in advance, as it will in a great measure relieve the inspired writer from responsibility for the various systems of chronology

which authors have sought to establish on the basis of Biblical data.

At first sight nothing seems easier than to build up a chronology of the patriarchs with the help of the dates in Scripture for the life of each one. To add twenty numbers, which express the ages of the successive patriarchs at the time when each ancestor begot his immediate descendant, seems all the work necessary to arrive at the date of the appearance of man upon earth as compared with the epoch of Abraham. In this manner, it seems, we may find the teaching of the Bible on the antiquity of man. The comparison of this result with the results of contemporary science upon the same question will show whether there is, or is not, harmony between faith and science.

Such an inference, however, would be decidedly hasty. In the first place, it would be wrong to assume a conflict between revelation and science in regard to a point not included in the teaching of the Church as it is actually formulated. The Biblical teaching, if teaching there be, on the antiquity of man, on the date of the creation of the first man as compared with the date of Abraham or the Christian era, has not until the present been the object of any formal definition, and probably will not be defined very soon. Furthermore, there has been disagreement on this subject among the recognized representatives of tradition since the beginning of Christianity; none of the doctors of the Church has considered any computations relating to the date in question as matter of faith. The question of chronology has therefore remained outside of the teaching of the Church; this is a point we must not forget.

But though the right of inquiry be unhampered by any authoritative definition, it would be extreme rashness to affirm that we have found the true Biblical chronology for the patriarchs anterior to Abraham. To keep clear of assertions destitute of solid foundation, it is necessary to solve three questions: First, what is the true reading of the Sacred Text? Second, has the sacred writer made any omissions? Third, what is the interpretation of the terms employed?

147. (1) THE GENEALOGICAL TABLES CONSTITUTE ONLY CHRONOLOGICAL ELEMENTS.—The restoration of the true text of Moses, dealing with the years which comprised the lives of the patriarchs anterior to Abraham, constitutes the first embarrassing question for the exegetist. Taking into his hands the genealogical tables as given in Genesis, he finds himself face to face with three principal readings, from which he may make a selection, or he may reject all in favor of a fourth reading more or less probable, on the supposition that the true reading has been lost in all the manuscripts of the Bible now known. These three readings are furnished to us: (*a*) by the text of the Hebrew (and the Vulgate) as the Massoretes have left it to us, and as Onkelos possessed it when writing his Targuma, in the first century of the Christian era (*b*) by the Greek version, or Septuagint; (*c*) by the Samaritan text.

These readings make known to us, besides the direct descent of the patriarchs, the age of each patriarch at the birth of his successor in the genealogical series. Thus, for instance, we see that Adam begot Seth in his 130th year, that Seth begot Enos in his 105th year, etc. Therefore, from the creation of Adam to the birth of Seth there are 130 years; from this epoch to the birth of Enos, 130 plus 105—or 235 years. By adding in this manner all the figures furnished by Genesis, it is easy to calculate the time which separated the first man from the epoch of Abraham.

What is the result? The calculations which the

chronologists have made, though starting with the same dates, arrived at different results. Why? Because the figures on which their calculations were based are not the same in the original texts which have come to us. There is a difference of about 1500 years between the Jewish, Samaritan, and Greek dates. The following genealogical table will show the respective chronologies of our three sources.

Names of the Patriarchs.	Age at the Birth of their Sons according to the		
	Hebrew Text.	Septuagint.	Samaritan Text.
1. Adam	130	230	130
2. Seth	105	205	105
3. Enos	90	190	90
4. Cainan	70	170	70
5. Malaleel	65	165	65
6. Jared	162	162	62
7. Henoch	65	165	65
8. Mathusala	187	167	67
9. Lamech	182	188	53
10. Noe	500	500	500
From Noe to the Deluge	100	100	100
Total	1656	2242	1307
1. Sem, two years after the Deluge, begot	2	2	2
2. Arphaxad	35	135	35
3. Cainan	..	130	..
4. Sale	30	130	130
5. Heber	34	134	134
6. Phaleg	30	130	130
7. Reu	32	132	132
8. Sarug	30	130	130
9. Nachor	29	79	79
10. Thare	70	70	70
Abraham's vocation	75	75	75
From Arphaxad, or from the Deluge to the vocation of Abraham.	367	1147	1017
From the creation of Adam to the vocation of Abraham	2023	3389	2324

148. DISCREPANCIES BETWEEN THE THREE AUTHORITIES.—Thus, according to the Hebrew-Massoretic text, from the creation of Adam to the Deluge there were 1656 years; according to the Hebrew-Samaritan, 1307 years; according to the Greek Septuagint, 2242 years. From the Deluge to Abraham the difference is no less apparent. The Jews count 367 years, the Samaritans 1017 years, the Septuagint 1147 years. Before the Deluge the Samaritan falls short of the Hebrew text. After the Deluge it diverges from the Hebrew and approaches the Septuagint, from which it differs only by the omission of Cainan.

Some of the discrepancies which appear in the figures of these three sources are due to the copyists; others may be due to design, as suggested by St. Augustine.[1] Indeed, the Samaritan and Septuagint texts add 100 years to the Hebrew dates. What is the reason for this difference between the Jewish text on the one hand and the Greek version on the other? How does it come that the Samaritan now agrees with the Hebrew and then with the Greek? Efforts have been made to solve these problems since the first centuries of Christianity, but without success; attempts to find a plausible solution have failed so far, and the words of St. Augustine always remain true: "We give no explanation where the explanation would be unsatisfactory."[2]

Besides, we need not here look for the cause of these discrepancies; it is only important to remark that they are the cause of the differences in Biblical chronology. When we investigate the different systems of the chronologists, we find that one expresses himself in favor of the Septuagint, another in favor of the Hebrew and Vulgate, and a third favors a combination of the different dates according to his own method.

[1] "De Civitate Dei," xv. xiii. i. vol. xl. col. 453.
[2] *Ibid.*, xvi. x. 2 vol. xli. col. 489.

149. THE SEPTUAGINT AND ITS VENERABLE AUTHORITY.—The Septuagint version is one of the most venerable authorities. Its tables served to establish the era or date of the creation of the world adopted by the patriarchal churches. This date is fixed for the year 5504 by the Church of Alexandria, 5490 by the Church of Antioch, 5510 by the Church of Constantinople, and 5199 by the Church of Rome. (*Martyrologium Romanum*, December 25th.) The Chronicon Paschale, based also on the Septuagint, fixes the date for the year 5507. The first fathers of the Church likewise adopted the tables of this version; those of the Greek Church took them directly from the Septuagint; those of the Latin Church received them through the Itala, an early Latin translation made after the ancient Greek version. George Syncellus[1] and Hesychius also reckon the time from the creation of man to the Incarnation of Christ on the basis of the Septuagint.[2]

Among modern authors who have declared in favor of the Septuagint are P. Morin,[3] P. Martin,[4] P. Pezron,[5] a professor of the Protestant Academy at Saumur, Louis Cappel, in a controversy on this point with John Buxtorf, Jr., Isaac Vossius, another Protestant writer, who maintained the same thesis against George Horn, Alphonse de Vignoles, Hales, Jackson, Panvinio, and others.

The tables of the Hebrew-Jewish text enjoy the authority which many claim they possess owing to the fact of their being arranged by the Massoretes. They are also

[1] Chronogr. ed. Dindorf., vol. i., p. 590.
[2] Cardinal Baronius observes: "Sanctam Dei Ecclesiam antiquitus consuevisse supputare annos ab origine mundi non secundum Hebraicam editionem, sed, secundum Septuaginta duos interpretes." Apparatus ad Ann. Eccl., § 118.
[3] "Exercitationes Biblicæ," Paris, 1669.
[4] "Sinicæ Historiæ Decas," Munich, 1658.
[5] "Chronologie de l'Histoire Sainte," 1738, vol. i., p. 2.

supported by the Targum of Onkelos, which establishes the high antiquity of this reading, and especially by the adoption of the Latin Vulgate as the authentic version by the Council of Trent. The Jews of to-day adopt the tables of their own text. The chronology based on these tables has prevailed since the sixteenth century, thanks to the authority of Joseph Scaliger, who laid the foundation of modern chronological science in his book, "De Emendatione Temporum," 1583, and who attributed exaggerated value to the Hebrew text. Bossuet, Petavius, Usher (Usserius), and Clinton calculate the date of the creation of man after this Hebrew text, or the Vulgate.

The tables of the Hebrew-Samaritan text have not attracted very much attention. However, they were adopted in ancient times by the author of the Apocryphal writing, called the "small Genesis," and in modern times by Lepsius, the German Egyptologist.[1]

The tables of the Septuagint have the highest and strongest authorities in their favor; the choice, however, remains absolutely free between them and the Hebrew texts. The scientific critic undoubtedly has the right to study these numbers and to seek the true reading, the figures written by Moses himself. This right is not disputed; it remains to be seen whether the task is or is not beyond his powers. Many authors have no hope that a satisfactory result can ever be reached.

150. CONSEQUENCES RESULTING FROM BIBLICAL CHRONOLOGY.—What have we to conclude from all the facts under consideration? In the first place, the Church does not guarantee the correctness of either of the two chronologies (Septuagint and Hebrew), and her authority does not oblige us to adhere rigorously to the text transmitted by tradition or to the sense attributed to it.

[1] "Chronologie der Aegyptier," Berlin, 1849, vol. i., p. 397.

151. IMPOSSIBILITY OF FIXING THE DATE OF THE CREATION OF MAN.—Another consequence is that it is impossible to fix with certainty the date of the creation of man. The most competent authors are unanimously agreed on this subject. "The number of years passed from the Creation to the nativity of Christ is uncertain," says Pagi, the learned annotator of Cardinal Baronius. . . . "We can never know for certain what was the age of the world at the time of the Incarnation." P. Petavius, who consecrated so many vigils to clear up this chronological question, makes the following confession in his "De Doctrina Temporum:" "We have no certain means of knowing at what date the Creation took place, and we would need a special revelation from God in order to know it. They are in error who dare not only to determine it with certainty, but also to treat with contempt those who believe that they can add or subtract from the numbers given in Scripture."

The reason for this uncertainty is that even supposing the genealogical lists of Genesis to be complete, it is impossible in the present state of the text to know the real figures written by Moses. We have no decisive reason to prefer the Septuagint to the Hebrew or the Hebrew to the Samaritan. All attempts of the learned to arrive at a solution have been unsuccessful; nay, more, perhaps all the three tables are false, and the figures have been changed in all the texts. The latter hypothesis is far from being improbable, for, as Molloy and Brucker have justly observed,[1] it is impossible to prove that some generations have not been omitted intentionally or accidentally, perhaps by the copyists, or by the sacred writer himself. Therefore, we have to conclude with Bishop Meignan: "It appears to us that the exact

"La Controverse," March 15, 1886.

date of the appearance of man upon earth cannot be fixed with certainty."[1]

"However," says the Abbé Vigouroux, "we may hold with probability that whatever the alterations of the numbers in the book of Genesis may be, they cannot be very considerable; and consequently when we do not assign a fixed date to the origin of the human species, and place man between 4000 and 6000 years before Christ, we may rest assured that we are not mistaken. But here a new question presents itself to our mind. It is perfectly true that mankind cannot be older than about 8000 years, if the tables of the antediluvian and postdiluvian patriarchs are without omissions in the text, but it is different if they are fragmentary and incomplete. May we not be permitted to assume this? Are we sure of possessing the entire catalogue of all the descendants of Adam until Abraham in a direct line?"[2] This is what we must inquire into.

152. (2) THERE ARE OMISSIONS IN THE GENEALOGICAL TABLES OF SCRIPTURE.—Criticism has unquestionably established omissions in the genealogical tables which the various books of Scripture contain. Let us take, for example, the genealogy of the Saviour, after the twenty antediluvian and postdiluvian patriarchs. The generations of Esron, who appears to have been born in Chanaan (Gen. xlvi., 8–12), of Aram, and of Aminadab, seem insufficient to fill up the interval of time which elapsed from the establishment of the Israelites in Gessen to their migration in the desert, during which Naasson was phylarch (chief) of the tribe of Juda. At least this is the opinion of those authors who reject as an interpolation the words, "and in the land of Chanaan" (Ex. xii., 40), in the Septuagint and in the Sa-

[1] "Le Monde," etc.
[2] "Les Livres Saints," etc., vol. iii., p. 238.

maritan text; and these authors become more numerous every day. Among those in the sixteenth century we find Eugubinus Stenchus and Guilbert Genebrard; in our days, Dr. Haneberg, Abbé Vigouroux, P. Brucker, M. Halévy, etc.

Naasson died in the desert. He, together with Salmon, who married Rahab after the taking of Jericho; Booz, Obed, Jesse, and David, in all six generations, fill up the time from the Exodus to the building of the Temple, about the beginning of the reign of Solomon. Now this interval was 480 years in length. Lequien, a Jesuit father, concludes from this that there are omissions for this epoch in the genealogical tables of Ruth iv., 18–22; I. Paralipomenon ii., 11–15; Matt. i., 4, 5; Luke iii., 31–33.

We add several other examples to confirm the above. Even in the Pentateuch, Laban, grandson of Nachor, is called his son, owing to the omission of the name of Bethuel, his father; Jochabed, the mother of Moses, is called the daughter of Levi, though Levi was certainly dead long before her birth.[1] In the first book of Paralipomenon, Suebal, contemporary with David, is called the son of Gersom, who was the son of Moses, and lived several centuries before him. In the third and fourth books of Kings, and also in the second of Paralipomenon, Jehu is named the son of Namsi; yet he was Namsi's grandson. In Esdras, Addo, who was only Zacharius' grandfather, is called his father. There are other genealogical omissions in the same book; for instance, between Azarias and Maraioth he omits five members— Johanan, Azarias, Achimaas, Achitob, and Amarias.[2]

[1] Gen. xxix., 5, and xxxviii., 5; Num. xxvi., 59.
[2] I. Par. xxvi., 24; I. (III.) Reg. xix., 16; II. (IV.) Reg. ix., 20; II. Par. xxii., 7; II. (IV.) Reg. ix., 2–14; I. Esd. v., 1; Zach. i., 1–7; I. Esd. vii., 3; I. Par. vi., 7–14.

From the fact thus established we may draw the conclusion that there is a possibility of many similar omissions in the genealogical tables. Two Jesuits, P. Von Hummelauer and P. Brucker, have taken up this point. The views of P. Brucker, in favor of omissions in the tables of the twenty patriarchs, have met with opposition among the learned members of the Oratory of Rennes. In "La Controverse" (1886) the Abbé Ch. Robert has submitted for the consideration of the learned Jesuit many judicious observations, and the Abbé Hamard, without positively rejecting his views, for excellent reasons justifies those who refuse to admit them.

153. THE MOST REMARKABLE EXAMPLE OF OMISSION.—The most remarkable example of omission, as the Abbé Vigouroux observes, is that which is drawn from the Gospel of St. Matthew. The sacred author purposely excludes from the genealogical list of Our Saviour three well-known royal names: Joas, Amasias, and Azarias. This suppression deserves our attention the more, as it serves to reveal the motive for the systematic omission of certain links in the genealogical chain. In fact, they seem to have been omitted as a means of aiding the memory; as the table of generations was learned by heart, recourse was had to various means to assist the memory and to retain these dry lists of names. With this in view, the evangelist subdivided[1] the series into three great groups, each of fourteen numbers, and because the second number would have contained seventeen, instead of fourteen names, the harmonious order of his distribution would have been destroyed; therefore he eliminated three members.

Analogous mnemonic reasons may have modified the patriarchal genealogies. Indeed, they seem to have been arranged on a simpler system; for there are ten patri-

[1] Matt. i., 17.

archs before, and ten after the Deluge, a number easily retained, which corresponds to the fingers of the two hands, upon the number of which the decimal system is founded.

To sum up, the arrangement in groups of ten of the patriarchs before and after the Deluge, the Oriental custom of suppressing intermediate members in their genealogical tables, suggests to us plausible grounds for admitting the probability of omissions in the lists which Moses has transmitted to us of the direct descendants of Adam until Abraham. If this be the case, the date of man's creation may be much more ancient than has been believed hitherto, on account of the longer duration of life among the patriarchs omitted in the catalogue of Genesis; consequently, the epoch of man's appearance on earth is altogether uncertain, not only because we do not know the real figures written by the author of the Pentateuch, but also because there may be omissions in the genealogical series. If the corruption of the figures modify the antiquity of man only in a limited degree, this is not the case if generations have been omitted; for if these omissions are numerous the date of man's creation may be put back many centuries.

154. MANKIND VERY PROBABLY OVER 8000 YEARS OLD.—Thus, if we consult the Bible alone, we find ourselves in almost complete darkness as regards the antiquity of man. It is possible that man's creation dates back only 6000 years, according to the actual Hebrew text; it is possible that it dates back 8000 years, according to the Septuagint; but it is also possible that a longer period has elapsed, on account of the omissions that may exist in the genealogical tables. Such is the final conclusion of chronological critics, and such is the conclusion to which a critical study of the Sacred Text leads us, for with all our facts and speculations we must admit our

ignorance and uncertainty at the very threshold. Still the question of omissions will continue to occupy the minds of the learned in chronology, and quite new views will suggest themselves, as we notice in the case of P. Bourdais, an eminent French commentator.

155. NEW VIEW ABOUT THE GENEALOGICAL LISTS.— "According to formal testimony," says P. Bourdais, "of St. Jude,[1] St. Paul,[2] Jesus, Ben-Sirach,[3] the Roman Ritual,[4] on the existence, not only of Adam and Noe, ancestors *par excellence* of the first and second humanity, but of the other primitive patriarchs, such as Henoch, it does not seem to us reconcilable with orthodoxy to deny the individual existence of the twenty patriarchs. However, we admit without difficulty that the names designating these patriarchs in the tables of Genesis have such a comprehensive sense that they may designate both individuals and ethnic groups more or less extensive and connected with these names. The ethnographic table of the tenth chapter of Genesis is interpreted to-day in an analogous manner, with the difference, however, that the individuality of the ancestral progenitor of a people in a certain number of cases disappears there almost altogether. According to our system, the twenty Biblical patriarchs would be separated in the course of the centuries anterior to Abraham, and between each of them would be placed an undetermined number of unknown generations. Such is the broad concession we would make to the partisans of omissions in the genealogical tables in question above.

"Thus, instead of understanding these lists to mean that each patriarch represents a genealogical group included with him under his name, we should assign to the several groups the number of years given in the tables.

[1] Ep. Cath., 14.   [2] Heb. xi., 5.   [3] Ecclus. xliv., 16.
[4] "Litanies of the Prayers for the Dying."

In the series of numbers in which Moses gives the chronology of the time before Abraham it is hard for us to admit omissions. Certainly, if we adopt this view, the advantages to be gained for the defence of the Bible from the hypothesis of omissions in the tables of the twenty patriarchs would disappear. But criticism also has imperative demands. These compel us to reject the hypothesis of elasticity in the numbers marking the age of the twenty patriarchs. The comparison of Biblical chronology with Chaldean tradition leads us to this conclusion. The Chaldean tradition may have changed more or less; it is unquestionable, however, that it was derived from the same source as the facts of Genesis at a time when the tradition was still unadulterated. Taken as a whole it agrees with Genesis in a striking manner, particularly on primitive chronology." [1]

156. (3) CHRONOLOGICAL TABLE OF THE TEN ANTEDILUVIAN PATRIARCHS.—From Adam to Noe, that is, from the Creation to the Deluge, the Bible counts ten patriarchs. The Chaldean traditions also give ten antediluvian kings. It is impossible not to recognize in the number "ten" a survival of the primitive tradition, for it appears with remarkable persistency in the legendary traditions of many nations. The principal human races always speak of ten primitive fathers, the founders of their institutions, the root from which they sprang. Among the Iranians they are the ten Peshdadian monarchs, "the men of the ancient law," who lived on the pure *homa*, or draught of immortality; among the Hindoos, the nine Brahmadikas, who, with Brahma, their author, are called the ten Pitris or fathers; among the Germans and Scandinavians, the ten ancestors of Odin; among the Chinese, the ten emperors who partook of the

[1] Cf. "Dictionnaire Apologétique," by Jaugy, article "Chronologie des Patriarchs."

divine nature before the dawn of historical times; among the Arabs, the ten mythical kings of the Adites, the primitive inhabitants of the peninsula comprised between the Red Sea and the Persian Gulf, etc. The Phenician Sanchoniathon also gives ten generations of primitive patriarchs. This constant occurrence of the number ten is the more striking because it is connected in no way with religious or philosophical speculations on the mystic value of numbers.[1]

The Babylonian tradition in the time of Berosus attributed to the reign of each antediluvian king a marvellous duration, if we are guided by the computation of the sar—a period which Chaldean historians make use of in their chronology. The sar is generally estimated at 3600 years, and thus we arrive at the enormous number of 432,000 years from the first king to the Deluge. In this calculation we have only a remembrance of the longevity of primitive men.

Moses of Khorene, the national historian of Armenia, speaking on the history of Berosus and the Chaldean kings, says: "The ancient writers have changed the names and duration of life of the antediluvian patriarchs. Whether led by their fancy, or by other motives, what they say about the origin of things is a mixture of truth and falsehood. Thus, in speaking of the first created being, they make a king of him instead of a simple man, give him a barbarous name without meaning, and finally attribute to him 36,000 years of life. . . . So, also, they give Noe a different name and assign to him a life of immense duration."[2]

Moses of Khorene, in attributing to the sar the value of 3600 years, only copied the Chaldean historian Aby-

[1] Lenormant, "Manuel de l'Histoire ancienne de l'Orient," vol. i., pp. 19, 20.
[2] Cf. "Collection des Historiens de l'Armenie," de V. Langlois.

denus on the subject of the ten antediluvian monarchs. He also says, "The sar contains 3600 years, the ner, 600 years, the soss, 60 years."[1] Eusebius, resuming Berosus, after Apollodorus or Polyhistor, says: "The time during which these ten kings reigned was 120 sars, that is, 432,000 years."[2]

However, as regards the opinion of Berosus and his abbreviators on the value of the sar in his antediluvian chronology, it is not certain that we should attribute to it a duration of 3600 years. A precious passage in Suidas teaches us that the sar also represented among the Babylonians the period of eighteen years and six months. "The sars," he says, "of the Chaldeans are both a measure and a number; 120 sars, according to the calculations of the Chaldeans, make 2222 years, for the sar contains 222 lunar months, which is equivalent to 18 years and 6 months."[3]

The sar, therefore, had a double value—an astronomical one, corresponding to 3600 years, and a civil one, viz., eighteen years and six months. Following this suggestion of Suidas, it seems plain that the 120 antediluvian sars of Berosus were civil sars, for to take the 120 sars at their astronomical value would extend to a fabulous length the time which the history of Babylon assigns to the period which preceded the great cataclysm. Now, if we give to the sars the value of eighteen years and six months, we find that between the Biblical and the Chaldean chronology there is a harmony, the more striking because we arrive at it in different ways; the former being founded on the age of the patriarchs at the birth of their first-born sons, and the second on the duration attributed

[1] "Historicorum Græcorum Fragmenta," vol. ii., p. 499. Cf. Migne, "Patrologia Græca," vol. xix., col. 121.
[2] *Ibid., loc. cit.*, col. 113–114.
[3] Suidas, "Lexicon," edit. Kuster, vol. iii., p. 289.

to the reign of each of the ten antediluvian kings. In this manner we use different figures and obtain an almost identical result, as may be seen from the following table:

Biblical Antediluvian Patriarchs.[1]	Year of birth of the first-born son of each patriarch according to—			Sars.			Chaldean Antediluvian Kings.[2]
	Hebrew and Vulgate.	*Samaritan.*	*Septuagint.*	*At 18 years and 6 months.*	*No. of Sars.*	*At 3600 years.*	
Adam........	130	130	230	185	10	36,000	Adorus.
Seth.........	105	105	205	55½	3	10,800	Alaparus.
Enos.........	90	90	190	240½	13	46,800	Amillaroas.
Cainan.......	70	70	170	222	12	43,200	Ammenon.
Malaleel.....	65	65	165	333	18	64,800	Amegalarus.
Jared........	162	62	162	185	10	36,000	Daonus.
Henoch......	65	65	165	333	18	64,800	Edoreschus.
Mathusala....	187	67	167	185	10	36,000	Amempsinus.
Lamech......	182	53	188	148	8	28,800	Obartes.
Noe..........	600	600	600	333	18	64,800	Xisuthrus.
Totals......	1656	1307	2242	2220	120	432,000	

When we compare Chaldean chronology with that of the Bible, the numbers do not agree, and nevertheless the sum total of years from the creation of man until the Deluge, as given by Babylonian chronology, the value of the sar given by Suidas being assumed to be correct, differs only by 22 years from the chronology of the Septuagint, while the Septuagint differs by 575 years from the

[1] Petau, " De Doctrina Temporum," l. ix., c. viii., edit. 1703, vol. ii., p. 11.
[2] Berosus, in Eusebius, " Chron. Arm.," l. i., c. i.; Migne, " Patrologia Græca," vol. xix., col. 107-108.

Hebrew and Vulgate, and by 945 years from the Samaritan version. This agreement between the chronology of the Septuagint and the Chaldean computation might seem fortuitous, but as the Chaldeans had so many traditions in common with the Hebrews, it cannot well be purely accidental.

According to Lenormant, the ten antediluvian kings of Babylon, whose names have nothing in common with those of the Biblical patriarchs, are personifications of the signs of the zodiac, of the Mazzalôth or "solar mansions," which infidel Hebrews at the time of Assyrian supremacy adored along with the sun, the moon, and the whole celestial army.[1] "We believe it to be more exact," remarks Vigouroux, "to say that the names of the ten primitive kings, however disfigured, were given to the signs of the zodiac, just as the Latins gave to plants the names of their gods, and as in the Middle Ages, and even to-day, popular language gives to constellations Biblical names, as the name of 'Chariot of David' to the Great Bear, and 'The Three Magi' to the Belt of the Orion. There are more than ten signs of the zodiac, and the ancients did not know ten planets."

We do not know the exact duration which Berosus attributed to the reigns or lives of the postdiluvian Chaldean patriarchs, because we possess only fragments of his Babylonian history. However, we may assume that he counted the duration of their reigns also according to the Babylonian sar, that is, according to its civil value of eighteen years and six months per sar.

P. Bourdais, following his own system, according to which he holds that the names of the patriarchs in the genealogical tables of the Bible designate both an in-

[1] II. (IV.) Kings xxiii., 5; Lenormant, "Essai de Commentaire de Bérose," pp. 233-238.

dividual and an ethnic group, arrives at the following conclusion:

"In the table of Chaldean antediluvian patriarchs," he says, "the sum of the numbers of the column on the left (the sar = 18 years and 6 months) seems to be equal, not in its figures, but in the length of time, to the sum of the numbers on the right (the sar = 3600 years). The average number of years in the life of each patriarch is a cyclic day, exactly the duration of each of the works of the hexahemeron. Certain numbers belong to corresponding periods of time, whether natural or conventional, and appear to be their ideographic signs, like the 365 years of the life of Henoch. Authors begin to regard the whole system of the primitive chronology of the Bible as an arrangement of numbers having a cyclic character, a vague value and a figurative sense, instead of being used in their literal sense, with a precise value and a positive character. Consequently the Bible does not furnish us the elements of a scientific chronology of primitive times."[1]

157. COSMIC DAYS IN THE CHALDEAN AND BIBLICAL CHRONOLOGIES.—Let us observe that the exegetists known to be respectful towards the Sacred Text, even the most timorous, admit to-day this figurative sense, this vague value of the days of creation which have also a cyclic character, and constitute, in the whole of the week which they form, a system of cosmogonic chronology. Fr. Lenormant has proved this in a scientific manner.[2] The Chaldeans preserved the tradition of the hexahemeron in the week of creation, and saw in each day

---

[1] "Essai de Commentaire," pp. 238, 240.
[2] The Chaldeans, for the history of the origin of the world, had devised a day of long duration, counted after the manner of the ordinary day, that is, a day of twelve hours, six for the night and six for the day; sixty minutes for each hour and sixty sec-

the twelve hours or great sars of 3600. Thus they attributed to each nycthemeron the value of 43,200 years, and for them the whole week of creation formed 259,200 years. The creative days of Moses, with their evening and morning, are cycles copied after the nycthemeron or ordinary natural day, but their subdivisions are less extended. To judge of the length of life of the antediluvian patriarchs according to Moses, compared with the duration of the reigns of the antediluvian kings of Berosus, the Mosaic day, the twelve hours of the Biblical text are the fiftieth part of the corresponding Chaldean periods. P. Bourdais is of the opinion that the total duration of the hexahemeron according to Moses is about 259-200/50-5-184 years. "A conscientious exegetist," he says, "will not reject these figures for the interpretation of the six days of creation. But all exegetists will grant to the geologists that these days, if taken in a figurative sense, can be extended and have as such the value of an undetermined period. It is thus that we establish the system of 'epoch days' for the reconciliation of revelation and science in matters of cosmogony.'

We have amplified the third section of our subject to show the bearing which this chronological system of the Chaldeans has on the interpretation of the genealogical tables of the twenty patriarchs as given in Genesis. The time may come when it will be impossible for the Christian exegetist to prove that the chronology of the Septuagint, even allowing the omissions referred to before, is sufficient to satisfy the just claims of both geology

onds for each minute. Each second of the cosmic day represented an ordinary year, each minute sixty years, and each hour 3600 years; the cosmic day itself, having twelve hours, represented 43,200 years. Cf. Lenormant, "Essai de Commentaire," pp. 185-217.

and paleontology. In this case the system of P. Bourdais would not fail to satisfy any chronological claims for the antiquity of the human race.

158. Conclusion: The Bible Teaches Nothing Definite about the Antiquity of Man.—In concluding this chapter the reader will not fail to observe that Holy Scripture does not teach anything definite about the age of man. But if Scripture does not teach anything explicitly and authoritatively, is there not another source from which we may learn? Does profane science enlighten us on this question? Does it remove the doubts which the comparative study of primitive texts and of the Biblical genealogies leave to us? These are the questions which remain to be answered.

In the true spirit of inquiry it is our right to make use of the lights which paleontology on the one hand, and the history of ancient nations on the other, furnish us in order to interpret more intelligently the Sacred Text: then it will be easy to show that the short chronology which is drawn from the Hebrew text is insufficient, and that that of the Septuagint in its postdiluvian table is perhaps also too restricted. It follows from this that the existence of omissions in the genealogies of Genesis becomes quite probable, and that it is only by this means, together with the aid of those ancient monuments, whose testimony is unquestionable, that we are put in possession of facts and knowledge that enable us to reconcile the Mosaic account with the data of modern research.

CHAPTER IX.

THE ANTIQUITY OF MAN AND GEOLOGY.

The claims of science.—Antiquity of man according to geology.—Alluvions.— Peat-moors.— Stalagmites.— Antiquity of man according to physical geography.—Antiquity of man as inferred from climatic changes.— These changes are exaggerated.—Valuable hints from ancient writers.—Antiquity of man as indicated by changes in the fauna.—Alleged prehistoric animals.—We cannot draw a line between the age of the mammoth and the reindeer.—Man contemporary with many extinct animals. — Tertiary and quaternary man. — The age of the acerotherium, halitherium, and elephas meridionalis. — Quaternary man. — What is tertiary and what is quaternary?—Powerful catastrophes.—Antiquity of man judged by the progress of his industry.—Five types of primitive man.—The ages of stone, bronze, and iron are not consecutive. —No necessity of extra-scientific hypotheses. — Conclusion.

THE materialistic school claims unlimited authority; it proclaims publicly and aggressively the insufficiency of the time accorded to man by traditional or Biblical chronology; it laughs to scorn the six or eight thousand years which span the generations of the human race, and it rebukes the obstinate and retrogressive ideas of Christians for not keeping abreast of the spirit of progress and enlightenment. Every day this demand grows louder, this assertion more forcible, till Christian scientists submit to and accept the new dogma. This excessive docility and submission to the behests of materialistic science is condemned by true science itself, for science must not dogmatize nor assume authority on any question without due confirmation of the proofs submitted.

159. WHAT DOES SCIENCE TEACH US ABOUT THE ANTIQUITY OF MAN?—It is curious to note the readiness of some men to accept everything new and startling, and to efface and destroy the old landmarks of time and history, merely because somebody has said they are fogyish. Men have never been more rebellious against religious dogma than in our days, and yet they have never bowed with more humble submission to assertions put forward in the name of science by self-styled savants. When we are told "science has spoken" the case is settled. Everything must give way to science; everything have her seal and approbation. But has science spoken? Are we sure that these misguided sceptics, infidels, and materialists do not err in their speculative theories like many other weak and diseased minds which trespass on the domain of theology? What is there in scientists to claim immunity from error? Scientists must bring forward their proofs and support them, and not only must their proofs support their conclusions, but in their terminology they must maintain exactness of definition; they should not coin new phrases to lend a subtle charm and varnish to fanciful theories. We call scientists to the bar of judgment; we shall try them before an unbiassed jury; and we are willing to submit the verdict to the intelligence of our readers.

Prehistoric man has been a favorite theme of amateur scientists and over-zealous materialistic theorists, who attempt to justify their erroneous speculations by calling to their aid long periods of time. If man's reasoning power is at fault in dealing with social and business questions, with religious and political issues, what guarantee have we that his ideas on scientific questions are exempt from error or fallacy? Man does not know himself; his active mind is ever planning, ever scheming, ever craving to reach above and beyond the tangible and the visible. Beyond the limits of history he can roam at will and indulge in all manner of extravagant speculations. History denies him flights of fancy, self-styled science encourages him to ignore everything that is incompatible with its teachings. He may be the veriest crank upon earth or the most consummate humbug, still so-called science will shield him from either appellation, and the world knows him as an "advanced thinker."

Has science good grounds and solid facts on which to build its teaching on man's prehistoric advent? What are the leading points in its affirmations? Science says they can be reduced to the following: Considerable changes have taken place upon the surface of our globe since the advent of man; the earth's physical geography has changed; here, the land has risen and encroached upon the sea; there, it has sunk, and the waters have spread over the land; enormous deposits of gravel or peat have been formed on the uplands or in the valleys; the Arctic climate, which formerly extended over large tracts of the earth, has been modified; glaciers have receded towards the poles; gigantic animals, like the elephant, formerly lived in company with man; man, himself a savage, has modified his implements at different times, and slowly improved the industrial arts and the resources of his own development, which presupposes a long period of time.

If we accept these loose assertions about the physical changes of the earth's surface from the time of man's advent as a savage to his present development, certainly traditional or Biblical chronology would fail to supply a full and consecutive genealogical history of the human race. But is there no exaggeration in the long periods so boldly claimed? Could not these thousands and tens of thousands of centuries be curtailed within reasonable limits and still be sufficient to account for all these changes? We think so, and we shall endeavor to prove our opinion by the testimony of eminent authorities.

Owing to the importance of our subject, to avoid confusion we shall treat the question under six heads: (1) geology, properly speaking; (2) orography and physical geography; (3) climate; (4) fauna; (5) archæological discoveries; (6) the implements of man.

160. (1) ANTIQUITY OF MAN ACCORDING TO GEOLOGY.—Before going further we must first answer the following question: Since what epoch has man made his appearance on earth?

Natural science is in accord with the Bible in proving man the most recent of God's creatures. No fragment of a human body, no product of human art or industry has been found within the stratified rocks which contain the organic remains of extinct animals down to the last layers of the pliocene. Man, at most, has been the contemporary of the mammoth, mastodon, cave bear, etc.; it is certain he did not antedate them. Nay, more; he was not created till a long time after these animals, for only when the age of the cave bears closes do we find the remains of both man and bear commingled. Until now no decisive proofs of the existence of man in the tertiary epoch have been produced. Heterodox savants themselves acknowledge this. "The existence of tertiary man," says the German rationalist, Virchow, "is a problem." It is therefore useless to stop and discuss a question which does not rest upon solid proof; but we may inquire into the value of direct arguments in favor of the high antiquity of man.

Let us study the nature of geological deposits. These deposits are of mechanical origin, like the alluvial deposits; or of organic origin, like the peat-moors; or of chemical origin, like stalagmites and other concretions resulting from the precipitation of carbonate of lime kept in solution by water; or, finally, of archæological origin, like human bones or objects of art buried in alluvial soil. Hence we have four quite natural divisions.

161. (*a*) ALLUVIONS.—The evidence so anxiously looked for that is to condemn traditional chronology is not found in the quaternary or the alluvium. If there were evidence of deposits formed regularly at the bottom of seas or lakes, such testimony should be furnished; but the formations to which our attention is directed by the advocates of man's vast antiquity on earth are evidently due to violent phenomena, the most frequent being immense inundations, of whose great excavating and cutting power modern times give us hardly any idea. It is sufficient to witness some of these sudden scoopings out, to learn the devastating action and the transporting power of water. It has been calculated that this transporting power increases at least as the square of the rapidity of the current. Thus we understand that waters habitually calm and hardly charged with clay could, at certain periods, transport not only gravels and bowlders, but also pieces of sandstone and granite.

One of the most remarkable localities, illustrating the power of water and the accumulation of alluvium, is the valley of the Somme in France, in the vicinity of Amiens. Here the first, and perhaps the most ancient, traces of quaternary man have been found. When we look at the thickness of these deposits, and the depth of the valley whose base they cover, we can hardly believe that this is the work of the modest river which rolls its quiet waters at the bottom of the basin. The fact is, we might allow thousands of years for their accumulation by the river in its present state without reaching the cutting power and the action needed to explain the immense excavations and transportations caused in a comparatively short time. But it is not necessary to go back very far in the past to establish the fact that the Somme did not always have the present volume and force. According to M. de Mercey, who has made this river his special study,[1] its waters at the Roman epoch were fifty times more abundant than in our days; hence the deposits which have been formed since that time are very considerable. In certain places they have attained several yards in thickness, and present great similarity to the alluvia in which the axes of St. Acheul and the famous jawbone of Moulin Quignon were found. However, we can have no doubt regarding the age of these deposits, for quite at the bottom of them is found, with bowlder stones and marine shells, pottery which M. de Mortillet himself does not hesitate to attribute to the end of the Roman epoch.

The presence of marine shells and other deposits proves that the sea at that time must have extended to Amiens. The whole region was, undoubtedly, sinking, which caused a momentous submersion. A remarkable discovery in the Departement du Nord tends to prove this. Below a marine deposit nine feet thick remains of the Roman epoch have been found, especially coins, whose most recent date bears the effigy of a prince who died A.D. 267. We may conclude from this that the sea, at this epoch, covered the country around this locality, and remained long enough to deposit nine feet of sediment. However, this overflow could not have been of long duration, for since the seventh century some villages have been established on the shores. It is, therefore, within the time of two or three centuries that so considerable a deposit was accumulated.[2]

[1] "Bulletin de la Société Géologique," 1876–1877, p. 347.
[2] "Compte rendu du Congrès Scientifique de Lille," 1874, p. 60.

These instances of phenomenal erosions and deposits could easily be multiplied. An analogous case, of the same epoch, has been noticed at Lille. Here a layer of turf clay about eight feet high replaces the marine deposit; but the date is the same, for below is a fluvial deposit in which have been found coins bearing the image of a Byzantine emperor. This deposit proves the occurrence of a violent inundation, for it contains bowlders of flint and pieces of chalk as thick as a hand. The river Deule, a sleepy stream, hardly able now to carry its ordinary alluvium, cannot have transported these bowlders.[1]

To sum up: these facts show that a great inundation laid waste this locality at the end of the third century. History confirms this, for it tells us that the neighboring country had been thickly peopled, but was then suddenly deprived of its inhabitants.

It is not surprising that a locality, overwhelmed by a violent catastrophe, should present considerable alluvial deposits. After all, the deposits which cover human remains do not seem anywhere to have a depth of more than twenty-one feet. This may appear much; it is little, however, when we take into consideration that remains of the Roman epoch, among which is a medal of Marcus Aurelius, have been found in this neighborhood at a depth of twenty-five feet, under a triple bed of reddish clay, muddy slime, and peat mixed with sand.[2] If, taking this as a basis, we should calculate the age of the other deposits containing products of human industry, we should refer them to the sixth century before the Christian era.

We should be justified in rejecting the results of some

[1] Cf. Gosselet, "Compte rendu du Congrès Scientifique de Lille," 1874.
[2] "Matériaux pour l'Histoire de l'Homme," 1878, p. 136.

calculations on the antiquity of the deposits we have mentioned, based on the age of similar deposits taken as criteria; for formations of this kind are quite irregular. However, if we admit that deposits increased uniformly before and after the Roman epoch, we grant too much, for all geologists allow that such deposits accumulated more rapidly in the quaternary period than during the period of rest which followed.

What we have said about the alluvia of the Somme Valley applies equally to those of other countries. Two centuries have sufficed for the Simethe (the Giaretta of to-day), the small river in Sicily that skirts the base of Etna and empties into the Mediterranean south of Catana, to dig out a passage one hundred feet wide and fifty deep through the hardest volcanic rocks. The Kander, in the canton of Bern, Switzerland, while changing its course in 1715, carried into Lake Thun, into which it flows, from one hundred and twenty to one hundred and fifty million cubic feet of matter in twenty days. Hence the thousands of years, and even centuries, which certain geologists claim do not rest on a solid foundation.

162. (*b*) PEAT-MOORS. — Another argument for the antiquity of man is taken from the formation of peat moors or bogs, and the successive increase of the forest products which they contain, amid which are met human remains.

The argument has but little weight, for peat is formed at the bottom of marshes in consequence of the decomposition of vegetable matter, and may form with great rapidity. Thousands of years have been claimed for the formation of the Somme peat-bogs, which contain human remains. These calculations are imaginary. The destruction of a forest through a storm, towards the middle of the seventeenth century, gave rise to a peat-bog at Lochbroom, Rosshire, England, and the inhabitants of the locality were cutting peat therefrom in less than a half century after the catastrophe. Lyell, the ardent champion of long periods of time for man, in his "Principles of Geology," says: "All the weapons and implements (coins, axes, etc.) found in the peat-moors of France and the Grande Bretagne are Roman. A great part of the peat formations of Europe do not date further back than the time of Cæsar. . . . Data for determining the age of peat can only be attained by multiplying such observations and carefully comparing them. But up to the present no such careful observations have been made in order to determine what is the minimum time requisite for the formation of a certain amount of peat."[1] In the most ancient times, during the Bronze and Iron Age, peat must have formed more rapidly than in our days, because the accumulations of vegetable matter in primitive forests must have been very abundant.

In answer to those who hold that the forest products which the peat contains go back to a very remote period, Lyell says:

"By collecting and studying a great variety of objects of human industry discovered in the peat, the Danish archæologists were led to establish a chronological succession of periods, which they named ages of stone, bronze, and iron, according to the nature of the materials which served for the manufacturing of implements. The Stone Age coincides with the period of the first vegetation, that of the Scotch pine, and, in part at least, with that of the second vegetation, or of the oak. A considerable portion of the oak period ought to coincide with the Bronze Age, for swords and shields of this metal have been found where the oak abounds. The Iron Age corresponds more correctly with the period of the beech."[2]

[1] "Antiquity of Man," p. 156.   [2] *Ibid.*, p. 10.

It is supposed that the Scotch pine dates back 6000 years. A flint knife has been found under one of the trees in the most ancient zone, and this has led to the conclusion that Denmark was inhabited 6000 years ago. Professor Hitchcock has observed that the first forests of Scotch pine in Denmark might have been destroyed by fire during a single season, as often happens in North America, and been replaced later on by other vegetation. The long periods of time which geologists claim are needed in order that the oak and beech should replace the pine, are therefore not at all necessary. It is even probable that the different forest products of the peat-beds of Denmark existed at the same time, but were of different heights. Accidents and the extension of swamps, for instance, may have caused these products to superpose themselves upon one another, and thus give rise to the arrangement witnessed by the naturalist.

From these observations we can understand that there is no immediate prospect of obtaining a chronometer to calculate the growth of peat. Even in the same country, peat will grow in one place a foot and in another an inch, during the same period. Much depends on the condition of the soil and the plants which grow and accumulate there.

Archæology confirms the rapid increase of ancient peat-beds. In various parts of France and England we find ancient Roman roads covered with a thick layer of peat, covered sometimes by deposits of another nature. In London has been found under the ancient walls a bed of peat from six to nine feet thick, which must have been formed entirely during the Roman period, for we find there at different depths traces of this period. Not only quantities of Roman coins and other ancient remains have been found in the peat-beds of Scotland, but also Roman axes, still sticking in the trees, buried in the peat, suggesting at once the probability that the Roman soldiers cut their way through these forests.

We have been furnished with still more remarkable facts. The corpses of two persons who died in Derbyshire in 1674 were discovered twenty-seven years afterwards under three feet of peat. Coins of Edward IV., who died in 1483, have been found recently at a depth of eighteen feet. Finally, in Ireland, the most favored country of all for the production of peat, thanks to the humidity of the climate, small butter-tubs and a leather shoe have been found at a depth of fifteen to twenty feet, objects which do not seem older than the seventeenth century.[1]

It is said that the peat-bogs of Ireland grow five centimetres (about two inches) per year. The facts we have related and other similar facts make this assertion very probable. At this rate a bank of peat thirty feet thick—much thicker than that of the Somme Valley—could have formed in two hundred years. This conclusion is almost admitted by competent geologists. We read in the "Prodromus of Geology," by M. Vezian, that "a century is sufficient for such humble plants as the mosses to produce a bank of peat nine feet high." R. de Neuville goes a step further. "It seems to be proved," he says, "that, under favorable circumstances, the thickest beds of peat could have formed in the space of one or two centuries, even where it does not grow to-day because the necessary conditions for its development are wanting."[2]

[1] For all these facts see Lyell's "Principles of Geology," vol. ii.; Southall, "The Recent Origin of Man," *passim;* De Nadaillac, "Les Premiers Hommes," vol. ii.
[2] "Matériaux," 1876, p. 358.

We are far, it is plain, from the thousands and tens of thousands of centuries claimed by the adherents of long chronologies for the accumulation of peat.

163. (*c*) STALAGMITES.—The stalagmite is a deposit of calcareous matter, which is deposited at the bases of caverns, and often covers the products of human industry. It is produced by the evaporation of water which falls from the vaults of caves, and deposits on the soil the carbonate of lime which it holds in solution.

If we knew the rate of accretion of stalagmites, it would be an easy matter to deduce the approximate age of the débris they cover up. This has been tried without success. Unfortunately, the data of the problem are exceedingly uncertain. The growth of stalagmites varies greatly according to times, places, and conditions. Hence the astonishing diversity of the results to which calculations have led. One author believes himself quite liberal in attributing only one million years to the formation of two stalagmite layers which have been found superposed in a cave in Kent, near Torquay, England, claiming that these layers together are fifteen feet thick. At the same time an American author observes that the stalagmites of the caves in Virginia increase five millimetres per year, and there is no reason to think that the Kent stalagmites did not form with equal rapidity. At this rate, a thousand years would suffice for their formation.

We have to add that the lower stalagmite, by far the most considerable, may have existed previous to the advent of man. The few flints found below are of a very doubtful shape, as well as rough-looking; besides, there is reason to question their authenticity on account of the many diggings and the attempts to build a long chronology on the deposits of this grotto. However, our American caves are not the only ones that prove the rapidity of such formations under favorable circumstances; we also find a grotto in the county of York, England, where the annual increase is nine millimetres, and Reclus mentions other facts of this kind, especially in one of the grottoes of Adelsberg, Austria.

Undoubtedly, many of the stalagmites do not form as rapidly nowadays, but climatic conditions are not at present so favorable for this formation. It was quite different in the quaternary epoch. At that time there was more vegetation and greater humidity, charged with carbonic acid, the result of the decomposition of plants, and the water had more effect on the limestone. Therefore it would be imprudent to base any calculations on stalagmites, as they do not offer us anything reliable for even approximate dates on the advent of man in any country, no more than the peat-beds or river gravels.

164. (*d*) HUMAN BONES AND OBJECTS OF ART.—Another argument brought forward in favor of man's great antiquity is derived from human bones and objects of art buried in alluvia. In the lower part of the Nile Valley no organic remains of extinct species have been found, but fragments of pottery and baked bricks have been met everywhere. Mr. Horner, from borings in the mud of the delta, found a piece of pottery at a depth of thirty-nine feet; immediately it was inferred that the pottery had been buried 13,000 years. Sir John Lubbock and Sir Charles Lyell, accepting this conclusion, drew wonderful inferences, read in various papers before learned societies; they concluded that the bricks and pottery of Egypt date back from 12,000 to 60,000 years. Unfortunately for all this fine speculation, Sir R. Stephenson found in the delta near Damietta, at a greater depth than Mr. Horner had reached, a brick bearing on it the stamp of Mohammed Ali.[1] Mr. Hor-

[1] Southall, "Recent Origin of Man," p. 474.

ner, moreover, rated the growth of the mud deposits in a given spot at only three and a half inches in a century, but a description of the same spot by a Mohammedan writer, only six centuries ago, shows that the mud is deposited at the rate of over eighteen inches in a hundred years.[1] No wonder that even the *Anthropological Review* pronounces Mr. Horner's evidence as preposterous, and laments that Sir Charles Lyell should have thought it worth his while to notice such absurdities.[2]

Indeed, all these calculations, together with those that have been made on the deltas of American rivers,— the Mississippi, for instance,— rest on arbitrary and false foundations. They suppose that these deposits were always made in a regular and constant manner, which, however, is not the case at all, for they must have been formed much more rapidly formerly when the masses of water were more abundant. Thus in Egypt, especially, movements of the soil have been shown to have taken place which destroy all these "airy hypotheses." These movements produced depressions in some parts of the Nile Valley, whilst it remained unchanged elsewhere. The Nile in a very short time filled up the hollow places with the slime which is at present carried into the sea. Calculations based on the hypothesis of a uniform progress in deposits rest upon a false foundation.

A very curious fact is related by Mr. J. Ferguson, an English resident in India. He says: "From these data it will be perceived how fallacious any conclusions must be which are drawn from borings into the strata of deltas

---

[1] Southall, *op. cit.*, p. 474.

[2] "Pieces of brick stamped with a Grecian honeysuckle, and, therefore, at the earliest dating from the time of Alexander the Great, have been obtained from as great a depth as that of Mr. Horner's borings.' Saville, "On the Truth of the Bible," p. 26.

and calculations formed from local superficial deposits. I myself have seen the bricks which formed the foundation of a house I had built carried away and strewed along the bottom of a river at a depth of thirty or forty feet below the level of the country. Since then the river has passed on, and a new village now stands on the spot where my bungalow stood, but forty feet above the ruins; and any one who chooses to dig on the spot may find my *reliquiæ* there, and form what theory he likes as to their antiquity or my age."[1]

The gentlemen who insist that long periods of time have elapsed since man's advent are not supported by geology, for geology does not solve the antiquity of our species. All it teaches is that man appeared in the quaternary period, and rather towards its end than towards its beginning. But let us remember that this age differed from ours. The causes which modified the surface of the land, and which manifested themselves with unusual intensity, make it impossible to infer its duration from the phenomena which distinguish it. The only criterion which geology offers is the thickness of deposits. As to the time it required to form these deposits, geologists are not agreed.

The present state of science, therefore, authorizes only a negative conclusion. Nevertheless, of all the calculations referred to, the least well-supported is that which so generously distributes its thousands and millions of years among the various periods of the quaternary epoch. In spite of much talk it has been impossible hitherto to prove the insufficiency of the ancient chronology. In the geological facts which they hold up to us, and which we have reviewed and summed up, "we see absolutely nothing," says M. de Lapporent (and

[1] "Quarterly Journal of the Geological Society," Aug., 1863, p. 327.

we agree with him), "which justifies the large figures before which certain authors do not flinch."[1]

165. (2) THE ANTIQUITY OF MAN ACCORDING TO PHYSICAL GEOGRAPHY. — Considerable changes have taken place, we are told, in the distribution of land and sea and in the configuration of the continents since man first occupied the countries of western Europe. According to Lyell,[2] the English Channel did not exist at that time. Mortillet goes a step further, and avers not only that France was in direct communication with England, but that it was also united to Africa and America. According to these views, considerable sinking and submersion of countries must have taken place at intervals since that epoch.

On the other hand, it is claimed that the land has risen. Lyell shows us on the coast of Wales marine shells of quaternary origin at a height of 1200 feet. In Norway he finds marine sediment of the same age at a height of 600 feet. In Sardinia, near Cagliari, marine shells have been found associated with pottery 170 feet above the level of the sea, according to the same author.

All these movements of the earth which are supposed to have occurred after man's advent must have gone on with extreme slowness. Lyell asserts that the rate of rising was not more than seventy-five centimetres per century, because this would be the measure of the oscillations established in our days on the coasts of Sweden. Now, the basis of this calculation is not exact, for observation rather proves a mean rise of three feet per century on the Scandinavian coasts. Moreover, this movement is far from being uniform. It differs not only according to localities, however close to one

---

[1] "Traité de Géologie," 2d ed., p. 1284.
[2] "Antiquity of Man."

another they may be situated, but it varies at different times in the same places. This has lately been again proved in the case of the rock of Pitea, in the north of the Gulf of Bothnia. This rock, which rose only ninety-three centimetres in more than a century (from 1750 to 1851), has risen fifty centimetres in thirty-three years; that is, from 1851 to 1884.

We can show that considerable variations have been observed in other localities. The shores of Scotland, for instance, have risen from five to fifteen millimetres per year; the Cape of Spitzbergen, according to Lamont, has risen over six feet during four hundred years. About one-half of the islands of the Pacific Ocean are believed to be rising continually; the same can be said of the West Indies and the whole of the western coast of America. Among the most remarkable slow movements are those of the southern portion of Greenland; the numerous coral-reefed islands and atolls of the Pacific; the coasts of Holland, Belgium, Denmark, and the south shore of the Baltic Sea. The coast of Newfoundland, in the neighborhood of Conception Bay, and probably the whole island, is rising out of the ocean at a rate which fairly promises, at no distant day, to materially impair, if not render useless, many of its best harbors. At Port de Grave a series of observations have been made which unquestionably prove the rapid displacement of the sea-level in the vicinity. The island of Sicily has also been considerably elevated in recent times; at some places the coast is two hundred feet above its former sea-level.

All these changes can be easily established on the coasts because of the consequences which the least change of level causes. Here, the land has encroached upon the sea; there, on the contrary, it is the sea which has gained on the land. This latter phenomenon has taken place notably upon the northern coast of France, where, at low-water mark, undoubted proofs are met with that the continent formerly extended quite a distance beyond the present coast-line. Here there has been an encroachment of the sea at a recent period.

This increase and decrease of land along the coasts of certain countries are frequently observed. The waters have gained on the ancient coast of England. We know from Diodorus of Sicily that Cornish grain and tin were carried to the Isle of Wight at low-water mark on the backs of beasts. Perhaps it would not be going too far to say that a few centuries prior to this time the British islands were united to the continent.

However, if this rising of the land extended over the whole northern portion of France, it must have been interrupted at times by a contrary phenomenon; for we have proof that a part of this territory was lower towards the end of the Roman epoch than in our days. Some pages back we spoke of the state of alluvial deposits in the Departement du Nord, and of coins with ancient effigies found under a marine layer nine feet thick. We must infer from this that the sea covered this country for some time towards the beginning of the third century of our era, and how could it do this, if the soil was at its present level?

An analogous statement has been made by M. de Mercey regarding the Somme Valley. The discovery of marine shells and of bowlders associated with Roman relics has led this geologist to believe that the sea ascended to Amiens about fifteen centuries ago. Now, the spot where the discovery was made is to-day sixty feet above the level of the sea. Here, again, we would have more than three feet increase per century, if the rising took place uniformly. But there is reason to believe that it took place suddenly. We cannot otherwise explain the violent phenomena which accompanied the receding waters and the traces left behind, even in the city of Lille.

In spite of the denials of certain scientists, these sudden movements are not rare; indeed, they may be even more frequent and better established than slow movements. If space would permit, we could cite numerous instances of the kind which have taken place, even in the last two centuries, from earthquakes and volcanic eruptions, not to speak of other phenomena. We shall mention a few to show how fallacious are theories put forward by scientists who assume to dictate to and guide all.

166. SUDDEN AND GRADUAL UPHEAVALS AND DEPRESSIONS.—The small island of Santorin (Cyclades) sprang up suddenly from the bosom of the water at different periods, especially in 1707 and 1866; the island Nyon rose in 1783 and disappeared again in less than a year afterwards; the island of Julia, or Graham, appeared with the same rapidity to the south-east of Sicily in 1831, only to sink beneath the waves at the end of some months; the Jorullo, a volcano, rose suddenly in 1759 to a height of about 1500 feet in the midst of the Mexican plains; a notable portion of New Zealand rose nine feet in one night, January 23, 1855; the coast of Chili was agitated in our century by movements which had the result of raising the shore and adjoining islands from six to nine feet; a portion of India, representing nearly one square mile, was suddenly buried under the waters of the sea, whilst a chain of hills sprang up about two miles away in the midst of a plain; Calabria sank here and there, to rise afterwards during the terrible shocks of earthquakes which it experienced in 1783; in the valley of the Mississippi lakes eight miles in extent formed in the space of an hour in 1812; a quay of Lisbon sank

suddenly from under a crowd of people at the time of the earthquake in 1775, and engulfed them beneath four hundred and fifty feet of water; finally, the recent catastrophe of the Sonda Islands caused the submersion of other islands, and modified the physical geography of that portion of the globe so that navigators were obliged to somewhat change their course.

The reader can see by this hasty and partial enumeration whether violent phenomena, sudden movements of the earth, are rare in our days. There is every reason to believe that they were still more common during the geological periods, especially during the last, or quaternary period. We do not think that any reliable geologist will question this.

We cannot, therefore, judge of the duration of the quaternary period by the greatness of the oscillations which took place therein. It is well to observe, however, that these oscillations, supposing that they were only three feet per century, would not seriously affect the antiquity of man. Although marine sediments have been found at a height of six hundred feet in Norway, and of twelve hundred feet in Wales, there is nothing in these finds which proves that man existed at the time of their formation. Only in Sardinia have products of human industry been met in sediments of this nature, but at a height which does not exceed two hundred and seventy feet. Undoubtedly, even this is a good deal, if we suppose that the rise has been three feet per century on the average; on this hypothesis we must conclude that man lived in Sardinia nine thousand years ago, which is not in agreement with traditional chronology. But the rate of three feet per century, which has not been adequately established anywhere, is altogether inapplicable to a region so frequently agitated by volcanic eruptions and commotions as the islands on the coast of Italy. Moreover, as we saw before, it is pretty well established that similar risings of land took place in other localities, for instance, on the coasts of Scotland and Sweden. E. Dumas sees in the pottery and heaps of shells found in these places remains of cookery analogous to the Kjökken möddings' of Denmark.

The objection drawn from the ancient connection of Spain with Africa at Gibraltar, and with America by a continent now sunk, does not merit serious attention. It is a hypothesis far from proven, especially as regards the connection of Europe and America. If these countries were connected, it was before the appearance of man, as their fauna prove. It is remarkable that naturalists who admit the junction of Europe and America when there is question of multiplying the proofs of the antiquity of man, are the first to deny the existence of Atlantis (an island of the Atlantic Ocean) when there is question of explaining the peopling of the New World from the Old. Such are the contradictions to which party spirit leads!

167. MODIFICATIONS IN PHYSICAL GEOGRAPHY DO NOT OBLIGE US TO EXTEND TRADITIONAL CHRONOLOGY.—The few considerations which we have already submitted should be sufficient to prove that the modifications in physical geography and the frame of the globe since the beginning of the quaternary epoch do not in any manner force us to extend human chronology. Either these movements took place before man appeared on earth, or they may be explained without accumulating centuries to explain them, as we shall show further on. When we reflect on the phenomena of this nature which have taken place, so to say, before our eyes, during the historic period; when we recall that the description given by Cæsar of the

¹ E. Reclus, "La Terre," vol. i., p. 120.

coasts of France does not agree with its actual shores; when we bear in mind that the quaternary period was much more irregular in its phenomena of convulsion and more agitated than our times, we are astonished that no more considerable changes have taken place in the configuration of the land during the five or six thousand years which have elapsed since man occupied western Europe.[1]

168. (3) THE ANTIQUITY OF MAN AND CLIMATIC CHANGES.—Some scientists are pleased to insist on the slowness with which important climatic changes have taken place in the world since the appearance of man, that is, since the quaternary period. We shall strive to prove that these changes have been exaggerated, and that they do not date back to as remote a period as is pretended.

169. (*a*) CLIMATIC CHANGES HAVE BEEN EXAGGERATED.—The quaternary period, at least in part, is identical with the glacial period, so called because it was characterized by the existence of considerable glaciers. Traces of ancient glaciers are still apparent in the mountainous districts of France, such as the Pyrenees and Auvergne, the Vosges, and particularly the Alps and the contiguous country. 'One of these icy rivers, the least studied of all, did not measure less than three hundred miles in length; it extended from Haut Valais to the hillock of Fourviers, near Lyons, filling in the whole valley of the Rhone—the lake of Geneva included.

However, it is certain that there is much exaggeration in dealing with prehistoric subjects. One school, which is designated the glacial school, teaches that the whole of France, if not all Europe, was covered with an immense mantle of ice. Had this been the case they

[1] Cf. "Dictionnaire Apologétique," article "Antiquité de l'Homme."

ought to be able to establish an interruption in the vegetable and animal life, for, evidently, plants and animals could not have lived under such conditions. Now paleontology does not show anything of the kind. The species which lived before the glacial period for the most part still exist. Among the fifty-seven species of mollusks discovered in the strata ante-dating the glaciers, fifty-four live in our day. All our wild animals, and a certain number which have disappeared, date from the quaternary epoch and were contemporary with the great glaciers. Vegetation, too, in the quaternary period was extremely vigorous. We know this from the little that is left us, but more especially from the presence of a number of herbivorous animals—stags, horses, elephants, rhinoceroses, etc., which enlivened the plains and valleys, not only of Europe, but also of America, at that time. Evidently they could not have lived and propagated themselves without abundant vegetation.

What has most deceived the adherents of the glacial theory is the fact that rocks, gravels, and other materials have been found spread here and there at long distances from the mountains whence they came. The transportation of the so-called erratic rocks has appeared to them inexplicable in any other manner, and the piles of rocks and gravels have been considered as so many moraines, that is, deposits of materials transported by glaciers. They forget that, besides ice, other agents of transportation exist; water in liquid state has often produced analogous effects, and it has been the error of the glacialists to attribute to one the effects of the other.

Erratic rocks and moraines are undoubtedly the ordinary indications of ancient glaciers, but, unless confirmed by other evidence, they are not sufficient proof. In order to convince us, they should be accompanied by striated rocks, as we find them in the neighborhood of our actual glaciers. When all these signs are present together there is hardly any possibility of error; but one alone is not enough, because it may be the effect of other causes.

Because scientists now understand this they are inclined to reduce considerably the extension of the ancient glaciers, and the lowering of the temperature of the quaternary epoch. We must not, however, fall into the opposite excess, and assert, as some have done, that the temperature has rather been reduced since that epoch. It is not only the extension of the glaciers which proves that it was colder in the quaternary period than now; quaternary animals also are a proof of this. At that time lived, on the plains of Europe, particularly on those of France, the reindeer, the glutton, the camel, and the marmot, which are not found to-day except in higher latitudes or at more considerable heights. The mammoth and rhinoceros are no exceptions to this statement, for we know they were organized to live in cold countries.

170. THE TEMPERATURE WAS AT MOST FOUR DEGREES LOWER.—It seems, therefore, that the temperature was really lower in the quaternary period, that is, at the time when man appeared in Europe; but the difference is not so great as some pretend. A lowering of four degrees is sufficient, according to Ch. Martin, to explain the ancient extension of the glaciers. We may even take this figure as a maximum, for it is proved to-day that mankind played the chief *rôle* in the glacial phenomena. The beds of rivers and alluvia tell us that not all water was in a solid state then; the glaciers were much more extended than in our days, and the courses of water were infinitely more voluminous.

The above statement, with regard to the temperature, agrees also with the most recent discoveries. Lately,

Torell, a Swedish naturalist, has discovered our ordinary oyster, *Ostrea edulis*, in a fossil state at various points in northern Germany. It was found imbedded in the so-called cypridina clay, strata which immediately precede the first glacial period. This same oyster lives to-day in the North and Baltic seas, and penetrates northward to the Polar circle. Here, the bottom temperature of the sea is 6° C.; the surface temperature ascends in summer to at least 21° C. Hence, when the *Ostrea edulis* became fossilized in the cypridina clay, the temperature must have been at least as low as it is at present in the Polar circle.

But on the cypridina strata are superposed other strata, which are partly previous to the glacial period, partly posterior to it. They have as guiding fossil a shell called *Yoldia arctica*. The yoldia is at home to-day in the northern Polar sea in places where the bottom temperature varies between 0° and 2° C., whilst the upper surface of the sea does not exceed 5° C. It cannot live in warm waters. From this it follows that, during the glacial age also, especially after the first glacializing in Germany, the climate must have been similar to that on the northern coast of Siberia.[1]

171. (*b*) THE GLACIERS DO NOT DATE AS FAR BACK AS SOME THINK.—It might be thought at first sight that a state of things so different from ours presupposes a very considerable lapse of time and brings us to a remote period. Nothing of the kind. To trace climatic conditions such as we have described, there is no need of taking refuge in the darkness of prehistoric times; it is sufficient to go back fifteen or twenty centuries. All the information we possess about this epoch is sufficient to show us that all Europe and the neighboring countries of Asia and Africa were colder and damper then than now.

[1] "Jahrbuch der Naturwissenschaften," 1889-1890, p. 372.

172. TESTIMONY OF THE WRITERS OF ANTIQUITY.— To the writers of antiquity we are indebted for valuable information regarding this subject. Herodotus describes for us the climate of Scythia as similar to the climate of Lapland and Greenland to-day. He describes the country as completely frozen over during eight months of the year; the Black Sea, for instance, was frozen up so that it bore the heaviest loads; the region of the Danube was buried under snow for eight months, and was watered in summer by abundant rains, which gave to the river its violent course.

Herodotus adds that the ass cannot live in Scythia on account of the extreme cold which reigns there. In the following century Aristotle makes the same remark regarding Gaul. His contemporary Theophrastus also tells us that the olive-tree did not prosper in Greece more than four hundred furlongs from the sea. We need not add that in our days neither the ass nor the olive has any trouble to live in the countries mentioned.

Three centuries afterwards Cæsar speaks frequently and emphatically of the rigor of the winters and the early setting in of cold weather in France; of the abundance of snow and rain. He also dwells on the number of lakes, marshes, and swamps which every moment became obstacles to the marching of his army. He speaks of being cautious to undertake any expedition except in summer, owing to the severity of the climate and the suffering of his troops.

Cicero, Varro, Posidonius, and Strabo also speak of the rigor of the climate in Gaul, which allowed neither the culture of the vine nor that of the olive. Diodorus of Sicily confirms this information. "The cold of winter in Gaul is such," he says, "that almost all the rivers freeze up and form natural bridges, over which numerous armies pass quite safely with teams and baggage;

in order to prevent the passengers from slipping on the ice, and to render the marching more secure, they spread straw thereon."

Virgil and Ovid in turn describe the intensity of cold in the region of the Danube. The former shows that this river was crossed by teams, and that the miserable inhabitants of these countries withdrew into caves, and covered themselves with the skins of wild beasts. We might almost say that the poet describes a scene in the quaternary epoch.

Ovid, who passed several years of his life in that region, is more precise in his description: "The Danube," he says, "this large river, which empties into a vast sea, freezes so as to conceal its fall into the bosom of the Pontus-Euxinus [Black Sea]. Men march with firm step where vessels floated. The waves, frozen by the cold, re-echo under the feet of the horses, and the oxen of Sarmatia roll their heavy carts over these new bridges. I have seen this, yet it can hardly be believed, although my account merits full belief, for I have no interest in disguising the truth. I have seen ice cover the whole extent of the Pontus-Euxinus. It is little to have seen it. I have myself marched over these frozen waters. The wine has changed here into a solid, frozen mass; it is given to be drunk by pieces." And as he fears to be accused of poetic exaggeration, he appeals to the testimony of two ancient governors of Maesia, who could establish the facts like himself. We can see that Ovid took every precaution to be truthful and precise in his statements. The author who would speak thus of the Black Sea in our days would risk his reputation for veracity.

Italy, too, in early days experienced its share of the cold which reigned more severely in the north. Virgil tells us of the snows heaped up, the rivers which carried the ice along, the sad winter which split the stone and bound up the course of large streams, and all this in the warmest part of Italy—at the very base of the walls of Taranto. Horace shows us Soracte, a mountain near Rome, whitened by thick snow; "the rivers stopped by the bitter frost and suspending their courses;" the country covered with snow. To-day the snow lies on Soracte but a very short time.

During the following four or five centuries writers indicate the same severity of the climate in North Italy. Owing to want of space we cannot reproduce their testimony. However, we believe we may draw the legitimate conclusion from the writers we have cited that our climate has modified sensibly since the beginning of the prehistoric period. This is the pronounced view of an eminent author who has made a careful study of this question: "If there was ever a fact demonstrated in history," says M. Fuster, "it is the extreme rigor of the climate of ancient Gaul. All the witnesses, all the opinions, every circumstance, proclaim aloud with one voice the intensity of its cold, the superabundance of its rains, and the violence of its storms. It is in vain to struggle against this fact by opposing to it false notions or prejudices which are supported by nothing; this fact will triumph sooner or later as the truth."[1] We may add that geology and archæology join their testimony to that of history. The learned studies of M. de Mercey on the Somme, of M. de Rossi on the Tiber, of M. Belgrand on the Seine, and of M. Rosemont on the Rhone, have proved that these rivers two thousand years ago rolled much greater masses of water than now.

The same is true of the Danube, of the Rhine, and of other rivers of Central Europe. Algiers was much damper than at present, owing to the humidity of its

[1] "Des Changements dans le Climat." 1845.

abundant vegetation, which has almost totally disappeared. Asia and North America possessed a much more humid and colder climate fifteen to twenty centuries ago. Everything goes to prove that the rivers carried larger volumes of water, the level of the lakes was higher, and the flora was more abundant and varied.

173. CLIMATIC CHANGES DO NOT IMPUGN THE TRADITIONAL CHRONOLOGY.—From these facts we conclude that considerable changes have taken place in twenty centuries. If the volume of water and the intensity of cold were not at that time as great as they must have been in quaternary times, the difference was slight; and we are convinced that many of the phenomena attributed by geologists to the quaternary epoch really took place in historic times. In any case, when we consider the short space of time sufficient for all these climatic modifications, it must be admitted that in order to obtain (if there be any need of it) a degree less in the temperature of the seasons, it is not necessary to go very far back in prehistoric times; surely traditional chronology affords us plenty of time to account for all these changes.

174. (4) ANTIQUITY OF MAN AS INDICATED BY CHANGES OF FAUNA.—Another argument brought in favor of the antiquity of man is the disappearance of the greatest part of the quaternary fauna. It is supposed that this disappearance took place in a slow and gradual manner; and as it is known that man lived at the same time as these animals, it is inferred that man must have appeared upon earth at a very early time.

175. ALLEGED PREHISTORIC ANIMALS COULD EASILY LIVE DURING THE HISTORIC PERIOD.—It is now generally acknowledged that man existed in Central Europe at a period when it was inhabited by animals that are now either extinct or that do not live there at present.

The fact that human remains have often been found mixed with the bones of animals, sometimes with one kind, sometimes with another, does not justify us in dividing the time of man's existence into periods, as some naturalists have done, and in calling these periods after the animals with whose bones human bones are found associated—*e.g.*, the periods of the mammoth and the reindeer. At any rate, we must not imagine these periods to have been so clearly defined that on the day of the death of the last cave bear the first generation of the mammoth appeared. The reindeer and aurochs undoubtedly existed in the mammoth period; it is only called the mammoth period because the mammoth died out in that period, whereas the reindeer and aurochs continued to exist. In order to convince ourselves of this, it is sufficient to cast a rapid glance, first on the animals which disappeared in prehistoric times, and secondly on the species which man has seen disappear in the historic epoch.

The species which have been considered contemporary with man, and which have disappeared in ancient times, are the mammoth (*Elephas primigenius*), the woolly rhinoceros (*Rhinoceros tichorinus*), the great bear, or cave bear (*Ursus spelæus*), the cave lion (*Felis spelæa*), the Irish stag (*Cervus megaceros*), the cave hyena (*Hyæna spelæa*), and the reindeer (*Cervus tarandus*). We shall briefly discuss the antiquity of each.

The co-existence of the elephant with man in Europe perhaps surprises us most, for this animal no longer lives in Europe. Nevertheless, the African elephant at one time roamed over Spain and France, and existed in Hanno's time in North Africa, whilst to-day it is found only in Central Africa. Paleontologists may, at some future day, find the bones of this animal in all of the above-mentioned countries. In Central Africa they may find its remains alongside of a musket-ball; in North Africa, with Carthaginian weapons; then they may surprise their contemporaries by various profound theories about a remote "period of the *Elephas africanus*," during which the North Africans understood the working of iron, the Central Africans knew even the use of the shotgun, whilst, on the contrary, the Gallic plains were apparently a wilderness untrodden by man.

There are two or more species of the elephant which, in the quaternary or post-glacial epoch, seem to have overspread the plains of Europe and Asia in vast herds. One of these (*Elephas primigenius*) we know, from the perfect specimen found imbedded in the frozen soil of Siberia, lived till a modern period. It was covered with long hair, fitting it for a cold climate. There were also three or four species of rhinoceros, one of which (*Rhinoceros tichorinus*) was clad with wool, like the great Siberian mammoth. Mr. Brodie, an English author, observes that it is not yet 3,000 years since the aborigines were hunting this animal in the marshy plains of France together with the mammoth.

These two animals are, to all appearance, the most ancient which have co-existed with man. It was believed for a time that the great bears or cave bears preceded them; but, besides the fact that this species is not always easily distinguished from specimens belonging to existing species, there is now every reason to believe that it did not appear until a recent epoch. Remains of these bears have been found in different localities associated with remains of existing species, and even with those of our domestic animals. Perhaps it is to this species we are indebted for the remarkably large specimens which we find described in documents of the Middle Ages.

The lion, too, is one of the animals which Parthenopex of Blois designates among the inhabitants of the forests of France. The song of "Rôland" also makes it live in the woods of the Ardennes. All we know outside of these documents is, unfortunately, destitute of authority. However, it is certain that the lion was more common then than in our times. Greek writers tell us that it inhabited the mountains of Thrace, Macedonia, and Thessaly. It abounded in Africa, where the Romans captured hundreds of lions for the games of the circus. There is no positive proof that this animal did not inhabit some unfrequented recess of Europe at this time, where it needed not to dread the approach of man as much as in Africa at the present day.

The Irish stag is also one of the species which have totally disappeared, but whose extinction does not seem to date back very far. It has been said of this animal that it was represented upon the monuments, sought after by the Romans for its savory flesh, and imported from England. We place no confidence in this account, though it is far from being wholly improbable. Remains of the Irish elk have been found in peat-beds of recent formation, and the naturalists who are most disposed to make the so-called quaternary species very ancient acknowledge that there is reason to make an exception for this species.

The cave hyena need hardly detain us, for it is probable that it is not an extinct species. It is, say Chantre and Lartet, confounded with the striated hyena, and we must not be surprised to find it all over the world, under a climate relatively cold, for it has a very extensive habitat, and lives in some places, in the Altai, for instance, at a very low temperature. It is not the cold which caused it to abandon Central Europe, but rather the inroads of man and the constant dread of his presence. Besides, its disappearance from Europe is relatively recent.

176. WE CANNOT DRAW A STRICT LINE BETWEEN THE AGE OF THE MAMMOTH AND THAT OF THE REINDEER.—The age of the reindeer is another open question. Here we have a species which is not extinct, but which has merely emigrated to other countries. The reindeer lives in our days in the Arctic regions. What is contested is the date of its disappearance from Central Europe. "It seems to us, however," says M. Hamard, "that it would be easy to come to an understanding on this question, if we abstract for a moment from the prejudice that the reindeer is exclusively a quaternary species, and that the quaternary epoch ended long before the historical era. We quote the clear description which Cæsar gives of this animal: 'There is,' he says (in the Hercynian Forest), 'an ox similar to a stag, which carries in the middle of the head, between the ears, one single horn, bigger and more straight than those we know of, and whose upper extremity is divided into long branches similar to palms. Both male and female have the same type; the form and shape of their horns are the same.'"[1]

Hamard and Geoffroy Saint Hilaire find that this description "bears, even in its errors, the traces of direct and profound observation." The reindeer is the only animal of the stag kind both the male and female of which have antlers, the only one which presents a fulness of the forehead that resembles the ox, and the only one whose horns terminate in long, palm-like branches. There is, however, in Cæsar's description an inexactitude which evinces superficial observation; the antlers of the reindeer do not project from the middle, but from each side of the head. 'A casual observer might have been deceived on account of the divergent disposition of the horns, and especially of certain specimens which

[1] "Bello Gallico," vi., 26.

show a basilar branch that extends in front and gives the horns the appearance of having their roots in the centre of the forehead. Besides, Cæsar speaks of the reindeer by name in another passage. The Germans, he says, make use of small leather cloaks made of the skin of the reindeer. At least, this is the natural translation of the words, "*parvis, rhenonum tegumentis utuntur,*" which it is difficult to explain in any other manner.

177. IT IS CERTAIN THAT THE REINDEER WAS CONTEMPORANEOUS WITH MAN IN EUROPE.—From the statements of Buffon, Cuvier, P. Gervais, in fact of all naturalists that are not influenced by the prejudices of the new archæological school, the reindeer cannot be classed among the animal species which disappeared in prehistoric times. These species number about half a dozen, if we take into account only well-established facts. But let us suppose that they are more than twice as numerous: what is this compared to the forty or fifty species of mammalia and birds which have, to our knowledge, become extinct in the course of historic times?[1] If the proportion of lost animal species were the same in both periods, not ten or fifteen species would have disappeared in prehistoric times, but at least one hundred, because this period must have been three times longer than the historical era, according to the current chronology. Moreover, the destruction of species towards the end of prehistoric times must have been much more rapid than in our days, for some species fell helpless victims to the first occupants of the soil. To be convinced of this we need only remember the very rapid extinction of the American buffalo.

According to Pictet, the post-glacial beds of Europe afford ninety-eight species of mammals, of which fifty-seven still live there; the remainder are either locally

[1] Pozzy, "La Terre et le Récit Biblique," p. 144.

or wholly extinct.¹ According to Boyd Dawkins, in Great Britain about twelve pliocene species survived the glacial period and reappeared in the British Islands in post-glacial times. To these add forty-one species, making in all fifty-three, whose remains are found in the gravels and caves of the latter period. Of these, in the modern period, twenty-eight, or rather more than one-half, survive; fourteen are wholly extinct and eleven are locally extinct.

The results obtained by archæologists also prove that we should not speak about a mammoth or reindeer period. These animals, with various other species, were more or less contemporary. The carefully made researches of M. Dupont in seven Belgian caves, distant from one another, brought to light the bones of the following animals, mixed more or less: mammoth, eighteen bones; rhinoceros, twenty-nine; cave lion, four; hyena, forty-two; cave bear, one hundred and seven; reindeer, eighty-two. Mr. C. Struckman, treating on the fossil remains of the quaternary mammals in the north-west of Germany, found in the alluvions of the province of Hanover and neighboring countries the remains of fifty-five species of undoubted mammals; of these, thirty-five belong to the present fauna of said province, twelve still live in other countries, and eight have died out altogether: these are the mammoth, the one-horned rhinoceros, the aurochs, the Irish elk, the cave bear, the cave hyena, the mountain lion (*Leo barbarus?*), and the cave lion, if the last is not, as is very probable, identical with our lion.²

178. MAN CONTEMPORARY WITH MANY EXTINCT ANIMAL SPECIES.—That man was contemporary with many extinct animals in France and Germany is clearly

¹ Pictet. "Paléontologie."
² "Jahrbuch der Naturwissenschaften," 1885-1886. p. 258.

proved. The same fact is established for Lower Austria. While Much was building a railroad at Stillfried (1872), on the river March, a high wall of loess was cut off almost perpendicularly, and in its débris were discovered many bones, flint implements, coal and ashes. The bones, with the exception of pieces of an antler, belonging to the *Cervus nobilis*, and of smaller pieces, difficult to assign, belonged partly to small, partly to large mammoths. Twelve molar teeth, of which two have a masticating surface of twenty centimetres in length and seven and one-half in breadth, are well preserved, whilst the incisors or canine teeth, and many other bones, fell apart when they were exposed to the atmosphere. However, it was remarked that a great many of them had been broken off by human hands, probably to extract the marrow, as the early troglodytes used to do, according to the general opinion. A small incisor is covered all over with deep, connecting scratches, made either intentionally for the purpose of getting a firmer hold of the tooth, or caused by its being used as a mallet. Among undoubtedly human implements are the so-called prismatic flint knives, two scrapers, one well shaped, two so-called *nuclei* (stone kernels), from which the knives and scrapers were broken off, as also great numbers of waste slivers. The finds show very clearly that the implements, coals, and bones are contemporary. A layer of loess was already deposited when man erected his dwelling-place on the shore of the March; the layer, however, which covered up the old place of encampment is a good deal thicker than the lower and more ancient, so there cannot be any doubt that man lived with the mammoth in Lower Austria at the time when the loess began to form.'

The eminent American naturalist, J. W. Dawson,

¹ "Jahrbuch der Naturwissenschaften," 1886, pp. 259, 260.

after having shown that the elephant, rhinoceros, hippopotamus, Irish elk, machairodus, cave bear, and cave lion all, or nearly all, survived in the human period, adds:

"If we now turn to these animals which are only locally extinct, we meet with some strange and, at first sight, puzzling anomalies. Some of these are creatures now limited to climates much colder than that of Britain; others now belong to warmer climates. Conspicuous among the former are the musk sheep, the elk, the reindeer, the glutton, and the lemming; among the latter we see the panther, the lion, and the cave hyena. That animals now so widely separated as the musk sheep of Arctic America and the hyena of South Africa could ever have inhabited the same forests seems a dream of the wildest fancy, yet it is not difficult to find a probable solution of the mystery. In North America, at the present day, the puma or American lion comes up to the same latitudes with the caribou or reindeer and moose, and in Asia the tiger extends its migrations into the abodes of boreal animals in the plains of Siberia; even in Europe, within the historic period the reindeer inhabited the forests of Germany, and the lion extended its range nearly as far northward. The explanation lies in the co-existence of a densely wooded country with a temperate climate, the forests affording to southern animals shelter from the cold of winter, and equally to the northern animals protection from the heat of summer. Hence our wonder at this association of the animals of diverse habitudes as to climate is merely a prejudice, arising from the present exceptional condition of Europe. Still, it is possible that changes unfavorable to some of these animals were in progress before the arrival of man, with his clearings and forest fires and other disturbing agencies. Even in America, the megalonyx, or gigantic sloth, the mammoth, the mastodon, the fossil horse, and many other creatures, disappeared before the modern period; and on both continents the great post-glacial subsidence or deluge may have swept away some of the species. Such a supposition seems necessary to account for the phenomena of the gravel and cave deposits of England, and Cope has recently suggested it in explanation of similar storehouses of fossil animals in America." [1]

The dinornis and epiornis, gigantic birds which formerly lived in New Zealand and Madagascar, have completely disappeared in our days. On the island of Rodriguez, in the Indian Ocean, east of the island of Mauritius, the ornithological fauna seems to have disappeared only towards the middle of the last century. It still existed in 1730; thirty years later it was on the decrease. A sailor who visited this island in 1760 tells us that the solitaire, one of the birds described by Leguat, who visited this island in 1807, had become extremely rare. Hence we ascribe the date of its disappearance to the middle or last half of the eighteenth century.

From what we have said it is reasonable to conclude that it is wrong to draw a line between the mammoth and reindeer periods, because they are more or less contemporary; secondly, that the prehistoric and quaternary animals could very well have continued to live during the historic period in some part of the East, whither they withdrew gradually from western countries; thirdly, that the number of these animals is in reality very small, and much inferior to that of the species which have disappeared, so to say, under our eyes during the last two thousand years. Therefore, instead of proving the great antiquity of man, the arguments here adduced confirm the recent origin of man.

[1] J. W. Dawson, "The Story of the Earth and Man," pp. 302, 303.

179. (5) ANTIQUITY OF MAN AS SHOWN BY THE TERTIARY AND QUATERNARY FINDINGS.—How would the ancient historian and archæologist Hecatæus feel to-day in the presence of the galaxy of scientists who have shed a halo of light on ancient history and archæology! He claimed relationship with a divine ancestor in the sixteenth degree, and induced the taciturn Hierodulos of Thebes to lead him into the inner sanctuary—that grand hall where the three hundred and forty-five colossal wooden statues of earth-born high priests were found in unbroken series, who bequeathed their sacred dignity from father to son. Similar feelings must arise in the novice when he enters the sacred domain of archæology and passes through the long series of types which scientists are pleased to call quaternary—the man of Neanderthal, St. Acheul, Clermont, etc., and again, when one of the Archimedes of primitive history opens the inner sanctuary, and suddenly shows him the row of tertiary men rising upward to himself, or rather descending downward to the incomparable—to the primitive pithecoid! In fact, all the members of our venerable series of grandsires have not yet been discovered; but singularly misty forms are already dawning in the extreme horizon, and therefore we suggest patience, for soon the sun of science will reach its zenith, and then we may warmly shake hands with those shaggy old fellows, and being free "from blind, authoritative faith," we may revel in knowledge and science.

180. MEANING OF THE TERMS TERTIARY AND QUATERNARY MAN.—But, before going any further, we must explain what we understand by tertiary and quaternary man. To believe in tertiary and quaternary man is to believe in the existence of our species in the respective geological epoch which bears that name.

We know that the history of the earth since the apparition of life upon its surface is generally divided into four epochs of unequal and decreasing durations, called Primary, or Age of Transition, Secondary, Tertiary, and Quaternary. The first two, which were incomparably the longest, undoubtedly preceded the advent of man. Nobody ever pretended seriously to have found in the deposits of these periods the least remains of a human skeleton, nor the least trace of man's industry. No existing animal species goes back to those remote times, and it would be strange indeed were our species to form an exception.

With regard to the quaternary epoch, the most recent and shortest of all, it is quite different. It is certain that man co-existed with some, at least, of the species which characterize the quaternary in France and certain parts of Germany; for example, with the elephant called mammoth, with the *Rhinoceros tichorinus*, its regular companion, and with the reindeer, which lives to-day in other latitudes. But while admitting the existence of man in quaternary times, we do not mean on that account to go beyond the traditional chronology. The quaternary epoch, as it is understood by geologists, extended to times which are not so very distant from ours, perhaps even to the Christian era, for one of the animals which characterize it, the reindeer, as we saw, seems to have lived in Cæsar's time, in the Hercynian forest near the Danube.

The existence of man in the tertiary epoch would involve grave consequences. If it were proved it would undoubtedly, according to all the geologists, be incompatible with traditional chronology. The existence of tertiary man, it is true, would prove nothing against faith, because the so-called Biblical chronology is not imposed upon us by the Church. Excellent Catholics think that we can extend it indefinitely, for they hold the opinion that there are omissions in the Biblical genealogies.

Now let us throw a glance at the arguments which are alleged in favor of the apparition of man in the tertiary epoch. After having done this we will consider his appearance in the quaternary epoch.

181. TERTIARY MAN.—Some years ago there existed a regular "type disease," especially in France and Western Europe. It has not yet quite died out, for symptoms appeared as late as 1884 in the Congress of Blois.

Archæology teaches us that man raised himself gradually from the state of barbarism to civilization; that he passed through a series of industrial phases succeeding one another; that his implements became more and more perfect; at first man employed nothing but stone implements, and these gradually gave way to implements made of bronze and iron. This is not all. The three ages of stone, bronze, and iron are themselves, they pretend, divisible into a certain number of sub-periods, all, or nearly all, prehistoric and marked, as we shall see later on, by industrial progress. The age of stone alone comprises seven periods, of which the first two belong, we are told, to the geological period called tertiary, the following to the quaternary epoch, and the last to the beginning of the present epoch. After these follow two periods of the bronze age and two periods of the iron age; only after all these periods the Roman epoch, the historical epoch, properly speaking, opens. All these industrial stages represent so many different types of primitive mankind. The representatives of this "type disease" at present are Mortillet and Hamy. The latter divides the Tertiary Age as follows:

182. (*a*) THE AGE OF THE ACEROTHERIUM.[1]—This, geologically, is associated with the limestone of Beauce;

[1] A kind of extinct *Sirenia* from the early tertiary.

paleontologically, with the acerotherium and different species of the rhinoceros; archæologically, with the scrapers of Thénay.

183. (*b*) THE AGE OF THE HALITHERIUM.—This is geologically distinguished by the sand deposits of Orléanais, an ancient province of France, which forms the largest part of the departments of Loir-et-Cher, Loiret, and Eure-et-Loir; paleontologically, by the mastodon, dinotherium, halitherium, and monkey (*Hylobates antiquus*); archæologically, by attempts in the art of pottery and by scrapers.

184. (*c*) THE AGE OF ELEPHAS MERIDIONALIS.—This is geologically distinguished by the sand and gravel deposits of St. Prest; paleontologically, by the *Elephas meridionalis;* archæologically, by certain spear points, and by bones, which show traces of human work.

185. INQUIRY ABOUT THE AGE OF THE ACEROTHERIUM.—It is a law in most countries to demand a passport from a stranger who intends to enter or pass through them. If this document is not found in proper order, he is turned back. Now it happens sometimes that officials appointed to inspect these passports do not care much whether the papers of travellers are in order or not. Certainly, this is wrong, and the reader understands that a passport in proper order is quite an important thing, except, perhaps, if he met the passport officer of the Austro-Italian frontier who, after finding out that a traveller had no passport, observed with an air of indifference: "Well, it is just as good; if you had a passport, of course you would be obliged to show it." However, we shall not follow the example of this officer, but firmly demand a passport, made out in proper form, and authoritatively signed, from this tertiary man, who is a stranger to us all. The reason, of course, is that we cannot always rely on the mere assertions of people,

who, like the officer, are indifferent whether one has a passport or not; so we find some archæologists who insist on making us believe many things which do not carry authoritative proofs with them.

186. TERTIARY MAN'S PASSPORT.—Now let us ask: What is the condition of the tertiary man's passport, and where is the authority therefor? Let us see his bones or his works. With regard to the bones, it is generally admitted that none can be produced. Some savants pretend to have discovered human bones in 1844, on the slope of the extinct volcano Denise, near Le Puy (Haute-Loire). Here they found human bones in volcanic tufa, while in the opposite slope, in a similar site, were discovered the remains of a tertiary pachyderm (*Elephas meridionalis*); hence, it is claimed, the human bones are of the tertiary epoch. However, it is not proved that the volcanic débris in both places are derived from the same volcanic eruption; on the contrary, J. Robert furnished proof that the tufa which contained animal remains of the tertiary owes its origin not to the volcano Denise, but to the extinct volcano of St. Ann opposite,[1] while the tufa on the opposite slope, besides human remains, also conceals the bones of the mammoth and other quaternary animals.

With regard to the skeleton found on the Colle del Vento, not far from Savona, in a pliocene stratum, even Hamy assures us that "this pretended fossil man from the lower pliocene of Savona appears to have been buried in the layer in which it has been found much later than the layer itself was formed, to which some naturalist had assigned it without sufficient proof."[2] Thus we are informed only of the works of tertiary man, and

[1] B. Pozzy, "La Terre et le Récit Biblique de la Création," Paris, 1874, p. 299.
[2] "Précis de Paléontologie Humaine," p. 63.

these are of a very doubtful nature. For a long time tertiary man was held up as the most formidable obstacle to harmony between science and divine revelation, and yet the person who raised this question about tertiary man is an excellent French priest, the Abbé Bourgeois. To-day this subject, after having caused a good deal of excitement among the savants of Europe, may be considered as scientifically settled.

In a geological excursion along a hollow road which cuts through the hill on the left shore of the river Thénay (Loir-et-Cher), in France, the Abbé Bourgeois, director of the College of Pont Levoy, perceived at the base of the slope, in a tertiary clay, a fragment of black flint. He picked it up, examined it with much emotion and curiosity, and believed he saw thereon all the signs which indicate the action of man: the engravings, the symmetrical grooves, the traces of percussion and wear and tear, the action of fire, and, finally, the reproduction of certain perfectly known characters.[1] . . . This humble flint stone was destined not only to emit sparks of fire, but to cause a real tempest of fiery discussions. It is unnecessary to relate the consequences of this discovery further than to mention the prolonged hesitations, the incertitudes, the solemn discussions of the savants called together to express their views, the hasty conclusions of some and the determined obstinacy of others. However, we shall continue our rôle as apologists, and pass to the doctrinal objection, which may be resumed in the form of a dilemma.

Either the flint instrument belongs to the ancient layer, was cut by human hands, and man must have existed thousands of centuries ago, or it was fashioned by an intermediate being—a being between the anthro-

[1] See the account written by the Abbé Bourgeois himself in the "Revue des Questions Scientifiques," October, 1877.

poid monkey and man. If by the latter, it is a new and indisputable proof of universal transformism, and the animal descent of man. The adversaries of religious belief do not hide their preference for the latter alternative.

Eloquent apologists and eminent controvertists, alarmed by the accounts given by geologists of the antiquity of the tertiary strata, admit the possible existence of an animal able to invent and preserve fire, to cut stone, and to prepare tools.

With all the respect we owe to such men—our masters—we believe we have a right to protest against a useless concession, the consequences of which seem perilous.

187. IF THE TERTIARY FLINTS ARE TRUE INSTRUMENTS, THEN THEY ARE THE WORK OF BEINGS SIMILAR TO US.—If the tertiary flints are true instruments, cut, as is pretended, by the help of fire, artificially engraved; if they bear evident traces of intentional work, they are the work of beings similar to us—the work of man. To admit the contrary would be filling up the abyss which separates the rational being from the animal; it would be preparing the way for biological evolution applied to the soul; for to make implements is proper to man, because it is proper to man to reflect, to reason, to have general ideas of cause and effect, of the end to be attained, etc. By digging up the earth, by descending from layer to layer, other wonderful débris have been met with, more and more perfect organisms; but it is always the same world of living beings, always the same animality. In presence of a roughly-cut flint, we are astonished, stop, meditate, and say to ourselves. An absolutely new being, a reasonable and free being, has lived here millions of years ago.

If we reject the second alternative, we are face to face with the former: that is, in presence of the astonishing antiquity of man. Grave alternative, truly serious difficulty, if it were based upon well-established facts. It made the eminent Abbé Moigno say: "Indeed, I had lost my foothold; I found myself as drowned in an ocean of uncertainty—on the point of being grieved and full of anguish. . . . Then I made a new effort in my researches, and regained the light." To regain the light and the most perfect serenity it will be sufficient to expose the results of the latest researches, the most recent verdict of the prehistoric sciences.

"About twenty discoveries," says the Abbé Hamard, "have been announced successively which proved the existence of man in the tertiary epoch. We have heard of cut flints, of engraved or perforated bones, and even of human skeletons found in the miocene or pliocene. The most of these discoveries have not stood attentive examination. Even M. de Mortillet admits that none of the skeleton remains in question is authentic. The engraved or perforated bones have been made, not by man, but by the teeth of the dog-fish or by other marine animals. There remain the flints claimed as the work of man. Three localities are said to have furnished them: the commune of Thénay, the neighborhood of Aurillac (Cantal), the vicinity of Lisbon. Everything in the flints of Portugal is contested—their cutting, their origin, and their age. There is no real guarantee of the authenticity of the flints of Cantal, nor of the age of the strata to which they are attributed, nor of the nature of their cutting."[1] Professor Hébert, of the Geological Institute of Paris, declared repeatedly in public that "assertions like those of the Abbé Bourgeois [with regard to his finds] are likely to bring science into discredit." F. Chabas also says: "That the pretended stone implements were not fit for use; some might be

---

[1] "Le Congrès de Blois et l'Homme tertiaire," in "La Controverse et le Contemporain," Nov. and Dec., 1884.

taken as piercing instruments, but their point is so short that it cannot pierce even a piece of leather." Then he directs attention to the laws and forms according to which stone cracks when exposed to the air, and contends that it is very probable that a great number of objects which have been held to be human products originated in this manner.[1] Indeed, Dr. Ratzel proved, from stones exposed to the air and sun, that F. Chabas was correct in his views; for similar slivers, especially from flint stones, broke off like the "human products" of the Abbé Bourgeois. With regard to the markings which, according to the Abbé, were produced by the action of fire, Sir John Lubbock was right in saying that "the action of fire does not absolutely prove the presence of man, as fire may be due to lightning."

We give here an extract from an unbiassed author, M. Cotteau, an eminent French geologist and paleontologist, on the slivers of the Abbé Bourgeois, which had already caused so much excitement among savants, and were supposed to prove the tertiary existence of man. This author says:

"The most interesting question of geology which was studied at the Congress of Blois [in 1884] was the question of man's existence in the tertiary period. . . . Forty members of said Congress, belonging partly to the section of anthropology, partly to that of geology, made a journey to study the geological situation of Thénay and its cut flints. . . . At first they examined the surroundings and established in a positive manner the superposition of the layers. . . . The first part of the question was settled; the situation of Thénay is certainly in the deep strata of the tertiary.

"With regard to the second part, it appears to us that we have almost found a definite solution during this excur-

[1] "Revue des Questions Scientifiques," 1ier année, p. 565.

sion. In spite of the practical diggings on a large tract, and the number of flints brought to light; in spite of the very careful researches of the forty members of the Congress, only two flints offering the appearance of some kind of scratchings were met. The cracked flints are more numerous, but the discussion showed that the cracks attributed to fire and to the action of man may have been produced by physical causes unknown to us. The greater part of the members who took part in the excursion, bearing in mind the enormous antiquity of the strata, remained convinced that man did not yet exist when they were formed. To prove his existence at so remote a time, proofs more convincing are required than a few cut flints, the use of which cannot be defined, which have no surface for striking, and which offer, as evidence of intentional work, only a few irregular scratches, undoubtedly due to chance."[1]

A distinguished anthropologist, noted for his clear and critical mind, writes as follows in the "Revue des Questions Scientifiques:"[2]

"After having read this important discussion, I went to see the vast deposits of flint clay at Maconais.... I gathered cut flints in various strata of this locality; some have a head, and even traces of scratchings that we would not hesitate to attribute to man if these flints were found in quaternary ground. Cracked flints, absolutely identical with those of Thénay, are found by the thousands on the surface of our clays.... It is difficult to explain the strong faith of some anthropologists except by prejudice. For, certainly, without the supposed cut flints, nobody would ever have dreamt of tertiary man, and this proof being unsatisfactory, the hypothesis has no other support."

Many physicists, many archæologists, famous uphold-

[1] "Revue Scientifique," Oct. 25, 1884.   [2] Jan., 1885.

ers of rationalist science, declare that the action of water, sand, and wind, the abrupt changes of temperature, pressure, etc., can alter the shape of flints and give them forms apparently the result of human work. Professor Tyndall possesses a collection of such flints. "If they were met," he says, "along with human remains, we should class them in some period of the stone age." Dr. Virchow expressed the same opinion at the Congress of Lisbon, of which he was president, and supported his views by analogous facts. He said: "Ten years ago I put this question to myself: Can we recognize in a few splinters of flint whether their form is or is not the result of intention? . . . This question is likely to call forth the discussions of several congresses. . . . Here we disagree, and there are many naturalists who deny that the form of these flints is the work of man. . . . For myself I question it, and at the next Congress I will submit samples, with all the characters claimed, which I collected under conditions such that man could not have had anything to do with them."

188. INQUIRY INTO THE AGE OF THE HALITHERIUM.—We will leave the age of the acerotherium to find, if possible, more solid ground in the age of the halitherium. Vain hope! Here we meet in the sand deposits of the Orléanais the same doubt-suggesting stones that were found at Thénay. But this time the chief piece is a stony mass, consisting of a hard gray clay mixed with coal, in which small stones are imbedded. The Abbé Bourgeois concludes therefrom that man knew the use of fire at that early age; yea, that he made attempts in the art of pottery. Hamy is a little more careful; he believes that this mass may have been the product of fire accidentally enkindled through human agency. "But why by man," asks the Jesuit Father Hummelauer, "and not by lightning?"

The Abbé Delaunay[1] noticed, at Pouance (Maine-et-Loire), in two fragments of the thigh bones of the halitherium (a fossil whale) deep incisions corresponding to those which would be produced with a knife or a saw. Here, it seems, we have caught miocene man in *flagrante delicto*. Hamy sees, in spirit, these primitive Frenchmen, standing on about the same level of rudeness as the Australian Papuan negroes of to-day, falling greedily upon a dead halitherium swept ashore, cutting with stone knives its meat from the bones, and then devouring it raw. But in this case also the illusion is short. M. Delfortrie made the incisions, which are repeated in fossil bones at Leognan, near Bordeaux, a subject of his especial studies. "We notice them," he writes, "on almost all the bones of the Aquitanian miocene, on the jawbones of the halitherium and squalodon, and the ribs and vertebral spinals of whales; the pelves and loricæ of turtles are literally covered with them." The number awakens suspicion. Certainly, either the population of Aquitania was very numerous, and then we must be astonished that not even a little bone has come to us from all these men; or it was not, and then their appetite, which led them to gnaw off all the bones in the land, does not cause less astonishment. All these incisions, further explains M. Delfortrie, are of the same nature. "Incisions are not wanting which one might attribute to human effort at first glance; others, straight and deep, look just like those which could be produced with a stone implement; then others follow with a suspicious appearance, bent and turned; and every doubt and deception disappears completely when we look at certain parallel, slightly bent strokes which correspond exactly

---

[1] Let no person in future tell us that the clergy are averse to scientific progress, for here we have two famous Abbés who stood godfathers to miocene man.

to the teeth of a predatory fish (*Sargus serratus*) found just there."[1] Even the Abbé Bourgeois became convinced by Delfortrie's arguments, and abandoned the hypothesis of the Abbé Delaunay.[2] Besides, we do not need to go to Leognan in order to find the key of the phenomenon of Pouance. In this very place, as in many similar places of Chavagnes (Maine-et-Loire), a great number of teeth of different fishes of the shark family are found; they had a good time on the dead halitheria swept ashore.[3] With regard to the dicroseros bones at Sansan (Gers), they have the same value as those of Pouance. The incisions in the rhinoceros bones at Billy (Allier) G. de Mortillet declares to be merely geological impressions.

189. INQUIRY INTO THE AGE OF THE ELEPHAS MERIDIONALIS.—Now let us look at pliocene man. Our road leads us to St. Prest, not far from Chartres (Eure-et-Loir). Here, in 1863, M. Desnoyers found bones of the *Elephas meridionalis* with oblique incisions, which he attributed to man. Sir Charles Lyell became suspicious, and caused some fresh animal bones to be put into the cage of porcupines in the Zoölogical Gardens at London, and after a few days the same oblique lines were noticed on them—the traces of those gnawers. Sir John Lubbock produced further proof of the pliocene man of St. Prest,[4] but only in order to doubt its force forthwith. "Among the bones of the deer were several crania, all of which have been broken in one way, namely, by a violent blow given on the skull between, and at the base of, the horns. Mr. Steenstrup has noticed fractures of

[1] Pozzy," La Terre et le Récit Biblique de la Création," p. 231 *sq*.
[2] "Congrès International," sess. 6, Brussels, 1872, p. 91.
[3] " Études Réligieuses et Philosophiques," etc., v. series, vol. x. Lyon, Paris, 1876, p. 194 *sq*.
[4] " Prehistoric Times," 2d ed., p. 411.

this kind in other less ancient skulls of ruminants, and at the present day some of the northern tribes treat the skulls of ruminants in the same manner. Through the courtesy of M. Desnoyers I have had the opportunity of examining some of the scratched bones from St. Prest. The markings fully bear out the description given by him, and some of them at least appeared to me to be probably of human origin; at the same time, and in the present state of our knowledge, I am not prepared to say that there is no other manner in which they might have been produced."

The pliocene fossil found near the Arno, which showed incisions similar to those of St. Prest, is no better authenticated. The perforation of the carcharodon teeth found in the pliocene crag of Suffolk, according to J. M. Hughues, Quatrefages, and Hamy, was probably effected by natural causes, for instance, by some animal.

The discovery of stone implements in gravel beds in the bluffs of the Delaware River, near Trenton, New Jersey, raised the question of the antiquity of man in America, as these gravel deposits were believed to have been formed by glacial action. The genuineness of these pliocene remains, however, is far from well established. Even on November 21, 1876, Professor Hughues, in a speech before the Cambridge Philosophical Society, expressed his doubts about the existence of man in preglacial times. J. C. Southall says: "Dr. Abbott (the person that first called attention to the relics in the Trenton gravel) was quite astonished to find together implements of such various characters of workmanship; he concluded that the polished pieces descended from the Indians who lived on the Delaware a few centuries ago, the rougher, on the contrary, from the Autochthones of the paleolithic time. But this is a wrong conclusion altogether, as there cannot be any doubt that all the pieces come from the same time."[1] When Dr. Abbott attributes to pieces found in the same place a higher antiquity or different epochs, merely because they are more or less rudely worked, his opinion cannot gain our confidence.

190. TERTIARY MAN NEVER EXISTED.—It is certain from all the evidence, pro and con, found up to the present that pliocene man has failed to furnish proofs of his existence. But there is another ray of hope in the distance. J. Capellini, an Italian archæologist, tells us that he found in Tuscany, at Monte Aperto, not far from Siena, in a blue pliocene clay, fish skeletons which undoubtedly bear traces of human action. A number of paleontologists and zoölogists acknowledged them as such. The discoverer exposed the pieces before the Congress at Buda-Pesth in 1876. After examining them, Dr. Broca declared that, while he refused to admit man's existence in the tertiary period as long as it was based on the finds of Abbé Bourgeois and others, he now for the first time felt his doubts disappear. Warning his associates to be careful, and advising them not to express a definite judgment on a fact implying such important consequences, he at the same time expressed his inclination to let these rib incisions pass as proof of the existence of tertiary man. Even Quatrefages shared the views of Capellini. But alas! the bones found by Capellini met the same fate in the course of time as the flint implements of the Abbé Bourgeois and so many others. To-day one of the greatest naturalists of France, the Marquis de Nadaillac, declares the rib incisions on the bones discovered by Capellini to be nothing but traces of the teeth of some animal.

We may sum up the result of our inquiry in the

[1] "The Epoch of the Mammoth," London, 1878, p. 237.

following propositions: (1) The proof of the existence of miocene man has not been furnished so far. (2) The existence of pliocene man, according to the present state of science, cannot be maintained with any probability.

191. QUATERNARY MAN.—Now let us look for man's existence in the quaternary age. But before doing this, we first put the question: What is tertiary and what is quaternary? Lyell, who has many followers, distinguishes four sub-divisions in these tertiary epochs, to which he gives rather strange names. He calls the oldest strata of the cainozoic period the eocene, that is to say, the dawn of a new period; the two following sub-divisions he calls miocene and pliocene; that is, less recent and more recent. The most recent strata he formerly called pleistocene; that is, the most recent. In his later writings, instead of this name he makes use of the word post-pliocene, and includes the post-pliocene and the recent strata under the name post-tertiary. I will mention only the simplest among the countless other divisions and names: the eogene formation, neogene formation (molasse), and the diluvium.

This brings us to the question: In what relation do these divisions stand to each other, and which are included in the tertiary and which in the quaternary period? In fixing the boundaries between the two periods, Lyell relied principally on the comparison and the percentage of shells. It is evident that this mode of proceeding is arbitrary; even in the oldest tertiary strata there are shells similar to those now existing. Meyer classes the tertiary formations according to the different kinds of mammals found in them; but even by this means no definite line can be drawn between the tertiary and diluvian formations.

"It cannot be denied," he says, "that there are places

where the mammalia of the molasse (miocene) period are found intermixed with those of the diluvian formations, although usually these formations and those of the molasse can be clearly distinguished." "It is most probable," says Reusch, "that the diluvian (the name diluvian is universally given by modern geologists to a whole geological period and formation, which is supposed to be the last of the many geological revolutions that have been produced by violent eruptions of water after the ice age) was not a simultaneous and general inundation of the whole earth; modern geologists believe that instead of this a series of geological events took place which occurred partly in the human and partly in the pre-human period." "Further," says Reusch, "there is no proof of a clear separation between the primeval and the recent fauna and flora; on the contrary, it seems as if, by degrees, long before the first appearance of man, many species of plants and animals had died out, and had been replaced by others; and that this took place in consequence of geological convulsions, changes of climate, and other causes, and occurred at different times and in different countries."

From what we have said it follows that no strict line can be drawn between the tertiary and quaternary epochs. This conclusion is confirmed by the Jesuit Father Hummelauer,[1] who proves that it is highly probable in the first place that the pliocene and the ice age were contemporaneous, at least for central Europe; secondly, that on the whole we have to conceive the post-pliocene or diluvian as contemporaneous with the pliocene or ice age.

Hummelauer bases his hypothesis upon the following facts: In the basin of Balerna (Tessin) and in the

[1] Cf. "Stimmen aus Maria-Laach," 1878, vol. i., pp. 490, 493.

vicinity of Eucciago (province of Como) A. Stoppani found stones and blocks which, on account of their being ground, he recognized as moraines from the ice age, mixed up with a blue, incontestably pliocene clay. While the moraines consisted of primitive rocks from the Alps, especially from Monte Rosa, over forty Mediterranean or pliocene shell species were found in the clay. That the soil where these observations were made was virgin soil, is firmly established. Among other professional men, the eminent and learned Desor, Martins, and Schimper, who deserve great praise for their inquiries into the ice age, have acknowledged the correctness of Stoppani's observations. The glaciers of the Swiss ice age extended their moraines up to a pliocene sea, which just at that time covered the Lombardic plain and reached to the foot of the Alps. Here we have a striking proof, confirmed by other facts, that the pliocene and the ice age were contemporaneous, at least in central Europe. Pliocene flora and fauna developed in low grounds; pliocene waters formed their deposits on the ground beds of the sea, while the glaciers of the ice age reached their greatest extension. "If it is once proved," remarks Dr. J. A. Bianconi, "that the lake which extended to Balerna existed in the ice age, then it is also proved that the torrents of Setta and Reno, which flow in pliocene soil, are torrents of the ice age. Thus pliocene soil appears in quite a new light, namely, as soil formed in the bosom of the sea mostly from the ground rubbish of the glacial epoch. Two phenomena which until the present were conceived as separate are brought into such close relations as to melt, so to say, into a single one."[1] After a careful inquiry into the primitive Swiss world, Dr. O. Heer drew

[1] "Matériaux pour l'Histoire Primitive et Naturelle de l'Homme," Toulouse, 1876, vol. i., p. 230.

attention to the fact that pliocene strata, properly so called, were wanting between the eocene, miocene, and post-pliocene slate coal. He believed he had found the reason for this in the grinding activity of the glaciers, which might have carried off as grinding rubbish the existing pliocene formations. From what we have said it appears that the reason for this may have been simply that there was no pre-glacial pliocene in Switzerland.

192. RELATION BETWEEN THE PLIOCENE AND POST-PLIOCENE.—It is likewise difficult to establish the relation between the post-pliocene or diluvian and the pliocene or ice age.

"There is no sharp line," says E. Lartet, "between the tertiary and the diluvian formations." The same great mammals lived before, during, and after the glacial age. The extension of the glaciers, which cannot be denied, did not bring any essential changes in the fauna and flora. Unessential changes are not excluded, but pliocene and post-pliocene do not appear anywhere as two separate periods in the earth's history. Hence we must conceive the post-pliocene or diluvian as contemporaneous, on the whole, with the pliocene or ice age. The diluvian in the main is the grinding product of the glacial epoch, or of those submersions and elevations about which we spoke in another chapter, and apart from the glaciers. We said these formations were "on the whole" contemporaneous. Locally, the pliocene, ice age, and post-pliocene may appear in some places as three epochs separate in time; in certain places a pliocene flora and fauna may have first developed itself, been afterwards removed by the advance of the glaciers, and when these retreated, may have returned, very little or not at all changed. We can hardly attribute a general chronological meaning to that triple division.

Thus, inside of these formations there is no room for

the geological separation of the tertiary and quaternary periods. The appearance of man does not mark such a separation, because geology has not yet settled finally the date of his appearance; there is room for such a separation between the diluvium and the alluvium, which is acknowledged to be later. Here, at least, great catastrophes have drawn a marked geological boundary.[1] About the latter Dawson says:

193. POWERFUL CATASTROPHES.—"It seems not improbable that it was when the continents had attained to their greatest extension, and when animal and vegetable life had again overspread the new land to its utmost limits, that man was introduced on the eastern continent, and with him several mammalian species, not known in the pliocene period, and some of which, as the sheep, the goat, the ox, and the dog, have ever since been his companions and humble allies. These men, at least in the west of Europe, were the 'paleolithic' men, the makers of the oldest flint implements; and, armed with these, they had to assert the mastery of man over broader lands than we now possess, and over many species of great animals now extinct. In thus writing, I assume the accuracy of the inferences from the occurrence of worked stones with the bones of post-glacial animals, which must have lived during the condition of our continents above referred to. If these inferences are well founded, not only did man exist at this time, but man not even varietally distinct from modern European races. But if man really appeared in Europe in the post-glacial era, he was destined to be exposed to one great natural vicissitude before his permanent establishment in this world. The land had reached its maximum elevation, but its foundations, 'standing in the water

[1] Hummelauer, "Stimmen aus Maria-Laach," vol. xiv., pp. 492-494.

and out of the water,' were not yet securely settled, and it had to take one more plunge-bath before attaining its modern fixity. This seems to have been a comparatively rapid subsidence and re-elevation, leaving but slender traces of its occurrence, but changing to some extent the levels of the continents, and failing to restore them fully to their former elevation, so that large areas of the lower grounds still remained under the sea. If, as the greater number of geologists now believe, man was then on the earth, it is not impossible that this constituted the deluge recorded in that remarkable 'log-book' of Noah, preserved to us in Genesis, and of which the memory remains in the traditions of most of the nations. This is at least the geological deluge which separates the post-glacial period from the modern, and the earlier from the later prehistoric period of the archæologists."[1]

194. MAN TOWARD THE END OF THE ICE AGE.—That man already lived in Europe toward the end of the ice age, *i.e.*, in an epoch when mighty glaciers covered a great part of the European continent, when animals of the cold North and warm South roamed plains without ice, must be considered as an incontestable fact. For even if we doubt, with the careful Dawkins, that most eminent investigator of caves, that any of the skulls found in Europe belong to quaternary times, nevertheless a great number of witnesses remain which evidently prove man's presence at that time. The great archæological find which was made in the year 1886, near the Bodensee, not far from the Abbey of Schussenried, is alone sufficient to prove the existence of diluvian or quaternary man.

Lately, Penk made minute investigations in the localities in which, until now, unquestionable remains

[1] J. W. Dawson, "The Story of the Earth and Man," pp. 289, 290.

of quaternary man have been found, and arrived at some very beautiful results.

It is known that the glaciers of the ice (quaternary) age were subject to considerable fluctuations; colder periods, during which the masses of ice moved forward, were succeeded by warmer ones, during which they withdrew. The first periods of the ice age are the glacial periods, properly speaking; the later, that is, the periods near the end of the ice age, are the so-called inter-glacial periods. Both periods are authenticated by the presence of northern (reindeer, glutton) and southern (mammoth, hippopotamus) animals. Man was contemporary with both animal groups; his remains are found, for instance, at Taubach, Thuringia, with the animals of warmer climates, of the inter-glacial period; at Schussenried with those of the glacial age. At the time of the greatest extension of the glaciers, between the great ice-fields of Northern Europe, which radiated from Scandinavia and the glacial streams of the Alps, advancing towards Central Germany, only a small strip of land in Germany was uncovered by ice. During the ice age this was the only habitable spot for man and animal, surrounded by glaciers; it is the only territory where we find human remains. On the other hand, all places in which human remains are found in countries which were buried during the ice age under the inland ice belong to a later post-glacial period, when mankind had already given up the huntsman's life for agriculture and the breeding of cattle, in the so-called neolithic time. This is the reason why France is much richer in quaternary human remains than Germany. The latter country, at the time of the greatest extension of the glaciers, was covered with ice over much more than one-half its territory, while in France, on the contrary, glaciers covered only one-fiftieth part of the area. In the North German lowlands, in the highlands of South Germany, we do not find any human remains of the quaternary epoch, for the glacier districts and the localities where we meet with remains of quaternary men exclude each other, because the glaciation and the appearance of man took place simultaneously.

Now, on examining the distribution of the places where human remains are found, we remark that they lie not only in the non-glacier districts, but also—and they are the most remarkable here—in the so-called older moraines. For the glaciers of the ice age show chiefly two extensions of the ice, marked by the so-called terminal moraines, between which lies a time of recession, an inter-glacial period. The former extension of the ice reached further down the valley than the latter. Hence all glaciated districts are surrounded by a double wall of moraines, an older exterior and a younger interior one. The places where human remains are found are outside the older wall, and also between the older and younger. From these facts it follows that quaternary (paleolithic) man did not precede the latter (less extensive) glacial period; he rather lived during the inter-glacial and during the last glacial period, hence in a warmer as well as in a colder time,[1] as is also clearly indicated by the varying character of the animal fauna whose remains are found together with those of man. With the end of the last glacial period the early quaternary period ceases and the alluvium begins, introducing the men of the later stone age (neolithic time).[2]

195. EXISTENCE OF QUATERNARY AND DILUVIAL MAN.—From the foregoing the attentive reader will see that it is proven that man lived during the quaternary and

[1] To-day it is almost the unanimous opinion of geologists that there were at least two glacial periods. This is certainly true of Sweden and Norway.

[2] "Jahrbuch der Naturwissenschaften," 1886-1887, pp. 348, 349.

diluvial periods. M. de Nadaillac concludes the first part of his studies of the first men and prehistoric times thus: "The facts abundantly answer the objections against the reality of prehistoric discoveries. . . . A simple flint, cut by man, is as unanswerable proof of his existence as his skeleton would be. To-day the number of human bones incontestably dating back to the quaternary epoch and paleolithic times is considerable enough to allow us to affirm that man lived in Europe with the great bears, the great feline species, the mammoths, etc., when the physical and climatological conditions were absolutely different from those now existing. . . ."[1]

196. (6) ANTIQUITY OF MAN JUDGED BY HIS INDUSTRIAL PROGRESS.—This is another argument brought forward in support of man's great antiquity. Like the other assertions, it has no foundation in fact, as we shall presently show.

Archæologists teach us that man raised himself gradually from the state of barbarism to the state of civilization; that he progressively passed through a series of industrial phases; that his implements, at first of the simplest and roughest description, were gradually perfected; stone, the first material employed, made room for bronze, and iron succeeded bronze. This is not all. The three ages of stone, bronze, and iron have been divided into a certain number of sub-periods, and all, or nearly all, are ascribed to prehistoric times.

197. MORTILLET'S DIVISIONS OF THE STONE AGE.— The stone age alone, according to Mortillet's school, comprises seven sub-periods. The first two belong to the geological period, called tertiary; the following to the quaternary, and the last to the beginning of the present epoch. After this there come two periods of the

[1] Nadaillac, "Les Premiers Hommes," chap. iii., Conclusion.

bronze age and two periods of the iron age; after all these the Roman period, the only properly historical one, begins.

These divisions are based upon the hypothesis that a considerable time must elapse before man—if there was such a being as man in the proper sense of the word—could pass from the savage to the civilized state. Mortillet's various types of primitive mankind may be reduced to the five following: 1. Type of St. Acheul (Somme); 2. Type of Moustier (Dordogne); 3. Type of Solutre (Saône-et-Loire); 4. Type of La Madeleine (Dordogne); 5. Type of Robbenhausen (Switzerland). These types have an archæological foundation; that is, they rest on various finds, such as flint knives, scrapers, spears, etc.

198. FIVE TYPES OF PRIMITIVE MAN.—The archæologists who have adopted Mortillet's view conceive the primitive man of St. Acheul—*the first type*—as on the lowest scale of human development. He knew, indeed, how to give an edge to stone, but he did not know how to fasten it to a handle, in order to increase the strength of his blows. When he wished to build a hut out of the branches of a tree, he sharpened a stone in order to cut off the larger branches, and when this rude implement became blunt and useless, he sharpened another stone for the same purpose. With a cudgel in his hand he fought against wild beasts, and as the man of St. Acheul looked greatly like a gorilla, a chimpanzee, or a baboon, he was obliged to be very careful not to get mixed up with these animals and mistake them for individuals of his own race. But when the man of Moustier—*the second type*—learned how to fasten a handle to his sharp stone, he became a much-feared warrior, and went forth to conquer, armed with a spear and a battle-axe. However, all these implements were yet very imperfect. The man of Solutre—*the third type*—knew enough to

give a point to his laurel-shaped spear and to sharpen the edges. He also exchanged the grater for a regular scraper, but could not yet make any engravings on stone. Now comes the man of La Madeleine—*the fourth type*—who abandoned stone for bone and horn, made implements of reindeer antlers elaborately carved, sometimes with admirably designed figures of animals thereon. Very probably the man of La Madeleine already farmed a little, for he had mortars for grinding wheat. However, in spite of the great progress man continually made, it is strange that our ancestors of La Madeleine did not succeed in giving to the stone hammer a flat face instead of a half-round one. Harpoons he now worked beautifully, and fishing must have become a source of pleasure for him, rather than a means of obtaining his livelihood; of course, Mortillet does not tell us this, but he says the man of La Madeleine knew how to make needles. Whether his ancestors had attained this high degree of progress or not, we get no information from Mortillet's previous types. Henceforth primitive man's progress is very rapid in every respect. The man of Robbenhausen—*the fifth and last type*—invented the art of pottery. He even learned to gamble, it seems, for the type of Robbenhausen had pieces of ivory, on which lines at different distances were marked. Very probably they indicate gambling sticks, like those of the modern Haidas on the west coast of America; or did the man of Robbenhausen use these things for calculation, and keep accounts?

While Mortillet's system found many ardent adherents, especially in France, it met with as many vehement opponents, and, indeed, his subdivisions are not only without foundation, but are opposed to well-established facts. His different industrial types are mostly found mixed up in the same layer of earth. When they are superposed, it is often in the order contrary to that which Mortillet's theory requires. Thus, to quote only the most recent example, A. Gaudry has found in the grotto of Montgaudier (Charente) the industry of La Madeleine associated with the quaternary animals considered to be the most ancient (rhinoceros, lion, cave bears), and superposed on fauna apparently less ancient than the times when the reindeer, bison, and horse flourished.

199. THE AGES OF STONE, BRONZE, AND IRON ARE NOT SUCCESSIVE.—The mistake of Mortillet's school is that it considers the ages of stone, bronze, and iron as successive, whereas they were more or less contemporary. There can be no doubt that for the most part they succeeded one another in the order named. Men used stone and bone before they used metal. Nevertheless, the use of stone long survived the introduction of bronze and iron.

Therefore we must not assign every stone or non-metallic implement to the stone age, for stone implements have been used at the same time as those made of metal, and it cannot be proved that any nation, or series of nations, passed through these three periods contemporaneously or successively, and thus we must not strictly distinguish one from the other.

"Spears with points of stag's horn," says O. Fraas, "arrows with sharp flint heads, and especially stone axes, stone chisels, and stone hammers are found among the Germans, even down to the time of the Franks, and the same is true of races well known to the historians of the classical age. According to Herodotus, Ethiopians accompanied the army of Xerxes who were so savage that they possessed only weapons of stone and bone, and who were dressed in the skins of wild beasts; they had long bows made of the ribs of palm leaves, and reed arrows with pebble points; their javelins were pointed with the horns of gazelles." [1]

Five hundred years later Tacitus mentions tribes, whom he calls Fenni, and of whom he says: "They have no (iron) weapons. Their only means of attack are arrows, to which, having no iron, they give a bone point." "The Homeric heroes," says Vogt, "who knew bronze, or rather copper and iron, in spite of this used to hurl huge stones at one another's heads, and the sling was, until not very long ago, a regular weapon. It is proved by several facts that stone implements, after they were no longer in general use, were used at religious ceremonies, because it was supposed that the metals, the preparation of which required much human work, were to a certain extent unclean." [2] In Sweden, with the exception of a few arrows of bronze, the missile weapons were all made of stone, and these are found alongside of handsomely worked swords and other bronze weapons. Metal was probably too costly to be generally used for missile weapons. [3] Besides, it is quite possible that in many ancient nations only the leaders, the rich and powerful men, had metal weapons, whilst the common soldiers had for the most part weapons of stone, bone, and horn, just as in the Middle Ages only the knights wore steel armor.

The theory of widely separate ages for old and new stone tools, and for bronze and iron, is one of those scientific fancies which further investigation overthrows. To use the words of the Duke of Argyle: "There is no proof whatever that such ages existed in the world." [4] "The negroes of Central and South Africa," writes

[1] O. Fraas, "Die alten Höhlenbewohner," p. 30.
[2] "Archiv für Anthropologie," vol. i., p. 8.
[3] Nilson, "Die Ureinwohner," etc., p. 89.
[4] "Primeval Man," p. 181.

Lenormant, "have never known bronze, and work hardly any copper. Instead of this, they manufacture iron wares in large quantities, and for this purpose make use of a process which was not communicated to them from the outside. Hence they themselves discovered the method of manufacturing iron, and when they gave up the use of stone implements they passed to the manufacture of this metal."[1] Iron ore, as Sir Samuel Baker informs us, is so common in Africa, and of a kind so easily reducible by heat, that its value might well be discovered by the rudest tribes.[2]

Aside of the facts above quoted, we will add the following testimony. Cæsar tells us[3] that the Gauls, when besieging Alesia (52 B.C.), made use of stones and pebbles; Pliny, that the barbarians of the north had spears pointed with the horn of the aurochs;[4] Varro, that in order to grind the grain they employed, as is done in Spain to-day, a plate armed with stone teeth;[5] an epic poem of the fifth century describes two warriors battling with stone axes;[6] St. Ouen, bishop of Rouen in the seventh century, speaks of flint hatchets in his "Life of St. Eligius." The annals of Ireland make mention of projectiles of stone on the occasion of a battle against the Danes, near Limerick, about the year 920. According to William of Poitiers, similar projectiles were used at the battle of Hastings in 1066. It even appears that, more than a century later, the Scots of Wallace made use of stone arms.

The Mexicans and Peruvians, when first visited by the Spaniards in the sixteenth century, were familiar with the working of copper as well as of gold, although totally

---

[1] "Die Anfänge der Cultur," vol. i., p. 57.
[2] Cf. C. Geikie, "Hours with the Bible," vol. i., p. 135.
[3] "De Bello Gallico," vii., 81.   [4] *Ibid.*, ii., 43.
[5] "De Re Rustica," i., 52.   [6] Ampère, "Histoire Litteraire."

ignorant of iron; they retained for common purposes many of the primitive stone weapons and implements. Greece passed from its bronze to its iron age within the period embraced in its literary history; and the history of the art of working iron is traceable with tolerable clearness in the early history of Rome, that is to say, up to the time when the Romans came in contact with the Transalpine barbarians.

Stone, moreover, is rare in some countries, as, for example, in Mesopotamia, and hence it is not surprising to find stone implements of a very rude character co-existing there with advanced civilization in agriculture and commerce.[1] Each "age" in fact runs into the other, and tools of stone, bronze, copper, and iron were used at the same time in not a few places. For instance, a well-made bronze pin was found on the Isle of St. Jean, near Mâcon, France, which till then had yielded only remains of the polished stone period, and M. Chabas found iron under similar circumstances elsewhere.[2] The age of bronze must be limited more and more, says Professor Desor. Iron is found throughout the so-called age of bronze. In Holland, tumuli known as hunnebedden (the graves of the Hunni) are common. Beneath a layer of soil are found rough casings of unhewn stone covering chambers of stone, regularly squared and smooth, with a flooring of broken granite. Under this funeral urns are met with, as well as numerous flint tools and weapons, such as polished hatchets, chisels, arrow-heads, hammers, etc. Some of these are rough, that is, of the oldest age; others are partly polished, still others polished perfectly. Along with these occur samples of pottery, often of elegant shapes, and finely ornamented by means of instruments of wood or

[1] Rawlinson, "Two Great Monarchies," pp. 119, 120.
[2] "Études," p. 552.

bone. Fifty of these barrows have been opened without finding any trace of metal in them, and yet scientific men are of opinion that they are not older than the Roman period, when the country began to rise above the vast floods which till then had covered it nearly every year. Holland and the neighboring low countries seem, indeed, to have been formed from the vast beds of soil worn off the Alps and other mountains by the glaciers, which formerly reached to the North Sea, but had now retreated to Switzerland, and from deposits by the waters of the Rhine, Meuse, Scheldt, Ems, and Yssel. At first only the sand-hills and other elevations, natural or artificial, were habitable, and these in Cæsar's time were so many small islands, whose savage (*silvatici*) and brave inhabitants were believed to live on fish and the eggs of birds.[1] About the beginning of our era the Batavians took possession of the country, but the Hunni lingered among them even during the Roman period, and have left these tumuli apparently remotely prehistoric, but, to give the words of M. Pleyte, dating from the commencement of our era to A.D. 500.

The Chevalier de Rossi has found equally striking proofs of the lateness of the stone age in Italy.[2] "The whole evidence," he says, "proves to demonstration that the neolithic age was very near to historical times." This conclusion is confirmed by the discoveries so frequently made, and every day becoming more numerous, of stone weapons mixed with objects of bronze. C. Geikie found early uncoined money (*aes rude*) along with polished stone weapons; and a number of flint knives have been obtained from Etruscan graves. Indeed, a piece of coined copper money, marking a

[1] "De Bello Gallico."
[2] "Comptes Rendus du Congrès International d'Archéologie Préhistorique," 1871, p. 464.

still later period, has been found in an Etruscan tomb alongside of a stone knife, undoubtedly of the neolithic or new stone period. Not less striking are the results of excavations on the sites of the Romano-Gallic cities in France. Thus at Bibracte, the largest, richest, and most important town of the Ædui,[1] scientific explorers have discovered remains of pottery, jewelry, ornamental work, work on metal and coins, mingled with flint arrow-heads, polished stone axes, and a flint knife. The same results have been obtained on the site of Gergovia, near Clermont; weapons, vases, and large pins of bronze, pieces of jewelry, and Gallic coins have been found along with stone knives, arrow-heads, axes, etc.[2] Similar stone weapons and tools have also been met with on the site of Alesia, in the Jura, in conjunction with the skeletons of Gauls, their personal ornaments, and weapons of bronze and iron, and even the remains of their armor.

The lateness of the stone period has received further illustration by the discovery that the ancient Egyptians, though they already possessed and used all the metals, and enjoyed a high civilization, systematically used stone tools for mining and other purposes. Brugsch found such stone instruments along with remains of ancient pottery in the turquois mines of Midian.[3] They are met with, moreover, so often throughout Egypt, that it appears as if they continued to be used freely in common life.[4] M. Mariette found in the tombs of the ancient Egyptian empire at Saqqara, and the pyramids, bas-reliefs showing workmen cutting wood with a tool exactly resembling the

[1] "De Bello Gallico," i. and iv.
[2] Chabas, "Études," p. 377.
[3] Brugsch, "Wanderungen nach den Turquis Minen," p. 71.
[4] "Leisure Hour," 1870, p. 423 *sq.*

stone axes of the Polynesian Archipelago. There is a stone knife in the British Museum bearing an inscription which shows that it is not older than the sixth century before Christ, another at Athens has a Greek inscription, while a third, at Copenhagen, has one in Runic characters. There is, indeed, no distinct stone age in Egypt, but stone tools are found abundantly along with those of iron and other metals, as if the Egyptians used them for many of the same purposes, and almost as commonly, as the barbarous peoples around them, who did not know the metals or were unable to procure them. Mr. Keast Lord found in his minute explorations of the mines of Midian that the veins of metal had been worked with stone tools exclusively, many of which he brought away with him; and he mentions, also, that owing to geological changes the lake from which the miners received water, both for drinking and for their mining operations, is now gone, though the shells of the freshwater mussel, used for food by the miners, still remain in the old lake beds. Moreover, their huts of rough dry stone without mortar, bearing every proof of the highest antiquity, are still standing; yet the inscriptions show incontestably that these works, and the lakes themselves, date within the strictly historical period, and even as late as the twelfth century before Christ. But for these inscriptions, the mines would certainly have been referred to unknown antiquity, accompanied as they are by the vanished lakes and archaic huts. But it cannot be said that the stone period is even yet a matter of the past, for M. Mariette, having noticed his Arab laborers shaving their heads with razors of flint, and the Arabs of Qournah having showed him Bedouin lances tipped with flint, justly says that he fancied himself transported to the stone period, and arrived at the conclusion that the age of stone survived in Egypt under the Pharaos, the Greeks, the Romans, and the Arabs, and finally that, in a certain measure, it survives in our day.[1]

We must also take into consideration that some nations, for a time, retrograded in culture on account of external circumstances; thus the Polynesians, whose stone axes we mentioned before, are a branch of the Malay race, which separated from the Malays only a few centuries before Christ, and must have been well acquainted with the working of metals. But the island groups of the Pacific Ocean, which they first peopled, did not furnish any metals, and thus after a few generations the secret of metallurgy was lost; consequently wood and stone were once more brought into requisition as materials for weapons and tools.[2] The same can be said about the Guanchoes, an offshoot of the Vandals, on the Canary Islands, who lost the use of iron and boats.[3] The Finlanders, on the contrary, learned the working of bronze in their northern home.

200. CONCLUSION: SINGLE FINDS OF STONE OR IRON DO NOT ESTABLISH A CHRONOLOGICAL ORDER.—In conclusion, the practical lesson which the archæologist must draw from all we have said is: Single finds of stone or iron do not, as a rule, establish a chronological order.

The division into stone, bronze, and iron ages, says Lindenschmidt, is of no more use to us than the division of the products of nature into minerals, vegetables, and animals. Pullman, again, says: "Such a division only benefits the careless directors of antiquarian museums; it enables them to divide the antiquities according to the materials of which they are made (stone, bronze,

---

[1] Chabas, "Études," p. 396; cf. C. Geikie, "Hours with the Bible," vol i., pp. 135–138.
[2] Quatrefages, "Les Polynésiens et leur Émigrations," Paris, 1866.   [3] *Ibid.*

and iron), just as the careless librarian classes his books according to their size; but for chronology nothing is gained by this classification."

201. PALEOLITHIC AND NEOLITHIC AGES.—Of the three periods of culture, the stone, the bronze, and the iron ages, only the first can be subdivided in a somewhat general way into a paleolithic and a neolithic period, *i.e.*, an ancient and a recent stone age. In the first, it is supposed, roughly-worked stone implements were used; in the second, polished stone implements. However, of them also holds good what we have remarked above; they do not appear everywhere, much less contemporaneously in all places. Here the paleolithic, there the neolithic stage is wanting. When both are found, they sometimes follow each other immediately; at others, are separated by longer or shorter intervals of time. Here, also, the truth probably lies in the middle. Their relations in various places have been different, and can be established only by local investigations.

To review our study, we trust we have sufficiently proved the worthlessness of the arguments taken from the modifications which have taken place since man's appearance in the superficial layers of the globe, in its physical geography, its climate, its fauna, and in the implements of man. When we compare the modifications which have taken place in the course of the historic period with those which must have taken place previously, we are astonished that the latter are not more considerable. Far, therefore, from establishing the great antiquity of our species, the arguments we have investigated tend to prove the contrary; they confirm the recent date of man's origin and appearance upon earth.[1]

[1] Hamard, "Dictionnaire Apologétique," article "Antiquité de l'Homme."

202. It is Needless to Have Recourse to Extra-Scientific Hypotheses.—Therefore it is not necessary, in order to reconcile the accounts of science with the chronology of the Bible, to have recourse to extra-scientific hypotheses. Believing, on the one hand, in the great antiquity of many objects made by man, and especially of the flints found in tertiary strata, which some savants, like the Abbé Bourgeois, maintain to be cut after some design, and refusing, on the other, to admit the existence of man at so remote a period, some apologists came to the belief that a being similar to us, although different from our nature in essential qualities, may have lived long before Adam. This unknown being was not a man, but, like man, cut flints in the form of knives and arrows. P. de Valroger was the first who set up these ideas, and P. Monsabré preached them from the pulpit of Notre Dame, in Paris.

203. We Have to Admit that Man is More Ancient than was Formerly Believed.—Whatever there may be in this theory, we could not pass it over in silence; but as it does not rest upon facts and is generally rejected, and as there is no necessity whatever to admit it in the present state of science in order to reconcile paleontology with the Bible, it is sufficient for us to have mentioned it. As long as geologists do not discover a chronometer worthy of confidence to determine the antiquity of our race, they have no right to oppose their unproven affirmations to the teaching of Scripture, and we should not attach more value to their figures than they really deserve. However, while rejecting the exaggerations of several geologists, we admit the following point as established: Man is more ancient than was believed before the progress of geological studies. Paleontology proves it, and its teachings are confirmed by other sciences. Mankind has existed for many ages;

we find the principal races, such as they are to-day, represented upon the most ancient monuments of Egypt. Mankind, therefore, was even then very ancient; because, though sprung from a single pair, it had had time to modify itself so markedly. Philology obliges us to draw a similar conclusion; for at a very remote epoch we meet a number of languages completely different from one another, which could not descend from one primitive language except after centuries. Hence, everything goes to prove that we must put back the appearance of man upon earth further than was formerly done.[1]

However, we cannot determine the time needed for these changes and revolutions in the language and physical conformation of man, our chronometers being entirely defective. Thus we can arrive only at vague results, which do not permit us to draw categorical conclusions regarding the chronology of the Bible and of primitive times. The historical monuments which have come down to us, and of which a great number have been discovered in this century, will put us in the condition to be a little more precise. We shall examine and discuss these monuments in our next chapter.

[1] Vigouroux, "Les Livres Saints," etc., vol. iii., pp. 257, 258.

CHAPTER X.

THE ANTIQUITY OF MAN AND THE CHRONOLOGIES OF INDIA, CHINA, EGYPT, AND CHALDEA.

Chronology of India.—Its great chronological pretensions are not justified.—Chronology of China.—Facts against the credibility of the Chinese chronology.—Chronology of Egypt.—Increasing difficulties in face of new information from the monuments.—Chief authorities.—Contradictory accounts.—The monumental lists.—Chaldea and Assyria offer more precise chronological figures.—Canons or eponymous lists.—The account from the cylinder of Nabonidos.—If it is correct, even the chronology of the Septuagint is too short.—Conclusion.

204. THE CHRONOLOGY OF THE SEPTUAGINT PREFERRED.—As early as the seventeenth century the Jesuit missionaries in China declared themselves in favor of the chronology of the Septuagint, by means of which they could reconcile the annals of China, which they were evangelizing, with Holy Scripture. From the beginning of their mission they had paid attention to it, because "some missionaries believed that Chinese chronology was contrary to Holy Scripture; and although they tried to make the Chinese understand that their chronology agreed with the chronology of the Septuagint, authorized by the Church, these missionaries had always some scruple of conscience."[1] To solve the question, Father Adam Schall drew up a memoir, in which he gave an account of the foundations of Chinese chronology, and sent it to Rome, where it was examined. We are

[1] A. Gaubil, " Traité de la Chronologie Chinoise," pp. 283, 284.

not informed whether it was examined at St. Peter's, but a letter written from Rome the 20th of December, 1637, in answer to the inquiry, declared, "that the Chinese chronology may be followed without scruple, even though it places the reign of the Emperor Yao in the year 2357 B. C., because it does not contradict the Septuagint, whose chronology is supported by the Fathers and the Church."[1]

When Sanscrit studies began to be cultivated in Europe at the beginning of the present century, the scholars who devoted themselves to the literature and history of India claimed a high antiquity for India. But subsequently Egyptologists and Assyriologists, the savants who decipher hieroglyphics[2] and the cuneiform[3] characters of the Assyrians, claimed even greater antiquity for Egypt and Assyria. We shall therefore examine successively the chronology of India, China, Egypt, and Chaldea.

205. (1) THE CHRONOLOGY OF INDIA.—Those who claim a great antiquity for India are mistaken. The best Sanscrit scholars of to-day acknowledge this; they say that their predecessors exaggerated the antiquity of the history and literature of India. Those best versed in Hindoo literature agree that the Hindoos were destitute of the historical instinct. "The Hindoos,"

[1] *Ibid.*, p. 285.
[2] The figure of any object, as an animal, tree, weapon, staff, etc., standing for a word or syllable, or a single sound; a figure representing an idea, and intended to convey a meaning, thus forming part of a system of writing. The name, which has its origin in the idea that the sculptured symbols were exclusively sacerdotal, is now given to any writing of similar character, as that of the ancient Mexicans, Peruvians, etc.
[3] Having the shape or form of a wedge; also called "arrow-headed characters." This term is applied to the inscriptions of the ancient Babylonians, Assyrians, and Persians.

says Kreuse,[1] "do not possess any historical works. They have wrapped ancient events in a poetical cloak of myths, without any attempt at chronology." Hence we cannot draw anything precise or certain from their mythology. "The astronomical tablets," says Klaproth,[2] "to which they ascribed a mythical age, were made up in the seventh century by the ordinary computation of time, but later on were dated back to an earlier period and designated as the work of the gods." The Hindoos, says B. St. Hilaire,[3] have neither chronology nor history; their astronomy is a plagiarism from the Chinese and Greeks; they began to make use of writing only towards the middle of the Sutra period (440 B.C.);[4] they recited their hymns by memory. Their Vedas in the present form were probably not composed before the seventh century before Christ; at all events, not much earlier.

206. VALUE OF HINDOO CHRONOLOGY.—It is generally supposed that the separation of the Aryans and the Indo-European migrations, starting from Bactria, took place towards the year 2500 B.C.[5] This is only a hypothesis, but quite probable. The antiquity which the Hindoos claim for themselves is therefore fabulous.

Talboys Wheeler commences their history only about 1500 before the Christian era, and he has nothing to say about the date of the legends, which he extracts from the Mahabharatam.[6] The famous German Sanscritist, Lassen, places the victory of the Pandavas over the Kouravas later than the year 1000 B.C. This victory ended the

---

[1] "Indiens Alte Geschichte," p. 2.
[2] "Asia Polyglotta," p. 397.
[3] "Journal des Savants," vol. iii., p. 31.
[4] Max Müller, "History of Sanscrit Literature," p. 517.
[5] F. Lenormant, "Manuel d'Histoire Ancienne," vol. iii., p. 431.
[6] T. Wheeler, "A Short History of India," p. 1.

war related in this great epic poem. He holds that the history anterior to this war is fictitious, and that it is impossible to reduce it to a true chronology.¹ Duncker assures us that we give it some credence only to the year 800 B.C.² Biot has proved³ that the numbers from which the Hindoos calculated their world periods were purely imaginary; they are based upon certain astronomical conjectures, and were borrowed, with the astronomy itself, from the Chinese. Cardinal Wiseman says: "A million of years are as soon invented as a thousand, . . . and your readers will believe it all, if you can only get them over the first step—that of believing the kings to have been the descendants of the sun and moon, or some such unearthly progenitors. We cannot indeed help pitying those who have been deceived into the belief of such absurdities."⁴

207. EPIGRAPHICAL MONUMENTS OF INDIA.—The most ancient dated monument on which we find the Hindoos mentioned is the trilingual inscription of Darius, King of Persia, at Persepolis. The son of Hystaspes mentions the land of the Hindusch, India, as one of the countries under his dominion.⁵

208. THE FIRST FOREIGN WRITER ON THE HISTORY OF INDIA.—The first foreign writer who speaks of this country, after seeing it, is the Greek Megasthenes; he was sent, about the year 300 B.C., as ambassador by King Seleucus Nicator to the king of Magadha, Chandragupta, whom he calls Sandracottos, and on his return he wrote his Indica, of which only some fragments have

¹ "Indische Alterthumskunde," 2d ed., p. 611.
² Duncker, " Geschichte des Alterthums," 5th ed., vol. iii., p. 11.
³ "Journal des Savants," 1860, p. 605.
⁴ "Lecture on the Connection between Science and Revealed Religion," vol. ii., pp. 31, 32.
⁵ Fr. Spiegel, "Die Altpersischen Keilschriften," 2d ed., 1881, p. 54.

come down to us.¹ What he narrates of the state of the country, while exaggerated, is generally correct; the 6402 years which he, repeating native stories, attributes to the kings who reigned from Dionysos or Bacchus to Sandracottos are fabulous.² In the country itself no historical monument dated anterior to the third century before Christ has been found. The inscriptions of Açoka (250 B.C.) are the first to make us acquainted with historical facts of certain date;³ they are the most ancient Indian inscriptions from which we can learn the dates.⁴

209. HINDOO LITERATURE.—Indian literature does not permit us to go back any further than Indian history, and it is not nearly as ancient as was believed formerly.⁵ Max Müller distinguishes four epochs in the composition of the Vedas. The first, that of the Chandas, to which the most ancient hymns belong, he places between 1200 and 1000 B. C. He does not find any trace of authentic history in the indigenous literature of India before this time.⁶ According to this savant, the Hindoos did not themselves conceive the idea of chronology; this notion came to them from the outside, like their alphabet and their coinage; it was their relations with the Greeks that led them to date their historical documents.⁷ Therefore, Sanscrit literature

[1] C. Müller, "Fragmenta Hist. Græc.," vol. ii., p. 397 *sq.*
[2] M. Duncker, *op. cit.*, vol. iii., p. 56 *sq.*
[3] Cf. R. Swell, "A Sketch of the Dynasties of Southern India," Madras, 1883, p. 1.   [4] See the summary in M. Duncker, *op. cit.*
[5] Cf. Max Müller, "A History of Ancient Sanscrit Literature so far as it illustrates the primitive religion of the Brahmans," London, 1859; Summary by St. Hilaire, "Journal des Savants," 1860-1861.
[6] Klaproth puts the beginning of true chronological history in the countries of the Ganges only in the twelfth century before Christ. Cf. "Asia Polyglotta," p. 412.
[7] "Ancient Sanscrit Literature," pp. 301-305; see also Max Müller's "India, What it Teaches," p. 292.

THE CREDIBILITY OF CHINESE CHRONOLOGY. 335

cannot furnish us any important data on the antiquity of man.[1]

210. (2) THE CHRONOLOGY OF CHINA.—Quite different from the chronology of India is that of China, which presents to us a long series of regular annals. The Jesuit missionaries, who were the first to study this chronology, were very much surprised by the connection which they remarked therein; the most accepted it without hesitating, and they carried with them several European Sinologues in the seventeenth and eighteenth centuries. Fathers Cibot and Premare, however, had doubts on the authenticity of the dates contained in Chinese histories, and these doubts were shared by Des Guignes, Klaproth, Renaudet, and some others. This division of opinion continues even to-day.

P. Gaubil, S.J., known by his learned works on the chronology of the Celestial Empire, and as the translator of the Shu-king, places the reign of Hoangti (and he does not belong to the first dynasty) anterior to 2400 B.C., and in another place he is not disinclined to put the first year of his reign in 2677 B.C. The Jesuit De Maillac believed that Fohi's reign falls about the year 2941 B.C., although, according to the figures in the Vulgate, the Flood took place towards 2600 B.C., or even later.

211. FACTS AGAINST THE CREDIBILITY OF CHINESE CHRONOLOGY.—However, Chinese dates and calculations are very suspicious, and every means of checking them is wanting. The early inhabitants of the Celestial Empire had no era, properly speaking, like that of Nabonasar or of the Seleucides; the era of Hangti, commencing in the year 2367, was officially adopted by the Chinese government at a time when it was impossible to verify it; it is not universally accepted even by the Chinese themselves. "Who knows what passed in remote antiquity?"

[1] St. Hilaire, " Du Budhisme," in the " Journal des Savants," 1861.

asks the Chinese Yangts, "because no authentic document has come down to us. Whoever will examine the old histories will come to the conclusion that it is very difficult to believe them, and a serious discussion of them will convince him that they are unworthy of belief. They did not preserve any historical document in primitive times."[1] Certainly no European or American author can be more exacting than the Chinese themselves.

212. THE MOST ANCIENT CLASSIC BOOK OF CHINA.—The Shu-king, the most ancient of Chinese classics, contains various historical documents, which, according to M. Legge, its last translator, extend from 2357 to 627 B.C.[2] approximately. "But," observes the learned Sinologue, "however favorable to the antiquity of China, the Shu itself does not furnish us the means to establish a system of chronology for the long period of time it embraces.[3] It teaches that the dynasty of Kau succeeded that of Chang (or Yiu), and the Chang dynasty that of Hia, and that before Yu, founder of the Hia, Chun and Yao had been reigning. . . . Before the dynasty of Han, a list of kings and the duration of their reigns were the only means the Chinese had to determine the duration of their national history. This means would be sufficient had we a complete catalogue, worthy of belief, of the kings and the years of their reigns, but we do not possess this."[4]

Charles Gutzlaff, for many years a Protestant missionary in China, in his history of this country says:

[1] In W. Williams' "The Middle Kingdom," London, 2d ed., 1883, vol. ii., p. 137.
[2] "The Sacred Books of China," Oxford, vol. iii., p. 1.
[3] He admits that Yao reigned during the twenty-fourth century before Christ.
[4] "The Sacred Books of China," pp. 20, 21. For proof, see *Ibid.*, pp. 21–27.

"All those who have written about China are agreed that the Chinese are a very ancient nation. But that the nation existed before the Deluge, or even before the era we assign to the creation of the world, is just as extravagant and ill-founded as the mythological fables of the Romans and Greeks. It is our belief that the Chinese astronomical notions were like those of the Chaldeans and Egyptians, and we give great credit to their calculations of eclipses; but we doubt very much the correctness of their chronology, which the supporters of the antediluvian existence of the empire wish us to believe. Not only the fabulous part of Chinese history is very uncertain, but even as regards the two first dynasties, those of Hia and of Chang, there are grievous difficulties which have never been entirely cleared up. In fact, the authentic history of China should be dated from Confucius, 550 B.C., and the duration of the period previous to this ought to be looked upon as altogether uncertain."[1]

213. CHINESE ASTRONOMICAL CALCULATIONS ARE NOT TO BE TRUSTED.—The astronomical calculations by which it was attempted to fix the antiquity of China are unreliable, except the calculations of the eclipses. M. G. Schlegel, in his "Chinese Uranography, or direct proofs that primitive astronomy originated in China, and that it has been borrowed by the ancient peoples of the West from the Chinese," ascribed the invention of the signs for the two equinoxes and the solstices to the year 16,916 before our era; but his conclusions have no better foundation than those of Dupuis, who attributed an almost equal antiquity to the zodiac of Denderah, which, in fact, dates only from the Roman epoch.

Thus the Chinese annals, considered in themselves,

[1] Ch. Gutzlaff, "Sketch of Chinese History," London, 1834, p. 72.

allow of much criticism. In their most ancient parts they have no chronology; they attribute to their first kings reigns of unlimited time, they are often self-contradictory, and even the Chinese themselves do not agree in regard to their primitive history.

214. ANOTHER REASON AGAINST THE CREDIBILITY OF THE CHINESE ANNALS.—Another circumstance which stands against the credibility of the Chinese annals is the destruction of all the historical books of the empire, which took place in the year 213 B.C. by the order of Chi-koang-ti, founder of the dynasty of Tsin.[1] This prince commanded them all to be thrown into the fire, threatening the disobedient with death. We are told that this command was obeyed by all, except one man, and, thanks to a copy of the Shu-king he had hidden inside of a wall, Chinese scholars were enabled to restore the history of the empire; others say that the Shu-king was dictated by an old man who knew it by memory. The savants of China never have doubted the destruction of the monuments of their ancient literature,[2] and if they are right, all they relate about the times anterior to the dynasty of Tsin deserves little confidence. However, European critics, without contesting the partial fulfilment of the imperial will, believe that a certain number of copies of the Shu-king, and other historical books, must have escaped the flames in a vast empire like China.

But some of those who think it probable that the destruction of Chinese historical literature was not complete have another grievance against Chinese chronology;

---

[1] Gaubil, " Traité de la Chronologie Chinoise," p. 64.
[2] " As the ancient books describing the ancient times were burned by Tsin, why, asks Yangts, should we represent these remote ages inaccurately and show ourselves satisfied with fables?" In W. Williams' " The Middle Kingdom," vol. ii., p. 137.

ancient monuments are wanting to confirm and check it. One of the most recent historians of China, S. Fries, divided his work into two parts: the mythological and the historic period—the latter commencing in the year 775 B.C. Not, says he, because all the events related after this date are historical and all those previous to it fabulous, "but because this is the first fixed point for a comparative chronological study, whilst all prior dates must be considered as estimates."[1] Klaproth, also, denies that Chinese history is deserving of unquestioned belief before the building of Rome, *i. e.*, before the time when Hebrew literature began to decline.[2]

215. OLD CHINESE MONUMENTS.—True, the Chinese appeal to some ancient monuments in support of their historians, but these monuments bear no critical examination. The authenticity of the tablet of Yu, which, as they say, was discovered in 1212 B.C., of the "stone drummer," ascribed to the dynasty of Chu (827–882 B.C.), and of the seventy-two tablets engraved, they say, by order of the seventy-two predecessors of Fo-hi, is justly looked upon with suspicion. Thus we do not find in the Celestial Empire any really authentic document upon which we can build an ancient date.[3]

What we do not meet in China itself we do not find outside of it; we have no foreign testimony in favor of the high antiquity of the Chinese. The Chinese inscription supposed to have been found on a vase of baked clay, discovered by Schliemann in his excavations at Hissarlick,[4] is, according to Mr. Sayce,[5] a Cypriot inscription. The commercial relations which, as we are assured,

[1] S. Fries, "Abriss der Geschichte China's," 1884, pp. ix, x.
[2] "Asia Polyglotta," p. 406.
[3] Th. Fergusson, "Chinese Researches," Shanghai, 1880, pp. 7–12.
[4] H. Schliemann, "Troy and its Remains," p. 23.
[5] See his letter in the "London Times," June 11, 1879.

existed since 3000 years between the Celestial Empire and Egypt, and which were carried on by means of caravans travelling irregularly from the one country to the other by way of India, are not remote enough to justify the pretentions of the Chinese. Small china vases of Chinese origin are said to have been found in the ancient tombs of Egypt.[1] But if Chinese objects—which do not bear any date—have reached the valley of the Nile, it is certain that the workmen who produced them were unknown there. Chabas has shown that the monuments of ancient Egypt do not contain any mention of the Celestial Empire, although the names of many other ancient nations known at that time are found there.[2] The Chinese themselves acknowledge, as Tcheng-ki-tong has done,[3] that their relations with outside nations are comparatively modern.

From what we have said it follows that the primeval history of the Middle Kingdom is a sealed book,[4] and that Chinese chronology does not prove that the Celestial Empire is as ancient as Noe; the chronology of the Septuagint is sufficient for the development of its history.[5]

216. (3) THE CHRONOLOGY OF EGYPT.—The difficulties of Egyptian chronology have increased with the new information furnished by the monuments. The statements of ancient writers were easily reconciled with half knowledge, but better information shows discrepancies which are in many instances beyond the hope of solution. It may be said that we know something of the outlines of Egyptian chronology; but Egyptian history is in a great

---

[1] W. G. Hunter, "Bits of Old China," London, 1885, p. 131.
[2] "Études sur l'Antiquité," Paris, 1873, ch. iv., p. 94.
[3] "Les Chinois peints par eux-mêmes," Paris, 1884, p. 272.
[4] F. H. Balfour, "Waifs and Strays from the Far East," p. 11.
[5] Gaubil, "Traité de la Chronologie Chinoise," p. 277.

measure a mass of conjecture, at least before the time when the Egyptian lists can be checked by what we know of Hebrew and Assyrian history.

217. THE CHIEF AUTHORITIES FOR THE EGYPTIAN CHRONOLOGY.—Our information on the chronology of ancient Egypt comes from three sources: (1) from the accounts of Greek travellers who visited Egypt; (2) from a history written in Greek, a little after the conquest of Alexander the Great, by an Egyptian writer of great reputation, named Manetho, a priest of Sebennytos, in the reign of Ptolemy Philadelphus (about 317 B.C.); to Manetho we owe a list of thirty dynasties, and the length of time each ruled, to which, at least in some cases, the duration of the individual reigns is added; (3) from the monuments, inscriptions, papyri, discovered in the valley of the Nile since the beginning of the present century.

218. THE GREEK WRITERS ATTRIBUTE TO EGYPT A HIGH ANTIQUITY.—The priests of Heliopolis related to Solon that their monarchy had lasted 8000 years.[1] One century later the priests of the same temple told Herodotus[2] that the annals of their kings dated back 11,340 years; that is, 3340 years more. According to Varro (116-26 B.C.), on the contrary, the Egyptian monarchy, in his time, had lasted a little short of 2000 years.[3] Diodorus of Sicily, who visited Egypt in the reign of Augustus, places the reign of Menes, the first human king of Egypt, a little less than 5000 years before his time.[4]

These contradictory accounts are far from satisfactory.

[1] Plato, "Timaeus," ed. Didot, ii., p. 201.
[2] Herodotus, ii., p. 142, ed. Didot, pp. 118, 119.
[3] De Buttafoco, "Études Historiques," p. 9. We do not know on what the calculations of Varro are based, because his work is lost.
[4] Diodorus, i., p. 14, ed. Didot.

The figures given by the Greek travellers deserve only moderate confidence. They could communicate with the Egyptians through interpreters only, and therefore may have misunderstood their information, and we have no more satisfactory guarantee of the truthfulness of those who furnished it. On the other hand, it is evident that their testimony ought to be confirmed by indigenous documents.

219. THE HISTORY OF MANETHO.—Of the latter we possess only one which is prior to recent discoveries, namely the history of Manetho, mentioned above. This author's history itself is lost, but its chronological part has been preserved to us. Manetho attributed to Egypt an antiquity of 30,000 years before Alexander the Great. Here is the summary of his chronology, as it has been transmitted to us by Eusebius:[1]

1. Reign of gods................	13,900 years
2. Reign of heroes.............	1,255 "
3. Reigns of other kings........	1,817 "
4. Reigns of thirty Memphites..	1,790 "
5. Reigns of ten Thinites.......	350 "
6. Reigns of Manes and heroes..	5,813 "
7. Reigns of thirty dynasties...	5,000 "
Total	29,925 years

The reigns of the gods and demi-gods, with which Manetho's list of kings begins, throw discredit upon it, as is but natural; however, after rejecting the first six categories of kings, most critics justly consider the thirty dynasties beginning with Menes and ending with Nectanebo II. as historical.

220. THE VALUE OF MANETHO'S STATEMENTS.— Manetho, writing in the third century before our era,

[1] "Chronicus Canon," i. 1, c. xx., Migne, "Patrologia Græca," vol. xix., col. 182 and *sq.*

proposed to give not only the Egyptian dynasties, but also most of the names of the kings in the order of their succession, with the exact duration of their reigns. These lists, supposing that the kings they enumerate were not contemporary, cover a period of about 5000 years. However, it appears that Manetho's method is often not strictly chronological. As far as we can see, he makes up the sum of each dynasty, except the twelfth, by adding the individual reigns, where these are stated, taking no account of the fact that some of them overlap; in other words, Manetho enumerates as successive reigns which it is certain were wholly or partly contemporaneous. Moreover, he never makes two kings reign conjointly. But from the monuments we know that several kings reigned together for a time. The best known example is that of Ramses II. of the nineteenth dynasty; he was associated in the kingdom with his father Seti at the age of eleven years, and reigned conjointly with him for about twenty years. Afterwards he continued to reign alone for about thirty-six years. Manetho assigns to these two kings 121 years, the monuments 77.

Finally, Manetho frequently increases the length of reigns. Of thirty-seven cases, in which we can check his figures by those of the papyrus of Turin, his numbers are greater 22 times and less only 6 times. The total of these thirty-seven reigns according to him is 984 years, and according to the papyrus, 615, making an excess of one-third.[1]

Hence it follows that the authority of Manetho, although it should not be disregarded altogether, must be checked by the monuments.

221. ORIGINAL MONUMENTS OF EGYPT.—The authentic original monuments for Egyptian chronology are, in

[1] G. Rawlinson, "The Antiquity of Man," London, 1883, p. 20.

the first place, the four royal lists. (1) The papyrus of Turin is the most important; it includes the kings from the gods to the shepherd kings. Unfortunately the papyrus, entire when discovered, was broken into 164 pieces while being transported to Turin, and hence is no longer complete. (2) The tablet of Abydos, discovered in the temple of Osiris, at Abydos, in 1864, by Dümichen, represents King Seti I. and his son, Ramses II., offering homage to 76 kings, their predecessors. The 76 cartouches of these kings are placed in chronological order. Scholars have remarked intentional omissions therein.[1] (3) The tablet of Saqqarah, found by Mariette in the tomb of Tunrei, an officer of Ramses II., at Saqqarah, and at present preserved in the Museum of Boulak, contains 45 royal cartouches, arranged in the same manner as those on the monument of Abydos. In the middle there is a vacant space sufficient for at least five kings. The tablet begins with the sixth dynasty. (4) A similar tablet, found at Karnak, preserved in the "Cabinet of Medals," at Paris, shows us Thotmes III. rendering homage to his predecessors, 61 in number; however, the royal cartouches in this case are not arranged chronologically. Nevertheless, it has the advantage of giving more fully than the other lists the names of several kings from the thirteenth to the seventeenth dynasty, and a great number of names of the eleventh dynasty.

Besides these four great royal lists, we possess a number of shorter ones, dating mostly after the eighteenth and nineteenth dynasties. The hieroglyphic inscriptions on the walls of the temples relating the exploits of Egyptian monarchs, the stelæ of the court officers and different other personages, the Apis stelæ and all kinds of figured monuments, allow us to complete and check, in part, at least, the facts furnished by the royal lists.

[1] "Zeitschrift für Egyptische Sprache," 1864, p. 84.

222. WHAT THESE MONUMENTS TEACH US.—These monuments supply us with an almost complete series of the kings who reigned from the beginning of the eighteenth dynasty, with which commences what Manetho calls the New Empire. The number of kings of this period furnished by the monuments is 63, which is about the same as that given by Manetho. The reigns of several of them were short; some princes reigned conjointly.

For the time preceding the New Empire the monuments present considerable omissions. We have no contemporary documents of the 1st, 2d, 3d, 7th, 8th, 9th, 10th, 14th, 15th, and 16th dynasties of Manetho. The most ancient Egyptian monument is that of Snefru, first king of the fourth Manethonian dynasty. Next in age are the pyramids, and the tombs of this epoch are very numerous, as also those of the fifth and sixth dynasties. Afterwards they are wanting altogether, until the eleventh dynasty. This dynasty furnishes a small number; the twelfth a great number. The Turin papyrus is the principal source for the history of the thirteenth dynasty; then follows complete darkness until the end of the seventeenth dynasty. We have, therefore, contemporary accounts of the 4th, 5th, 6th, 11th, 12th, 13th, and 17th dynasties. According to Josephus,[1] Manetho attributed to them a duration of 511 years; according to Julius Africanus,[2] 955 years. The monuments seem to disprove so long a duration. The Ancient Empire embraces the first six dynasties. According to Manetho, the first lasted 268 years; according to the Turin papyrus, 102 years.

223. NO COMPLETE EGYPTIAN CHRONOLOGY.—Thus, in spite of all these sources of information, we have no

[1] "Contra Apionem," i., p. 14.
[2] Apud Syncellum, "Chronographia," i., pp. 113, 114.

fixed Egyptian chronology. The difficulty the monuments present is that they are incomplete and we have no complete series of them. The Egyptians had no era, consequently had no system of chronology.[1]

The accounts they have left us teach us how many years each king reigned, but without informing us of his relation to the reign of his predecessor and successor. They recorded carefully the length of each sovereign's reign and the life of each Apis; but here they stopped. They failed to indicate the lapse of time between one Apis and another; they did not distinguish the years during which a prince reigned alone from those when he was merely an associate on the throne. Thus, if a king reigned ten years with his father, thirty-two years alone, and three with his son, the monuments ascribe the ten and the three years respectively to his father and to his son, but at the same time assign forty-five years to the king himself. This is no imaginary example; it applies, so Brugsch[2] tells us, to Osortesen I., to whom the Turin papyrus attributes a reign of 45 years. Nay, more, contemporary dynasties, if legitimate, are enumerated as if they had been consecutive; whilst, on the contrary, usurping dynasties are neglected entirely.

Generally speaking, the monumental lists of Egypt are not chronological at all; the papyrus of Turin is the exception. It gives the years of each reign, but, as we have seen, the state of the document permits us to make only a limited use of it.[3] In the first part of the papyri the chronology is defective. It is only after the beginning of the twenty-sixth dynasty that we possess the means to establish a correct chronology.

[1] Lenormant, "Histoire ancienne de l'Orient," vol. i., p. 322.
[2] "Geschichte Ægyptens," p. 40.
[3] G. Rawlinson, "History of Ancient Egypt," 1881, vol. ii., p. 2.

224. DIFFERENCES AMONG MODERN HISTORIANS.—
What we have said explains the great disagreement
which exists among the modern historians who have
dealt with this question. Between the highest and
the lowest of their calculations there is a difference of
no less than 3936 years.[1] "It is," observes G. Rawlinson,
"as if the best authorities on Roman history would tell us,
the one that the republic was founded in 508, the others
in 3508 B.C." These differences are caused in part by
the uncertainty of the length of the reigns of the several
kings, but chiefly by the varying number of contemporaneous dynasties assumed by the authors of these calculations. It is admitted that several dynasties ruled at
the same time, but how many we do not know.[2] All the
chronologies are, therefore, hypothetical, and the one
has no surer foundation than the other. All Egyptologists who have studied the question acknowledge this.

225. THE DATE OF MENES NOT CLEARLY ESTAB-
LISHED.—Nothing is less certain, says Vigouroux, than
the date of Menes' reign. The shortest chronologies
are doubtful and suspicious; the longest are certainly
false. Egypt is somewhat in the same position as China;
their historical documents and dates do not permit us
to construct a satisfactory chronology, and therefore do

[1] *The beginning of the reign of King Menes is put by*

Henne	in the year...6117 B. C.	Lepsius	in the year...3852 B. C.
Lesueur	" ....5773 "	Bunsen	" ....3623 "
Böckl	" ....5702 "	Röckerath	" ....2782 "
Unger	" ....5613 "	Seyffarth	" ....2762 "
Brugsch	" ....4455 "	Poole	" ....2717 "
Lauth	" ....4157 "	Wilkinson	" ....2691 "
Pessel	" ....3917 "	Prichard	" ....2400 "
Lieblein	" ....3893 "	Hofmann	" ....2181 "
Ebers	" ....3892 "		

[2] Lenormant supposes only two contemporaneous dynasties,
Brugsch, five; Lieblein, seven; Wilkinson and Poole, twelve.
Cf. Vigouroux, "Les Livres Saints," vol. iii., p. 289.

not prove that the chronology drawn from the Septuagint is too short. The savants who demand more time base their demand on mere conjectures and hypotheses and nothing obliges us to accept these.

When P. Pierret places the reign of Menes 5000 years before our era, and asserts that 4000 years must have passed' when Menes united Upper and Lower Egypt under one sceptre, he states what is simply an opinion, and one far from being established. We must admit, however, that Egypt existed as a state before this king. All unbiassed Egyptologists admit this. It is supported by a number of well-authenticated facts; for, no matter how far we trace back the history of Egypt, we find it in possession of advanced civilization, of the art of monumental writing, and of religion. We know nothing of its rise and of its infancy. When Egypt becomes known to us its civilization is at full maturity. The Exodus of the Hebrews took place under the nineteenth dynasty; Abraham's visit to the valley of the Nile probably took place during the twelfth dynasty. Egypt was already very ancient at that time; its pyramids had been built a long time before. But here, as in prehistoric paleontology and archæology, we lack reliable chronometers; we can attain no sure results, and must repeat that Genesis, if correctly explained, does not conflict with the results of Egyptological research.[2]

226. (4) THE CHRONOLOGY OF CHALDEA.—Chaldea and Assyria present to us more precise figures than Egypt. They are transmitted to us, not by ancient authors, but by the monuments discovered during the last twenty or thirty years. We have no native historical

[1] "Cours d'Archéologie Égyptienne," Paris, 1883, p. 42. Owen assumes 7000 years for the Ancient Empire. Others claim 10,000, 15,000, and 20,000 years.

[2] Cf. Vigouroux, "Les Livres Saints," vol. iii., pp. 290, 291.

accounts except those contained in the Chaldean history of Berosus, priest of Bel, at Babylon, in the time of Antiochus II., King of Syria (261-246 B.C.); but what the fragments of Berosus tell us of Babylonian chronology is mostly fabulous and was not believed even by the Greeks and Romans. Of the Chaldeans Cicero says: "We should find the Babylonians guilty of folly, of vanity, or of ignorance, and pronounce them liars, when they assert that their monuments include the history of four hundred and sixty thousand years." [1]

227. THE MONUMENTS OFFER MORE PRECISE CHRONOLOGICAL ACCOUNTS.—Indeed, the cuneiform documents, especially the Assyrian, present us with new accounts of Babylonian chronology. The Assyrians are the first people of antiquity who show chronological intelligence. The historical inscriptions which they have left us, and which contemporary explorers have unearthed from the ruins of their capitals, contain the most precise details and are carefully dated. This people did not, like the Egyptians and Chinese, count by the reigning years of their sovereigns, but by *cponymous* officers called *Limmi*, who gave their name to the year, like the Archons at Athens and the Consuls at Rome. They set up canons or eponymous lists, and some of these documents have been found and published. Unfortunately, thus far we possess only a small number of them; however, we have the certainty that the institution of the *Limmi* goes back at least to the fourteenth century before our era, for an inscription of Binnirari I. is dated in the eponymy of Salmankarradu.

228. CUNEIFORM ACCOUNTS.—Thanks to this system of chronology, the Assyrians furnish us more precise dates than we have met with among other ancient nations. We shall call attention to three cuneiform

[1] "De Divinatione," i., 19, 36.

accounts. Sanherib, Sargon's son and successor on the Assyrian throne (705–681 B.C.), and the enemy of Ezechias, in one of his inscriptions reports a fact which took place 418 years before him, under Tiglath Pileser I. (about 1130 B.C.); Tiglath Pileser in turn relates that he restored a temple at Khalah-Shergat, built by Samsi Bin, son of Ismi Dagon, 641 years before. Assurbanipal, nephew[1] of Sanherib, and king 668 B.C., reports an invasion of the plains of the Euphrates by Kudur Nakhunti, King of Elam, 1635 years before the conquest of Elam by himself; that is to say, in the year 2276 before our era.[2] Herewith agrees a fragment of Berosus, preserved by Polyhistor, according to which the Elamite dynasty reigned at Babylon about 2300 B.C. But Berosus knows of more than 30 earlier rulers whose ruined buildings were restored by the Elamite dynasty.

229. THE CYLINDER OF NABONIDOS.—We are brought to a still more remote time, even to the extreme limit of the fourth thousandth before Christ, by an inscription on a cylinder of Nabonidos. This inscription was discovered at Abou-Alba by Hormuzd Rassam, and is at present preserved in the British Museum. Mr. Pinches, in the year 1882, laid before the Society of British Archæology a translation of this cylinder; this translation was approved by Sir Henry Rawlinson. On this monument we read that Nabonidos (about 550 B.C.) disinterred the *timin*, corner-stone of the temple of the sun at Sippara, from a depth of 32 feet, and here he found the tablet of Naram Sin, son of Sargon I., which had not been seen by the eyes of men for 3200 years. It recites that Sargon I. had built said temple of the god Samas (the sun)

---

[1] Vigouroux calls him "son" of Sanherib.
[2] Ménant, "Annales des Rois d'Assyrie," p. 18; *Idem*, "Babylon et Chaldée," p. 55. Cf. Wetzer und Welte, "Kirchenlexicon," 2d ed., Art. "Chronologie."

at Sippara 3200 years before the reign of Nabonidos; that is, about the year 3750 B.C.[1] This elder Sargon, who was formerly believed to have lived 2000 B.C., is brought in connection with the Deluge, and was afterward deified. A summary of the events of his reign, found by Nabonidos on an astrological tablet, proves him to have been a historical person. Hence, according to the cylinder of Nabonidos, the Deluge took place about 4000 years B.C.

230. VALUE OF THE CYLINDER OF NABONIDOS.—If we admit this date we must acknowledge that the postdiluvian chronology based on the Bible, even that of the Septuagint, is insufficient, because it gives us less than 4000 years between the Deluge and the advent of Our Saviour. But although the date given by Nabonidos has been strongly maintained by some Assyriologists,[2] we should accept it only on condition that it be confirmed by future documents. Indeed, it is very hazardous to assume the correctness of calculations made for such long periods, whether by Nabonidos or by those who furnished him this date. Even the fact that it is given in round numbers is suspicious. "I confess to feeling considerable hesitation myself," says Mr. Sayce, "in accepting it (this date) on the strength of one single, unsupported statement of Nabonidos."[3] Mr. Peters remarks: "If such a number met us in the Bible we should certainly refuse to regard it as accurate; why not here also?"[4] If we do not accept contradictory dates given by contemporary chronologists, we should

[1] "Cuneiform Inscriptions of Western Asia," vol. i., pl. 64; J. Latrille, "Der Naboniduscylinder" in "Zeitschrift für Keilschriftforschung," 1885, vol. ii., pp. 350–357.

[2] See H. Rawlinson, "Athenæum," Dec. 9, 1882, p. 781.

[3] Sayce, see "Academy," Nov. 24, 1883, p. 351.

[4] "Proceedings of the Society of Biblical Archæology," May, 1886, p. 142.

certainly hesitate to accept those which Babylonian chronologists give us for a period so remote from them. We find the Assyrians had a chronological canon, which is a guarantee of their calculations, but we must remark that thus far no trace of a similar canon has been found among the Babylonians. But how could Nabonidos compute so accurately the time which separated him from Naram Sin? Did the priests of Sippara not exaggerate the antiquity of their temple, and is not the date of the inscription fabulous or exaggerated, as so many dates in Berosus?

231. EXACT CHRONOLOGY OF CHALDEA.—For Chaldea and Babylonia an exact chronology begins only with the era of Nabonassar, in 747 B.C. The canon of Ptolemy, the royal lists of Babylon,[1] the synchronisms of the Assyrian monuments, and finally the numerous tablets of the family of Egibi (from Nabuchodonosor until Darius, son of Hystaspes), furnish us sure and reliable dates for this epoch, but we have no means to check earlier dates, except the Assyrian documents, which, however, do not go back far enough.

232. CONCLUSION: IF THE CYLINDER OF NABONIDOS IS CORRECT, THE CHRONOLOGY OF THE SEPTUAGINT IS TOO SHORT.—The cuneiform documents are, among all the ancient monuments, those which furnish us the most precise and complete dates. If the date to which Nabonidos assigns Naram Sin is correct, the chronology drawn from the Septuagint is much too short, and we must admit that there are breaks and omissions in the Biblical chronology. But while waiting for new discoveries to confirm or refute the King of Babylon, there is

---

[1] All the Babylonian royal lists may be found in Sayce, "Ancient Empires of the East," pp. 292-299. The Babylonian cuneiform inscriptions have been published in the "Proceedings of the Society of Biblical Archæology," Dec., 1880, Jan., 1881, May, 1884.

no positive proof to show that the figures of the Greek version of the Old Testament are insufficient.

The authentic history of India, and even that of China, can, without much difficulty, be reconciled with the chronology of the Greek and Latin fathers.

The extreme antiquity of Menes, the first king of Egypt, is far from being proved, and there are many reasons to lower his date. The civilization which flourished in Egypt and Chaldea at the time of the most ancient kings known to us, it may be said, requires a longer time to develop than that furnished by the chronology of the Septuagint; and recent paleontological discoveries also demand a greater lapse of time. Only very lately we hear that proofs are not wanting that before the erection of the great pyramids other structures had stood on the site where they now stand.[1] The cultivation of flax in Egypt between 3000 and 4000 B.C. is proved beyond a doubt. We need not, therefore, be astonished to find that the lake-dwellers whose remains are found in Lakes Pfäffiker, Niederwyler, and Constance knew well how to cultivate and use this plant. They knew how to work flax thread, not only into rough twine, fish nets, and mats, but also into fine products like fringes, blankets, embroideries, and hair nets. Samples of textile and tress-work prove the skill of the colonists of Robbenhausen in the working of flax; and to judge from the numerous remains of thin and thick cloth that have been found, we draw no rash conclusion when we say that these people dressed not in furs, but in garments of flax, and this not only in the so-called bronze age, but even in that of stone. A further example of the artistic taste of these people is a nicely worked hair net and a piece of cloth "which is so worked by means of a needle that it forms various

[1] "Jahrbuch der Naturwissenschaften," 1889, 1890, p. 436.

designs." Their taste in dress is proved from an idol of clay. It wears a dress open under the neck, but neatly closed from the breast downward. Its edges, as also the seams of the sleeves, are adorned with square ornaments, with a cross in the middle.[1]

From all we have said it follows that the civilization of Asia must be very ancient. However, as it is impossible to fix dates, we need only repeat. Prove the antiquity of man, and the Bible will not contradict you. The genealogies in Genesis are probably incomplete, hence they cannot serve as a basis for chronology. It is not the end of Holy Scripture to inform us of the precise date of the creation of our first parents, nor of the day and year when heaven and earth were created. It leaves all these questions to the discussion of men, provided they keep within the limits of a wise criticism. Let us always bear in mind the words of Sacred Writ found in Ecclesiasticus: "Who hath numbered the sand of the sea, and the drops of rain, and the days of the world?"[2]

[1] "Jahrbuch der Naturwissenschaften," 1889, 1890, p. 437.
[2] Ecclus. i., 2: cf. Vigouroux, "Les Livres Saints," etc., p. 298.

CHAPTER XI.

UNITY OF THE HUMAN SPECIES.

Importance of the subject.—La Peyrère, the inventor of polygenism.—His system.—Criticism.—The Preadamites.—Historical side of the question.—The strongest polygenists are found in the United States.—The polygenists confound races with species.—Influence of climate and heredity.—The classification of the human species is not yet settled.—The influence of climate and heredity upon man's body is unquestionable.—Examples.

THE unity of the human species, or its descent from one pair, is, from the dogmatic point of view, one of the most important truths derived from the account of man's creation. Nevertheless this doctrine has found a great number of adversaries in our days.

233. IMPORTANCE OF THE SUBJECT. — The theory which affirms the plurality of human species is called *polygenism*, in contradistinction to *monogenism*, the Catholic doctrine which teaches its unity. "It is a very curious illustration of the vagaries of the human mind," says Cardinal Gibbons, "that, while Darwin refers all living creatures, man included, to one, or at most, to a few original types, another school of philosophers has endeavored to trace the human family not to one single pair, but to different sources. Thus while error runs to both extremes, truth rests between them."[1]

In denying that all men descend from one original pair, polygenism evidently contradicts Christian teaching. Revelation teaches us that Adam is the common

[1] "Our Christian Heritage," p. 284.

father of all men. The Church proclaims this doctrine expressly when she sends her missionaries to all parts of the world to baptize unbelievers without distinction of color or physical formation. If, as polygenists pretend, the negroes of Africa, the yellow race of Asia, the Redskins of America, do not descend from Adam, these races could not inherit original sin. Then, what good would it be to administer to them the sacrament of baptism?

Hence the Church would err, and with her all Christians, including heretics and schismatics, if science proved that the whole human family is not descended from Adam, from one common father. By such a discovery the whole economy of Christianity would be modified.

234. THE FATHER OF POLYGENISM.—The father of polygenism is La Peyrère (1594–1676). This author maintained: 1. That the first and second chapters of Genesis relate different facts, and that the man of Gen. i., 27 is not the Adam of Gen. ii., 7. But it is especially from the history of Adam and his posterity that he seeks to draw his proofs of the existence of Preadamites. 2. Cain, he continues, after the murder of Abel, having been condemned to roam upon the earth, expressed the fear of being killed: hence other men existed who were not children of Adam, for the third son of Adam, Seth, was not yet born. 3. When Cain departed he took his wife along. Whence came this woman, if Adam and Eve were the only human beings then living? 4. Soon after the birth of his son Henoch, Cain built a city. He could not have built this city, much less people it, if his father and mother, together with Seth, had formed the whole human family. 5. Finally, the Bible tells us that besides the race of the children of God, there was also the race of the children of men, and that "the sons

of God, seeing the daughters of men, that they were fair, took to themselves wives of all which they chose, and giants were upon the earth in those days."

235. ARGUMENTS OF THE POLYGENISTS.—Let us examine these arguments. In the first place, it is not true that Genesis speaks of different human species. When La Peyrère distinguishes the man whose creation is related in the first chapter of Genesis from the one spoken of in the second chapter, he wrongly interprets the text; for in both cases the Hebrew calls by the name of "Adam" the reasonable creature that proceeded from the hands of God. Even Morton, an American polygenist, is forced to confess that "the sacred text, according to its literal and obvious sense, teaches that all men descend from one pair."[1] Moses, in the first book of the Pentateuch, sets forth in the account of the earthly paradise the history of our first father, whose creation he had only mentioned in the general account of creation.[2] Afterward he continues the history of the children of Adam, without troubling himself about filling in a certain number of omissions, because the matter he had omitted was understood and could raise no doubt in the mind of the common reader. He supposed it useless to state in express terms that Adam and Eve had daughters as well as sons, and that the brothers had taken their sisters as wives; everybody would understand this without being told.

But, say the polygenists, if no other men existed except the Adamites, how could Cain, after committing fratricide, be afraid of being killed by those whom he would meet? We answer: because he knew that men would multiply, and as remorse of conscience rendered him suspicious, what is there astonishing in his being

[1] Morton, "Crania Americana," Introduction, Philadelphia, 1839.
[2] Vigouroux, "Manuel Biblique," vol. i., p. 329 *sq*.

afraid that his crime would be revenged as soon as the children of Adam had become more numerous?

But, again, they tell us, "Cain built a city and called it by the name of his son, Henoch."[1] Voltaire remarked on this passage: "Cain built a city immediately after he had killed his brother. We may ask what workmen had he to build his city, what citizens to people it, what arts, what instruments to construct the houses?"[2] These workmen, these citizens, could not have been children of Adam.

All this reasoning rests on a false supposition. It gives to the word "city" a meaning which it has not in this passage of Genesis. Gesenius, a rationalist, explains this word as follows: "This word has a very extensive signification, and it can be applied to camps. . . . In Genesis iv. 17 we must not understand a city any more than a cave, because a cave is not built. The words of this passage signify nothing but a camp of nomads, shielded by a ditch, or an intrenchment, against the attacks of wild beasts."[3] Cain, therefore, did not build a city, properly speaking, but a "place of refuge," in which he believed himself secure against those who might seek to kill him.

The last argument, drawn from the expression "the sons of God and the daughters of men" is worthless, because it is not necessary to assume that "the sons of God" were not Adamitic men. The descendants of Adam were the creatures of God and, consequently, the sons of God, as much as any other species of men that can be conceived. It is generally believed that the sons of God are the descendants of Seth, who had remained faithful to the Lord, whilst the daughters of men are

[1] Gen. iv. 17.
[2] "La Bible enfin Expliquée," Œuvres, vol. vi., p. 339.
[3] Gesenius, "Thesaurus Linguæ Hebrææ," p. 1005.

the Cainites, whose fathers had been ungodly persons; but whatever the exact meaning of these expressions may be, the interpretation of the polygenists is not a logical deduction from the text.

The polygenists on the one hand pretend to follow the Bible, and on the other directly contradict it. If they really accept its authority, then they ought to admit the unity of human species, because it is evident that Holy Scripture teaches this, saying "God hath made of one all mankind."[1] If they do not accept its authority, how can they maintain that men existed before Adam, or that Adam ever existed, because his existence is known to us only through the Bible.

The error of La Peyrère gained very few adherents in truly Christian times like the seventeenth century. Its author himself abandoned it. And, what is better, he became a Catholic and died a Jesuit.

236. HISTORICAL SIDE OF THE QUESTION.—The thesis which La Peyrère maintained was not absolutely new. The ancients did not believe in the unity of origin of all men. According to their view, most nations were autochthonous; that is, they were supposed to have risen or sprung from the soil they inhabited. The migrations which gave rise to the various peoples of the world had been forgotten, and it appeared quite natural to them that they were born upon the soil they occupied. This was the belief of the Greeks, the Pelasgians, and the Trojans with regard to their own origin.

It was Christianity which taught the opposite doctrine, *i.e.*, the descent of all men from one common ancestor and, consequently, the fraternity of all men. If we except the heresy of La Peyrère, we find no traces of polygenism until the end of last century. The

[1] Acts xvii. 26; cf. I. Cor. xv. 45; I. Tim. ii. 13.

philosophers of that time, who used everything as a weapon to undermine Christianity, did not fail to attack the dogma of the unity of man's origin. "Only a blind person can doubt," says Voltaire, "that the whites, the negroes, the Hottentots, the Lapps, the Chinese, and the Americans are entirely different races."[1]

However, the naturalists of the time vigorously maintained the traditional monogenistic and orthodox opinion. It was reserved for our century to see the opposite view become popular with them. Verey, in his "Natural History of Mankind" (1801); Bory de Saint-Vincent, in an article printed in the "Dictionary of Natural History" by Deterville, which appeared in 1825; Desmoulins, in a volume published the year following, under the title of "Natural History of the Human Races," were the champions of the polygenistic theory.

237. THE STRONGEST POLYGENISTS ARE IN THE UNITED STATES.—More recently polygenism has found strong adherents in the United States. At the time when the slave-trade flourished in America, infidelity tried to propagate polygenism in Europe; in our country, political causes helped to increase the number of its advocates. The friends of slavery tried to prove that the brotherhood of man is idle talk, that the negro in particular has nothing in common with the white man, because he arose from a wholly different stock.

Among the more or less prominent savants who advocated this opinion we may mention Morton, Nott, and Gliddon. Morton divides the human race into twenty-two families, constituting as many groups of nations.[2] Nott and Gliddon maintain that "the surface of our globe is naturally divided into several zoölogical provinces, of which each forms a distinct centre of creation, possessing its own particular fauna and flora. . . . The

[1] "Essai sur les Moeurs."   [2] "Crania Americana," p. 4 *sq*.

human family does not form an exception to this rule; mankind is divided into several species, of which each constitutes a primitive element in the fauna of its particular province."[1] Gliddon speaks of no less than sixty-five families of mankind, embracing over 270 subdivisions.[2] Other Americans are still more extravagant. Knox carries the autochthonist theory so far as to assert that Frenchmen cannot live and prosper in Corsica; the European cannot transplant himself to America. Agassiz also held that men were created by nations, each one having its own language, which he compares to the song of birds and the cries of animals.

238. IN WHAT RANKS THE POLYGENISTS ARE FOUND.
—The polygenists of our country teach the fixity of species, and argue from the actual existence of human varieties to their primordial and original existence. The position has changed, however, and it is in the ranks of the scientists who maintain the variability of species that we must to-day seek the polygenists; that is to say, among materialists and atheists and defenders of transformism without limit. Man, they tell us, was not created man; he became man only through a series of transformations. The inferior species gradually perfected themselves; first, they acquired language and reason, and finally they became intelligent beings. Hence nature, by various means, produced various human species. Consequently, what Holy Scripture teaches about our origin is irreconcilable with the teachings of science. This is Haeckel's view, as appears from what follows:

"The hypothesis of the unity of the human species, which the Indo-Germanic nations borrowed from the

[1] "Types of Mankind," p. 465 *sq.*
[2] "Indigenous Races of the Earth," Philadelphia, 1857, pp. 618–637.

Semitic myth in the Mosaic writings, is absolutely untenable. . . . The great and never-ending debate on this point is based entirely on a wrong statement of the question. As it would be absurd to ask whether all hunting-dogs and all race-horses descend from one pair, so also it is absurd to inquire whether all Englishmen and all Germans come from a single pair, etc. There was no more one first pair than there was one first Englishman or one first German, one first race-horse or one first hunting-dog. Every new species always proceeds from a preceding species, and the slow work of metamorphosis includes a long chain of individuals. . . . It is impossible that the twelve human races or species¹ which we are going to examine should have gone forth from one single pair. . . . According to the Biblical account of Genesis, . . . these human races would all descend from one couple, Adam and Eve, and consequently would be varieties of a single species. Every impartial observer, however, will admit that the differences among these . . . races are as great and even greater than the specific differences laid down by zoölogists and botanists to distinguish animal and vegetable species. Therefore Quenstedt, a distinguished paleontologist, is perfectly right when he says: 'If the negro and Caucasian were snails, all the zoölogists would affirm unanimously that they are species, which could never have come from one and the same pair, from which they gradually separated.' "² Haeckel is the type of polygenetic transformists.

¹ Haeckel holds that there are twelve distinct human species (in his " Geschichte der Schöpfung," p. 598 *sq.*, and in his " Anthropogenie"). Formerly Haeckel contented himself with ten. See his Conference held at Jena, November, 1865, " Ueber den Stammbaum des Menschengeschlechts," in the " Gesammelte Populäre Vorträge," vol. i., 1878, p. 95.

² Haeckel, " Geschichte der Schöpfung." pp. 295, 296.

239. MOST NATURALISTS ARE MONOGENISTS.—Fortunately, science has other representatives who are less one-sided and better fitted to speak on this question. These never hesitated to declare their belief in the unity of the human species. Among them in the last century were Linnæus and Buffon; in ours, Cuvier, Müller, Humboldt, Prichard, Waitz, St. Hilaire, Steffens, Schubert, Rudolf, A. Wagner, Baer, Myer, Wilbrand, Flourens, H. Miller, J. Herschel, Lyell, Huxley, Quatrefages, etc. Burmeister said that those who defend the theory of the unity of mankind are "for the most part insufficiently acquainted with the results of natural science." Every unbiassed man must admit that most of these savants were no novices in natural science. If there are scientific men who need not be defended against the charge of insufficient acquaintance with the results of natural science, they are Alexander von Humboldt, Prichard, and A. de Quatrefages; the last of these is looked upon as the prince of anthropologists. It would be very unjust to accuse these men, as Burmeister does, of being prejudiced in favor of the Bible, because many of them are rationalists; Humboldt praises modern science because, on the Continent at least, it has at last thrown off "Semitic influences."

Let us now consider the arguments the polygenists bring in favor of their theory.

240. IN WHAT THE ERROR OF THE POLYGENISTIC SCHOOL CONSISTS.—The polygenistic school err in confounding *races* with *species;* they pretend that there is no difference between these terms. The monogenists, on the contrary, acknowledge that there are several races of men, but affirm, as the Bible teaches, that there is only one species. But what do we understand by species? *Species* is a collection of individuals having

the same essential characters, issued from one and the same primitive pair, and having the power to reproduce themselves indefinitely. A group of species having the same common characters is called a *genus*. Species is unchangeable in its essential characters, but its accessory characters may be modified under the influence of various causes, and thus give rise to *varieties* and *races*. *Varieties* are individuals of the same species, which are distinguished from the common type by accidental modifications. These modifications are not essential or specific, but changeable and unstable in their nature, although, under circumstances, they may become fixed and durable. By the action of the natural law of reversion, varieties return to the primordial type, at least when outside causes, and especially the union between individuals of the same variety, do not render these transient characters permanent, conformably to the law of heredity, which transmits to children the qualities that belonged to their parents. When the accessory qualities which constitute a variety have become fixed through generations, they form what we call a race.

241. ALL MEN FORM BUT ONE SPECIES.—Now, in applying to the human species these notions, accepted by all ancient naturalists, it will be easy for us to account for all the phenomena which mankind presents at the present time. The solution of the problem is this: All men who live upon earth form but one single species, but this species includes several races; all these races have, as starting-point, varieties, produced accidentally or naturally by various causes—varieties the characters of which have become hereditary. Varieties might manifest themselves sometimes through sudden change in individuals, but generally they are the accumulated result of gradual modifications brought on by circumstances. Hence the error of the polygenists

consists, as we have observed, in confounding races with species, and in pretending that the accessory characters which distinguish races are specific characters. We shall show that these characters are not really specific, but that they have, or at least can have, an accidental origin. Now, to prove that science is not in opposition to Holy Scripture as regards the unity of the human species, it is sufficient to show that this unity is scientifically capable of explanation, and that anthropology is unable to prove the plurality of human species.

242. NO CHARACTER IN THE RACES OF MAN IS SPECIFIC.—What establishes the possibility of the common origin of all men is that there does not exist in any race a distinctive character which is not found sometimes in individuals of another race. None of these characters, therefore, are specific, for otherwise we should meet them only in the species to which they properly belong. But since they appear accidentally in individuals of different races, it follows that they may have originated in the same manner, and that they have become common to certain parts of mankind by means of the "influence of environment and heredity." To convince ourselves of this, we need only study successively the various race characters, and show by the light of observation and experiment that they are all accidental and not essential to the species; consequently they are the result of circumstances, not qualities without which it is impossible to conceive an individual belonging to our species.[1]

243. NO CLASSIFICATION OF HUMAN RACES MADE SO FAR.—This is so true that race characters in mankind are not absolute, but relative, one might almost say, arbitrary; hence until now anthropologists have been unable to arrive at an understanding in regard to them.

[1] Vigouroux, "Les Livres Saints," etc., vol. iii., pp. 324, 325.

some adopting one character as sufficiently distinctive of race, others rejecting it, as subject to too many exceptions. This is the reason why, in spite of the facts accumulated by numerous savants, no classification of races has to this day been made which has been unanimously or even generally accepted. Blumenbach (1752–1840), the founder of anthropology, divides the human species into five races: The Caucasian or white race, the Mongolian (Asiatic) or yellow race, the Ethiopian (African) or black race, the American or red race, and the Malay or brown race. But Blumenbach himself acknowledges that his classification is arbitrary. St. Hilaire, like Retzius, divides nations into long-skulled and short-skulled (dolichocephalic and brachycephalic); among the first he includes elongated and oval skulls (Ethiopian and Caucasian races); among the second, pyramidal skulls (Mongolian race). Again, he divides both classes according to the position of the jaw, with which the formation of the forehead harmonizes, into straight-jawed and slanting-jawed races (orthognathic and prognathic). In this way he gets four principal types. To the long-skulled races with straight jaws belong the Celtic, Germanic, Romanic, and Hindoo races; to the round-skulled races with straight jaws, the Slavs, the Lapps, the Persians, the Turks, the Polynesians, etc; to the round-skulled with slanting jaws, the Tartars, Mongols, Malays, and several western American tribes; to the long-skulled races with slanting jaws, the Australians, Chinese, Japanese, negroes, Esquimaux, and most of the eastern American tribes.

Mr. Latham distinguishes three great varieties: The Mongolides, Atlantides, and Japhetides, which he subdivides again into a multitude of branches.[1] The Bel-

[1] R. G. Latham, "The Natural History of the Varieties of Man," p. 30.

gian naturalist, M. d'Omalius, of Holloy, classifying the races of men by the color of their skin, admits five: the White, Black, Yellow, Brown, and Red. The polygenists, as we saw before, propose the most various and most complicated divisions.

The classification of races is so difficult that Quatrefages, after having devoted the greater part of his life to anthropology, finally renounces every attempt at a scientific classification. It is acknowledged by every school that the classification of the human species is yet to be made, and all the efforts made thus far are open to criticism. A. Hovelacque says:

"It is very difficult to classify races; in doing so we must ignore characters, which are just as important as the color of the skin. There are, for instance, great differences between the Blacks of the southern Soudan and the Blacks of the Andaman Islands; between the Blacks of the south of India (Dravidians) and the Papuans of New Guinea. The nature of the hair, the cranial form, the height, are equally important characters; but they cannot serve as basis for an ethnographical classification. It is sufficient to recall to mind that some black races have crisp, others woolly hair; that some individuals of these races have oblong, and others round heads. It is equally impossible to adopt a linguistic basis. In fact, one and the same linguistic family very often embraces peoples very different from each other: for instance, the Lapps and Finlanders, so different in race, speak idioms which belong to the same family. Nor is a geographical classification acceptable. Asia, for instance, contains black races, like the southern Hindoos (Dravidians), white races, like a great number of the northern Hindoos, and people who belong to the so-called yellow races. Oceanica with its Papuans and Polynesians, Africa with its Blacks and Semitics, are in a similar position. Can they be classified according to their civilization by placing first the inferior races, and then passing to the pastoral people, to the agriculturists, and finally to the more cultivated peoples of Europe? This seems equally inadmissible. In fact, we need give only one instance to show the incorrectness of this method, for we must in that case separate from their relatives the American tribes that still lag on the lowest steps of the human ladder—such as the Botocudos of Brazil and the inhabitants of Tierra del Fuego."[1]

There is, perhaps, not a single negro tribe, if we may rely on Prichard's authority, in which all the characters ascribed to the negro are found fully developed. These characters are distributed among different tribes in various ways, combined in every instance with some of the characters belonging to Europeans or Asiatics.[2] The alleged persistence of the negro type, says Waitz, is mostly imaginary; this type is in reality confined to comparatively few peoples, and we find among negroes many other types, which may partly be considered as transitions to European forms and partly as variations and modifications of the negro type itself.[3]

Thus, according to the most recent works, there is no really scientific classification of the races of mankind. In other words, all the divisions that have been proposed are arbitrary; and thus far it has not been possible to discover any character peculiar to each race.

244. THE PRINCIPAL DISTINGUISHING CHARACTERS.—From the preceding statement it follows that the principal characters which distinguish men or nations

---

[1] A. Hovelacque, "Les Races Humaines," Paris, 1882, pp. 7, 8.
[2] Prichard, "Researches," etc., vol. ii., p. 340.
[3] Waitz, "Anthropologie," vol. i., p. 339.

from one another are differences in organic conformation—the color, the hair, and the language. These are the characters we shall now examine in order to find out whether they are original, or only accidental modifications of the primitive type that have become stable in the course of time.

245. INFLUENCE OF ENVIRONMENT ON THE CHARACTERS OF THE RACES OF MANKIND.—If we examine these characters we shall find that they may arise from the influence of environment and of heredity. By the influence of environment we understand the influence of climate, nourishment, mode of life, customs, civilization—in a word, all that is connected with the place and time in which man lives and that can exercise a certain influence upon the physical, intellectual, and moral development of the individual. The influence of environment is unquestionable. Here are a number of well-proven facts.

Vegetables whiten when they are excluded from the light; and they not only whiten on the surface, but the absence of light affects the texture of the plant, its taste, and the properties of its juice. The animals of the polar regions turn white at the approach of winter. The small and shabby bulls of Sologne, if transported into the valley of the Loire take an altogether different shape and quality in one or two generations. The Swiss bull transported into the plain of Lombardy becomes a Lombard bull in a very short time. Two generations are sufficient to alter the small brown bees of Burgundy into the large yellow bees of Bresse. In the warm regions of South America bulls transported from Europe lose their hair by degrees. Sheep lose their wool in the West Indies and Guinea, and are covered with hair. The dahlia sent from Mexico to the botancal garden of Madrid in 1791 produced a flower which was in no respect remarkable. It was cultivated, not as an ornamental plant, but because it was believed to be a substitute for the potato. However, its new environment transformed it entirely. In 1810 some dahlia flowers in a seed-bed attracted attention, and florists began to cultivate them carefully. In 1834 they had produced the varieties which to-day make the dahlia one of the chief ornaments of our flower-gardens. All the varieties of pigeons now known are descended from one species—the rock-dove (*Columba livia*). There are over 280 well-marked varieties to-day.

Dogs furnish the most striking examples of what environment can do. "A man had gone to live in the polar circle; his dog followed him, and developed the thick fur of the setter; the man went to the intertropical regions with his companion, and the dog lost all his hair, becoming the Guinea dog, improperly called the Turkish dog. It was changed not only on the outside; even the skeleton had been altered, the bony head like the rest. Who, even if he had never studied anatomy, would confound the skull of the bull-dog with that of the greyhound? ... If we estimate the number of canine breeds at 300, we shall fall far below the truth."

246. OTHER INFLUENCES THAT VARY THE CHARACTERS IN THE RACES OF MANKIND.—The influence of civilization and environment upon man is clearly established by a number of facts. If man does not always suffer as great changes from the action of climate as animals, it is because his intelligence furnishes him with the means to protect himself against its influence. He

---

[1] Quatrefages, article "Races" in the "Dictionnaire Encyclopédique des Sciences Medicales."

knows how to combat both the heat of the tropics and the cold of the polar circle. He carries along with him his regimen, customs, and mode of life, and thus neutralizes, in part at least, the modifying influence of climate and external conditions.

However, we must not believe that man can escape these influences altogether. Climate, social state, and mode of life have a greater influence upon the physique of man than is generally admitted. Want, slavery, and oppression tend to lower the human type to that of the beast. This has been observed in the geophagous tribes of Orinoco, who are reduced to feed on clay during a part of the year, and in the Digger Indians, formerly inhabiting the State of Oregon, who lived on insects and roots.

The settled Arabs of the Hauran are of high stature and have a very rich beard, whilst their nomad brethren, the Bedouins, exposed to all the vicissitudes of an unsteady life, are small and have hardly any beard. Their life in the open air with head uncovered explains the thickness of their skulls, as also their piercing look, though no difference between them and settled Arabs is remarked until the age of sixteen. The negroes of Brazil, who wrestle by knocking their heads against each other, have the front of the skull considerably harder and thicker than the hind part. It is said that Cuvier's skull had become almost transparent at his death, so thin had it grown on account of his continual mental work. This thinness of the skull is also noticed, as we are assured, in certain artists—particularly in musicians. In many countries varied and very marked differences have been proved to exist between the upper and the lower classes. Hence, the Arabs of the north compare their nobles with the palm-tree and the common people with the brier. When different modes of life produce such differences in physique in the same country, how much greater must be the effect when there is a complete change of environment.

By a wonderful disposition of Providence, man differs from animals by being able to live in every part of the earth; he bears the cold of Greenland and the heat of Senegal. But, although he can adapt himself to every climate, he cannot escape its influence. Man is born white in every latitude; the child among the tribes of the Upper Nile turns black only about a year after its birth. The negro type transported to another environment is modified very rapidly and very distinctly. Thus, the negro transported from the south to the north changes after a few generations; his color becomes lighter, his features change to his advantage; the characteristic odor gradually disappears, his blood loses its plasticity, and his intelligence becomes more developed. "In the space of 150 years," says Élisée Reclus, "the negro has overcome a full quarter of the distance which separated him from the white man in outside appearance. If other influences do not balance that of climate, it may well happen that, after a certain number of centuries, all Americans, from wherever their ancestors may have come, will have the color of the natives."

In Tasmania environment alone, very probably, has modified the negro type and formed at the same time a peculiar and homogeneous population. In the same way the native of Europe and his descendants undergo a transformation in America; their heads become smaller and incline toward the pyramidal form, their necks become longer, their jaws more massive, their cheeks hollow, their bones stretch, and their fingers need a special size glove. This is the so-called Yankee type, a new type, which approaches more and more that of the natives of his adopted country, the Hurons, the Iroquois—in a word, the Redskins. The same English type has changed so much in New Zealand and Australia that the eye can easily distinguish the children of the old soil from those of the new. The French who have dwelt in Canada for a number of years have changed their color, their physiognomy, and their hair.

Different environments produce different results. The Jew is white in the countries of the north, brown in Portugal, black in certain parts of Africa and Asia. The royal dynasty in England is of German origin, and has always intermarried with German families; nevertheless, to-day it has developed the characteristics of the English race in the highest degree. The influence of environment on the constitution is, therefore, unquestionable.

247. INFLUENCE OF HEREDITY ON RACE.—Heredity is another factor which explains many of the phenomena we are studying. It is the property of living beings to repeat or reproduce themselves with the same forms and same attributes. A white man transported into a warm country takes so dark a color that he might be taken for a black man; his son, however, is born white, and remains so as long as he is not exposed to the same atmospheric conditions as his father. Intellectual qualities are transmitted as well as physical characters; in the family of the great Bach there were thirty-two musicians.

An accidental quality, a spontaneous variation, may be transmitted by heredity, and thus constitute a race. We shall give some examples. In 1770 a bull without horns was born in Paraguay, which, in spite of every effort to suppress this peculiarity, on account of the difficulty with which these animals are caught with the lasso, gave rise to a numerous breed. The so-called

Ancon and Mauchamp sheep are also due to accidental deviations. The first originated in Massachusetts in 1751, and the second at Mauchamp, France, in 1828. In both cases, it is true, man interfered by isolating and skilfully crossing the animals whose characters he wished to perpetuate; but the first modification was spontaneous.

The abrupt variations which animals present may also be observed at times in the human species. In 1717 there was born in England Edward Lambert, whose body was partly covered with a shaggy skin, which gave him the name of the "porcupine man." Lambert transmitted this strange peculiarity to his six children and his two grandchildren, although his wife and daughter-in-law did not show the least trace thereof. The Colburn family is also remarkable, for during four generations its members had six fingers on each hand. There can be no doubt that if in these two cases selection had intervened so as to isolate the families by allowing the members to marry only persons who had these curious anomalies, races would have resulted with a shaggy skin and with six fingers. The Anamese are called Giao-Chi, a name signifying that the great toe of the foot is turned aside from the second. This trait distinguishes the true Anamese, and has distinguished them for centuries. Similar peculiarities, produced spontaneously, are numerous; and this law of heredity or transmission is admitted by all naturalists.

Frederick William and Frederick II., of Prussia, hunted for tall men throughout Europe; and it is said that if money could not buy them they stole them. By making these giants marry the tallest women of their kingdom, these two sovereigns produced a breed of tall men, whose descendants can still be seen at and near Potsdam.

248. THE INFLUENCES OF ENVIRONMENT AND HE-
REDITY MAY COMBINE.—The influences of heredity and environment may combine and work toward the same end, thus making nascent differences all the more stable. Environment leads insensibly to more or less considerable and marked changes; heredity fixes and perpetuates them in such a manner that modifications due to climate or to mode of life, for example, can be transmitted in a certain measure, even in another climate, with other habits and a different civilization. Finally, the crossing or mixing of races produces new modifications, or sub-races, able to perpetuate themselves with their new characters, when the circumstances are favorable.

With the help of these unquestionable principles, all the differences which distinguish the races of men may be explained without great difficulty, and in a satisfactory manner, as we shall show in our next chapter.

CHAPTER XII.

THE UNITY OF THE HUMAN SPECIES.—Continued.

Preliminary remarks.—Color of the skin.—Discovery of Dr. Malpighi.—Causes of different pigments in races.—Character of the hair.—Form of the skull.—Custom of some peoples to give the skull a certain form.—No part of the human body is more subject to change than the skull.—Causes.—Examples.—Cardinal Wiseman and the first series of generations.—Measurements of the skull.—Relation between talent and cranial capacity.—Volume of the brain.—Relation between intelligence and weight of the brain.—Comparative study of the human skeleton.—Different languages no argument against monogenism.—Rapid increase of mankind.—Geographical objections against monogenism.—Origin of the Polynesians.—Of the Americans.—Conclusion.

AFTER having explained how races may originate, we have now to prove that the same essential traits are found in all men, and that, consequently, we form but one single species. In fact, we resemble one another: firstly, in physical structure, and, secondly, from the moral point of view.

249. PRELIMINARY REMARKS.—Man, compared with other organic species, be they animals or plants, presents the least differences. Stature, color of skin, proportion of the different members, all the characters which polygenists adduce to disprove the unity of mankind, differ more in most animals than in man. The canine species, for instance, is divided into countless varieties, more marked than the races of men. The distance which separates the pug-dog from the bull-dog, the skull of the wild-boar from that of the domestic hog, is

much greater than that which distinguishes the negro from the European. As to color, it is so accessory a character that three years sufficed for the famous breeder, John Sebright, by skilful crossing, to give to pigeons the colors he chose.

The arguments against the unity of the human species to which polygenists attach the greatest importance may be reduced to the following: (1) the color of the skin; (2) the character of the hair; (3) the form of the skull; (4) the volume of the brain; (5) the plurality of languages; (6) the rapid increase of mankind; and, finally, (7) geographical objections—*e.g.*, those drawn from the origin of the Polynesians and Americans.

250. (1) THE COLOR OF THE SKIN.—It is especially the color of the skin to which polygenists appeal as an argument against the unity of our species. Pliny says: "Who would believe in the existence of the Ethiopians without having seen them?" When Herodotus, during the Olympic games, related that there are black and white races, and that we must draw a distinction between them, he caused immense enthusiasm. Voltaire, as we saw already, thought it could be believed only by blind persons, or by such as had never seen people of a different race, that all men are descended from one pair.

251.—THE CATHOLIC CHURCH AND THE COLORED PEOPLE.—Even to-day there are many persons, little acquainted, it is true, with natural science, who lay such stress on the color of the skin that they do not believe that the negro is the offspring of Adam. We find congregations that do not admit negroes as regular church-members. The Catholic Church knows no such distinction; she considers black and white as the children of the same Adam and as redeemed by the same Saviour,

Jesus Christ. Therefore, she never hesitated to receive the negroes into her fold. From the very beginning, she canonized the black man as well as the white, raised the images of both, side by side, upon her altars, and invoked the intercession of the one as well as of the other. At all times she sent out her missionaries to preach the Gospel to every creature, and at all times she received all, black and white, yellow and copper-colored, with open arms, into her communion, pressed them to her bosom, broke the same bread of life for them, and looked upon them all as the children of the same Father, who created them; of the same Son, who redeemed them; of the same Holy Ghost, who sanctified them.

As in the past, so in our days, the Catholic Church makes the greatest efforts to gather the negroes into her fold. Catholic bishops, the princes of the Church, lay their anointed hands upon the head of negro youths, to raise them to the sacred dignity of the priesthood, to bestow upon them the same power that they possess; that is to say, the power given to no angel of heaven, to offer upon the altar the unbloody and immaculate sacrifice of the Mass. While some Christian ladies would be shocked to kneel alongside of a poor negro woman, we see colored girls knocking at the gate of Catholic convents, asking to be received into the community. And if nothing else debars her from this favor, neither her poverty nor her color will be an obstacle. The poorest black girl is admitted as well as the noblest white lady. Both will receive the same welcome, and both may be seen walking side by side, partaking of the same privileges, kneeling at the same table to receive the same bread of life; there is no distinction, not even in dress.

In fact, why should the Church draw any line between man and man on account of their color? Does she not number among her greatest saints and most learned men members of the black race as well as of the white?

252. THE COLOR OF THE SKIN FORMS NO ARGUMENT AGAINST MONOGENISM.—Though the color of the skin furnishes an excellent race character, it forms no argument against monogenism, and cannot determine species. The yellow, red, and black colors have too many intermediaries and are not characteristic enough for this purpose.

Darwin himself acknowledges that there is nothing more changeable, or, to use his own expression, "more floating than color."[1]

We can find the whole color series in a single animal species. "The goldfish of China is yellow, with a mixture of black in all possible proportions, so that it may pass from pure yellow to absolute black, through a series of gradual transitions; however, it would be impossible to consider the series of intermediary colors as a genetical series, because experience proves that all these variations can be found in one generation, issued from the same couple."[2]

Even in the negro the black color is so little essential that at the moment of birth the negro is not black; he becomes so when he is exposed to the open air.[3]

Pruner-Bey found that the new-born negro does not show the color of his parents; he is of a reddish color mixed with bistre; the red is less pronounced than that of the new-born European. This color, however, is more or less dark in various parts of the body. From reddish it soon turns into a gray slate color, and finally corresponds to the color of the parents, the change being more or less rapid according to the environment in which the negro grows up. In the Soudan the

[1] Hartmann, "Der Darwinismus," p. 23.
[2] Blumenbach, "Einheit," etc., p. 149.
[3] Pruner-Bey, "Mémoires sur les Nègres," p. 327.

metamorphosis—that is, the development of the so-called pigment—is generally completed in one year; in Egypt it takes three years.

253. CAUSE OF THE COLORING OF THE SKIN.—The color of the skin is almost solely due to differences of temperature and climate. Where the heat is excessive, as in Senegambia and in Guinea, the people are entirely black; where it is somewhat less strong, as on the eastern coast of Africa, the population shows a less dark tint; where the climate is more temperate, as in Barbary, Mongolia, Arabia, men are brown; finally, in the temperate and cold parts of Asia and Europe they are white. Hence heat is the great cause which modifies the color of man, and although there are many races and sub-races, nevertheless there is but one species. Microscopic observation has taught us the following facts about the location of the coloring matter. The human skin consists of two layers, the outer skin (*epidermis*) and the inner skin (*cutis*). The former is divided into the cuticle (*stratum corneum*) and the *stratum mucosum*, or *rete Malpighii*, named after its discoverer. The cutis and the cuticle are the same in all races; differences appear only in the cells of the *stratum mucosum*, which are filled with a granular coloring matter. According as these color cells are confined to the bottom of the *stratum mucosum*, or become thicker, and in some few cases even stretch up into the cuticle, the color of the skin is lighter or darker. Certain parts of the body are more strongly colored in every man, as warts; freckles, moles, and stains in different parts of the body are produced by the same cause which produces the color of the negro; Europeans have been observed in whom the whole skin becomes quite dark, although only for a time.[1] The

[1] Peschel, "Völkerkunde," p. 91; Burmeister, "Geologische Bilder," vol. ii., p. 134.

skin, therefore, has a tendency to become darker, and we may consequently believe that in the youth of the human race, and under the influence of other climatic conditions, this tendency was developed and became permanent in the races which at present are not white.[1]

In negroes and persons with a dark skin the *stratum mucosum*, or pigment, as it is called very often, is more considerable in quantity than in whites. Consequently, the color of the skin in various races does not depend on a difference of structure, but solely on the amount of granular coloring matter in the cells of the mucous layer.

If the pigment is wanting, the negro is white. Indeed, there exist undoubted cases of albinism among negroes. "In the case of two albino children," says Pickering, "the negro aspect had so entirely disappeared that they might have passed for children of Europeans had it not been for the remarkable appearance of the hair, which I could compare only to a white fleece."[2]

254. THE CAUSE OF COLORING PIGMENT.—But what causes this difference in pigment in the various races? Certainly the climate is the main cause. "Color in the negro," says Lepsius, "is the work of the sun."[3] The ancients already noticed the influence of climate on the color of man. Theodectes of Phaselis, the ancient tragic poet, sang: "The Ethiopians owe to the god of the sun, who approaches them in his course, the dark brightness of the soot with which he colors their bodies."[4]

"In all races, whatever their color may be, except in the black, which is too dark to admit of deeper color, the skin colors under the action of the air, and especially

[1] A. Wagner, "Geschichte der Urwelt," vol. ii., p. 254.
[2] Pickering, "The Races of Man," London, 2d ed., p. 188.
[3] "Nubische Grammatik," Berlin, 1884.
[4] In "Strabo," xv., 24th Didot's ed., p. 593.

of the sun. Among the Hindoos everybody is colored, and here our views as to distinction of color are greatly modified. Mongolians, under the influence of the sun, have become as dark as negroes; while there are whites in tropical countries who might be taken for yellow-bronzed Mongolians."[1]

Heat produces the darkening of the skin, because it renders the secretion of the viscous liquid constituting the pigment more abundant. It is well known that the negro loses a part of this pigment when taken to a northern country. It is always in the prominent parts of the face, as the nose, ears, etc., that we first observe a lightening of the color in brown persons.[2] To the action of the sun we may add other less important causes; for example, exposure to open air and the mode of life, which act not only on the structure in general, as we saw in the preceding chapter, but also on the production of the pigment and the color of the skin.

The vegetable kingdom is governed by the same laws as the animal kingdom. The coloring matter of the black grape, for instance, is also a kind of pigment. For the black and the white grape are but one species.

255. THE COLOR OF THE SKIN IS NOT A SPECIFIC CHARACTER IN MAN.—We might cite numerous other facts, but the above are sufficient to show that the color of the skin is not a specific, but only a racial, character in man, which may arise from external and accidental circumstances, may change under the influence of climate and mode of life. By a wonderful disposition of Providence, man, unlike the animals, acclimatizes himself all over the globe; he is not confined, like the animal, to one country; he bears the glacial cold

---

[1] Topinard, in the "Revue d' Anthropologie," Oct., 1886, p. 594.

[2] Pruner-Bey, "Memoires sur les Nègres," p. 308.

of the north pole and the burning heat of the torrid
zone, although there is a difference of temperature of
more than one hundred degrees between the two.
Thus man has become cosmopolitan. Thanks to his
constitution, so much more plastic than that of other
animals, he is able to adapt himself to every zone and
climate.

In temperate regions, we sustain the changes of the
seasons by changing our garments and mode of life. In
other zones these means would not always be sufficient.
Our fellow-men, thanks to their physical constitution,
can live with the greatest ease even under the burning sun of the tropics, for the skin of the negro has
been harmonized with the country where he lives.[1]

256. (2) THE HAIR.—Closely connected with the color
of the skin are the color and character of the hair, for there
is nearly always a correlation between them; the black
man, for instance, has always black hair. Several anthropologists have attached great importance to the hair
in classifying human races. Some polygenists have
even made the attempt, as we saw before, to separate
men into species on this slight basis.

257. THE HAIR IS NO DISTINGUISHING CHARACTER
IN HUMAN RACES.—The color of hair varies so much
that it can hardly be considered as distinguishing races;
the character of the hair is more important, and some
modern anthropologists have laid great stress on this.
We can distinguish smooth or straight, curly or wavy,
frizzy or tufted hair. The form of the transverse section of single hairs differs; it is sometimes round, sometimes elliptical. If the largest diameter of the transverse section of a hair is 100, the smallest diameter sinks
from 95 in the South Americans to 34 in the Papuans
of New Guinea. The tendency to curliness and to friz-

[1] Vigouroux, "Les Livres Saints," etc., p. 343 *sq*.

ziness increases with increased flatness of the hair, with which greater fineness is also usually connected. Generally speaking, the Americans and Mongolians have round, straight hair, the European and Semitic races curly, and the negroes and Australians frizzy hair; tufted hair is found among the Papuans, Hottentots, Bushmen, and a few other African tribes. But here also we find gradual transitions, which make a sharp separation impossible. We find important differences also in the growth of the beard, and of the hair in other parts of the body; but these are not distinct and invariable enough to make them a distinguishing mark of race.

Dr. Waldey, professor of anatomy in the University of Strassburg, although he attaches great importance to the hair as a means of classifying human races, nevertheless says:

"It would be a great mistake to distinguish races by a single character, such as the color or form of the hair. By means of the hair alone we cannot make a sound and useful classification of the races; to use this means only would lead to a defective division." [1]

258. INTERESTING DISCOVERIES ON THE COLOR AND CHANGE OF THE HAIR.—Only very recently Dr. Fritsch, in a paper read before the "Society for Anthropology," [2] made some very interesting statements with regard to the color and change of the hair. The following is the substance of his essay.

"The color of the hair changes with age. This change takes place gradually, beginning at the root of the hair. Therefore, in childhood, when the color changes, the two ends of the hair are sometimes differently colored. In young Botocudos, savages whose hair

[1] "Atlas der Menschlichen und Thierischen Haare," 1884.
[2] Berlin, April 28, 1888.

is very dark, the ends of the hair are found not to show the same development of the pigment. A boy nine years old was decidedly of the blonde type; that is to say, his hair was light reddish. The hair of a blonde child differs, microscopically, very little from the white hair of the aged, as regards the pigment; only the hair of the aged has not the fineness and smoothness of the child's hair. It is also destitute of the soft and evenly-diffused pigment, which can always be recognized in light-colored hair. This pigment, under the microscope, does not appear granular like the ordinary pigment: it is much thinner; so that we are justified in asserting that red hair has no pigment, or at least very little. Hence red-haired men very often have a particularly white and fresh color of the skin, because the pigment is not so plenteous in the upper skin when it is lacking in the hair. Hair cut from the head of a living person, with its secretions undiminished, has quite a different appearance from the hair cut from a corpse. Any hair-dealer can tell at a glance whether hair was cut from a living or a dead person. With regard to the question why the hair turns gray, whether suddenly or gradually, it is now generally agreed to be due to the pigment withdrawing, either suddenly—through fright, for instance—or slowly, as in the case of old age."

Thus, in spite of differences of color and form, hair is essentially the same in all men, and it changes by insensible gradations.

Light hair prevails in the north, while the dark color is more common in the south; nevertheless, northern climates do not exclude altogether the dark nor southern climates the light color. Very often, tribes which are closely akin possess differently-colored hair.

259. THE HAIR OF NEGROES.—Besides, the hair of negroes differs from fair hair only in appearance. Ex-

amined under the microscope, true wool looks like a cylinder formed of imbricated scales, while the frizzled hair of the black presents the structure of the pileous form. Dr. Prichard, who made minute studies on this question, writes:

"To me it is clear that the negro has hair, properly speaking, and not wool. The chief difference between the hair of the negro and that of the European consists in this: the one is more frizzy and crisp than the other, and this is really only a difference of more or less, because in some Europeans the hair is also extremely crisp. Another difference . . . consists in the greater quantity of the coloring substance or pigment which the hair of the negro contains. . . . Besides, it is well to remark that even if the growth which covers the head of the negro showed under the microscope a structure different from that of hair and quite like to wool, this would not prove that the negro is not descended from stock the same as the white man, because we know that among some animal species there are races which have wool, while other races are covered with true hair."[1]

260. (3) THE FORM OF THE SKULL.—Of the different forms of the skull, Aeby says: "The fact that there is no interruption in the series of normal forms, because the extremes are connected by countless intermediate forms, and, furthermore, the fact that each normal form is the imaginary centre of a series of individual organisms, are of great importance. This continuity in the forms of the skull is the more remarkable, because it is in harmony with all the other features in man. If we break the organic connection of the extremes, they are no doubt sharply separated; and if any one, as is often

---

[1] Cf. Prichard's "Natural History of Mankind," the French translation by Roulin, Paris, 1843, vol. i., pp. 140, 141.

the case, contrasts the negro and the European, it is easy to make splendid school pictures in most vivid colors of the different races of mankind. But they are school pictures, and their outlines are remorselessly obliterated by the reality."[1]

261. THE FORM OF THE SKULL IS NOT A SPECIFIC CHARACTER.—Indeed, the forms of the skull can no more justify us in drawing the conclusion that men are of different species than the color of the skin or the character of the hair. They form no specific character, properly speaking. Even Haeckel acknowledges that the different forms of the skull are not sufficient to establish a basis for the classification of the human species. If we group the races of mankind according to the shape of the skull, we must except the pathological abnormities which occur in whole races, produced not naturally, but artificially. In many races, for instance, the custom prevails of pressing or binding up the skull directly after the birth of the child, so as to give it a shape approaching the ideal of beauty prevailing in those tribes; some try to flatten the skull as much as possible, others to make it as high as possible. These practices exist to-day among the American Indians, but they also occur in other countries, and were found in ancient times, as Greek and Latin writers tell us. Professor Retzius proved that these customs still exist in the south of France and in parts of Turkey. Not long since a French physician surprised the world by showing that in Normandy children's heads are pressed into a sugar-loaf shape by bandages and a tight cap, while in Brittany the head is rounded by similar means. No doubt this is done to-day.

262. THE CUSTOM OF TYING UP THE SKULL.—Here, then, is an unnatural practice, which has existed from

[1] "Die Schädelformen," p. 57.

high antiquity over vast regions of country, on both sides of the Atlantic, and which is perpetuated unto this day in races as widely separated as the Turks, the French, and the Flathead Indians. May not some similar custom explain both the peculiar fossil skulls that have been found and the various cranial forms that are met with to-day among the races of mankind? Savants are still discussing the question whether such artificial formations of the skull, if produced throughout a series of generations, may not become hereditary.[1] During the last ten years much time and labor have been spent in studying and measuring minutely cranial forms, without obtaining results worthy of notice. In fact, within the limits of the same race—in the Mediterranean, for instance—the forms of the skull may vary extremely.[2]

263. No Part of the Body More Subject to Change than the Skull.—No part of the human body is subject to greater change in its form than the skull. The reason is that it is composed of so many flat bones. Only an insignificant accident is needed to alter the form of a bone or to change its situation, and the resulting form will be quite different. If we bear in mind the strong natural tendency to reproduce forms, we can easily understand how certain types may spread by degrees in some races.[3]

264. The Influence of the Mode of Life on the Skull.—Besides, it is certain that the habits, the passions, the mode of life, exercise a considerable influence on the physical constitution of man, and especially on the form of the skull and on the features. The pri-

---

[1] Burmeister, "Geschichte der Schöpfung," p. 54; "Archiv für Anthropologie," vol. ii., p. 21.
[2] Haeckel, "Geschichte der Schöpfung," p. 596.
[3] Prichard, "Histoire Naturelle," 3d ed., vol. i., pp. 222, 426, 444.

vations of the people of Connemara, Ireland, in the year preceding the famine of 1847, led to a change in their whole physical appearance: the jaws became prominent, as in the negro, and the whole form was affected. Prichard quotes the following striking example.

"Two hundred years ago a great multitude of the native Irish were driven from the counties of Antrim and Down to the sea-coast, where they have lived ever since in unusually miserable circumstances. The consequence has been that they are still distinguished by very degraded features, being remarkable for open, projecting mouths, with prominent teeth and exposed gums; their projecting cheek-bones and depressed noses are suggestive of barbarism. They are five feet two inches in height on an average, pot-bellied, long-legged, and abortively featured. Low stature and abnormal thinness of limbs is everywhere the outward sign of low and barbarous conditions of life. This is seen especially in the Bushmen and in the aborigines of Tierra del Fuego and Australia."

Baer found in the Tartar races evident signs of the influence of the mode of life, and especially of the food, on the skulls and shape of the face. He says:

"The Tartars of Kasan have by no means broad faces and high cheek-bones; their faces are narrow, sometimes long, with large, projecting, and often hooked noses. Their skulls are of the medium form, in which no dimension preponderates over the others. I found that the Tartars on the Kur River were still handsomer, for they were without a certain vulgarity which I observed in the Volga Tartars. Why is it that other Tartars who live in the Volga-Ural steppes, not far from the Kasan Tartars, and who speak the same language, have broad faces and less projecting noses, and altogether a much ruder appearance? Like Prichard, I find the cause in their different mode of life; for I would especially emphasize the fact that this is no case of different peoples classed under one name by the ethnologist, but one people which looks on itself as one. The Tartars of Kasan and of the Kur, like their neighbors in the Trans-Caucasian provinces, are old inhabitants, live in regular houses, which, among the Kasan Tartars at any rate, are kept clean, and are engaged in agriculture and gardening, besides the cattle trade; the cereals, especially wheat and rice, form a considerable portion of their food. The Tartars of the steppes are nomads; they have, therefore, movable kibitkas, live only on animal food, and their confined dwellings give little opportunity for cleanliness. If we go further east and examine tribes who speak a language belonging to the Turkish Tartar family, although some of them go by different names, we find that the face grows broader and the cheek-bones more prominent. The prominence of the cheek-bones, which is usually found with breadth of skull, reminds us that carnivorous animals are distinguished from graminivorous animals by prominent cheek-bones, and suggests the same explanation for men with high cheek-bones, for I find that in all the tribes which live solely on animal food the cheek-bones are more prominent than in those which, like the Hindoos and the Indo-Germanic peoples, eat a great deal of vegetable food."[1]

265. WAS THE TYPE OF THE FIRST GENERATIONS MORE VARIABLE?—We do not mean to say that differences in races of men may be explained solely by the influence of climate, mode of life, and other outward conditions, but they show that these influences may produce great changes in mankind. And even if the races of mankind were now fixed, so that these influences would not produce this effect, as they must

[1] Baer, "Bericht," vol. ii., p. 229.

have done if they gave rise to the different races of mankind, the action still continues in several races of animals. It is possible that ages ago variations of species were developed, reproduced, and then remained fixed; that in early times such differentiation took place, and stopped when it had attained its natural limits.[1]

Cardinal Wiseman says: "In the child the circulation of the blood, the absorbing and digestive operations, all the functions of life, are the same as in man, with variations only in the degree of activity; they commence with being, and are regular through its duration. But in earlier stages there is besides a plastic virtue at work within us, traceable to no law of necessity, having no clear dependence on the general course of the ordinary vital powers, which gives growth and solidity to the limbs, characteristic shape to the features, gradual development and strength to the muscles, then to all appearance sinks into inertness and ceases to act, till age seems once more to call the extraordinary laws into activity, to efface the impression, and undo the work of their earlier operations. And, in like manner, we must allow that in the world's infancy, besides the regular ordinances of constant and daily course, causes necessary to produce great and permanent effects may have had a power now no longer wanted, consequently no longer exercised; that there was a tendency to stamp more marked features on the earth and its inhabitants, to produce countries as well as their vegetation, races as much as individuals."[2]

Baer also says: "It seems to me that we may justly assume that in the first series of generations the type was

[1] Reusch, "Bibel und Natur," p. 491.
[2] Wiseman, "On the Connection between Science and Revealed Religion," etc., p. 138.

more variable, and therefore could be more powerfully affected by the influence of nature."[1]

266. INTELLECTUAL AND MORAL INFLUENCES AFFECTING THE HUMAN RACES.—But climate, food, mode of life, etc., are not the only causes that lead to the formation of races; in man quite different and mightier influences are active—namely, his intellectual, moral, and religious life. A highly-developed intellectual life must exercise great influence on the brain, the most important organ of the thinking faculty; with the development of the brain, and, therefore, of the whole nervous system, a modification of the entire organism takes place, both in an ascending and a descending progression. The more the projecting chin recedes, the more prominent the forehead becomes; the cheek-bones no longer protrude when the frontal lobes of the brain extend over the forehead; the size of the mouth decreases as nobler instincts predominate.[2]

According to Frère, the skull of man grows until his fiftieth year, and does this according to the measure of the brain's development, because the membranes which unite the septa are elastic. The arch of the forehead with increasing education converges so as to flatten the occiput. In the formation of the civilized nations of history, sexual crossing and the exchange of ideas have always worked together. Marcel de Serres shows that the hair also changes in consequence of the activity of the brain.[3]

On the other hand, the body degenerates with the intellect. The Portuguese who live in the tropical part of Africa have not wholly resisted the influence of climate, but in the main they have preserved their Euro-

[1] Cf. "Jahrbuch für deutsche Theologie," vol. vi., p. 710.
[2] Hettinger, "Apologie," 6th ed., vol. ii., 1, p. 254.
[3] Marcel de Serres, "Die Mosaische Cosmogonie," etc., p. 262.

pean culture. Hence they have not the African form of skull; nor has their color become black, like that of the Africans. The North American slaves have met with a different fate.[1] Retzius has conclusively proved the effect of habit on the formation of the skull and bones.[2] The American Stephens, no friend of the negro, found Russian soldiers more degraded than the negroes in the Turkish army.[3] What oppression accomplished in this case is effected elsewhere by isolation. The white man would turn savage in the country of the negroes, were he cut off from all communication with his own race. The most striking proofs are not wanting. Let us recall the example of the Irish of the counties of Antrim and Down, related by Prichard. Some years ago the *Ausland* told of European savages on the Fiji Islands; M. Mundy found some in New Zealand.[4]

267. CAN TALENT BE MEASURED BY THE SIZE OF THE SKULL?—The measurements of skulls by Parchappe, R. Wagner, Lawrence, Tiedemann, Huschkle, and others, although differing in their results, in every case prove that intelligence does not correspond with cranial capacity. Thering says[5] that the influence of the form of the skull has been over-estimated. Lyell also has shown that the skull and the whole body of negroes, when associating with white men, resemble those of the whites more and more every generation; and American educators confirm this fact from numerous examples in their own country. Anthropology and ethnology furnish many instances from every part of the

[1] Quatrefages, "Histoire de l'Homme," p. 962 *sq.*
[2] Müller's "Archiv für Anatomie," 1885. For examples of improvement and degeneration, see Bastian, "Das Beständige in den Menschenrassen," etc., Berlin, 1873, p. 24 *sq.*
[3] "Incidents of Travel in Greece," etc., 1842.
[4] "Our Antipodes," 1852, vol. ii., p. 124.
[5] "Zeitschrift für Ethnologie," 1873, 3. Heft.

world, of improvement in the form of the skull and the features of the countenance, due to education. On the contrary, Perty reports that even to-day in Hungary we may meet with the frightful ugliness which characterized the Huns.

268. (4) THE VOLUME OF THE BRAIN.—The form of the skull, therefore, is not a specific character, nor can this be said of its cranial capacity or volume. We certainly find a very appreciable difference in this respect between the negro and the white man. But here, as in all the phenomena we have already examined, we meet all the intermediate steps in the other races. We cannot, therefore, decide that one race ends at the point at which another race begins. On the other hand, between the highest monkey and the most degraded man there is a difference which cannot be bridged over.

269. MAN'S INTELLIGENCE CANNOT BE MEASURED BY THE WEIGHT OF HIS BRAIN.—Besides, it is certain that neither man's moral worth nor his intelligence can be measured by the weight of his brain; therefore no conclusion can be drawn therefrom in regard to difference of species. The weight may be greater or smaller in consequence of disease, such as hydrocephaly or microcephaly. Vogt himself says of microcephaly:

"Microcephaly is a cessation of the development of the brain; for the more we study the brains of microcephali, the more certain it is that in all microcephalous persons the insula is open for a part of its lower surface, which is the normal condition of the human embryo at the age of about three months. This state has become permanent in the microcephalus; an essential part of the brain has ceased to develop."[1]

270. WEIGHT OF THE BRAIN.—In hydrocephaly the size of the brain is abnormal; but even in its normal

[1] Vogt, "Ursprung des Menschen."

state the brain is not a correct measure of intelligence. The most searching investigations have been made on the brains of individuals differing in race, sex, and talent. The general result is that the brain of the better educated does not differ from that of the uneducated by greater weight, but by more numerous and more minute windings and deeper furrows. According to Wagner, the average weight in the white race is, for men, 1,410 gr.; for women, 1,262; according to Huschkle, 1,424 and 1,272 gr.[1] It is said that the brain of Cromwell weighed 2,231 gr.; of Turgenieff, the poet and novelist, 2,020 gr.; of the giant Joachim, 1,935 gr. (his skull measured 1,950 cubic centimetres); of Cuvier, 1,830 gr.; of Byron, 1,807 gr.; of Schiller 1,785 gr.; of Agassiz, 1,512 gr.; of Gauss the mathematician, 1,492 gr.; of Dupuytren the surgeon, 1,436 gr.; of Broca the anatomist, 1,400 gr.; of Hermann the philologist, 1,358 gr.; that of Gambetta weighed only 1,165 gr. Certainly exceptions to the supposed rule that the brain is the measure of intelligence are not rare, and are the more intelligible because the investigators made success in life the chief, if not the exclusive, test of a man's intellectual work.

And this is hardly correct; the laborer, who has to wrestle against much greater obstacles than the man who was born amid wealth and prosperity, has often to use greater intellectual effort than the scholar. The brain of the Swiss lake-dwellers was larger than that of the modern Swiss. The brains of the Auvergnat and of the Breton, on the average, surpass the brain of the Parisian.

Certain dark tribes show a simpler superficial brain formation than cultured nations. Immediately it is in-

[1] Nadaillac, "Les Premiers Hommes," Paris, Masson, 1881, vol. ii., Append., p. 507.

ferred that the same is true of other peoples living in a state of nature. But this inference is not warranted. Among us there are men whose brain surface surpasses in simplicity of texture that of people living in a state of nature.[1] Kollmann examined the brains of Fuegians to discover whether their windings differed essentially from those of the European brain. After having hardened them in a solution of chlorine and alcohol and removed the *pia mater*[2] the weight of the brain was

in man .... 1,165 gr. = 100 per cent.
in woman .... 1,015 gr. = 87 "

He could not weigh these brains while fresh; he succeeded, however, in weighing immediately after death the brain of a Fuegean named Enrico. Together with the *pia mater* it weighed 1,403 gr. The capacity of the skull was determined with sand, millet-seed, and peas; the measurement with peas was found the most reliable. The result in the case of five persons examined was as follows:

Capitano .... 1,710 ccm. = 100 per cent.
Enrico .... 1,470 " = 86 "
Grete .... 1,400 " = 82 "
Wife of Capitano ... 1,370 " = 80 "
Liese .... 1,320 " = 70 "

The average is 1,454; in the men 1,590 ccm., in the women 1,363 ccm. In Enrico, the capacity of the skull being 1,470 ccm., the weight of the fresh brain together with the *pia* was 1,403 gr. The capacity of the skull of

---

[1] Seitz, "Zeitschrift für Ethnologie," 18, p. 284.
[2] The delicate fibrous and vascular membrane which invests the brain and spinal cord. It is the third or inmost of the three meninges, covered both by the arachnoid and by the *dura mater*. Also called *pia*.

1 cm. corresponds to 0.954 gr. of brain. From this we can calculate the fresh brain about as follows:

Capitano	1,631 gr. = 100	per cent.
Enrico	1,402 gr. = 86	"
Grete	1,336 gr. = 82	"
Wife of Capitano ...	1,307 gr. = 80	"
Liese	1,259 gr. = 77	"

The mean is 1,387 gr.; in the men, 1,516 gr.; in the women, 1,301 gr. After a description of the furrows and windings of the several brains, Seitz asks: "Where are the signs of inferior formation in the brains of these Fuegeans?" As far as he is able to judge, there is no proof of the kind. The weight is average; the measure is average.[1]

Hence we cannot draw any certain conclusion from the weight of the brain. However, it is true, as a rule, that the more intelligent a man is, the more developed is his brain. In men whose brain weighs less than 1,000 gr. the intelligence is generally weak; below 900 idiocy is complete.[2] How can we explain this difference in the races? By their intellectual work; at least in great part. Intelligence in the higher races has accumulated for centuries; it has developed their cranial capacity, and heredity has transmitted to the children the progress made by their fathers. It is in this sense that the words of Goethe must be understood:

"*Es ist der Geist der sich den Körper baut.*"
" The spirit 'tis that its own body builds."

We do not yet know the mysterious ties which Providence has established between intelligence on the one hand and the volume and circumvolutions of the brain on the other; but we do know that the volume of the

---

[1] Cf. " Jahrbuch der Naturwissenschaften," 1887-1888, p. 361.
[2] Hamard, in " Le Controverse," Jan., 1886, p. 152.

brain in man is not a specific character. M. Le Bon weighed one hundred brains from individuals dissected by Broca. His experiment showed how greatly cranial volumes differ in the same nation, for in Paris the weight of the brain varies from 900 and 1,000 grammes to 1,600 and 1,700 grammes.[1]

271. INFLUENCE OF SIZE ON THE BRAIN.—What influence has the stature on the brain? The differences of stature in races amount to very little when compared with the craniological differences we have studied. Undoubtedly, if we take the average height, there is a difference of stature in races. But everybody knows that this character is of little importance, because everywhere we meet dwarfs and giants alongside of men of intermediate sizes. Le Bon has shown that stature exercises very little influence on the weight of the brain.[2] M. Topinard acknowledges that "the stature varies, like other dimensions of the human body, with age, sex, individual, environment, state of health, and race. . . . Environment has a certain influence on the stature of the individual."[3] The French, for instance, have diminished in stature on the islands of Mexico; the English, on the contrary, increased in size in Kentucky and in the west of the United States.[4]

The osseous structure of the different races of men, as the comparative study of their skeletons shows, varies to some extent; but no race is in all respects superior to all others, and none in all respects inferior. In the length of the lower extremities as compared with

[1] Ch. Letourneau, "Bulletins de la Société d'Anthropologie," 1879, vol. ii., p. 380.
[2] *Ibid.*, p. 382.
[3] "Anthropologie," p. 326.
[4] Quatrefages, "Histoire Générale des Races Humaines," p. 211.

the upper, and of the thigh as compared with the upper part of the arm, the Europeans are nearer to the apes than the negroes. The Australians have certain peculiarities which place them in marked contrast to the monkey. These peculiarities are wanting altogether in the white and yellow races.[1]

We will not dwell on some unimportant peculiarities of an anatomical character, like the number of vertebræ, which are not essential characters of the species. Some families, for instance, have one more than the normal number of vertebræ. Vrolick mentions a family in Holland which has this peculiarity. Consequently we find nothing in the physical constitution of man which proves that the varieties of mankind have a right to be called species.

[1] *Table of the Mean Stature in Different Races.*

Patagonians	1 m. 78	Roumanians	1 m. 65
Polynesians	1 " 76	Magyars	1 " 63
Iroquois	1 " 73	Sicilians	1 " 61
Guineans	1 " 72	Finlanders	1 " 61
Caffres	1 " 71	Malays	1 " 59
Scandinavians	1 " 71	Lapps	1 " 53
Scotch	1 " 71	Papuans	1 " 53
Danes	1 " 68	Vedans	1 " 53
Arabs	1 " 67	Bushmen	1 " 40
New Caledonians	1 " 67	Negrilles of Africa	1 " 35

Cf. "Jahrbuch der Naturwissenschaften," 1888, p. 363. As regards the height of young men, the physical examination of recruits for the French army, according to the "Vossische Zeitung," 1888, has established some surprising results. Villerme had already shown that, as a rule, well-to-do Parisians were taller than those of the poorer classes. Now Dr. Manouvrier proves that this was also the case in 1881 and 1882. In twenty districts (Belleville) where the very poor live, the average was the lowest; in eight districts, comprising the Quartier des Champs Élysées, where the well-to-do live, the average was the highest. In the other districts it varies according to the circumstances of the people. Dr. Robert has proved the same fact for London.

272. (5) DIFFERENCES IN LANGUAGE.—Nor can language be used as an argument against the unity of species in mankind. The hundreds of languages which are known to exist at present are not so many independent systems, different in their origin, but simply varieties of higher units, the language groups; these, again, are differentiations of a small number of principal languages, which are called root languages. It is admitted that tribes that speak languages belonging to one root were originally one people, and that the growth of subordinate forms of language (families, tongues, dialects, etc.) was the result of the gradual division of this people. As philology has hitherto increased the extent but diminished the number of the co-ordinate groups, we are justified in expecting that further investigation will prove even the root languages, which at present seem to be disconnected, to be historical branches of one *summum genus* of language.

273. DIFFERENCE OF LANGUAGE IS NO ARGUMENT AGAINST MONOGENISM.—Ethnology, says Pott,[1] a disciple of Hegel, does not contradict the origin of all men from one pair. What appears especially remarkable is, that peculiarities of race and language do not at all coincide. Therefore, when Vogt[2] asserts that the great divisions based on the physical conformation of the races in general run parallel to the divisions based on language, in other words, that there are as many primitive language-groups as there are human races, he only proves his recklessness. Pott finds this entirely baseless assertion the more striking because ethnologists are "unable to tell us how many primitive races there are."

[1] Pott, "Die Ungleichheit der Menschenracen," p. 272.
[2] Vogt, "Köhlerglaube und Wissenschaft," p. 56.

274. CLASSIFICATION OF LANGUAGES.—From the morphological point of view, we divide languages into radical languages (like the Chinese), agglutinative (like the Turanian), and inflectional or organic (like the Aryan). Now, there are races which embrace nations belonging to different linguistic families and tribes; for instance, the Caucasian, which includes peoples speaking the Indo-Germanic as well as those speaking Semitic languages; again, the same linguistic family embraces nations belonging to different races: the Turanian family of languages, for instance, includes all the languages of Europe and Asia, with the exception of the Aryan, Semitic, and Chinese languages; therefore it comprises the languages of the Hungarians, Turks, Mongolians, Jakutes, Esquimaux, Mandchus, Tartars, down to the dialects of the Malays, Siamese, and Polynesians.[1] The most marked physiological and cranioscopical contrasts are found in peoples speaking languages belonging to the same family; the New Zealander linguistically belongs to the same family as the Dravidians of Farther India; the interior African tribes speak languages related to those of the Berbers in North Africa.[2] This is the reason, says Max Müller, why every attempt to classify the nations according to the races and languages must prove abortive.

275. LANGUAGES ARE VERY NUMEROUS AMONG SAVAGES.—Hence the hypothesis of the autochthonists is, from the linguistic point of view, altogether untenable. For historical facts and experience prove that the division of languages is largely the result of intellectual degeneration. Languages among savage races are extremely numerous; in cultured nations a language extends in area with the increase of education. Among

[1] Max Müller, "Wissenschaft der Sprache," p. 243.
[2] Quatrefages, "L'Unité de l'Espèce Humaine," p. 65.

the barbarous and scattered population of the island of Timor no less than forty languages are spoken, and among the cannibals some hundreds.¹ So also the language of Friesland is split up into numberless dialects.² Pliny³ speaks of three hundred languages in Colchis; and the missionary Gabriel Sagard⁴ relates that among the Hurons there is not one village which speaks the same language as its neighbor; even families, he says, have marked peculiarities in their language. Moreover, among savages language changes very fast; sometimes a language changes altogether after one generation.⁵

276. CAUSE OF THE MULTIPLICATION OF LANGUAGES.—If it be permitted to draw a conclusion from these facts, we find the cause of the multiplication of languages in the confusion of religious and social relations; and in this regard, too, the Biblical narrative is confirmed, which declares that when men became confused and divided in their knowledge of God, their language was divided and nations were formed.⁶ "The unity of mankind which preceded the separation," says Schelling, "and which we cannot imagine without a cause, could not be as well preserved by anything as by belief in one God. Hence, a spiritual crisis in man's heart must have preceded the separation of the nations, for this separation necessarily brought on a division of the language."⁷ The confusion of languages is only a consequence of the confusion of thought, says Hettinger, a confusion of man in the depths of his being, in his con-

¹ Crawford, "History of the Archipel." vol. ii., p. 79.
² J. G. Kolb, "Die Menschen und Inseln der Herzogthümer Schleswig und Holstein," vol. ii., p. 62.
³ Plinius, "Historia Naturalis," vi., 5.
⁴ G. Sagard, "Grand-voyage au Pays des Hurons," 1631.
⁵ Max Müller, *op. cit.*, p. 49.
⁶ Hettinger, "Apologie," vol. ii., 1, p 263.
⁷ Schelling, "Philosophie der Mythologie," Einleitung, p. 62.

sciousness of God. Therefore the multiplication of languages is a problem which cannot be explained by the wanderings of the nations, even when we add, as causes, climate, country, mode of life, habits, etc. Often nations living close together and descended from the same stock nevertheless speak different languages. Something must have taken place to separate them; philosophical speculations are here insufficient.[1]

277. THE RELATION OF THE VARIOUS FAMILIES OF LANGUAGES.—The relation of the various families of languages to each other is briefly set forth by A. von Humboldt as follows: "Though languages may at first sight appear very different, though their notions, humors, peculiarities, may seem very singular, nevertheless they betray a certain analogy, and we shall understand their numerous relations better according as the philosophical history of nations and the study of language become more perfect."[2] Pott speaks in the same terms.[3]

The last fifteen years have proved the correctness of this view to a great extent. The Mosaic account represents nations as related whose relationship antiquity was unable to recognize. The Romans and Greeks, in spite of their culture, never dreamed that they were nearer related to the Aryans and Germans than to the Syrians and Tyrians. What Holy Writ had stated the science of the nineteenth century has confirmed: Ionians, Aryans, and Germans are of common origin.[4] The study of language has proved that before the ancestors of the Hindoos and Persians emigrated

[1] Hettinger, *op. cit.*, p. 264.
[2] Klaproth, "Asia Polyglotta," p. 6.
[3] "Allgemeine Literarische Zeitung," 1839, Nr. 62. Cf. Bunsen, "Outlines of the Philosophy of Universal History," vol. i., p. 413.
[4] Cf. the testimonies of Ewald, Fürst, and Wüllner.

toward the south, and before the Greek, Roman, Celtic, Teutonic, and Slav colonies went to Europe, there was probably on the plains of Asia a tribe of Aryans who spoke a language which was not Sanscrit, nor Greek, nor German, but which called the Giver of light and life by the same name which to-day may be heard in the temples of Benares, in the basilicas of Rome, and in the cathedrals and churches of northern Germany.[1] All the Indo-Germanic languages, says Pott, were identical before their separation; they existed in the germ in one original language, which disappeared when they were differentiated from it.[2]

Max Müller and Hitzig[3] some time ago attempted to prove that, both in their material and their formal elements, the Turanian, Semitic, and Aryan families of language are related to one another.

A. Balbi, in his "Ethnographic Atlas" of 1826, counted 150 languages in Asia. Klaproth reduced this number to 23. Max Müller reduced the latter to four original languages, to which the 53 languages of Europe which Balbi gives are subordinate; the same is true of the Australian languages, of which Balbi counts 117.[4] The same author counted 423 languages in America, but they were related to one another and to the Turanian languages, as is becoming clearer every day that inquiry progresses.[5] "The historical comparative science of language," says Steinthal, "seems to find more and

[1] Cf. Max Müller, "Wissenschaft der Sprache," p. 177.
[2] Cf. Pott, "Etymologische Forschungen," 1833, vol. i., p. 28.
[3] Philologen-Versammlung zu Heidelberg, 1865.
[4] Cf. F. Bopp, "Ueber die Verwandtschaft der Malaisch-Polynesischen Sprachen mit den Indo-Europæischen," "Abhandlung der Berliner Akademie der Wissenschaften, Philosophische Klasse," 1840, p. 171.
[5] Prichard, "Histoire de l'Homme," p. 353; Prescott's "Mexico," vol. ii., p. 448.

more proof that all related languages have arisen from one single historic mother-tongue."[1]

278. THE MOSAIC ACCOUNT OF THE DIVISION OF LANGUAGES CONFIRMED.—Let us repeat: the Mosaic account, which tells us that the division of languages took place a long time after the Creation and brings this division into immediate connection with the division of mankind into different nations at the building of the tower of Babel, appears to be confirmed by the results of the science of language.

"But," says Hettinger, "even supposing that it could be proved that languages had not a common origin, it would not necessarily follow that we must assume different beginnings for the various races of men; for if language is natural to man, then, at various times and in different countries, languages may have developed among the descendants of one family and spread over other countries; but if language is an artificial invention, then it is hard to see why every succeeding generation should not have invented its own language."[2]

In conclusion, we hold that philology can neither prove that the different languages now met with have not their origin in a common mother-tongue, nor that the differentiation of languages did not take place in the manner described by the Bible in the wonderful narrative of the confusion of languages at the building of the tower of Babel.

Polygenists, when arguing against the descent of mankind from a single pair, bring forward not only the marked differences in the races of men, but also the rapid increase of mankind and the origin of certain tribes, especially the Polynesians and Americans. Let us inquire into the value of these arguments.

[1] Steinthal, "Ueber den Ursprung der Sprache," etc.
[2] Hettinger, "Apologie," vol. ii., 1., p. 269.

279. (6) THE RAPID INCREASE OF MANKIND.—"Whoever believes in the Bible," says Vogt, "must believe in the whole Bible. Whoever believes Adam to be the one father of the human race must admit the same of Noe, who, with his three sons, alone remained on the earth after the Deluge. But how wonderfully fecund must not the families of Sem, Cham, and Japheth have been to produce, in 500 years at the most, millions of descendants in Egypt alone, while the monuments of Khorsabad, Nineve, etc., also bear witness to the existence of very large nations, which peopled Asia a few centuries after the Flood. Even mice and rabbits must despair of a similar increase in so short a time. How could men increase so fast and reach distant islands? Furthermore, why did they not remain together on the luxuriant plains of the tropics, but emigrate to cold and dreary countries?"

"What a wonderful, what a curious disposition of fate," says Burmeister,[1] "to allow the earth to be peopled in the space of 4,000 years with 1,000 millions of men from one single point and one single pair!"

280. THE RAPID INCREASE OF MANKIND NO ARGUMENT AGAINST THE UNITY OF OUR SPECIES.—These objections can hardly be meant in earnest. We shall not refer again to the defective character of Biblical chronology. It is sufficient to remark that even if the time was as short as Vogt and Burmeister suppose, it would not be an argument against the descent of mankind from one pair. Assume that between the ages of twenty-five and fifty a married couple gives birth to six children on an average; in that case the number of men 450 years after the Deluge might have reached 800,000,000; that is almost as many as are supposed to exist on the earth now. Mankind, it is true, does not now increase

[1] "Geschichte der Schöpfung," p. 62.

at such a rate in any country; men need not have increased at this rate in the earliest times, but they probably did increase much faster than they do now. It may be that there is now no increase in the number of mankind, because the limit of the population which the earth can support has been reached, but that until this limit was reached the increase was more rapid and uninterrupted.¹ If we suppose that a yearly increase of only 2½ per cent. took place, and a similar increase takes place even now under favorable conditions in thinly-populated countries, 500 years after the Deluge 106,000,000 people might have existed; and if an increase of 3½ per cent. took place, 180,000,000 might have existed. We find instances of such increase in modern times. In the year 1780 the population of Java was 2,029,915; in 1824, 6,368,090; in 1838 it was 8,103,080. Thus the number of inhabitants had quadrupled in not quite two generations. It is asserted that from 1785 to 1788 the population of Ireland increased from 2,845,932 to 4,640,000, which would correspond to a yearly increase of 17½ per cent.² At the end of the last century a few English sailors and a few natives of Tahiti settled on an island of the Pacific Ocean. In the year 1800 there were nineteen children, one man and some women; in 1855, although several had died unexpectedly, there were 187 persons; this is an increase of more than 3½ per cent.³ It is said that on an island which was first settled by some shipwrecked Englishmen in 1589, and was visited in 1667 by a Dutch ship, a population of 12,000 souls was found—all the descendants of four mothers. Similar examples are mentioned by

[1] A. Wagner, "Geschichte der Urwelt," vol. ii., p. 278. Cf. Reusch, "Bibel und Natur," p. 432.
[2] Carey, "Socialwissenschaft," vol. iii., p. 368.
[3] "Natur und Offenbarung," vol. iii., p. 69.

Wiseman.[1] "In Europe," says Burdack, "four children on an average at present spring from one married couple. If only a single pair was created, which is very conceivable, and it propagated itself at this rate, then, after a thousand years, we should have a population twice as great as there is now upon earth."

Still more striking facts are found in the animal kingdom. Acosta, in describing the natural history of New Spain, one hundred years after its discovery, says that even before his time it was not uncommon for people to possess from 70,000 to 100,000 sheep; and yet before it was discovered by the Spaniards there were no sheep in New Spain, and all the sheep were descended from those which had been brought by the Spaniards. It is also well known that horses and cattle have existed in America only since its discovery by Columbus; countless herds are now found, both tame and wild. Acosta speaks of numerous herds of wild cattle which roamed over the islands of Hispaniola, and which afforded sport to the hunter; in 1585, 35,000 were exported from this island, and 64,000 from New Spain. From Paraguay and New Spain alone 1,000,000 of ox-hides were exported every year at the end of the last century; yet the cattle in these countries are the offspring of seven cows and one bull, which were left there in 1546. If these animals multiplied to such an extent in a comparatively short space of time, in spite of the depredations of men and wild beasts, why should not the human race have multiplied in a like degree, under more favorable conditions and in a longer period?

281. (7) GEOGRAPHICAL OBJECTIONS AGAINST MONOGENISM.—The primitive inhabitants of America are

[1] Wiseman, "On the Connection between Science and Revealed Religion," etc., p. 237; A. Wagner, "Geschichte der Urwelt," vol. ii., p. 280.

autochthonous, say the polygenists; they were born on the soil where the Europeans met them when they discovered the country. It is the same with the Polynesians, they tell us. Neither the one nor the other could arrive by way of emigration from the ancient world; therefore they not only form different races, but also different species.

These assertions of the polygenists are far from being proved. On the contrary, the more the question is studied, the more the proofs accumulate which show the connection between the inhabitants of the Old and the New World. The origin of the American Indians, it is true, is yet very obscure, but we know that the New World could be, and in fact was, peopled by races of the Old World.

282. THE ORIGIN OF THE POLYNESIANS.—Many investigations in recent years have proved that it is not impossible that the whole earth, including America and Polynesia, was peopled from one centre. Even those who, like Waitz and Giebel, do not actually believe that mankind did in reality spread from one centre, expressly acknowledge that this was possible. The former says:

"Man, even in his primitive condition, had so many favorable opportunities of wandering from one end of the world to the other, that we can hardly doubt the possibility of his having spread over it from one centre.

"We cannot admit that the difficulties in the way of migration afford a valid reason for disbelieving that mankind originally came from one spot on the earth. . . . These difficulties are evidently nowhere greater than in the Pacific Ocean, or even as great; and yet the Pacific Ocean affords abundant proof, not only that these difficulties are not insuperable, but also that they do not hinder either immigration from other countries or the spreading of the inhabitants from one group of islands to another. . . . The great similarity which exists in language, customs, tradition, and religion in Polynesia, from the Sandwich Islands to New Zealand, will not allow us to suppose that these islanders are of different races."[1]

The Main-myth proves just as conclusively as the common language that the Polynesian races were originally one. It is true, they are now divided, and marvellously scattered to far-distant islands. The Polynesians are probably the most nomadic race upon earth; they are the gypsies of the sea.[2] One of the most competent and learned authorities on the Polynesians is A. de Quatrefages, who made them his special study. His conclusions in regard to them are decisive; here they are:

1. The Polynesians were not created on the place; that is, they are not indigenous nor the spontaneous product of the islands on which they were discovered. 2. They are not the remains of a pre-existing population partly swallowed by some cataclysm. 3. Whatever may be the origin of the islands on which they were found, they arrived there by way of voluntary emigration or by involuntary dissemination, successively, and by proceeding for the most part from the West to the East. 4. They started from the archipelagoes on the eastern coast of Asia. 5. The parent race of the Polynesians is perfectly recognizable both in its physical characters and in its language. 6. The Polynesians settled at first in Samoa and Tonga; thence they passed to the archipelagoes of the immense ocean open before them. 7. When they landed on the islands which they came to people, the emigrants sometimes found them entirely desert; sometimes they met tribes more or less black,

---

[1] Waitz, "Anthropologie," vol. i., p. 225.
[2] Hochstetter, "Neuseeland," p. 56; Peschel, "Die Wanderungen der Südvölker," in "Ausland," 1864, p. 361.

evidently cast there by accident, as European travellers can prove. 8. Whether pure or allied to these Asiatic negro tribes, they have formed secondary centres from which new colonies started, which spread Polynesian customs more and more. 9. None of these migrations dates back beyond historic times. 10. The chief migrations took place a little before or after the Christian era."[1]

283. THE ORIGIN OF THE AMERICANS.—There is a growing belief in our days that formerly a large island existed in the Atlantic Ocean, opposite the mouth of the Mediterranean Sea. This island, it is supposed, was the remnant of an Atlantic continent, and is spoken of by Plato in his Timæus;[2] the island of Atlantis, it is assumed, perished in a terrible convulsion of nature, which sunk the whole island beneath the waters of the ocean, with nearly all its inhabitants; a few persons escaped in ships or on rafts to the American continent. Whatever may be the truth of this hypothesis, so much is certain: we have many ancient legends which mention a continent that may have been the cradle of some Central American tribes.

284. THE TRADITIONS OF CENTRAL AMERICA POINT TO AN EASTERN ORIGIN.—In fact, all the traditions of the civilized races of Central America point to an Eastern origin. The leader and civilizer of the Nahua family was Quetzalcoatl. "From the distant East, this mysterious person came to Tulan, and became the patron god and high priest of the ancestors of the Toltecs. . . . He was skilled in many arts; he invented" (that is, imported) "gem-cutting and metal-casting; he originated letters, and invented the Mexican calendar."[3] The

[1] Quatrefages, "Histoire Générale des Races Humaines," p. 145.
[2] See Plato's "Dialogues," ii., 517, Timæus. Plato describes Atlantis quite in detail.
[3] Ign. Donnelly, "Atlantis," New York, p. 166 *sq*.

Cakchiquel MS. says: "Four persons came from Tulan from the direction of the rising sun—that is one Tulan. There is another Tulan in Xibalbay, and another where the sun sets, and it is thence that we came; and in the direction of the setting sun there is another where is the god; so that there are four Tulans; and it is where the sun sets that we came to Tulan, from the other side of the sea, where this Tulan is; and it is there that we were conceived and begotten by our mothers and fathers." That is to say, the birthplace of the race was in the East, across the sea, at a place called Tulan; and when they emigrated they called their first stopping-place on the American continent Tulan also; and besides this there were two other Tulans.

Of the Nahua predecessors of the Toltecs in Mexico, the Olmecs and Xicalancans were the most important. They were the forerunners of the great races that followed. According to Ixtlilxochitl, these people—which are conceded to be one—occupied the world in the third age; they came from the East in ships or barks to the land of Potonchan, which they commenced to people.

In Yucatan traditions all point to an Eastern and foreign origin of the race. The early writers report that the natives believe their ancestors to have crossed the sea by a passage which was opened for them.[1] It was also believed that part of the population came into the country from the West. Lizana says that the smaller portion, "the little descent," came from the West. Cogolluda considers the Eastern colony to have been the larger. . . . The culture-hero, Zamma, the author of all civilization in Yucatan, is described as the teacher of letters, and the leader of the people from their ancient home. . . . He was the leader of a colony from the East.[2]

[1] Cf. Landa, "Relacion," p. 28.
[2] "North America of Antiquity," p. 229.

Samé, the most famous of the Brazilian legendary heroes, came across the ocean from the rising sun. The Samé of Brazil was probably the Zamma of Yucatan. The Quicheans speak of white men who came from the land of the sun.[1] The Peruvians attributed the origin of their civilization to Manco-Capac and Mama Oello,[2] his sister and wife, who had crossed the ocean to their country; the inhabitants of Bogota had preserved the remembrance of a white man who had taught them the art of building houses and of sowing, and who afterward disappeared.[3] So also the Brazilians. According to the account of the Shawnee Indians, the ancient inhabitants of Florida were white men. The Natchez believed that they had received their worship and laws from a man and woman sent by the sun; that is, from the East.[4] According to the Tuscaroras, their fathers were natives of the extreme North.[5]

285. HISTORY CONFIRMS THE ABOVE TRADITIONS.—History confirms the above traditions. Concordant testimonies, worthy of belief, show that numerous adventurers had preceded Christopher Columbus to America. The communication between Asia and the extreme north of America must always have been easy; they are separated only by Behring Strait. From the coast of Africa to that of Brazil the distance is hardly 1,500 miles; from Ireland to Labrador the distance is not much greater; Norway is separated from Greenland by only 780 miles.

286. THE AMERICANS AND THE RACES OF THE ANCIENT WORLD. — The greatest difficulty is to de-

---

[1] Brasseur de Bourbourg, "Histoire des Nations de Yucatan," p. 178.   [2] *Ibid.*
[3] Nadaillac, "Les Premiers Hommes," vol. ii., p. 95.
[4] Du Pratz, "History of Louisiana," London, 1763, p. 175.
[5] Nadaillac, *op. cit.*, p. 527.

termine the relations between the Americans and the races of the Old World. A migration may have taken place by way of Behring Strait, which, in the narrowest place, is only ten miles wide. Other tribes may have migrated by way of the Aleutian Islands.[1] Then, again, a series of island groups extends from Southern Asia toward South America. They succeed one another very closely for 100 degrees of longitude; for the remaining 50 degrees there are none. The resemblance among the inhabitants of these islands, in bodily structure, language, and habits, shows that this chain of islands, as far as the Sandwich Islands, was gradually peopled from Asia. If we assume that the gap which now exists was originally broken by intermediate islands, that the islands of this tropical chain are, as it were, the remaining pillars of a bridge originally stretching from Asia to America, it would be easy to understand how these tribes reached America. Again, the sailor who skirts the Aleutian Islands and goes from Kamtchatka to the peninsula of Alaska finds himself in the centre of a kind of archipelago, that makes it difficult to determine the limit of the two continents. The passage from the one to the other is very easy. The Tchouktchis, natives of Asia since immemorial times, camped on both shores of Behring Strait, which separates Asia from America. Now, if they crossed this strait, what hindered them from spreading on the American continent and thus becoming the progenitors, if not of the whole population of the western continent, at least of a part? The communication between both shores has been so easy at all times that even to-day these same peoples visit each other very frequently—sometimes as friendly neighbors, sometimes to treat on commercial affairs. In doing this,

[1] Peschel, "Völkerkunde," p. 428.

they make use of the same primitive means of navigation as formerly.[1]

287. SHIPWRECKS IN ANCIENT AND MODERN TIMES.—
It is possible, too, that the inhabitants of the Sandwich Islands, or of the eastern coast of Asia, reached America in boats, driven there, perhaps, by storms. In historical times there are numerous instances of ships thrown on the American continent, carrying men from different countries. Bancroft relates that from 1852 — that is, since the colonization of California by Americans — to 1875 twenty-eight Asiatic ships were picked up on its coast, of which only twelve were abandoned.[2] If such accidents can happen in our day, they certainly could take place in former times. Japanese boats are known to have been carried to the Sandwich Islands, and even to the mouth of the Columbia river.[3] Cardinal Bembo reports[4] that a vessel with blue-tattooed Esquimaux was found by a Norman sailor in the year 1508 on the shore of the Bretagne. Out of seven men, only one was alive. As late as the year 1682 Greenlanders were driven toward the Orkneys, a group of islands separated from Scotland by the Strait of Pentland. Captain Cook found on Otaheite three inhabitants of Wattero, who had been carried away in a boat for a distance of 550 nautical miles. In

---

[1] Dr. C. James, "Moise et Darwin," p. 230. "The whole shape of the Pacific Ocean, with its countless groups of islands, gives one the idea of a submerged continent, whose highest summits still reach above the surface of the sea; and judging from the frequency with which the lagoon islands occur, it seems as if the sea-bed was still sinking."—Vogt, "Geologie," vol. ii., p. 1005.

[2] "The Native Races of the Pacific States of North America," New York, 1875-1876, vol. v., p. 52.

[3] A. Wagner, "Geschichte der Urwelt," vol. ii., p. 233.

[4] " Historiæ Venet." vol. viii., p. 170 (Latetia, 1551). Cf. Humboldt, "Kritische Untersuchungen," vol. i., p. 471.

1696 two boats, which had left Ancorso with thirty persons, reached Samar, one of the Philippine Islands, after having been driven by storm 800 miles. In 1721 two boats with thirty men, women, and children, went from the Island of Faroidex to Guajan, one of the Ladrones Islands, a distance of 200 miles. Kotzebue made the acquaintance of a certain Kadu on the Radack Islands who had come from the Island of Ulea, 1,500 miles off.[1]

From these facts we can easily see that America may have been peopled by similar accidents; especially as the cold current which comes from the Arctic Ocean through Behring Strait carries to the coasts of the New World all the wrecked barges of the Pacific Ocean.

288. ANCIENT RECORDS AND LEGENDS.—In this way, therefore, Mongol and Malay immigrants may have reached America from the East; and it is not impossible that immigrants may have come from the West, *i.e.*, from Europe. If ancient records and legends are true, the Northmen were acquainted with our shores, from Newfoundland to Florida, five centuries before Christopher Columbus made his memorable voyages.[2] While several nations claim to have discovered America before Columbus, the Norse records deserve more than a passing notice. The voyage of Leif Erikson to "Vinland the Good" is recorded both in the Flatey Book and in

---

[1] Giebel, "Tagesfragen," p. 90. For other examples, see Rauch, "Die Einheit," etc., p. 343.

[2] A. v. Humboldt refers to the discovery of America by the Northmen as "undoubted." See Kosmos, ii., p. 6003. In regard to these Norse discoveries, Horsford quotes from a letter from Nordenskjold as follows: "The Norsemen made numerous long voyages out from Greenland for centuries, and established colonies on the American continent."—" Discovery of America by Northmen," Boston, 1888, pp. 17-19. Cf. E. A. Allen, "History of Civilization," vol. iv., p. 55.

the saga of Thorfinn Karlsefne, manuscripts dating back to the thirteenth or fourteenth century. The date of the discovery is fixed by the statement that Vinland was discovered by Leif the same year that Christianity was introduced into Iceland, *i.e.*, A.D. 1000. This was fourteen years after Bjarne discovered Vinland.[1]

It is quite likely, therefore, that in dim antiquity America may have been peopled from Europe, at least in part. In a book called "De Mensura Terræ," written by Dicuil, an Irish monk, in 825, we are told that as early as 795, that is to say, in the time of Charlemagne, Irish monks had gone to Iceland in order to introduce Christianity among the inhabitants who had come there from North America, and who, at a later date, withdrew to America again, flying from the Northmen and leaving behind Irish books, sacred bells, and croziers. In 861 the first Northmen were carried by storms to the shores of Iceland, and after Harold Harfagr's battle of Stafanger many migrations thither took place, so that toward the end of the ninth century the island was peopled by Norwegians and Danes, mixed with a few Swedes and Irishmen. Between 984–986 the west of the Greenland coast was peopled for the first time. In 986 Bjarne Herjulfson, driven out of his course on his way from Iceland to Greenland, came to Nantucket, Nova Scotia, Newfoundland, and to the mouth of the Taunton.

The Abbé Brasseur de Bourbourg, in a note to his translation of the "Popol Vuh," says:

"There is an abundance of legends and traditions concerning the voyages of the Irish to America, and their constant intercourse with that continent many centuries before the time of Columbus. We should bear in mind that Ireland was colonized by the Phœnicians (or by people of that race). An Irish saint named

[1] Cf. "North American Review," vol. xlvi., p. 185.

Vigilius, who lived in the eighth century, was accused before Pope Zachary of having taught heresies on the subject of the antipodes. At first he wrote to the Pope in reply to the charge, but afterward he went to Rome in person to justify himself; and there he proved to the Pope that the Irish had been accustomed to communicate with a transatlantic world." This fact, says Baldwin, seems to have been preserved in the records of the Vatican.

If ancient Irish records may be trusted, America was known and visited by Irishmen 1,000 years before Columbus.

The Irish annals preserve the memory of St. Brendan of Clonfert and his remarkable voyage to a land in the West, made A.D. 545. His early youth was passed under the care of St. Ida, a lady of the family of the Desii. When he was five years old he was placed under the care of Bishop Ercus. Kerry was his native home; the blue waves of the Atlantic washed its shores; the coast was full of traditions of a wonderful land in the West. He went to see the venerable St. Enda, the first abbot of Arran, for counsel. He was probably encouraged in the plan he had formed of carrying the Gospel to this distant land. He proceeded along the coast of Mayo, inquiring as he went for traditions of the Western continent. On his return to Kerry he decided to set out on an important expedition. St. Brendan's Hill still bears his name; and from the bay at the foot of this lofty eminence he sailed for the "Far West." Directing his course toward the southwest, with a few faithful companions, in a well-provisioned bark, he came after some rough and dangerous navigation to calm seas, where, without aid of oar or sail, he was borne along for many weeks. He had probably entered the same current which Columbus travelled nearly one thousand years later, and which extends from the shores of Africa and Europe to America. He finally reached land; he proceeded inland until he came to a large river flowing from east to west, supposed by some to be the Ohio. After an absence of seven years, he returned to Ireland, and lived not only to tell of the marvels he had seen, but to found a college of three thousand monks at Clonfert. There are eleven Latin MSS. in the "Bibliothèque Nationale" at Paris giving this legend, the dates of which vary from the eleventh to the fourteenth century, but all of them anterior to the time of Columbus.[1]

289. ANCIENT CHINESE ANNALS.—The most ancient Chinese annals make mention of a great continent situated about 20,000 li[2] from the East. They call it Fou-Sang, and, according to the Sinologues, Fou-Sang is America.[3] Marine currents, especially the Kuro-Chirvo, the black current of Japan, must formerly, like to-day, have thrown the sailors of the Celestial Empire on the coasts of America. From 1872 to 1876 forty-nine Chinese barks were carried along by the currents toward the Pacific Ocean; nineteen landed on the Aleutian Islands; ten on the shores of Alaska; three on those of the United States; two on the Sandwich Islands.

The Chinese interpreter at San Francisco lately wrote an essay, in which he makes the following statements drawn from Chinese historians and geographers: "Fourteen hundred years ago America had been discovered by the Chinese and described by them. They stated that land to be about 20,000 Chinese miles distant from China. About the year 500 after the birth of Christ, Buddhist priests repaired thither and brought back the

[1] Ign. Donnelly, "Atlantis," pp. 419, 420.
[2] One li is about 536 yards.
[3] Nadaillac, "L'Amérique Préhistorique," pp. 544–547.

news that they had met with Buddhist idols and religious writings in the country."[1]

290. ANCIENT RECORDS AND MYTHOLOGY.—When we turn to the ancient traditions, myths, and records of the Eastern world outside of China, we find much that points to an acquaintance with "Atlantis," or the "continent beyond the sea." Mythology refers to a great continent beyond the Cronian Sea, meaning the Atlantic; and it was beyond the waters that the ancients placed the Elysian fields. Theopompus, a famous historian and orator in the days of Alexander the Great, in his "Thaumasia" spoke of a continent beyond the sea, the dimensions of which were greater than Asia, Europe, and Africa together, and so fertile that animals of prodigious size were to be seen there. It is reported of one Hanno, that he made a voyage "beyond the Pillars of Hercules" (the Straits of Gibraltar) and visited a strange coast, which he reached by sailing due west over the ocean for thirty days. Homer, Solon, and Horace speak of the Atlantides as being islands situated at a distance of 10,000 stadia west of Europe and Africa.[2] Aristotle speaks of an island beyond the Straits of Hercules in these words: "It is said that the Carthaginians have discovered beyond the Pillars of Hercules a fertile island, which is without inhabitants, yet full of forests and navigable rivers, and abounding in fruit; it is estimated to be many days' voyage from the mainland." Plutarch also makes mention of a mysterious stranger who came from a distant country to Carthage about 300 B.C., where he lived many years. According to Cabrera, the first Carthaginian emigration to this western continent took place during the first Punic war. According to Sandoval, a succession of emigrations came from Ceylon, Java, and south-

[1] R. Shaw, "Creator and Cosmos," 2d ed., vol. i., p. 191.
[2] *Ibid.*, p. 193.

ern India to America many centuries before Columbus. In support of this, figures resembling the god Buddha seated on the head of Siva were found at Uxmal, Yucatan, etc.

291. SIMILARITY IN MANY POINTS.—At the time of the discovery of America, many points of similarity were found between its inhabitants and those of the Old World; for instance, in the arts, sciences, religious beliefs, habits, customs, and traditions. In the ruins of Gran Chimu idols of silver were found which are of the same type as Chinese idols.[1] The most curious analogies exist between the monuments, inscriptions, arms, modes of life, and customs of the ancient Americans and those of the Egyptians, Etruscans, Lybians, and Iberians. The Euscara language, the primitive tongue preserved by the French and Spanish Basques, resembles in a singular manner many native languages of America.

Quatrefages, who studied the question of the origin of the American people very carefully, believes that the New World was peopled by three races, the yellow, the white, and the black. The yellow race is still represented in Brazil by the Botocudos. The white race occupied mainly the northwest. The black race, less numerous, inhabited the Isthmus of Panama. Certain tribes of Florida, Brazil, and California also belonged to the black race.

292. CONCLUSION: IT CANNOT BE PROVED THAT THE EARTH WAS NOT PEOPLED FROM ONE CENTRE. — In concluding the discussion of this question, we shall quote Reusch, who says: "These observations show that it cannot be proved that the earth could not have been peopled from one centre. Former discussions have proved that it is physiologically possible that all the races of mankind have originated from one primitive

[1] Nadaillac, *op. cit.*, p. 106.

race; that the many important points of resemblance in all the races of mankind and their unlimited power of fruitful intermarriage are distinctly in favor of the specific unity of mankind; and that the differences which exist are no proof that the races are of different origin. The doctrine of the unity of mankind, *i.e.*, the doctrine that the races of man are not to be traced back to different ancestors, is therefore one which does not contradict the certain results of scientific inquiry. Hence, if the Bible teaches that mankind is descended not only from similar, but from the same ancestors, that is, from a single pair, this is a statement on which natural science can give no judgment, for it is purely historical."[1]

The Americans of both north and south, therefore, together with the Polynesians, do not form an exception to the general rule: they descend like ourselves from Adam and Eve. "He hath made of one all mankind, to dwell upon the whole face of the earth."[2]

[1] Reusch, "Bibel und Natur," p. 430.
[2] Acts xvii. 26.

CHAPTER XIII.

SPECIFIC UNITY OF MANKIND.

Preliminary remarks.—Anatomical organization of man.—Inner organs.—Man not confined to one kind of food.—Fecundity of mixed races.—Examples.—Man a cosmopolite.—All men endowed with intelligence and reason.—All are social beings.—All are endued with speech and free-will.—All are religious.—American Indians.—Negroes.—Conclusion.

293. SPECIFIC UNITY OF MANKIND.—Thus far we have seen that none of the characters which distinguish human races are specific characters. It remains for us to show that all the qualities which are proper to man alone, and which are not met with in animals, are found in all human races, and only in these.

Races form but one species when they all present the same essential characters; that is, when in each of them the qualities which distinguish them from one another are not specific differences. We shall try to prove in the present chapter that all human races have, 1st, the same anatomical organization, and, 2d, the same intellectual and moral qualities. By these they are distinguished from all animals and constitute a species by themselves.

294. (1) ALL MEN HAVE THE SAME ANATOMICAL ORGANIZATION.—The anatomical organization is essentially the same in all human races, both fossil and living.

"Dolichocephalous or brachycephalous, great or small, orthognathous or prognathous, quaternary man is always man in the full sense of the word. The more we study, the more we become convinced that every bone of the skeleton, from the largest to the smallest, carries with it, in its form and proportions, a certificate of origin which it is impossible to discredit."[1]

At all times and in all races we find the same anatomical structure of the body, the same mean duration of life, the same mean temperature of the body, the same mean rapidity of the pulse, the same duration of pregnancy; the catamenia everywhere take place in the same manner; dentition takes place at the same time; the number of teeth is the same in all. The peculiar development of the breast bone, which in childhood consists of eight, in youth of three, parts, that unite completely in adults, is found in all races. All men, too, are liable to sickness, although there are diseases to which the white races are especially subject, as yellow fever, for instance; but there is no disease which may not attack any race. The true skin is the same in structure in all nations; the age when manhood is attained is the same in all, as also the period when life begins to decline.

All men, without exception, have the same upright attitude. Except in the form of the skull and pelvis, the skeleton presents no noteworthy difference. Everywhere we find the same number of bones, similar in form and structure; the same covering of the skeleton with muscles, whose number and arrangement in every part of the body is the same in all men. The arms and feet of all men have powerful sinews; the thighs are common to them all; and the hips of all men are provided with rounded buttocks. The smooth, almost hairless, skin which covers the muscles, in spite of differences of color, shows no difference of function. The beard varies in its strength; the Caucasian race is the most favored, the American the least; but no race is entirely deprived of beard.

[1] Quatrefages, "L'Espèce Humaine," p. 220.

295. No Man is Limited to One Kind of Food.—
Camper says: "Every animal nourishes or feeds itself
in the manner nature has prescribed, as we see in the
carnivora. . . . Man, on the contrary, is omnivorous,
i.e., he feeds on all kinds of food. His nourishment, of
whatever nature it may be, does not cause any change
in his mental faculties, nor in his constitution, nor in
his prolific power. I am of the opinion that, excepting
intelligence and speech, we should consider as the greatest advantages with which nature has endowed man
above other creatures his ability to live on all kinds of
food, and to preserve everywhere the power of multiplying his species."[1]

296. Interracial Fecundity.—The last-mentioned
advantage is even more important than Camper thought;
it touches the very essence of our question. The
fecundity of all races and tribes, no matter how crossed
and intermarried, is proven by so many and so decisive instances that there cannot be any doubt of
its being unlimited. Two of the most important nations of Europe are mixtures. The English have
sprung from a mixture of Celts, Anglo-Saxons, and
Northmen; the French from Celts, Romans, and
Franks. The offspring of Arabs and Frenchmen are
inferior to their parents neither corporally nor intellectually. Negroes, Australians, and whites when
crossed bring forth children whose unlimited power to
propagate becomes the foundation of powerful families.
It is said that when Hottentot women marry men of
their own tribe they have three or four children; when
they couple with negroes this number of children is
trebled, and marriages with white men are even more
prolific.[2] Irish and Chinese, Malays and Hollanders,

[1] Camper, "Réponse à la Question de la Société Batave," chap. vii. [2] Quatrefages, "L'Unité de l'Espèce Humaine," p. 334.

intermarry extensively in Australia and on the South Sea Islands; a healthier and more numerous race is the result. From the union of Europeans with natives of the Philippines spring handsomer children than from the intermarriage of the whites among themselves.[1]

297. THE MIXING OF DIFFERENT RACES DOES NOT INTERFERE WITH THEIR FECUNDITY.—The mixing of different human races does not interfere with their fecundity—a clear proof that all mankind forms but one species. The Griquas, formerly called Basters, a population issued from the intermarriage of Hollanders and Hottentots, have become a fixed type. For more than two centuries they have dwelt upon the banks of the Orange River, and there they preserve their special features, intermediate between those of their ancestors. They form numerous tribes to-day. The same is true of the Cafusos of Brazil, who owe their origin to the crossing of Indians with negroes escaped from European settlements. The vigorous yellow population of Pitcairn Island (Pacific Ocean) is descended from a few English sailors and a dozen Tahiti women; it trebled in thirty-three years—a manifest proof that the mixing of races does not impair their fecundity.

Let us point out a few more mongrel races: The Papuas, whose color is chestnut and whose hair is flat, are a mixture of native woolly-haired negroes and Malays; the Malays themselves, who are undoubtedly sprung from the amalgamation of the white, yellow, and black races that have intermingled since remote antiquity in southern and eastern Asia; the Zulus, whom their language and physical characters, as also certain traditions, prove to be descended from a mixture of negroes and whites; some Senegambian tribes, who,

[1] Waitz, "Anthropologie," vol. i., p. 202.

according to M. Simonnot, owe their color to native negroes and their physical strength to the Moors.

Why not quote the millions of mongrels, mulattoes or others, who constitute one-fifth of the population of Mexico and Central America? Here Europeans as well as negroes crossed with native Indians to such an extent that tables were constructed to calculate the fraction of European blood which rolls in the veins of the mongrels; in Chili and Peru almost the whole population consists of mongrels, the progeny of Indians and Spaniards. In other parts of South America may be found mixtures of every shade and degree, descended from Indians, negroes, and whites; and these treble crossings are a most decisive proof of the prolific power of crossed races.[1] In all the States mulattoes, descendants of negroes and whites, are numerous; in the colonies they increase so fast that they bid fair to become dominant.

298. OBJECTION: BARRENNESS OF MARRIAGES BETWEEN WHITES AND AUSTRALIANS.—Polygenists object that the unions between whites and Australians remain barren in most cases. However, the fewness of such mongrels is disputed by Petermann and Quatrefages. Moreover, the barrenness of such unions can be explained by natural causes, such as prostitution and child-murder, drunkenness, syphilis, etc. Most of the women do not return to their tribe till the age of thirty, when their fecundity is exhausted. Another objection is equally unfounded. It was asserted that when the native women of America and Australia have conceived by a European, they are incapable of bringing forth another child by a man of their own tribe. But Wallace and Murray quote several examples which show that the power to conceive is unlimited.

[1] Darwin, "Descent of Man," vol. i., p. 198.

299. **MIXED HUMAN RACES AND BASTARD ANIMALS.—** We have laid special stress on the indefinite fecundity of individuals coming from parents of different races. This criterion proves that all men, to whatever variety they may belong, form one single species. It is true that mongrels are also begotten by nearly-related animal species, but these mongrels are mostly unfruitful. If now and then we find fecund individuals among them, fecundity is not transmitted to following generations, while, as we have seen, stronger and more prolific races result from the mixing of different human races. Let us conclude this subject with the words of John Müller: "The human races are forms of one single species, reproducing and propagating themselves; they are not species of one genus; if this were the case, their mixed breeds, when intermarried, would be barren."[1]

300. **MAN CAN LIVE UNDER ALL CLIMATIC CONDITIONS.—**We present another proof of the unity of the human race: Man can live under all climatic conditions, though animals cannot.

"The spot on earth is still to be found which cannot be inhabited or at least visited by man."[2] "It is undeniable that the same race can live successively in very different climates, and that this has in some cases occurred. This can be said of very few animals. Again, it is certain that the mode of life and the outward conditions to which a tribe is subject may, and often do, alter completely, while animals cannot bear such a change. Lastly, it is proven that a race may pass through various stages of civilization; not so the animals. Therefore, as the circumstances and conditions under which man can exist are so various, we see that

---
[1] J. Müller. "Handbuch der Physiologie," vol. ii., p. 773.
[2] Peschel. "Völkerkunde," p. 21.

it is in accordance with the laws of nature if the variation of his outward form is less limited than that of the animals."

We must, no doubt, assume that men spread over the earth gradually and very slowly, so that climatic changes were never abrupt. If we suppose this, the process of acclimatization is quite conceivable. Peschel says:

"If the transition to other climates takes place gradually and at long intervals, there is no doubt that the same race of men may people every zone of the earth. For no one denies that the high-caste Hindoo, whether his home be in Bengal, in Madras, or in Sinde, or in any other hot place of his native land, is of Aryan descent, just as much as the inhabitants of Iceland, and that the unknown ancestors of both must have inhabited a common home. All ethnologists are agreed that the aborigines of America, with the exception of the Esquimaux at most, form a single race, and this has succeeded in adapting itself to all climatic conditions, from the Arctic circle to the equator, and again to the 50th degree of south latitude. We find Chinese in Maimatchin on the Siberian frontier, where the mean temperature is below the freezing-point and the thermometer falls to 40 degrees below zero (Réaumur) in winter, and on the island of Singapore, which lies almost under the equator."[2]

301. (2) ALL MEN ARE ENDOWED WITH INTELLIGENCE AND REASON.—The intelligence of the so-called inferior races has been greatly undervalued; reason and intelligence exist in the least-endowed tribes, and there is between them a difference only of degree. All are susceptible of education and culture; all are distin-

[1] Waitz, "Anthropologie," vol. i., p. 213.
[2] "Völkerkunde," p. 21; Quatrefages, "L'Unité de l'Espèce Humaine," p. 206.

guished by greater or less intelligence. The animals, especially those of the superior species, are not wanting in a certain (animal) intelligence and memory, but all of them are devoid of reason, while there is not a single human race which has not the faculty of reasoning, abstracting, and generalizing.

302. ALL MEN ARE SOCIAL.—All men, even the most savage, are social. It is a long time since Aristotle defined man as a "political animal," that is, a social animal. Certain animal species are also social, especially the bees and ants; but their organization is not the work of reason; is not supple and flexible like ours; it has not the family as basis, and cannot accommodate itself to circumstances of time and place. Human association has the same end everywhere — security and mutual assistance, founded in part on the ties of friendship, in part on community of interests. It secures to the individual the means of existence, and special advantages which he could not possess in a state of isolation.

303. ALL MEN POSSESS THE GIFT OF SPEECH, AND WITH IT LIBERTY. — All human races are endowed with the gift of speech and with free-will; of this we have spoken in another chapter. We add the following.

All men have been endowed by the Creator with free-will, the black man as well as the white, the Redskin as well as the Mongolian. This is the greatest gift granted to us, because it enables us to raise ourselves above ourselves. The Creator, in spite of His infinite power, could not produce a perfect creature; as He could not create man perfect, He has created him perfectible. This is the grandest title of nobility, which all men have in common. It depends upon ourselves to elevate ourselves above ourselves. We are capable of progress, of intellectual and moral perfection: every day we can increase in science and virtue; every day we can turn toward the ideal of the good and the true and approach it more closely. We are a divine plant, which has the power to produce, if it wishes, the most beautiful flowers.

304. ALL MEN ARE MORAL BEINGS. — While this power makes us perfectible, it makes us at the same time responsible, and capable of merit or demerit. All men, in fact, and men alone, are moral beings.[1] No animal has a conscience like man; none distinguishes good from evil. On the other hand, there is no human race that has not an idea of duty, of vice and of virtue, of a life beyond the grave. The sentiment of filial piety exists everywhere; the idea of justice and mutual obligation is universal; the grave violation of the moral law among both savage and civilized peoples has as immediate chastisement remorse of conscience. The various elements of morality, it is true, are not equally clear and well developed in all races and nations; but this is less due to the influence of the race than to the greater or less progress in intellectual culture and in civilization, and to circumstances of every kind.

305. ALL MEN ARE RELIGIOUS. — The moral sentiment is inseparable from the religious. The religious character of man is so important that, in order to escape the inferences that follow therefrom, some polygenists deny its universality, others contest its value. But unbiassed savants who have studied the question acknowledge in clear terms that there is no people without religion. "The assertion that there ought to be peoples or tribes without religion," says Thiele, "rests either on inexact observation or on a confusion of ideas. Never has a tribe or a nation been found which

[1] Cf. Quatrefages, "Histoire Générale des Races Humaines," p. 253 *seq.*

did not believe in a superior being, and travellers who have denied this have been contradicted by facts."[1]

G. Roskoff, who has written a work on the religions of the so-called lower tribes, proves that even the most degenerate tribes are religious according to their notions.[2] We may consider the inhabitants of Tierra del Fuego as the most degraded American tribes. Nevertheless Darwin was surprised by features in their religious character which show how similar their mental faculties are to ours.[3] Traces of religion have been found even in the ruins which prehistoric men have left us.

Thus all human races are religious as well as perfectible, moral, industrious, social, endowed with reason, with speech and free-will. Nothing of the kind is found among animals, man alone possesses these qualities, and he possesses them wherever his home, under every climate and in every latitude.

306. CHARACTERS IN WHICH RACES DIFFER ARE SECONDARY. — Therefore there is no essential difference between human varieties; all characters in which they differ are secondary. All mankind forms one single species. When we read in the works of some naturalists the description of the various races of men, we are tempted to ask whether they are not different species, nay, whether they are human beings at all; but a closer acquaintance with the races so caricatured clears up the matter, and fills us with astonishment at the ideas of these writers. Who, for instance, that has come in contact with Indians, Chinese, Japanese, or negroes can seriously doubt that they are the same men as ourselves?

[1] Thiele, "Manuel de l'Histoire des Religions," 2d ed., 1885, p. 12.
[2] Roskoff, "Religionswesen der Rohesten Völker," 1880.
[3] Darwin, "Descent of Man," vol. i., p. 204.

307. THE AMERICAN INDIANS ARE CAPABLE OF CIVILIZATION.—The poor Indians in America, it is true, are more or less degraded, more or less hostile to civilization and Christianity; but who is to blame for this? Have not civilized Christian Europeans and Americans wronged them, by teaching them hatred, contempt, drunkenness, immorality—in a word, every vice, and no virtue? How can the Indian accept culture from the Anglo-American settler, who shoots him down like a wild beast, poisons his wells and his food, cuts off his means of living, robs him of his hunting and fishing grounds, constantly pushes him on toward the frozen north, and has brought him a number of fatal diseases, especially the small-pox, so deadly to the Indian?

And still, some tribes, like the Cherokees, take up agriculture. A son of this tribe, without possessing any higher education, composed an alphabet of wonderful simplicity and usefulness. The children of the Indians, when educated with white children, often show that they are not only the equal of the whites in mental endowments, but even their superiors.[1] That the Indians have talents like white men we can prove by numerous facts furnished by the Jesuit Fathers, who labor among them with so much zeal and success.

308. MANY NEGROES ARE THE PEERS OF THE WHITE MAN.—The same is true even in a higher degree of the negroes. Some tribes, it is true, are very degraded, especially in tropical climates, which exercise an enervating influence upon them; but some have reached a degree of civilization which proves them the equal of the white man in aptitude for education. According to Dr. Mann, the Caffres of Natal are capable of civilization. Robins describes the Banus, northwest

[1] Waitz, "Anthropologie," vol. iii., p. 240.

of the Niger, as very intelligent and industrious.[1] Magyar tells us that the Kimbunda negroes are very sprightly people, endowed with a very retentive memory, thanks to which they learn foreign languages without effort, as well as to read and to write.[2] The plea of A. Firmin, a negro of Hayti, in favor of the colored race, before the members of the Academy of Science in Paris, in 1885, is a proof of what we have said.[3] According to Decken, the East African tribe of the Wadschagga has made great progress in agriculture and the breeding of cattle.[4] Rohlfs and Barth tell us the same about the negroes of Bornu and Haussa.

That the negro can reach a creditable position in government, in art, and science, is proved by the clear-headed policy of Toussaint L'Ouverture, the dramatic ability of Ira Aldridge, the eloquence of the Caffre Tyo-Soga, and especially by the self-taught learning of the negro Banneker. The last became an astronomer without any teacher, aided only by a few books and instruments; he published astronomical almanacs from the year 1792 to 1802. He furnishes the proof that there are talents slumbering in the negro which need only be awakened and cultivated to place him on a level with his white brethren.

309. SOME EUROPEANS LITTLE SUPERIOR TO SOME NEGRO TRIBES.—These and many other examples we could adduce[5] refute the assertion that the negro is not capable of civilization, and that his inferiority is due to specific racial organization. Had he only animal in-

[1] "Ausland," 1886, p. 933; "Journal of Anthropology," 1866, p. 111.   [2] "Ausland," 1860, p. 879.
[3] Cf. "De l'Égalité des Races Humaines," Paris, 1885.
[4] Kersten, "Reisen in Ost-Africa," 1869.
[5] Cf. Tiedemann, "Das Gehirn des Negers;" Armstead, "A Tribute to the Negro;" Grégoire, "Die Neger. Ein Beitrag zur Staats- und Menschenkunde," from the French, 1869.

stinct, and no adaptability for intellectual development, no negro could reach the degree of intelligence which many consider the privileged endowment of the white man. The negro does not make the same progress in the sciences as the white man, but no doubt he would make greater progress if he devoted himself for a few generations to more systematic studies. Until now this was the privilege of a few individuals only. We must not forget that even in Europe, for instance, in Hungary, Ireland, England, Dalmatia, and in some provinces on the Danube, there are districts whose inhabitants hardly stand higher in civilization than some negro tribes in the Soudan. In our country we know from experience that, especially in some eastern and southern cities, where the negroes are, and were, allowed to live peacefully together with their white fellow-citizens for some generations, they have made great progress in education and civilization.

We conclude that the account of Genesis, which teaches that Adam and Eve are the first parents of all mankind, is confirmed by science, and that Hollard is right when he says, "Mankind constitutes only one species, and it varies within the limits of one nature."[1]

[1] "Dictionnaire Universel des Sciences Naturelles," vol. viii., p. 340.

CHAPTER XIV.

THE DELUGE AND THE TRADITIONS OF MANKIND.

Meaning of the word deluge.—The Biblical account of Noe's deluge confirmed by universal tradition.—Traditions in Asia.—Egypt.—Chaldea.—The account of Berosus.—Its striking resemblance with that of Genesis.—Is Ararat Armenia?—Poem of Izdhubar, claimed to be anterior to Abraham.—Comparison.—Legends of the deluge among other nations.—Account of the Arameans.—Hindoos.—Iranians.—Aryan races.—American traditions.—Conclusion.

310. WHAT IS MEANT BY THE DELUGE. — By the word deluge we mean the inundation which destroyed the entire human race, with the exception of Noe and his family.[1] Noe's Deluge was caused by the corruption of men; it was a chastisement of God. On account of the holiness of his life, Noe and his wife, his three sons, Sem, Cham, and Japheth, and their wives, were saved by means of an ark, which the Lord had commanded him to construct. It floated on the waters, and when the great cataclysm was passed, it landed probably not far from the place where it had been built, on the mountains of Armenia, which thus became the second cradle of mankind.

Noe, by the order of God, had taken with him into the ark of all clean beasts seven and seven, male and

---

[1] On this subject see Lambert, "Le Déluge Mosaique," 2d ed., 1870; Hettinger, "Apologie," vol. ii., 1, pp. 303–309; Vigouroux, "Les Livres Saints," etc., vol. iii., pp. 481–503; *Id.*, "Manuel Biblique," vol. i., pp. 517–540; Reusch, "Bibel und Natur," pp. 284–313; Güttler, "Naturforschung und Bibel," pp. 253–266; Pianciani, "Cosmogonia Naturale."

female; but of the beasts that were unclean, two and two, male and female; of the fowls also of the air, seven and seven, male and female: that seed might be saved upon the face of the earth.

311. THE DELUGE CONFIRMED BY UNIVERSAL TRADITION.—The historical reality of the Deluge is confirmed by the universal tradition of mankind. It is the tradition *par excellence* among all nations. A. von Humboldt says:

"The ancient legends of the human race, which we find dispersed throughout the world, like the fragments of a great shipwreck, are of the deepest interest to the philosophical inquirer into the history of mankind. Like certain families of plants, which preserve the common type of ancestry in spite of light and climate, the cosmogonic traditions of nations everywhere display a similarity of form and feature which moves us to wonder. The most various languages belonging to entirely isolated tribes give us the same facts. The essential part of the record, which treats of humanity destroyed and the renewal of nature, hardly varies at all, but each nation has given to it its own local coloring. On the continents and on the smallest islands it is always the highest and nearest mountain on which the remnants of the human race took refuge; and the event becomes more recent as the people become more civilized, so that what they knew about themselves covers a shorter space of time."[1]

312. ORIENTAL TRADITIONS.—Among the Chaldeans the account of the great cataclysm is so similar to that of Genesis that the two narratives must have come from the same source; the Hebrews, however, preserved it in all its purity. As regards the Egyptians, their monuments, so far, do not give us any account of the Deluge.

[1] "Reise in die Æquinoctial-Gegenden," vol. iii., p. 408.

The Hebrew traditions, which have so much in common with the Assyro-Chaldean traditions, are different from those of Egypt. Nevertheless, the Egyptians also have preserved a vague remembrance of the destruction of mankind by the gods. We see this from a mythological inscription on the tomb of Seti I., of the nineteenth dynasty at Thebes, published by M. Naville,[1] of which we subjoin the substance.

313. EGYPTIAN TRADITIONS.—Ra, the divine king, if not the first, is at least one of the most ancient. The beginning of his reign is anterior to the rising of the firmament, and consequently goes back to the first period of creation.[2] The inscription on the tomb of Seti I. appears to have formed a part of the sacred books of Toth, "the writer of the gods."[3]

Ra assembles the gods and says to them:

"Said by Ra to Nun: Thou the most ancient of the gods, from whom I am born, and you ancient gods, behold the men who were born through me; they express words against me; tell me what you would do with regard to such behavior; behold, I have waited and did not kill them before having heard your advice.

"Said by the Majesty of Nun: My son Ra, greater god than the one who created thee, I remain (full) of fear towards thee. Majesty, do thou reflect thyself (on what thou hast to do).

"Said by the Majesty of Ra: Behold they escape into the fields, and their hearts are afraid. . . .

"Said by the gods: May thy countenance permit us to strike these men, thy enemies, who plot evil things against thee, and may none live among them. . . .

"This goddess—a goddess under the form of Hathor,

---

[1] "Transactions of the Society of Biblical Archæology," June, 1875.   [2] "Zeitschrift für Egyptische Sprache," 1874, p. 57.
[3] De Rougé, "Notice des Monuments Egyptiens," p. 115.

whose name is lost—departed and killed the men upon earth. . . . And behold, Sechti, during many nights, trampled their blood under foot, even to the city of Hierapolis."

"Shall we admit that the destruction of these men implies the destruction of mankind?" asks M. Naville. "This seems evident to me," he answers.

After having massacred the men, the wrath of Ra was appeased.

"They put fruits into round vases . . . with the blood of men, and filled seven thousand pitchers of beverage thereof.

"Ra comes to inspect the vases: Said by the Majesty of Ra: That is right; I shall protect men on account of this.

"Said by Ra: I raise my hand, that I shall not kill mankind any more."

This offering of fruits and blood which appeased Ra and made him express a promise analogous to that of Genesis had been prepared by Sechti of Heliopolis, who had ground the fruits, while the priestess made them flow (?) into vases.

After this offering we read:

"The Majesty of Ra, the king of Upper and Lower Egypt, ordered the water from the vases to be poured out during the middle of the night, and thus the fields were completely submerged through the will of this god. The goddess, when arriving in the morning, found the fields covered with water. Her countenance became joyous, she drank abundantly thereof, and went away satiated. She did not perceive any men."

Further on in the inscription we see that not all men had been exterminated.

314. THE EGYPTIAN TRADITION RESEMBLES THE MOSAIC ACCOUNT ONLY VAGUELY.—This account, ob-

serves Vigouroux,[1] is very different from that of Genesis, and, nevertheless, there exists between both a general resemblance, which makes a deep impression: it does not seem possible to explain it as an accidental coincidence. In both the Hebrew and the Egyptian account men are punished for revolting against God. The Lord exterminates them, with the exception of a small number. A sacrifice is offered to Him. He promises not to destroy the human race again in that manner. This inscription on the tomb of Seti I. is best explained if we admit the historical character of Noe's flood and the destruction of men. The Egyptians had preserved its remembrance, but as the inundation of the Nile was wealth and life to them, they altered the primitive tradition; mankind, instead of perishing in the waters, was exterminated, and inundation, greatest blessing in the valley of the Nile, becomes to them the mark by which the wrath of Ra was appeased.[2]

315. TWO CHALDEAN TRADITIONS ABOUT THE FLOOD.—While the Egyptian tradition has only a general likeness to the Mosaic account of the Flood, the Chaldean tradition, on the contrary, bears a striking resemblance to it.

We have two versions of the Chaldean story, unequally developed, but exhibiting remarkable agreement. The one, more ancient and shorter, is the account taken by the Babylonian priest, Berosus, 260 B.C., from the sacred books of Babylon. He introduced it into his history which he wrote for the Greeks. The other ver-

[1] "La Bible et les Découvertes Modernes," vol. i., p. 260.
[2] Some Egyptian philosophers said to Solon, who asked them about their antiquity. "After certain periods, an inundation sent from heaven changed the face of the earth; mankind perished several times in different ways; this is the reason why the new race of men is wanting in monuments and the knowledge of times past."—Plato in Timæus.

sion was discovered by George Smith among the ruins of the library of Assurbanipal, in the historical epic of a hero called Izdhubar. Berosus wrote several centuries after the author of Genesis, while the heroic poem of Izdhubar is said to be older than Abraham. Both deserve our earnest attention. We will begin with the less ancient. The Flood, according to the Bible, took place under Noe, the tenth patriarch; according to Berosus, under Xisuthrus, the tenth antediluvian king. Here is what he says.

316. THE ACCOUNT OF BEROSUS.—"It is under Xisuthrus (Noe)," says Berosus, "that the great flood took place whose history is related in the Sacred Books. The god (Kronos) appeared to Xisuthrus in a dream, and warned him that on the fifteenth day of the month Daisius mankind would be destroyed by a flood. He bade him bury in Sippara, the city of the sun, the extant writings, first and last; and build a ship and enter therein with his family and his close friends, and furnish it with meat and drink, and place on board winged fowl and four-footed beasts of the earth; and when all was ready to set sail, Xisuthrus asked whither he was to sail, and was told, 'To the gods, with a prayer that it may fare well with mankind.' Xisuthrus was not disobedient to the vision, but built a ship five furlongs in length and two furlongs in breadth, and collected all that had been commanded him, and put his wife and children and close friends on board. The flood came. As soon as it ceased, Xisuthrus let loose some birds, which, finding neither food nor a place where they could rest, came back to the ark. After some days he again sent out the birds,[1] which again returned to the ark, but covered with mud. Sent

[1] So in Syncellus, "Chronographia," p. 54; but in the Armenian Eusebius we read "other birds." Chron., Can., i., 3, p. 15.

out a third time, the birds returned no more, and Xisuthrus knew that the land had reappeared; so he removed some of the covering of the ark and looked, and behold the vessel had grounded on a mountain. Then Xisuthrus went forth with his wife and his daughter and his pilot, and fell down and worshipped the earth, and built an altar, and offered sacrifice to the gods; after which he disappeared from sight, together with those who had accompanied him. They who remained in the ark and had not gone forth with Xisuthrus, now left and searched for him and shouted out his name; but Xisuthrus was not seen any more. Only his voice answered them, saying: 'Worship God; for because I worshipped God I am gone to dwell with the gods; and they who were with me have shared the same honor.' And he bade them return to Babylon and recover the writings at Sippara and make them known among men; and he told them the land in which they then were was Armenia. So they, when they heard all, sacrificed to the gods, and went their way on foot to Babylon, and having reached it recovered the buried writings from Sippara, and built many cities and temples, and restored Babylon. Some portion of the ark still continues in Armenia, in the Gordiæan (Kurdish) Mountains; and persons scrape off the bitumen from it to bring away, and this they use as a remedy to avert misfortunes.

"The earth was still of one language when the primitive men, who were of great stature and despised the gods as their inferiors, erected a tower of vast height in order that they might mount to heaven. And the tower was now near to heaven, when the gods (or God) caused the winds to blow, and overturned the structure upon the men, and made them speak with diverse tongues; wherefore the city was called Babylon." So far Berosus.

317. THE ABOVE ACCOUNT COMPARED WITH THE NARRATIVE OF GENESIS.—If we compare this account of Berosus with that of Genesis, we see that it has been altered in the course of time and lost several important traits; for instance, the moral cause of the Deluge, which was occasioned by the perversity of men, whom their crimes rendered worthy to perish. Moses did not, like Berosus, neglect this circumstance, which perhaps the more ancient form of the Assyrian tradition, in the poem of Izdhubar, had preserved, if we may understand some expressions of this document in a figurative sense. With this exception, the resemblance between the accounts of Moses and Berosus could not be more striking.

On this subject Rawlinson says:[1] "We have here a harmony with Holy Scripture of the most remarkable kind—a harmony not confined to the main facts, but reaching even to minute points, and one which is altogether most curious and interesting. The Babylonians have not only in common with the great majority of nations handed down from age to age the general tradition of the Flood, but they are acquainted with the most of the particulars of the occurrence. They know of the divine warning to a single man,[2] the direction to construct a huge ship or ark,[3] the command to take into it a chosen few of mankind only,[4] and to devote the chief space to winged fowl and four-footed beasts of the earth.[5] They are aware of the tentative sending out of birds from it,[6] and of their returning twice,[7] but when sent out a third time returning no more.[8] They know of the egress from the ark by the removal of some of its covering,[9] and of the altar, built,

[1] G. Rawlinson, "Ancient Monarchies," vol. i., pp. 147, 148.
[2] Gen. vi. 13.   [3] *Ib.*, vi. 14-16.   [4] *Ib.*, vi. 18.
[5] *Ib.*, vi. 20.   [6] *Ib.*, viii. 7.   [7] *Ib.*, viii. 9-11.
[8] *Ib.*, viii. 12.   [9] *Ib.*, viii. 13.

and of the sacrifice offered immediately afterward.[1] They know that the ark rested in Armenia,[2] that those who escaped by means of it, or their descendants, journeyed toward Babylon;[3] that there a tower was begun, but not completed—the building being stopped by divine interposition and a miraculous confusion of tongues.[4] As before, they are not content with the plain truth, but must amplify and embellish it. The size of the ark is exaggerated to an absurdity,[5] and its proportions are misrepresented in such a way as to outrage all the principles of naval architecture. The translation of Xisuthrus, his wife, his daughter, and his pilot—a reminiscence possibly of Enoch—is unfitly as well as falsely introduced just after they have been miraculously saved from destruction. The story of the tower is given with less departure from the actual truth. The building is, however, absurdly represented as an actual attempt to scale heaven; and a storm of wind is somewhat unnecessarily introduced to destroy the tower, which from the Scripture narrative seems to have been left standing. It is also especially to be noticed that in the Chaldean legends the whole interest is made narrow and local. The Flood appears as a circumstance in the history of Babylonia, and the priestly traditionists who have put the legend into shape are chiefly anxious to make the event redound to the glory of their sacred books, which they boast to have been the special object of divine care, and represent them as a legacy from the antediluvian ages. The general interests of mankind are nothing to the local etymology, and the Deluge an

[1] Gen. viii. 20.   [2] *Ib.*, viii. 4.
[3] *Ib.*, xi. 2.   [4] *Ib.*, xi. 4–9.

[5] The ark is made more than half a mile long, whereas it was really only 300 cubits, which is at the utmost 600 feet, or less than an eighth of a mile.

event which made the Babylonians the sole possessors of primeval wisdom."

318. IS THE ARARAT OF GENESIS ARMENIA?—According to the Bible, the ark "rested upon the mountains of the Ararat," and Berosus tells us that the vessel of Xisuthrus stopped in Armenia.[1] Rawlinson claims that Ararat is the usual word for Armenia in the Assyrian inscriptions.[2] In the original Babylonian text, whence Berosus drew his account, says Lenormant, the expression ought to be the same as in Genesis, for the most ordinary and most general name for Armenia in the cuneiform inscriptions is Urate or Ararti,[3] a name known to the Hebrews, but unknown to Greek and Latin geographers. St. Jerome, who was well acquainted with the Jewish interpretations of the Scriptures, translated Ararat by Armenia.[4] His translation shows that the sacred text does not designate the mountain on which the ark rested, but the country: "on the mountains of Ararat," and not on Mount Ararat, where Jewish and Armenian tradition have fixed the place.

What are we to conclude from the preceding facts? Is the Ararat of Genesis Armenia or a chain of mountains? This is a difficult question and cannot be solved to-day. Perhaps some future discovery will throw more light on the subject.

319. CUNEIFORM ACCOUNT OF THE DELUGE, SAID TO BE OLDER THAN MOSES.—Let us now examine the more ancient Chaldean document on the Deluge.

[1] The cuneiform account of the Deluge, which we subjoin, makes the vessel of Xisuthrus rest on Mount Nizir, but this indication is useless, because no such mountain is known.

[2] Rawlinson, "Ancient Monarchies," note 1, p. 147.

[3] "Essai de Commentaire de Bérose," p. 299.

[4] Gen. viii. 4. The name Ararat occurs four times in the Hebrew Bible. St. Jerome has translated it by the word Armenia: II. (IV.) Kings xix. 37; by Ararat: Is. xxxvii. 38; and Jer. li. 27.

"By the side of this version (of Berosus)," says Lenormant, "which, interesting though it may be, is after all second-hand, we are now able to place an original Chaldeo-Babylonian edition, which the lamented George Smith was the first to decipher on the cuneiform tablets exhumed at Nineve and now in the British Museum. Here the narrative of the Deluge appears as an episode in the eleventh tablet, or eleventh chant, of the great epic of the town of Uruk. The hero of this poem, a kind of Hercules, whose name has not as yet been made out with certainty, being attacked by disease (a kind of leprosy), goes with a view to its cure to consult the patriarch saved from the Deluge, Khasisatra, in the distant land to which the gods have transported him, there to enjoy eternal felicity. He asks Khasisatra to reveal the secret of the events which led to his obtaining the privilege of immortality, and thus the patriarch is induced to relate the story of the cataclysm.

"By a comparison of the three copies of the poem that the library of the palace of Nineve contained, it has been possible to restore the narrative with hardly any breaks. These three copies were made by order of the king of Assyria, Assurbanipal, in the eighth century before Christ, from a very ancient specimen in the sacerdotal library of the town of Uruk, founded by the monarchs of the first Chaldean empire. It is difficult to fix precisely the date of the original, copied by Assyrian scribes, but it certainly goes back to the ancient empire, seventeen centuries at least before our era, and probably even beyond; it was therefore written long before Moses and is nearly contemporaneous with Abraham.[1] Variations in the three existing copies prove that the original was written in the so-called hieratic characters—characters which must have become difficult to decipher as early

[1] Some claim that it was even anterior to Abraham.

as the eighth century before Christ; for copyists differed in regard to the interpretation to be given to certain signs, and in other cases reproduced exactly the forms they did not understand. Finally, from a comparison of these variations, it appears that the original, transcribed by order of Assurbanipal, must itself have been a copy of some still more ancient manuscript in which the primitive text had already received interlinear comments. Some of the copyists introduced these into their text, others omitted them."[1] With these preliminary observations we proceed to give the complete narrative ascribed in the poem to Khasisatra.

320. TEXT OF THE CUNEIFORM ACCOUNT OF THE DELUGE.—"I will reveal to thee, O Izdhubar, the history of my preservation, and tell thee the decision of the gods. The town of Shurippak, which thou knowest, is on the Euphrates. It was ancient, and in it (men did not honor) the gods. I alone was a servant of the great gods. (The gods took council on the appeal of) Anu:— (a deluge was proposed by) Bel, (and approved by Nebo, Nergal, and) Adar.

"And the god (Ea), the immutable lord, repeated this command in a dream. . . . 'Man of Shurippak, build a vessel and finish it (quickly). I will destroy life and substance (by a deluge). Cause thou to go up into the vessel the substance of all that has life. The vessel thou shalt build; 600 cubits shall be the measure of its length, and 60 the measure of its breadth and of its height. (Launch it) thus on the ocean, and cover it with a roof.' I understood and said to Ea, 'My lord, (the vessel) that thou commandest me to build thus, when I shall build it, young and old (shall laugh at me).' (Ea opened his mouth and) spoke: ('If they laugh at thee) thou shalt say to them, "He who has insulted me

[1] Cf. Lenormant, " Essai de Commentaire de Bérose."

(shall be punished), (for the protection of the gods) is over me." I will exercise my judgment on that which is on high and that which is below. . . . Close the vessel. . . . Enter into it and draw the door of the ship toward thee. Within it, thy grain, thy furniture, thy provisions, thy riches, thy menservants, thy maidservants, and thy young people, the cattle of the field and the wild beasts of the plain, which I will assemble and send to thee, shall be kept behind thy door. . . .' On the fifth (the two sides of the bark) were raised. The rafters in its covering were in all fourteen. I placed its roof and I covered it. I embarked in it on the sixth day; I divided its floors on the seventh, I divided the interior compartments on the eighth. I stopped up the chinks through which the water entered in. I poured on the outside three times 3600 measures of asphalt, and three times 3600 measures of asphalt within. Three times 3600 men, porters, brought on their heads the chests of provisions. I kept 3600 chests for the nourishment of my family, and the mariners divided among them twice 3600 chests. For (provision) I had oxen slain; I appointed rations for each day. In (anticipation of the need of) drinks, of barrels and of wine (I collected in quantity) like to the waters of a river; (of provisions) in quantity like to the dust of the earth. . . .

"All that I possessed I gathered together—of silver, of gold, of the substance of life of every kind. I made my servants, male and female, the cattle of the fields, the wild beasts of the plains, and the sons of the people, all ascend (into the ship).

"Shamas (the sun) fixed the moment, and he announced it in these terms: 'In the evening I will cause it to rain abundantly from heaven; enter into the vessel and close the door.' . . . When the evening of the day arrived I was afraid; I entered into my vessel and shut my door, and then confided to the pilot this dwelling, with all that it contained.

"Mu-sheri-ina-namari[1] rose from the foundations of heaven in a black cloud; Ramman[2] thundered in the midst of the cloud; Nebo and Shurru marched before— they marched, devastating the mountain and the plain. Nergal,[3] the powerful, dragged chastisements after him. Adar[4] advanced, overthrowing before him. The archangels of the abyss brought destruction. By their terrors they agitated the earth. The flood of Ramman swelled up to the sky, and (the earth), grown dark, became like a desert.

"They destroyed the living beings on the surface of the earth. The terrible deluge swelled up towards heaven. The brother no longer saw his brother: men no longer knew each other. In heaven the gods became afraid of the waterspouts, and sought a refuge; they mounted up to the heaven of Anu.[5] The gods were stretched out motionless, pressing one against another, like dogs. Ishtar wailed like a child; the great goddess pronounced this discourse: 'Here is mankind returned into earth; and theirs is the misfortune I have announced in presence of the gods.' . . . 'I am the mother who gave birth to men, and there they are, filling the sea like the race of fishes; and the gods on their seats, by reason of that which the archangels of the abyss are doing, weep with me!' The gods on their seats were in tears, and held their lips closed, (revolving) things to come.

"Six days passed and as many nights; the wind, the waterspout, and the deluge-rain were in all their strength.

[1] A personification of rain. [2] The god of thunder.
[3] The god of war and of death.
[4] The Chaldean and Assyrian Hercules.
[5] The upper heaven of the fixed stars.

At the approach of the seventh day the deluge-rain grew weaker; the terrible waterspouts, which had been awful as an earthquake, grew calm, the sea began to dry up, and the wind and the waterspout came to an end. I looked at the sea, attentively observing, and the whole race of man had returned to the earth; the corpses floated like sea-weed. I opened the window and the light smote on my face. I was seized with sadness; I sat down and wept, and the tears came over my face.

"I looked at the regions bounding the sea, towards the twelve points of the horizon, but there was no land. The vessel was borne above the land of Nizir; the mountains of Nizir arrested the vessel, and did not permit it to pass over. For six days they thus stopped it. At the approach of the seventh day I sent out and loosed a dove. The dove went, turned, and found no place to light on, and came back. I sent out and loosed a swallow; and it went, turned, and finding no place to light on, came back. I sent out and loosed a raven; the raven went, and saw the corpses on the waters; it ate, rested, turned, and came not back.

"I then sent out (the creatures in the vessel) towards the four winds, and offered a sacrifice. I raised the pile of my burnt-offering on the peak of the mountain. Seven by seven, I laid the measured vessels,[1] and beneath I spread rushes, cedar-wood, and juniper. The gods were seized with the desire of it—with a benevolent desire of it; they assembled like flies above the master of the sacrifice. From afar, in approaching, the great goddess raised the great zones that Anu made for the glory of the gods.[2] These gods, luminous as crystal, I will never leave; I prayed, in that day, that I might never leave them. 'Let the gods come to my sacrificial

[1] Vessels or vases with measured contents, for the offering.
[2] This is a metaphorical expression for the rainbow.

pile! But never may Bel come to it, for he did not master himself, but he made the waterspout for the deluge, and he has numbered men for the pit.'

"From far, in drawing near, Bel saw the vessel and stopped. He was filled with anger against the gods and against the heavenly archangels.

"'No one shall come out alive! No man shall be preserved from the abyss!' Adar opened his mouth and said: he said to the warrior Bel, 'Who other than Ea should have formed this resolution? for Ea possesses knowledge and (he preserves) all.' Ea opened his mouth and spake: he said to the warrior Bel, 'O thou, herald of the gods, warrior, as thou didst not master thyself, thou hast made the waterspout of the deluge. Let the sinner carry the weight of his sins; the blasphemer the weight of his blasphemy. Please thyself with this good pleasure and it shall never be infringed; faith in it (shall) never (be violated). Instead of thy making a new deluge, let lions and hyenas appear and reduce the number of men; let there be famine and let the earth be (devastated); let Dibbara[1] appear and let men be mown down. I have not revealed the decision of the great gods: it is Khasisatra who interpreted a dream and comprehended what the gods had decided.'

"Then, when his resolve (to destroy the remnant of men) was arrested, Bel entered into the vessel and took my hand and made me rise. He made my wife rise and place herself at my side. He walked round us and stopped short. He approached our group. 'Until now Khasisatra has been mortal, but now he and his wife are going to be carried away to live like the gods, and he will live afar, at the mouth of the rivers.' They carried me away, and established me in a remote place, at the mouth of the stream."

[1] The god of epidemics.

Such is the latest and best translation of this wonderful legend, from which only a few words of repetition have been omitted.

321. COMPARISON BETWEEN THE TWO CHALDEAN LEGENDS AND THE ACCOUNT OF MOSES.—When we compare the two Chaldean forms of the legend with the account of Genesis, we observe that they agree with it on several points and diverge on others.

Berosus tells us that the boat of Xisuthrus was five furlongs in length and two in width. The tablet of Nineve gives it in less exaggerated dimensions. They are expressed in cubits like in the Bible. The three writers agree in the main as to how the ark was built; but the two Chaldean narratives make several persons enter the boat with Xisuthrus and Khasisatra, while according to Genesis Noe, his wife, his sons and their wives alone were saved. Berosus and the author of the Izdhubar legend do not make any mention of the seven pairs of clean animals saved from the Flood. The Chaldean historian does not tell us the date when the Deluge began, which is given in the Bible. In reference to the duration of the Flood, there is a notable difference between Genesis and the inscription. According to the former, Noe remained in the ark one year; according to the latter, only nineteen days elapsed between the first rains and the last sending forth of the bird. Berosus is silent on this point. With regard to the place where the ark stopped, Moses, as we saw before, names the mountains of Ararat; the inscription, Nizir; Berosus, the Gordiæan (Kurdish) mountains. As there is no mountain known by the name Nizir, we cannot say whether the accounts agree on this point or not.

The three documents give the same account of the sacrifice offered to the divinity by the men saved from the inundation. The book of Genesis speaks of a promise made by God to man; so also do the inscription and the account of Berosus; the former vaguely, the latter very clearly. The ancient poem of Erech or Uruk relates that Khasisatra received the gift of immortality and was placed at the mouth of the rivers; according to Berosus, Xisuthrus at the end of the sacrifice disappeared from the eyes of those who were saved with him, and went to dwell with the gods, together with his wife, daughter, and pilot. The Bible says that Noe lived 350 years longer and died at the age of 950 years. Finally, one of the most remarkable features in the two stories is, that, abstracting from mythological amplifications, both give almost the same succession of incidents in describing the Flood.

For the Christian world the Chaldean version of the Deluge has a great importance. Moses' account of the Deluge is confirmed by these documents. And we can easily understand the great interest its publication caused in the whole Christian world. In this discovery we may see how God watches over His revealed faith. At a time when the hydra of infidelity raises its head everywhere, attacking Holy Scripture in the most vehement manner, God makes the Assyro-Chaldean monuments speak, holding up to the sceptics the words of Our Saviour: "I say to you that if these shall hold their peace, the stones will cry out;"[1] "The word of the Lord endureth forever."[2]

322. LEGENDS OF THE FLOOD AMONG OTHER NATIONS.—As regards the legends about the Deluge among other nations, Claudius says very truly:

"These traditions are like the children of one father, where each one has its proper features, but all have certain family traits. What children have that is peculiar to each they have, I believe, each from itself;

[1] Luke xix. 40.   [2] 1. Peter i. 25.

but what they have in common they have from the father."

323. ARAMEAN LEGEND.—The author of the treatise "On the Syrian Goddess" makes known to us the diluvian tradition of the Arameans, as it was narrated in the celebrated sanctuary of Hierapolis, or Bambyce. It was derived directly from that of Chaldea.

"The generality of people," he says, "tell us that the founder of the temple was Deucalion Sisythes—that Deucalion in whose time the great inundation occurred. I have also heard the account given by the Greeks of Deucalion. The myth runs thus: The present race of men is not the first, for there was a previous race, all the members of which perished. We belong to a second race, descended from Deucalion, and multiplied in the course of time. As to the former men, they are said to have been full of insolence and pride, committing many crimes, disregarding their oaths, neglecting the rights of hospitality, unsparing to suppliants; accordingly they were punished by an immense disaster. All on a sudden enormous volumes of water issued from the earth, and rains of extraordinary abundance began to fall; the rivers left their beds, and the sea overflowed its shores; the whole earth was covered with water, and all men perished. Deucalion alone, because of his virtue and piety, was preserved to give birth to a new race. This is how he was saved: He placed himself, his children, and his wives in a great coffer that he had, in which pigs, horses, lions, serpents, and all other terrestrial animals came to seek refuge with him. He received them all; and while they were in the coffer Zeus inspired them with reciprocal amity, which prevented their devouring one another. In this manner, shut up within one single coffer, they floated as long as the waters remained in force. Such is the account given by the Greeks of Deucalion.

"But to this, which they also tell, the people of Hierapolis add a marvellous narrative: that in their country a great chasm opened, into which all the waters of the Deluge poured. Then Deucalion raised an altar, and dedicated a temple to Hera (Atargatis), close to this very chasm. I have seen it; it is very narrow, and situated under the temple. Whether it was once large and has now shrunk, I do not know, but I have seen it, and it is quite small. In memory of the event, the following is the rite accomplished: Twice a year sea-water is brought to the temple. This is not only done by the priests, but numerous pilgrims come from beyond the Euphrates, bringing water. It is poured out in the temple and goes into the cleft, which, narrow as it is, swallows up a considerable quantity. This is said to be in virtue of a religious law instituted by Deucalion to preserve the memory of the catastrophe and of the benefits that he received from the gods. Such is the ancient tradition of the temple."

324. LEGENDS OF THE HINDOOS, IRANIANS, ARYANS, PERSIANS, GREEKS, CELTS, SCANDINAVIANS.—In India, as in Chaldea, we find two accounts of the Deluge, which, by their poverty in details, contrast strikingly with those of the Bible and the Chaldeans. The most simple and ancient form, which we will quote here, is found in the Çatapatha Brähmana of the Rig-Veda. It has been translated for the first time by Max Müller.

"One morning water for washing was brought to Manu, and when he had washed himself a fish remained in his hands and addressed these words to him: 'Protect me and I will save thee.' 'From what wilt thou save me?' 'A deluge will sweep all creatures away; it is from that I will save thee.' 'How shall I protect thee?' The fish replied: 'While we are small we run great dangers, for fish swallow fish. Keep me at first in a vase; when I become too large for it, dig a basin to put me into. When I shall have grown still more, throw me into the ocean; then I shall be preserved from destruction.' Soon it grew a large fish. It said to Manu: 'The very year I shall have reached my full growth the deluge will happen. Then build a vessel and worship me. When the waters rise, enter the vessel, and I will save thee.'

"After keeping him thus, Manu carried the fish to the sea. In the year indicated Manu built a vessel and worshipped the fish. And when the deluge came, he entered the vessel. Then the fish came swimming up to him, and Manu fastened the cable of the ship to the horn of the fish, by which means the latter made it pass over the Mountain of the North. The fish said: 'I have saved thee; fasten the vessel to a tree, that the water may not sweep it away while thou art on the mountain; and in proportion as the waters decrease, thou shalt descend.' Manu descended with the waters, and this is what is called the descent of Manu on the Mountain of the North. The deluge had carried away all creatures, and Manu remained alone."

Among the Iranians, in the sacred books containing the fundamental Zoroastrian doctrines, and dating very far back, we meet with a tradition which must assuredly be looked upon as a variety of the Deluge tradition, though possessing a special character, and differing in some essential particulars from those we have been examining. It relates how Yima, who, in the original and primitive conception, was the father of the human race, was warned by Ahuramazda, the good deity, that the earth was about to be devastated by a flood. The god ordered Yima to construct a refuge, a square garden (*vara*), protected by an enclosure, and to cause the germs of men, beasts, and plants to enter it, in order to escape annihilation. Accordingly, when the inundation occurred, the garden of Yima, with all that it contained, was alone spared, and the message of safety was brought thither by the bird Karshipta, the envoy of Ahuramazda.[1]

All the Aryan races—the Persians, Greeks, Celts, Scandinavians—had their legends of the Deluge. The Chinese say that Fo-hi, to whom they ascribe the origin of their civilization, escaped the great cataclysm with his wife, three sons, and three daughters.[2] The Phœnician mythology relates the victory of Pont (ocean) over Damaros (earth).[3] The medal of Apamea, representing the Deluge, is well known. On it is represented a square vessel, floating on the waters, which contains a man and a woman. Above the latter, the medal represents two birds, one roosting on the boat, the other flying toward the first one, carrying between its claws an olive branch. Noe and his wife are represented thereon in the attitude of going forth from the ark. All these details remind us of those which Genesis gives. The Armenians asserted that in the time of the emperor Augustus there were still remains of the ark in their country on the mountain Barris (ship). All these traditions keep close to the account of Moses, as also to the well-known tradition of the Hellenes concerning the Deluge of Ogyges.

325. AMERICAN TRADITIONS.—"It is a remarkable fact," says Maury, "that the American traditions of the Deluge come infinitely nearer to those of the Bible and the Chaldean religion than those found among any people of the Old World."[4]

[1] Cf. Lenormant, "Vendidad," vol. ii., p. 46.
[2] Klaproth, "Asia Polyglotta," p. 12.
[3] Wandsbecker, "Bote Thl.," vii., p. 105.
[4] "Revue des Deux Mondes," vol. xxvii., p. 643.

The most important among the American traditions of the Deluge are the Mexican; they appear to have been definitely fixed by symbolic and mnemonic paintings before any contact with Europeans. Among the many variations, not a few believed that a vulture was sent out of the ship, and that, like the raven of the Chaldean tablets, it did not return, but fed on the dead bodies of the drowned. Other versions say that a humming-bird alone, out of many birds sent off, returned with a branch covered with leaves in its beak. Among the Cree Indians of the present day, in the Arctic circle, in North America, J. Richardson found similar traces of the great tradition. He says:

"The Crees spoke about a universal deluge, caused by an attempt of the fish to drown one who was a kind of demigod, with whom they had quarrelled. Having constructed a raft, he embarked with his family and all kinds of birds and beasts. After the flood had continued some time, he ordered several water-fowl to dive to the bottom, but they were all drowned. A muskrat, however, having been sent on the same errand, was more successful, and returned with a mouthful of mud." From other tribes in every part of America, travellers have brought many variations of the same world-wide tradition; nor are even the scattered islands of the great southern ocean without versions of their own. In Tahiti the natives used to tell of the god Ruahatu having told two men "who were at sea fishing: Return to the shore, and tell men that the earth will be covered with water and all the world will perish. To-morrow morning go to the islet called Toamarama; it will be a place of safety for you and your children. Then Ruahatu caused the sea to cover the lands. All were covered, and all men perished except the two and their families."[1]

[1] Gaussin, "Du Dialecte de Tahiti," etc., p. 255.

In other islands we find legends recording the building of an altar after the Deluge, the collection of pairs of all the domestic animals to save them, while the Fiji islanders give the number of human beings saved as eight.[1]

326. WHAT DO ALL THESE TRADITIONS TEACH US? —Thus the story of the Deluge is a universal tradition among all branches of the human family, with the one exception, as Lenormant tells us, of the black. How could such a tradition arise, but from the ineradicable remembrance of a real and terrible event? It must, besides, have happened so early in the history of mankind that its story could spread with the race from its original cradle, for the similarity of the versions points to a common source.[2]

[1] Hardwick's "Christ and other Masters," vol. ii., p. 185.
[2] Cf. C. Geikie, "Hours with the Bible," vol. i., pp. 204, 205.

CHAPTER XV.

GEOLOGY AND THE DELUGE.

Geology has no facts that are at variance with the tradition of the Deluge.—Geological facts.—Erratic rocks.—Bone caves.—Osseous breccias. — Tufaceous limestone. — Geology confirms the Deluge.—Universality of the Deluge.—Three systems. — First: absolute universality. — Second: restricted universality.—This system is not in contradiction with the Sacred Text.—Arguments in its favor.—Important question.—Third: more restricted universality.—The Deluge did not cause the death of certain Mongolian and Ethiopean races.—Can such a view be maintained?—Conclusion.

327. GEOLOGY NOT OPPOSED TO THE TRADITION OF THE DELUGE.—The first geologists believed they had found direct proofs of the submersion of part, at least, of the earth in historic times. The English geologist Sedgwick at first defended the theory of the Geological Diluvium and Noe's Deluge, and then gave it up. In the speech in which he expressed his change of opinion, after giving the reasons against his former theory, he used the following striking language:

"Are, then, the facts of our science opposed to the sacred records? and do we deny the reality of a historical deluge? I utterly reject such an inference. In the narrative of a great fatal catastrophe handed down to us, not in our sacred books only, but in the traditions of all nations, there is not a word to justify us in looking to any mere physical monuments as the intelligible records of that event; such monuments, at least, have not yet been found, and it is perhaps not intended that they ever should be found. But there is a general accordance between our historical traditions and the phenomena of geology. Both tell us in language easily understood, though written in far different characters, that man is a recent sojourner on the face of the earth. Again, though we have not as yet found the certain traces of a great diluvian catastrophe which we can affirm to be within the human period, we have at least shown that paroxysms of internal energy, accompanied by the elevation of mountain chains, and followed by mighty waves desolating whole regions of the earth, were a part of the mechanism of nature. And what has happened again and again, from the most ancient up to the most modern periods in the natural history of the earth, may have happened once during the few thousand years that man has been living on its surface. We have therefore taken away all anterior incredibility for the fact of a recent deluge; and we have prepared the mind doubting about the truth of things of which it knows neither the origin nor the end for the adoption of this fact on the weight of historical testimony."[1]

Pfaff also says: "If the Deluge is supposed to have been a partial flood, only affecting the regions which were inhabited in the earliest times, and not a universal flood covering the whole earth, no objection can be made to it on the part of natural science. Natural science knows of the possibility, and history tells us of the reality of such floods in our ages."

Pfaff further explains the fact that geology does not afford any positive confirmation of the Biblical record, in the following manner:

"A passing flood which lasted only for a short time, such as the Deluge is represented to have been, would not leave any traces which would not be wiped out

[1] Address at the Anniversary Meeting of the Geological Society, 1831, p. 34.

again by the continued changes produced by the influence of the atmosphere and of vegetation. The occurrence of a flood can be proved only by stratified deposits, and the period in which these were found can be ascertained only by their organic contents. But we cannot possibly expect to find any deposits of that particular flood, however considerable it may have been, which could now, after thousands of years, be identified and distinguished from deposits produced by other causes."[1]

The Abbé Moigno speaks in a similar manner, adding that geologists can have no interest in the Deluge, nor have we a right to ask them for traces of it. The bodies of the men and animals that were destroyed in the Deluge were devoured by wild animals and birds, or decayed and were dissolved by the action of the atmosphere; and we should seek in vain for the antediluvian fossil man.[2] Besides, as Pfaff adds, it is precisely in those regions which probably were the dwelling-place of the first man and the principal scenes of the Deluge that no rigorous search for possibly existing traces has been instituted.[3]

Thus the geologists who believed they had found direct proofs of the submersion of a part at least of the earth in historical times, have to-day generally abandoned this idea. We admit that such an opinion is little probable, for an inundation of only one year could not leave on the soil traces characteristic enough to be distinguished from anterior inundations and to be recognized with certitude several centuries after. We remark, however, that geologists are not wanting who believe that, in fact, the Deluge or the effects of the Deluge did not pass away within the space of one year.

[1] Pfaff, "Schöpfungsgeschichte," p. 659 *seq*.
[2] "Les Deux Mondes," vol. xx., no. 1, May, 1869, p. 24.
[3] Cf. Reusch, "Bibel und Natur," p. 296.

They assume that its first shock took place only in Asia, that it afterward extended all over the world, and thus required many years before the last shocks had disappeared altogether.

328. GEOLOGICAL FACTS.—There exists between the tertiary strata and the modern strata almost everywhere on the globe a layer formed of gravel, clay, sand, and rolled pebbles; it is in this layer the first observers recognized traces of the Deluge. They attributed the sediments they met there to this great flood, and consequently they called the strata which contained these things *diluvium*. The geologists of to-day have kept the name "diluvium," but they give a different explanation of the formation of these deposits of sand and clay, which they refer to the quaternary and post-pliocene period. According to contemporary *savants*, the diluvium is not the work of one year and of one violent cataclysm, but the result of a long series of revolutions, conformable to the ordinary laws of nature, in which water played an important but not an exclusive part. If the Flood was a cause of these revolutions, it was not the only one.

329. ERRATIC ROCKS.—It is to this period that the erratic rocks belong of which we spoke in another place. These rocks are of various sizes, some measuring 40,000 cubic feet. They are found at very great distances from the rocks to which they originally appear to have belonged. They were transported and scattered over the whole North German plain as far as Poland and Russia; and it is unanimously assumed by geologists that they are not of local origin, but were carried there from the mountains of Scandinavia or Finland. They are identical with the rocks of these mountains in their formation. Similarly, blocks of granite which originally formed part of the opposite Alpine range are found in

the Jura Mountains. The same fact has been noticed in England, Belgium, Holland, France, in North America, and in the neighborhood of the Cordilleras. They are also met with on the Himalaya, Lebanon, Sinai, and in New Zealand. Erratic rocks are often detached from the highest summits of the Central Alps, and are scattered through Switzerland and Italy. Humboldt, von Buch, Deluc, Dolomieu, Cuvier, Buckland, Sedgwick (the latter for a time), and others, supposed that these rocks had been transported by the waters; so it was quite natural to see in them witnesses of the Deluge. But this explanation is abandoned to-day because, besides the difficulty of accounting for the removal of rocky masses measuring 40,000 cubic feet by means of a flood, it is in manifest conflict with the facts revealed by careful observation of the erratic blocks. Their angles are not broken and rounded, as they certainly would be if they had been rolled by the water. They have been carried away by glaciers; and these glaciers, not the Deluge, explain the existence of the erratic blocks on the tops of the highest mountains and in far-distant countries. Consequently, following Cardinal Wiseman,[1] we decline to see in these erratic blocks a geological proof of the reality of the Biblical deluge.

330. BONE CAVES AND OSSEOUS BRECCIAS.—It is equally difficult to regard bone caves and osseous breccias as proof of the Mosaic deluge, as several geologists attempted to do. We find, especially in limestones, natural caves, which are again narrowed into passages that lead into new chambers, and sometimes extend to vast distances underground. Masses of chalk, lime, sand, and all kinds of rolled stones, have been swept or fallen into these caves through the openings which connect them with the surface of the earth. Under

[1] "On the Connection between Science and Revealed Religion."

these rolled stones we find in many caves great quantities of bones, generally not petrified, but in their natural condition, often, however, covered with stalagmite or cemented together. It is possible that these bones have been washed into the caves with the rolled stones. But as the bones are not polished and have not lost their outline, as would be the case had they been washed down and rolled about by the water, we must suppose that animals got into the caves, that they decayed there, and that their skeletons were preserved, and a coating deposited on them which saved them from decomposition. If this be correct, either the animals lived in the caves and died a natural death there, or they were suffocated and buried by water which flowed in, or their corpses were washed in. It is supposed that the former occurred in those caves which contain chiefly the bones of one kind of animal; for instance, bears or hyenas. Thus, in a cave at Kirkdale, England, which was explored by Buckland, hyena bones were chiefly found. It is supposed that it was inhabited by hyenas, and the bones of horses, oxen, and deer, which were found with them, are those of animals which were dragged into the cave by the hyenas; it is said that whole layers of the excrement of hyenas were found there. Other caves contain the bones of graminivorous animals only, *e.g.*, horses, unicorns, sheep, and deer; and as these animals do not usually inhabit caves, it is supposed that they sought a refuge there, flying from the terrors of some convulsion of the earth, or, as is more likely, that the lair of these animals was in some neighboring place, and a stream of water washed them into the cave in which they were found. The bones of at least 1000 animals have by degrees been extracted from the Geilenreuth Cave in Bavaria, of which more than 800 were of bears, 130 of wolves, hyenas, lions, and wolverines. These animals cannot all have lived in the cave together; we must therefore suppose that their bodies were washed into it with all kinds of rolled stones and mud.

Besides the bone caves, there are the osseous breccias.[1] These are fragments of bones—the teeth of large and small mammals, besides shells, the remains of plants and wood, pieces of limestone, and other rubbish — which fill fissures in the older rocks and have been cemented into a solid mass by calcareous cement or clay.

The bone caves, of which many have been found in different countries, ours not excepted, lie in most cases so high above the neighboring rivers that the latter could not reach them when overflowing, so that their contents must have been deposited by very extensive inundations.. The fact that the animals whose remains are found in the bone caves belong not to the older formations, but the present animal world, or are very closely related to it, favors the supposition that these floods are identical with the deluge in the time of Noe.

331. TUFACEOUS LIMESTONE AT CANNSTADT. — We may also mention that to this class of geological facts belong the deposits of tufaceous limestone at Cannstadt, in which numerous mammoth bones and teeth are found; the enormous deposits of clay in the pampas of South America, with the skeletons of gigantic sloths, ant-eaters, armadillos, and the like; the "loess," a yellowish-gray sandy gravel, produced by alluvial deposits of several rivers, especially of the Rhine, in which such deposits are found as high as 600 feet above the level of the sea.[2] Of a similar character are the

---

[1] Nöggerath, "Geschichte der Naturwissenschaften," vol. iii., p. 159.

[2] Lyell, "Elements of Geology," vol. i., p. 119.

metalliferous deposits,[1] that is, those masses of conglomerate (gravel, sand, and lime) in which metals are found, especially gold, platinum, tin, and precious stones, which have been carried away from their original beds by flowing streams of water. It is supposed that metals and precious stones originally formed part of older formations; the rocks surrounding them were crushed and destroyed, the rubbish was dissolved and washed away with the precious stones and lumps of metal it contained, and deposited in valleys, ravines, and hollows. It is supposed that this washing and intermingling took place in the period of the Flood, because the gold, platinum, and ores found in the Ural Mountains contain the remains of the mammoth and rhinoceros, and those found in Australia, the bones of extinct species of the opossum. The ores found in the beds of rivers are in most cases probably produced by the uprooting and intermingling of older deposits; but these older deposits must in their turn be traced back to earlier important floods.[2]

332. IT IS POSSIBLE THAT SOME OF THESE DEPOSITS AND REMAINS ARE DUE TO THE DELUGE OF NOE.—It is possible, as Reusch says, and geologists cannot prove the contrary, that some of these deposits and remains of bones, skeletons, etc., are due to the great catastrophe related in Genesis, but this cannot be directly proved for any of them, and it is certain that some of these remains come from altogether different sources: partial inundations, the dwellings of the primitive men, caves, etc.

Geology, therefore, does not directly establish the reality of the Deluge. But it bears witness to many traces of partial inundations, of which it cannot determine the exact date.

[1] Nöggerath, *op. cit.*, vol. iii., p. 292.
[2] Reusch, *op. cit.*, p. 263 *seq.*

333. **The Universality of the Deluge.**—The extent of the Deluge has been a subject of animated discussion. Until within the last generation its universality was hardly questioned. At present minds are greatly divided on the subject. Still the majority doubts that the deluge covered the whole earth. The questions to be examined are: Did Moses mean that the Flood was universal? If so, in what sense did he mean this?

334. **Three Systems.**—The universality of the cataclysm described in Genesis can be understood in a triple sense:[1] 1. In the sense that the waters covered the whole earth, without leaving a dry spot on it. 2. In a restricted sense, *i.e.*, that the waters inundated only the inhabited earth. 3. In a yet more restricted sense, namely, that the Deluge caused the destruction of the race of Seth only, and not of the whole of mankind.

335. **First System: Absolute Universality of the Deluge.**—The ancient interpreters believed that the Deluge was universal in the widest sense of the word—that no spot on the globe was left above water. They accepted in the literal sense the words of the Sacred Text, "And the waters prevailed beyond measure upon the earth; and all the high mountains under the whole heaven were covered." The reasons which led them to this conclusion are: 1. The terms which Moses employs, and which do not seem to admit any exception. 2. The universality of the traditions of the Deluge.

336. **Second System: The Flood was Universal over the Inhabited Earth.**—The theologians of our days, however, do not interpret the words of the Bible so literally, and say that Moses wished to emphasize the destruction of the whole human race, with the exception of the eight persons in the ark, though

[1] Vigouroux, "Manuel Biblique," vol. i., p. 526 *seq.*

the waters did not cover the whole earth. In other words, they admit the universality of the Deluge for the part of the earth inhabited by the human race. The principal representatives of this view are: in Italy, P. Pianciani, S.J.;[1] in France, Maupied,[2] Marcel de Serres,[3] Lambert,[4] Schoebel,[5] Sorignet,[6] Godefroy,[7] Salmon,[8] Vigouroux,[9] Duihle;[10] in Belgium, P. Bellynck, S.J.,[11] P. Delsaux, S.J.,[12] P. Schouppe, S.J.;[13] in Germany, Dr. Hettinger,[14] Lorinser,[15] Veith,[16] Zschokke,[17] P. Bosizio, S.J.,[18] Reusch,[19] Michaelis,[20] Güttler;[21] in England and America, C. Geikie,[22] J. W. Dawson,[23] etc.

337. THE SECOND SYSTEM IS ADOPTED BY MOST SCRIPTURAL EXEGETISTS.—This view is adopted by most authorities who have recently written on the harmony between the Bible and the natural sciences,

[1] "Cosmogonia naturale comparata col Genesi," Rome, 1862.
[2] "Dieu, l'Homme, et le Monde," vol. iii., p. 803 seq.
[3] "Cosmogonie de Moise," etc., p. 154 seq.
[4] "Le Déluge," etc., p. 370 seq.
[5] "De l'Universalité du Déluge," Paris, 1854.
[6] "La Cosmogonie de la Bible," Paris, 1878.
[7] "Cosmogonie de la Révélation," p. 293 seq.
[8] "La Sainte Bible," Paris, 1878.
[9] "Manuel Biblique," 6th edition, Paris, 1888, p. 526 seq.
[10] "Apologie Scientifique," Paris, 1885, p. 441 seq.
[11] "Études Religieuses," etc., 1868, vol. ii., p. 578.
[12] "Revue Catholique," Louvain, 1876, vol. xli., p. 295.
[13] "Cursus Scripturæ Sacræ," Bruxelles, 1876, vol. i., p. 178.
[14] "Apologie des Christenthums," vol. ii., 1, p. 303.
[15] "Das Buch der Natur," Regensburg, 1877, vol. ii., p. 249.
[16] "Die Anfänge der Menschenwelt," Wien, 1865, p. 369.
[17] "Historia Sacra Veteris Testamente," Wien, 1863, p. 20.
[18] "Geologie und Sündfluth," Mainz, 1877, p. 105.
[19] "Bibel und Natur," 3d edition, Freiburg, 1870, p. 288 seq.
[20] "Quotes," Güttler.
[21] "Naturforschung und Bibel," Freiburg, 1877, p. 272.
[22] "Hours with the Bible," vol. i., p. 210 seq.
[23] "Story of the Earth and Man," p. 290 seq.

But we find opinions in favor of the non-universality of the Deluge in Christian antiquity also. As adherents of this view we count the ancient ecclesiastical writers who held the opinion that Paradise was left untouched by the Flood. Some excepted certain high mountain summits; for instance, during St. Augustine's time such an exception was claimed for Mt. Olympus. But as they based their claims upon physical objections, the holy doctor was perfectly right when, according to the estimate of physical science in his time, he tried to refute these objections by pointing to the omnipotence of God.[1] Later, Cardinal Cajetan interpreted Genesis by suggesting that by "all the high mountains under the whole heaven" were understood only the mountains under the cloudy region. The interpreters, mentioned by the pseudo-Justin,[2] who taught that the Deluge extended only to "the part of the earth inhabited by men," were not on such firm ground. Theodore of Mopsuestia favored only a partial deluge, and the Irish pseudo-Augustine, in the second half of the seventh century, without exactly adopting this view, calls its defenders *learned and ingenious scholars.*[3] An error in the figures of the Septuagint leads to the result that Mathusala died fourteen years after the Deluge, and there were commentators who, basing their view on the Septuagint, admitted that Mathusala may really have survived the Deluge; this would do away with the universality of the Deluge, even for the whole of mankind, and is against what St. Peter tells us, 1 Peter ii. 20. Of course this solution of the difficulty was erroneous; but it proves, like the preceding interpretations, that it was not believed nec-

---

[1] "De Civ. Dei," lib. xv., c. 27.

[2] "Quaestiones ad Orthodoxos," 9, 34, p. 412, edition Otto, iii., 248.

[3] "De Mirabilibus Scripturæ Sacræ."

essary to maintain the absolute universality of the Deluge.

The doctrine of the non-universality of the Deluge came more into favor during the so-called Reformation. In 1659 the Protestant Isaac Vossius, in his "*Dissertatio de Vera Mundi Ætate,*" expressed the opinion that the Deluge was not universal over the earth. At first Vossius met with great opposition within his own camp, but soon several of his co-religionists adopted his opinion; for instance, Stillingfleet (1663), Polus (1669), and others; in recent times nominal Protestants have taken the same view: Pfaff, Nägelsbach, Delitzsch, Zollmann, etc. On account of this opinion in connection with other doctrinal views, the book of Vossius was placed on the Index, and the Roman Congregation of the Index asked the famous Maurine Father Mabillon[1] for an opinion concerning Vossius' hypothesis. After having carefully examined the arguments for and against the universality of the Deluge, Mabillon, in 1686, gave it as his view that the opinion denying that the waters of the Deluge covered the whole earth was neither against faith nor against morals. "My opinion," he says in conclusion, "is that the interpretation of Vossius and others may be tolerated without any danger."[2]

Thus, in spite of contrary appearances, this second system is not in contradiction with the Sacred Text. It is a rule of hermeneutics, admitted by all interpreters of Holy Scripture, that in order to determine the sense of a passage the epoch when it was written must be considered, and that it must be understood as the author and those whom he addressed understood it.

338. WE MAY HOLD THAT THE DELUGE WAS A PARTIAL INUNDATION.—The exegetist is therefore at

[1] "Œuvres Posthumes," Paris, 1728, vol. ii., p. 60 *seq.*
[2] Cf. "Stimmen aus Maria-Laach," vol. xvi., p. 162 *seq.*

liberty to hold that the Deluge was a partial inundation of the earth's surface; for neither the aim of the Flood as expressed in Genesis nor the text of the Biblical account forces us to maintain the universality of the Deluge as to the whole earth.

339. PURPOSE OF THE DELUGE.—The purpose of the divine judgment is stated to be the punishment of man: " And God seeing that the wickedness of men was great on the earth, and that all thought of their heart was bent upon evil at all times, it repented Him that He had made man on the earth. And being touched inwardly with sorrow of heart, He said: I will destroy man, whom I have created, from the face of the earth."[1] The purpose of the Deluge, therefore, is the punishment of men; on them judgment is executed; it is directed against them. This causal relation between the destruction of men and the devastation of the earth is clearly expressed in the words of the Lord: "The end of all flesh is come before Me; the earth is filled with iniquity through them, and I will destroy them with the earth."[2] But now suppose—and who would find such a supposition inadmissible?—a considerable part of the earth's surface, perhaps entire continents, was not inhabited by any human being at the time of the Deluge.[3] Was it necessary for the complete attainment of the end indicated to bring on a simultaneous inundation of the entire surface of the earth?

340. THE LETTER OF THE BIBLICAL ACCOUNT DOES NOT TEACH THAT THE DELUGE WAS UNIVERSAL.— However, the letter of the Bible does not say that the Deluge was universal. But does not Holy Scripture say clearly that " the whole earth " should be inundated, that

---

[1] Gen. vi. 5.   [2] *Ib.*, vi. 13.
[3] " When the great catastrophe took place, the whole earth was not peopled," says Pianciani.

"all the high mountains under the whole heaven" should be put under water?[1]

We are not obliged, says Reusch, to take the expression "all the high mountains under the whole heaven" in a strictly literal sense, because similar expressions occur elsewhere in Holy Scripture where they cannot be taken literally. For instance, God says in Deuteronomy to the people of Israel: "This day will I begin to send the dread and the fear of thee upon the nations that dwell under the whole heaven; and when they hear thy name they may fear and tremble, and be in pain like a woman in travail."[2] Of course this does not speak of all the peoples of the earth absolutely. In the same way, only the countries with which the Egyptians came into contact are meant when it is said in the history of Joseph that there was famine "in all the lands," or, "the famine prevailed in the whole world," and that "all provinces" came to Egypt in order to buy corn.[3] According to the account of the Book of Kings, " King Solomon exceeded all the kings of the earth in riches and wisdom. And all the earth desired to see Solomon's face, to hear his wisdom, which God had given in his heart."[4] We must not take this geographical statement literally, any more than the saying of Our Saviour, that the Queen of Saba "came from the ends of the earth" to hear the wisdom of Solomon.[5] It is said in the Acts that at the time of the descent of the Holy Ghost there were people "out of every nation under heaven" dwelling at Jerusalem.[6] I know no exegetist, continues Reusch, who would suppose that Chinese and New Zealanders were there. In the same way we may understand the expression, "all the high mountains under

---

[1] Cf. "Stimmen aus Maria-Laach," vol. xvi., pp. 34, 35.
[2] Deut. ii. 25. [3] Gen. xli. 54–57.
[4] III. Kings x. 23, 24. [5] Matt. xii. 42. [6] Acts ii. 5.

the whole heaven," so as not to include the mountains which lay outside of Noe's horizon,¹ such as Chimborazo or Dhawalagiri.² We find analogous expressions in St. Paul; for instance, when he says that the faith of the converts at Rome was spoken of "throughout the world,"³ he could not have meant the whole globe, but only the Roman Empire. And would any one think of taking in the modern geographical sense his declaration that at the time he wrote to the Colossians the Gospel had been preached to every creature under heaven?⁴

Pianciani says: "The general statements and the word '*col*,' *omnis*, which occurs repeatedly in the history of the Deluge, must not and cannot be taken literally in the language of the sacred writers, and especially of Moses. . . . We are not unjust to Noe, I think, and his sons, or to the deliverer of Israel, if we assume that, like their contemporaries and later generations, they knew nothing of the existence of America or Australia; that they had no knowledge and no idea of the species of animals peculiar to those lands, and to distant parts of the Old World—for instance, the Cape of Good Hope; and that they knew no more of geography and zoölogy than did Aristotle, Hipparchus, Ptolemy, and Pliny. If this is so, Noe and his family might speak in their narrative, and Moses in his record of this great event, of the 'whole earth, of all the animals, of the high mountains which were under the whole heaven;' and yet we may perhaps understand these expressions to refer to those portions of the earth's surface, to the animals and mountains, which were more or less known to them. . . . We revere Moses as an inspired writer, but we find even in the inspired writers hyperbolical statements, and words

---

¹ "The Hebrews were ignorant of the existence of the two hemispheres."—Vigouroux, *op. cit.*, 529.
² Reusch, *op. cit.*, pp. 289, 290.   ³ Rom. i. 8.   ⁴ Col. i. 23.

which must not be understood in their most obvious and most comprehensive sense; and we believe that they were silent about many things, and did not know many other things, which were not necessary for the (religious) teaching of others. God left the Biblical writers in ignorance of much which it was interesting, but not necessary or useful, to know. He also allowed them to make use of expressions in their writings of which the most obvious sense is not always that which is confirmed by the context, or by a comparison of parallel passages,[1] or by the progress of human knowledge, which last sometimes furnishes an approximate and necessary commentary on the words of Holy Scripture, where the sense is not explained by the infallible exposition of revelation."[2]

341. IN WHAT SENSE THE DELUGE WAS UNIVERSAL.—Thus the account of Genesis does not oblige us to assume that the Deluge was universal in the sense that all the mountains on the earth were covered with water. The Flood no doubt was universal, but in another sense. Genesis repeatedly and distinctly asserts that all mankind, with the exception of the eight who were in the ark, was destroyed. God points this out as the real object of the Deluge, and it is repeatedly said that this object was attained, for the last time, at the end of the narrative, in these words: "These are the three sons of Noe: and from these was all mankind spread over the whole earth."[3] "By these were the nations divided on the earth after the Flood."[4]

[1] "The word translated 'earth,'" says Geikie, "in our English version has not only the meaning of the world as a whole, but others much more limited. Thus it often stands for Palestine alone (Joel i. 2; Ps. xxxvi. 11, 22, 29; xliv. 3; Prov. ii. 21; x. 30), and even for the small district round a town (Jos. viii. 1), or a field or plot of land (Gen. xxiii. 15; Exod. xxiii. 10)." Cf. "Hours with the Bible," vol. i., p. 219.

[2] Pianciani, *op. cit.*, pp. 543-545.   [3] Gen. ix. 19.   [4] *Ib.*, x. 32.

The terms employed by Genesis in the account of the Deluge refer, therefore, only to the earth known at the time of Noe and the Hebrews—to the mountains which they had seen, to the animals which were familiar to them and of which they had heard. Consequently, nothing obliges us to assume that the highest summits of the Himalaya, the volcanoes of Central and South America, and the mountains of the interior of Africa were covered by the waters, because the ancients did not know them. All the mountains Noe and Moses knew were inundated.[1]

342. IT IS NOT NECESSARY TO HOLD THAT THE ARK LANDED ON THE HIGHEST PEAK OF ARARAT.—If by the statement that the ark landed on Ararat we are to understand that the highest summit of Ararat in Armenia was covered with water, the Flood must have been very great; for the summit of Ararat is 16,000 feet above the level of the sea. Even if, as some suppose, some lower mountain in Armenia was the landing-place of the ark, a flood which spread over the Armenian highlands must have been of a very great extent. Pianciani says: "It is not necessary to assume that the ark landed on the highest peak of Ararat. It may have rested in a valley between the peaks."[2]

343. DID THE FLOOD LAST MORE THAN A YEAR?— But there is another question to be examined. May we assume that the changes caused by the Deluge on other points of the earth lasted more than a year? Father Hummelauer answers as follows: "Even if we do not take the Flood described in Genesis as universal, nevertheless we need not conceive it as a local inundation, such as a lasting inundation of the

---

[1] Cf. Nicolai and Pianciani, "Cosmogonia" in the "Civiltà Cattolica," July, 1862, pp. 316, 317; Reusch, *op. cit.*, p. 391.
[2] Pianciani, "Cosmogonia," p. 538.

Mesopotamian lowlands, caused by an extraordinary swelling of the twin streams, the Euphrates and Tigris. For the statement that the waters reached 45 feet above the summit of the 'mountains of Ararat,' whether we understand the great Ararat itself, or Armenia in general, or the mountains of Kurdistan, shows that the flood was much more extended. Without the most powerful commotions and changes of the earth's surface, without extensive elevations and depressions of continents and ocean beds, events like those described in Genesis, apparently by an eye-witness, are simply inconceivable. A sudden sinking of the land, which was formerly, perhaps, less elevated above the level of the sea than at present, explains best the rushing in of the ocean over the continent, and this was followed by an elevation of the land after the flowing off of the waters and the drying of the ground. But could such an event take place in Western Asia without affecting the whole earth? Therefore men have not been wanting in our time who believed that the immense changes of level that took place toward the end of the glacial age were caused by the Biblical Deluge. According to them, the convulsions in the Armenian mountain chains are only an isolated section of the great change on our planet the traces of which we can pursue in the recent elevations of the Alps and Himalaya, in the unfettering of the volcanic powers on so many other points of the earth, in the laying dry of the Sahara ocean, the Aral and Caspian seas, and the inner Asiatic ocean, as also the lower Rhenish plain; in the separation of the Malay island world, and also, perhaps, the sinking of Atlantis.

"The question whether and how far the above events were really connected with the Biblical Deluge may never be answered. However, supposing the reality of this connection, must we assume that the Flood, with all its consequences, was over within the space of one year? The Sacred Text does not support any other supposition; but it is possible that the catastrophe in Western Asia was only the first shock which was followed by other shocks on other parts of the globe; it is possible that in some localities shocks had preceded that in Asia. In any case, the drying of the lowlands must have progressed much more slowly than that of the 'mountains of Ararat.' Centuries may have elapsed before the last scene of the oscillating terrestrial drama found its conclusion. This suggests the possibility of a final reconciliation between the older hypothesis of Cuvier, who ascribed the whole diluvium to the Deluge, and the more recent view of Sedgwick and Buckland, who questioned the simultaneousness of the different diluvial layers; between the older conception of the Deluge as a catastrophe which extended over the whole earth and the more modern view which accepts only a local inundation. If we admit this view, then certainly the Deluge, in the widest sense of the word, that is, in so far as it embraced the above-mentioned changes of the earth's surface, extended over the whole earth and was, therefore, in a certain sense, universal, even as regards our globe; while, on the other hand, in the narrower sense, we may also call it local— that is, an inundation of the locality mentioned by the Bible. We must ascribe, at least in part, the formation of the diluvium to the Deluge; but this would diminish very considerably the age of the various diluvial deposits; thus almost complete harmony would be established between the Bible and science, and full liberty would be secured to science."[1] Let us hope to see the day when this harmonious view will prevail.

[1] "Stimmen aus Maria-Laach," vol. xvi., pp. 43-45.

344. THIRD SYSTEM: THE DELUGE DID NOT CAUSE THE DEATH OF ALL MEN EXCEPT NOE AND HIS FAMILY.—We must be careful not to confound the second system just explained with the third one, which denies the universality of the Deluge for the human species, and excepts certain branches, as the Mongolians and Ethiopians, from destruction by the Flood. In other words, this opinion asserts that the Deluge need not be regarded as a universal one, in the sense that all mankind, with the exception of Noe and his family, was destroyed; but that only the inhabitants of the countries known to Noe perished; so that certain Mongolian and Ethiopian tribes, which had already separated from the mass of mankind which inhabited Asia and had become strangers to Noe and his family, were not affected by the Deluge.

345. ON WHAT THIS THEORY IS BASED.—This theory is based on the belief that before the Deluge mankind had already spread over a great portion of the earth. On the contrary, the view that all men, except Noe and his family, were destroyed by the Flood, supposes that only a part of Asia was peopled. Genesis does not contain any information about the dispersion of mankind before the Deluge, and neither geological nor historical investigations have produced satisfactory information upon this point.

346. CAN THIS VIEW BE MAINTAINED?—Cuvier, Quatrefages, Schoebel, and the Abbé Motais maintain this opinion. Omalius of Halloy, a Belgian savant, also taught it in 1866, in his "Discourse to the Class of Sciences" at the Belgian Academy.[1] Professor Scholz, of Wurzburg, did the same. What are we to think of this

[1] P. Bellynck, a Belgian Jesuit, without positively adopting the view of Omalius, considers his opinion tenable.—"Études Religieuses," vol. i., 1868, p. 578.

opinion? We have seen that, according to Genesis, God caused the annihilation of all the descendants of Adam, whose genealogy it gives us, because they had all become corrupt; and St. Peter in his two Epistles expressly says: "In the ark (of Noe) few, eight souls, were saved by water."[1] "God preserved Noe, the eighth person, the preacher of justice."[2] The unanimous tradition of the Fathers, and the universal teaching of the theologians, interpret these words of St. Peter in the sense that only eight persons were saved —that is, Noe, his wife, his three sons, and their wives. No sufficient reason is given for departing from the interpretation accepted by the Church until at present. The formation of the various human races, and the numerous languages spoken upon earth in dim antiquity, the progress civilization had made long before Abraham, we are told, are so many proofs that some races escaped the Deluge and preserved their characteristic features, language, and arts. The supporters of this opinion suppose that a relatively short time elapsed between the Deluge and Abraham; but when treating on Biblical chronology we saw that very probably this time is longer than was generally believed. However, in our next chapter we shall meet this objection.

[1] I. Peter iii. 20.   [2] II. Peter ii. 5.

CHAPTER XVI.

CAUSES OF THE DELUGE.—ANSWER TO OBJECTIONS.

Why natural science cannot bring serious objections against the Deluge.—Linguistic and zoölogical objections.—Size of the ark and number of animal species. — Experiments. — Repeopling of the earth by animals. — Causes of the Deluge.—Torrential rains.—Invasion of seas.—Subterraneous fountains.—Upheavals and depressions.—Combination of the different systems.—Conclusion.

347. THE OPINION THAT THE DELUGE WAS RESTRICTED TO THE INHABITED EARTH DISPOSES OF MANY DIFFICULTIES.—If we hold that the Deluge was restricted to the inhabited part of the earth, most of the difficulties alleged against the Mosaic account disappear. Pfaff says: "The discussions on the Deluge have become useless, because theologians admit that the narrative of Genesis may signify, not that all the mountains on the surface of the globe were simultaneously inundated, but that all mankind was annihilated by a mass of water. This admission means that the Deluge was a partial submersion of the globe. The learned have no objections to make against the Deluge thus explained; it is impossible for them to prove that a partial flood, whose occurrence, in fact, is affirmed by the traditions of almost all the nations, could not have taken place, or did not really take place."[1]

348. OBJECTION AGAINST THE OPINION THAT THE DELUGE COVERED THE INHABITED EARTH.—Thus the physical and natural sciences have no serious arguments

---

[1] Pfaff, "Schöpfungsgeschichte," p. 750.

against the reality of the Biblical Deluge. The objections brought forward in the name of ethnology and linguistics are not convincing. It is impossible, we are told, that all men, except the family of Noe, were destroyed in the great inundation related in Genesis, because as far back as our investigations go, we find the races of men such as we know them, the languages that they speak already existing. But if all men now living upon earth are descended from Noe, we must admit that these races and languages are posterior to the Deluge, which in fact is inadmissible.

"But why inadmissible?" asks Vigouroux. "The difficulty is a chronological and not a scientific one; the question is, At what epoch did the Deluge take place? If it occurred at a time remote enough for the descendants of Noe to transform themselves—some into negroes, others into Mongolians or Redskins, etc.; if the number of centuries was sufficient for the language of primitive man to split up into several tongues, as happens in our days, the difficulty falls to the ground. These changes could take place since the Deluge as well as since the creation. We saw when discussing Biblical chronology that we do not know the date when God punished mankind by this terrible chastisement, and we have shown that we can put back its date as much as the historical and archæological sciences require. These, therefore, cannot bring any serious argument against the Mosaic account." [1]

349. HOW COULD NOE GATHER FOREIGN ANIMALS INTO THE ARK?—The most serious difficulty raised against the old interpretation of the account of the Deluge is that which zoölogists make. "Every beast according to its kind," says Genesis,[2] "and all the cattle

---

[1] "Les Livres Saints," etc., vol. iii., p. 499.
[2] Gen. vii. 14, 15.

in their kind, and everything that moveth upon the earth according to its kind; and every fowl according to its kind, all birds and all that fly, went in to Noe into the ark, two and two of all flesh."

This passage was understood to refer to all animals, known and unknown,[1] instead of referring only to the animals known at the time of the Deluge. Thus, it becomes very difficult to explain, without multiplying miracles, how Noe could gather into the ark animals which were separated from him by the immense ocean, and how animals living, perhaps, on islands could return there after the inundation.

The Deluge being, according to the Bible, a punishment for the sins of mankind, it follows that all men should perish in order to atone for their sins; but this was not true of the animals; hence there was no reason why they also should perish. Thus we must admit the universality of the Deluge for the human species, the Mongolian and Ethiopian tribes included; but nothing proves that we must admit its universality for the animals, any more than for the terrestrial globe. And just as it is conformable to the rules of good criticism to understand by the "whole earth" the earth known at the time, it is equally correct to understand by "all the animals" only those which were known to Noe and Moses. Pianciani says:

"It does not necessarily follow from the fact that human sinfulness was the moral cause of the Deluge that the part of the animal world which inhabited the

[1] However, even long ago interpreters excepted some animals, for instance, St. Augustine ("De Civitate Dei,"l. xv., c. xxvii., 4, vol. xli., col. 475). "In arcam," says Cornelius à Lapide, who with the ancients admitted spontaneous generation, "non sunt inducta animalia quæ ex putrefactione, uti mures, vermes, apes, scorpiones . . . nascuntur."—In Gen. vi. 19; "Cursus Completus Scripturæ Sacræ," vol. v., col. 275.

countries then unknown to man must have been spared by the Deluge. But we may gather therefrom that it is impossible to argue from animals to man, and *vice versa;* and that because all men died who were not in the ark, it does not necessarily follow that all animals died likewise; while, on the other hand, if it were proved that certain kinds of animals survived the Deluge, it would not follow that any man had been saved. Lastly, it must be noted that in the ten chapters of Genesis which follow the first, Moses tells the history of mankind, and not of the animal world; and that he nowhere says that all existing kinds of animals spread over the earth are descended from the animals which came out of the ark."[1]

350. ONLY THOSE ANIMALS PERISHED THAT WERE KNOWN TO NOE.—Hence we may admit that only those animals perished which were known to Noe and Moses. Those which Noe did not know did not exist for him. We have no reason to suppose that God revealed supernaturally to Noe the existence of animals which he never had occasion to see, and of which he had never heard. Neither does anything prove that God ordered him to gather others than those which lived in his own country.

"Noe was not commanded to do anything impossible, and he did no more than he could. If the command to assemble all the animals had been given to one possessed of much greater resources than Noe—for instance, to Alexander the Great, or Augustus—he would no doubt have collected together the most comprehensive menagerie that had ever been seen; and yet all the animals then unknown in Europe, and existing only in America and Australia, would have been wanting. Is Noe's collection likely to have been more complete?"[2]

[1] Pianciani, "Civiltà Cattolica," September, 1862, p. 34.
[2] Pianciani, *op. cit.*, October, 1862, p. 293.

It is evident that if God had wished, nothing would have been easier for Him than to assemble in the ark, by supernatural means, all the existing animal species; but, as Pianciani remarks, we must not multiply miracles without reason. As the animals which lived in regions not inhabited by man were thereby saved from the Deluge, and had no need of taking refuge in the ark in order to be saved, nothing obliges us to suppose that they entered therein.

It has been asserted quite seriously, even by men of science, that after the Deluge all living things went forth from Ararat and peopled the whole earth. In the time of Moses such an assertion was justifiable (although Moses does not make it), and we do not dispute its truth according to the knowledge of that age. All animals which were then known to the Jews, and in which they were interested, may have spread from Ararat.[1]

351. IF THE DELUGE BE RESTRICTED TO THE INHABITED EARTH, THE ARK WAS OF SUFFICIENT SIZE.— The hypothesis we have set forth at the same time meets the difficulties raised against the possibility of enclosing all species of animals in so small a vessel as the ark. The ark, it was shown, could contain without excessive inconvenience all the species of animals known of old. Since the discovery of so many new species in America, the question has been more difficult, and a vessel of the dimensions of the ark would hardly suffice to contain all animals on the earth.[2] But the

[1] Geibel, "Tagesfragen," p. 72.
[2] It is supposed that the ark was a vessel of 80,000 tons burthen. The most ancient book known treating on the number of animal species is the "Pirkê of Rabbi Eleezer." This author makes Noe bring into the ark 32 species of birds and 365 of other animals. Johnston in his "Physical Atlas" (1856) gives

difficulty vanishes if Noe assembled only the animals which were known to him.

In that case, the ark was able to fulfil the purpose for which it was constructed, and large enough to hold the family of Noe and the animals destined to be saved from the cataclysm. Experiment has proved this. In the year 1604 a Dutch Anabaptist, Peter Jensen, built a ship according to the proportions and form of the ark. It was not suitable for navigation, but it could contain one third more than the cargo which could be put into a boat of the ordinary form and of the same cubic capacity.

352. ANOTHER OBJECTION MET BY THE HYPOTHESIS OF A DELUGE RESTRICTED TO THE INHABITED EARTH.—Another objection raised by naturalists falls to the ground, if we admit that the Deluge did not destroy all animals. How could the animals contained in the ark spread all over the earth? they say. How could the mammalia overcome the difficulties they must encounter by land and sea to reach the furthest regions?

Pianciani answers this objection as follows: "It is not likely that whole species of land animals crossed the Atlantic, or any other ocean, for the pleasure of settling in America. Certainly the men that first peopled America and Australia and did not take with them cattle and horses, would not take to the new continent a fauna which is quite different from that of our continent. Neither is it likely that so many animals that are not found in the Old World travelled over icebergs to the warmer regions in the New World; although in the north the reindeer and polar bear, etc., could have passed in this way from one country to another."[1]

1,658 species of mammalia; Lessen admits 6,266 species of birds; Ch. Bonaparte, 642 species of reptiles; Sir John Lubbock states that the total of all species of animals surpasses the enormous figure of 700,000.   [1] "Cosmogonia," p. 556.

Linnæus believed that all animals had started from one centre, but to-day naturalists teach that each continent has more or less its peculiar fauna. Cuvier has remarked that when the Spaniards first penetrated into South America they did not meet there a single species of quadrupeds found in Europe, Asia, and Africa: the jaguar, the tapir, all the monkeys, etc., were animals unknown to the Spaniards. New Holland and the neighboring islands also had animals unknown to the first European settlers—such as kangaroos, ornithorhynchi, etc. New Zealand, which appears to possess no indigenous mammal except a species of rat, has very many species of birds which are proper to it. These countries which are peopled by a peculiar fauna to-day, have also a fossil fauna altogether different from ours. The kangaroos of Australia, for instance, had as predecessors kangaroos twice as large as the largest of to-day.[1]

Hugh Miller tells us that many animals are confined to certain places. This is especially true of the fauna of Australia; for example, its quadrupeds of all kinds, strange to say, are marsupials—that is, provided with a pouch in which to carry their young. The fossil remains of the great island continent show, moreover, that existing species are the direct descendants of similar races of extreme antiquity, and that the surface of Australia is the oldest land of any considerable extent so far discovered on the globe. It dates back to the tertiary geological age at least; since then it has not been disturbed to any great extent. But this carries us to a period immensely more remote than Noe.

Nothing forbids our admitting that the animals known to the Hebrews could spread from Mount Ararat to other Biblical lands; but that they scattered into other coun-

[1] Hugh Miller, "Testimonies of the Rocks," p. 332 *seq.*

tries beyond seas and oceans can hardly be maintained.

353. CAUSES OF THE DELUGE AND ANSWERS TO OBJECTIONS.—In regard to the causes of the Flood, difficulties were advanced in the name of natural philosophy which appeared very serious to some savants. Those who tried to explain the manner in which this terrible phenomenon took place were unable to arrive at an agreement among themselves. 1. Some attributed it to immense torrential rains, and alleged the words of Scripture, "The flood-gates of heaven were opened." 2. Others attributed the Deluge to an invasion of the seas, and appealed to the words, "All the fountains of the deep were broken up."[1] 3. A third opinion supposes an elevation of the surface of the globe, which destroyed the equilibrium of the waters, and thus brought on the inundations of the continents. 4. Finally, some hold that all these causes, or at least the first two, acted simultaneously. We know of no explanations except those we have enumerated. But these give rise to difficulties.

354. (1) EXPLANATION OF THE DELUGE BY TORRENTIAL RAINS.—Nothing is easier than to quote numerous examples of rains the abundance and duration of which caused considerable inundations. But supposing that the most violent torrential rain of which we have any record lasted for forty days, we should have a layer of water only 2,400 feet in depth; but the peaks of the Himalaya have a height of 27,520 feet. Again, assuming that such a rain fell over the whole world, it is said that the physical laws governing the world do not allow a simultaneous submersion of the two hemispheres. To produce such a rainfall, a sudden, simultaneous, and considerable fall in the temperature of the atmos-

[1] Gen. vii. 11. Compare Gen. viii. 2.

phere must take place, which the present state of the atmosphere would not permit. Rain falls when the humid air, having cooled, can no longer keep in an invisible, vaporous state all the water with which it is charged. The excess of water turns into vapor, forming clouds and fogs, or into drops which form rain. The air cools either by mingling with cooler air or by contact with cooler parts of the globe, or, finally, by dilation due to diminution of pressure, which in a manner determines atmospheric movements. These phenomena are necessarily local, and generally counterbalanced by contrary phenomena in other parts of the atmosphere; it is, therefore, impossible that rain should fall simultaneously over the whole earth, especially with a violence sufficient to bring on a deluge like that described in Genesis.

In reply we may say with Dr. Reusch, that what is impossible after the Deluge may have been possible when the Deluge took place; but such an answer does not remove the difficulties. A change in the essential laws governing the atmosphere that surrounds our globe supposes a change in the conditions of life upon earth—a change of which we do not discover any trace in the organisms of living beings.

Moreover, the entire mass of water which fell during the forty days' rain must have been suspended in the atmosphere before the beginning of the torrential rain or precipitate; for during the general rain a supply of water vapor could not rise from the ocean. Hence, before the rain an atmospheric pressure five and one-half times greater than normal would have lain on men and animals. After the rain this must have been removed and replaced by the normal atmospheric pressure. Furthermore, it would follow that formerly organic beings must have been accustomed to greater atmospheric pressure, or this pressure must have been temporarily lessened before and during the Flood. But whoever, while ascending a high mountain or witnessing experiments with a diving-bell, has noticed the noxious effects a relatively insignificant diminution or increase of pressure has on man and beast, will hesitate to admit these hypotheses.[1] In that case, the preservation of the men and animals in the ark can be explained only by a miraculous change in their organisms—an assumption, however, which contradicts empirical inquiry and finds no support in the words of the Bible. The same men and animals that went into the ark also went forth from the same.[2] Thus the explanation by torrential rains causes difficulties which seem insoluble.

355. (2) EXPLANATION OF THE DELUGE BY AN INVASION OF THE SEAS.—If, on the other hand, we ascribe the Deluge to an inundation of the seas and the bursting forth of subterranean springs we are face to face with difficulties of another kind.

"If we assume that no country, island, or mountain was left untouched by the Flood, and that the water stood 45 feet deep not only on all the mountains of Armenia, but also on all the great heights of Asia and America, it is very difficult to find a satisfactory answer to the question, 'Whence did so much water come?' We may unhesitatingly admit that subterranean waters burst forth, but will that suffice? May we assume that enormous stores of water existed in subterranean caverns, when we know that the mean specific gravity at the centre of the earth is much greater than that of the portion of the earth's crust known to us, and perhaps seven times greater than that of water? It is, of course, possible to assume that more water was created by God,

[1] Cf. Pfaff, *op. cit.*, p. 651.
[2] Güttler, "Naturforschung und Bibel," p. 267.

and was afterward destroyed again, or that the water came from regions beyond our atmosphere and returned whence it came. These things certainly do not exceed the almighty power of the Creator, but I do not know how far they are in harmony with His wisdom and His usual mode of working; and these assumptions would involve a risk of exposing the work of God to the ridicule of men of science, which, as St. Augustine and St. Thomas have observed, should be avoided as much as possible." [1]

Without even taking into account the fissures and hollows which exist on the earth's surface, in order to completely inundate the earth a volume of water of depth equal to the height of the highest mountains would be needed—that is to say, of a depth of 27,000 feet, the height of the peak of the Himalaya. Now, assuming that the quantity of water was not miraculously increased, the question arises whether there is on earth sufficient water to cause an inundation like the Deluge of Noe? We could answer this question in the affirmative if we assumed that God caused the Deluge by transferring the waters of the ocean to the continents, while the seas were dry. But such a suspension of the law of equilibrium is not probable.[2]

In the North Atlantic Ocean soundings have reached a depth of from 25,000 to 30,000 feet; in some cases the lead did not reach bottom at 40,000 feet. The Hima-

[1] Pianciani, *op. cit.*, p. 551.
[2] " Dana calculates the mean depth of the sea at 15,000–20,000 feet. Humboldt reckons the mean height of the land to be 1,000 feet. If, therefore, we wished to fill up the sea with all the land, and equalize all the unevenness of the surface of the earth, the sea would not lose more than about 375 feet of its mean depth, all continents would have disappeared, and besides this, the water would stand about 15,000 feet over all the earth."—Frass, " Von der Sündfluth," p. 89.

laya mountains, the highest in the world, could be buried at the bottom of the ocean, and our largest ships could float over their highest peaks without touching them.

356. (3) EXPLANATION OF THE DELUGE BY UPHEAVALS AND DEPRESSIONS.—These explanations of the Deluge are therefore subject to grave difficulties from the point of view of the laws of physics. Equal difficulties are involved in the hypothesis of Leonhard and Hugh Miller, who seek to account for the Deluge by the rising of great mountains—for example, the chain of the Cordilleras—or by a profound depression of the soil.

Of course these changes are only hypothetical. Genesis gives no account of them, because they do not come within the purview of its narrative; nor can we prove scientifically that they took place. But these hypotheses are welcome to Biblical scholars, as they make the narrative of Genesis more plausible. They may stand before the judgment-seat of natural science, if it can be proved that they do not go beyond anything that men of science have themselves admitted to be possible. We subjoin a few of these hypotheses.

Klee[1] thinks it probable that the inclination of the earth's axis to the plane of its orbit was not always the same as it is now. If the axis round which the earth revolves daily were at right angles to the plane of the orbit in which it revolves round the sun, there would be no alternation of the seasons; all parts of the earth would have equally long days and nights. The change of the seasons and the difference between the zones as they exist is caused by the fact that the axis of the earth varies $23\frac{1}{2}°$ from a horizontal position. If the axis had formerly been perpendicular to the plane of its orbit, or more upright than at present, the climatic conditions would have been materially different from what they

[1] " Der Urzustand der Erde."

are now; and if the change in the position of the axis had taken place suddenly, it might have sufficed to produce catastrophes as considerable as the Deluge. An English geologist is inclined to the belief that the earth was originally a ball, and received its present spheroidal shape by a sudden upheaval under the equator. Of course we are dealing with mere suppositions, for Genesis gives no account of them. But do they assist us to remove the difficulties? Hear what Pianciani says:

"Moses mentions neither volcanoes, upheavals of mountains, nor settlements of the land, nor any other phenomena which may have preceded, accompanied, or followed the Deluge; but he does not exclude the possibility of any of these phenomena, and we may therefore admit that they may have occurred without in any way contradicting his narrative. Perhaps these events took place in regions far from the dwelling-place of Noe's family. If at that time the great chain of the Andes was upheaved in America, Noe would hardly have known about it, and there is no apparent reason why God should have revealed physical events of this kind to Moses; but even if we suppose that the sacred historian did know of them, there is still no reason why he should have recounted them." [1]

There is no doubt that such upheavals and depressions of parts of the earth's surface occurred in the past. Geologists are the last people to object to them; for such upheavals and depressions play an important part in every system of geology. "We have many proofs," says one, "that important sinkings of the land took place at a comparatively recent epoch." [2]

According to Vogt,[3] a settlement of the land followed

---

[1] "Civiltà Cattolica," 1862, p. 519.
[2] De la Bèche, "Manual of Geology," p. 172.
[3] "Lehrbuch der Geologie," vol. i., p. 622.

the glacial period in the north of Europe and America, and the land subsequently rose again. According to the theory of the elevation of mountains which Élie de Beaumont first proposed, and which has been supported by many modern geologists, it is assumed that the highest mountains are the most recent; the Cordilleras, one of the most extensive and highest mountain ranges, being perhaps the most recent of all.[1] Burmeister[2] places the most violent and tremendous of these convulsions in the period immediately preceding the historical age. Even if they occurred singly and were of slight extent, could not such settlements and upheavals have taken place in historical times and caused inundations? The facts that in the year 1822, 1,000 miles of the coast of Chili were raised four feet in one night by an earthquake,[3] and that in 1819 more than 90 geographical square miles of the delta of the Indus were turned into a lake by a settlement of the land following an earthquake, show that this is not impossible, and that important upheavals and settlements do still occur.[4]

But whatever may be the value of these hypotheses for the purpose of explaining the causes of the Deluge, we must account for the presence of water on the land, and to do this we must have recourse to rain or to the sea.

357. (4) EXPLANATION OF THE DELUGE BY A COMBINATION OF THE DIFFERENT SYSTEMS.—Some scholars have attempted to explain the Deluge by the simultaneous action of all the causes we have mentioned, but all the difficulties inherent to the three explanations already set forth evidently hold good against the fourth system.

[1] "Schöpfungsgeschichte," p. 265.   [2] *Ibid.*, p. 272.
[3] "Natürliche Geschichte der Schöpfung," p. 127.
[4] Mantell, "Wonders," vol. i., p. 81; cf. Reusch, "Bibel und Natur," p. 311.

358. Conclusion: It is Impossible to Tell by what Means God Produced the Deluge.—Hence it is impossible to tell by what means God produced the Deluge, because He did not reveal it to us. But it matters very little whether we know it or not. It is sufficient to show that the laws of physics do not prove the impossibility of the great Flood as related by Moses. Nothing is easier than this if we assume—and we have proved that the teaching of the Church allows us to do so—that the Flood extended only to the inhabited earth. By this hypothesis all difficulties disappear. For the objections suppose that the waters covered the whole earth. If they covered only the part of our globe then peopled, man was exposed to no excess of atmospheric pressure, because rain was localized and did not fall in abnormal amount; the rivers would not mingle their waters with the waters of the sea, and the fish would not perish, because part of the earth would remain undisturbed; finally, so great a quantity of water would not be needed, and mankind could have been submerged by means of rain or water from the sea.

Even on this supposition we do not know the means God made use of to inundate the inhabited earth. All we know from Genesis is, that rain was one of the principal, if not the only, means He employed.[1] We may admit that He caused the seas to overflow and new springs to burst forth, according to the explanation given by certain exegetists.[2] Finally, nothing is opposed to the hypothesis of some great revolution of nature, which, geology proves, took place, and which God used as a means to bring about the great cataclysm.[3]

[1] Pianciani, "Civiltà Cattolica," July 17, 1862, pp. 315-317.
[2] Gen. vii. 11. The word "thehôm" employed by the Hebrew text may well mean the sea, and applies to the sea rather than to the atmosphere. [3] Cf. Vigouroux, "Manuel Biblique,' p. 537.

CHAPTER XVII.

MAN'S COMPONENT ELEMENTS. THE EXISTENCE OF THE SOUL.

Definitions.—Life. — Life-spring.— Soul.—Organisms.—Vegetative, sensitive, and intellectual life. — The highest form of life, the soul, appears in man.—The essence of the principle of life.—What is an organism?—Without accepting a soul-principle, we cannot explain organisms.—Nature of the human soul.—Teachings of Holy Scripture.—Three steps in the creation of man.—The distinction between the body and the soul and the intimate union of the two clearly expressed in Holy Scripture.—Hebrew psychology.—Man's soul is not a complex of his corporal organs.—Mental diseases prove nothing against the existence of the soul.—From corporal indications no certain conclusions can be drawn on the condition of the soul.

FROM our anthropological studies we have learned that man differs essentially from animals, both in origin and history; he also differs from them in his nature: this will form the subject of our last investigation.

359. WHAT IS MAN?—The question "What is man?" surely deserves our fullest attention. The knowledge of God and correct self-knowledge have at all times been considered as the end of all wisdom. In pagan antiquity men's opinions of man were often enveloped in thick darkness, the result of false opinions and strong passions; however, the idea of man is so intimate to us that it was never wholly unknown. But it was only by Christianity that our full dignity was revealed to us. The Church always saw in man a being composed of two substances—a spiritual substance and a corporal substance; she always distinguished the soul

from the body. This is also the teaching of the Vatican Council, which, renewing a dogmatic declaration of the fourth council of the Lateran, has expressly defined that "God made from nothing both creatures, the spiritual and the corporal, the angelical and the material, and afterward man, formed by the union, so to say, of a body and of a spirit."[1]

These two substances, the spiritual and the corporal, so different from each other, God has joined together in man by a tie incomprehensible, but very visible and very real. Thus man is a mixed creature. For this reason the philosophic and spiritualistic school of the beginning of the present century, by defining man as "an intelligence provided with organs," fell into error; for this definition does not sufficiently express the way in which spirit and matter combine individually and equally to form man. It is best to adhere to the more ordinary definition, "Man is a reasonable animal;" for this expresses very clearly that man is a being compounded of a body and a soul, both of which form part of his essence.

But before entering more into detail about the constituent elements of man, let us ask, What do we mean by a soul?

360. WHAT IS LIFE?—The answer to this question becomes clearer when we ask, What is life? What do we call "alive"? Life, being alive, generally speaking, is to move one's self, to be animated; life is the existence of a being which develops an activity from within itself. In a more limited sense life is the sum of the activities of so-called organic bodies. These are so called because they consist of heterogeneous parts that serve as instruments (organs) of activity. Hettinger says:[2]

[1] Constitution "Dei Filius," cap. 1.
[2] Hettinger, "Apologie," vol. i., 1, 336 *seq.*

"What moves we call alive. Therefore to live means to move—that is, to move one's self from within, so that the thing moving and the thing moved are one and the same thing, in contradistinction to the motion which does not proceed from within, but is caused by an impulse from without. The living body moves itself; cause and effect meet in one and the same body. The animal, for instance, approaches its prey through the power dwelling within itself; in the same way it flees before its enemy; while the motion of the stone through the air does not proceed from within itself, but from the hand that threw it; the animal, therefore, we call a living, the stone a dead, being."

361. THREE KINDS OF LIFE.—We distinguish three kinds of instruments of activity, three kinds of life: (1) Vegetable (plant) life, with the functions of growth and nourishment (development and preservation of the individual) and reproduction (preservation of the species). (2) Animal life, which, besides the vegetative functions, includes also the functions of sensation, desire, and motion. The life of the organism is conditioned by one combined, vivifying, moving power, or principle of life—life-spring—and ceases as soon as this power is separated from the organism; this separation we call "death." (3) Intellectual life, in which a spirit is the organic principle of life.

"In the organism of plants this principle of life is bound absolutely to the organs themselves, operates through the organs and their chemico-physical constituent parts, powers, and laws, and extends to the organism proper its nourishment, growth, and reproduction; however, this principle stands above the power of matter, because it is active from within and makes use of its organs according to immanent aims and laws. After the vegetative life proceeding from it, we call this principle the vegetative (vegetable) soul. In animals the principle of life, the life-spring, is tied to the corporal organism, makes use of it, but does not operate merely through its corporal qualities; its effect does not extend merely to its own body, as is the case in the plant, but also to sensible objects. This second principle of life we call a sensitive (animal) soul, because sensation and self-movement proceed from it."[1]

362. THE HIGHEST FORM OF LIFE APPEARS IN MAN.—The highest form of life reveals itself in man, in whom his spirit operates as the organic principle of life.

A spirit is a simple, incorporeal, supersensible substance, endowed with intellectual faculties (understanding, reason, and free will). From its simplicity follows its indestructibility and immortality. God is the highest, most perfect spirit. The angels are called "pure spirits" in contradistinction to the human spirit, which, incorporeal in itself, is nevertheless essentially united with a body into one nature; therefore we call the human spirit "soul."

In man this spirit operates not only as the organic principle of life, but exercises, besides the vegetable and animal functions, the higher spiritual functions, as we have just observed. For this reason we distinguish in man a corporal (organic) and a spiritual life. While the principle of life in the plant and animal (vegetative, animal soul) perishes with the separation of the organism, the human soul, on the contrary, being a spirit, continues to live after death, and continues to exercise the spiritual functions of life.

"The highest form of life appears where the principle of life operates neither through a corporal organism nor through corporal qualities, but directly, and is active

[1] Hettinger, "Apologie," vol. i., 1, pp. 339, 340.

through itself alone; its action, therefore, extends not only to the sensible and perceptible, but to the entire domain of truth. This is the reasonable soul, which, essentially united to the body in man, besides the vegetable and sensitive functions, possesses the faculties of thinking and free-will. As the animal unites in its sensitive soul also the vegetable principle of the plant, so the reasonable soul unites in itself the lower forms of life of both the plant and the animal. Man nourishes himself and grows like the plant, has the feeling and movement of the animal; that which distinguishes him as man is the third form of life, proper to him—the life of intelligence and liberty proceeding from the self-conscious spirit. In consequence of this unity of the principle of life or soul in man we ascribe to the same subject different and opposite activities, because the various functions reside in one and the same principle; on this account man's faculties influence each other; a violent passion checks clear thinking, profound reflection removes or weakens the lower soul powers. For this reason both Holy Scripture and the Church call the souls of the departed merely 'souls,' because they were formerly united with the body as principle of its organism, and are destined to be re-united with it. The angels, on the contrary, we call 'spirits,' because the principle of their activity—consciousness and liberty—is not, as in man, at the same time the principle of growth and sense perception. So Holy Scripture speaks of animal souls whenever it wishes to designate the principle of animal life."[1]

363. THE ESSENCE OF THE PRINCIPLE OF LIFE.—Having shown that man has a soul or principle of life, it remains for us to learn what science teaches with regard to the essence of our soul.

[1] Hettinger, "Apologie," vol. i., 1, pp. 341, 342.

Many physiologists, especially those of the materialistic school, assert that life is nothing but the result of a combination of physico-chemical forces. In what this combination consists, how it works, and how it produces life, materialism does not know and cannot satisfactorily answer. What is the essence of the organic principle of life? In answering this question, Hettinger says: "In saying that man has a soul we ascribe to him a principle of activity which surpasses the powers of mere matter, and produces phenomena which cannot be explained by the physico-chemical qualities of the body."[1] In other words, all organic life, be it human, animal, or vegetable, requires a life-spring, a soul, which stands like a new, higher creation above the powers of dead matter. And with this assertion we have touched the heart of materialism; for this either stands or falls with the declaration, "The process of life, with all its functions and activities, is nothing but the result of mechanical and chemical processes, the product of matter, which produces life by a peculiar combination." "The soul," says Burmeister, "is a complex of faculties and forces which animal or human organisms reveal."[2] "If science were compelled," says Büchner, "to acknowledge a vital force, then the universality of natural laws and the unchangeableness of the mechanical order of the universe would break down; we must admit that a higher hand has control of the laws of nature, and creates exceptional laws which are not subject to calculation; a rift would appear in the building of nature; science must despair of itself, and every natural and spiritual inquiry would cease;"[3] that is to say, materialism would be impossible. "But," continues Hettinger, "if we

[1] *Op. cit.*, p. 343 *seq.*
[2] Burmeister, "Geologische Bilder," vol. i., p. 251.
[3] Büchner, "Kraft und Stoff," p. 245.

cannot explain the organic unity of the most simple vegetable organism by a mere 'mixture of matter,' but only by a new, higher principle, much less can we explain sensation and human thought without such a principle."

364. WHAT IS AN ORGANISM?—And such a principle exists as a matter of fact. For what is an organism? "We have compared organisms," says John Müller, "with a system of parts united for a certain end, whose efficiency depends on the undisturbed harmony of the composing members. An organism is similar to a mechanical work of art in being a combination for the accomplishment of a certain end; but in the case of the organism it produces the mechanism of the organs in the germ and afterward reproduces it. The working of organic bodies does not depend on the harmony of the organs, but that harmony is an effect of the organic bodies themselves; and every part of this whole has its cause not in itself, but in the cause of the whole. A mechanical work of art is produced to perform certain work in accordance with the idea in the mind of the artist. Every organism also is based on an idea or type, and in accordance with this idea its organs are organized. But this idea exists outside of the machine, whereas it works in the organism and works of necessity."[1] Thus, not matter, taken from outside, causes the unity and harmony of an organism, but the unity and harmony precede it. The unity and harmony exist in the germ, before the later parts (previously undistinguishable) of the whole exist as such, and it is they (unity, harmony) that really produce the members essential to the idea of the whole.

Hence, that which makes the organism what it is, is the typical idea of the plastically operating force im-

[1] "Physiologie des Menschen," p. 23.

manent in the body. The germ, Müller continues, which is a simple cell, is the whole *in potentia;* with the development of the germ the parts arise *in actu.* This first formation and development of the cell is a proceeding which has its parallel nowhere in inorganic nature; in its essentials it is the same in plants and animals, and here the initial unity reveals itself in a striking manner by the power and activity that creates them.

365. TO EXPLAIN ORGANISMS WE MUST ACCEPT A SOUL, OR PRINCIPLE OF LIFE.—It is this organic principle of life, the soul, which makes the body what it really is. Therefore, wherever there is life there is the principle of life, a soul. Were organisms nothing but the result of material powers, then, by the proper combination of them, we ought to be able to produce a living body. But, in spite of all progress in natural science, nobody has yet dreamt of bringing forth a living body out of the crucible, not even a plant or a leaf.

The elements, the chemical constituent parts, found in the animal body are known; the relations in which they stand to one another can be expressed in arithmetical formulæ; but science has not succeeded in producing an organism. Were it only a mixture of matter, we ought to be able to imitate it, because the proportions of the mixture are known. The reason why this is impossible is evident. A principle not in the domain of science is wanting—the principle of life, the soul, which God granted to living beings at their creation. Science operates only with the physico-chemical properties of organic and inorganic matter. When men tell us that science does not yet know all the means by which nature works, this is a worthless subterfuge. When they speak thus they postulate the unknown force—evident from its effects—which operates in nature and which we have characterized as the principle of life—the soul. They do the same when they tell us that, "under certain relations," "through certain combinations," "under certain peculiar circumstances and conditions," organic life arises from the simultaneous action of material elements. When we ask, What are these peculiar conditions which constitute the general physical laws for the appearance of the individual life? they answer: They are conditions required in the organization of the being. But what light does this answer shed on the problem? It is only introducing another term, in order not to be obliged to accept the principle of life—the soul. But it is precisely this principle of life which arranges and governs the material elements found in the body, and which makes use of the lower material forces for the benefit of the whole, which forms by their means the individual whole. Thus only is the unity of the body well established. Hence, as soon as the principle of life escapes, corruption takes the place of vital action; the body, as an organism, perishes; and the chemical elements being no longer governed by the principle of life and used in accordance with its laws, the general forces of matter overpower the organic formation. The law of capillarity, of endosmosis and exosmosis, especially proves this. If asked to explain the fact that the blood in a living blood-vessel does not clot, physiology knows no other answer than this. "It is caused by the influence of the sides of the living vessel;"[1] because a mutual anastomosis (inosculation of vessels) of the sensor and motor nerves does not take place, but every irritation of the sensible nerves operates only upon the motor nerves

---

[1] Wundt, "Physiologie," § 110.—"Why does the stomach not digest itself, if chemico-physical powers only are at work?" asks Cl. Bernard (Criticism of Janet, "Causes Finales," "Journal des Savants," 1877)

through the medium of the gray matter of the spine, the "reflex movement"[1] cannot be explained by the mechanism of the conducting media (*Leitungsverhältnisse*). As the action of a mechanism cannot explain the regenerative power which produces essential organs (head, tail) in inferior organisms, and operates in higher ones as a natural healing force, so the animal instinct, this objective conformability, cannot be produced by physico-chemical forces.

366. DIFFERENCE BETWEEN ORGANIC AND INORGANIC BODIES.—Certainly there are physico-chemical forces active in the organism, but it does not follow that the organism is merely the effect of these forces. St. Thomas observes that the vegetative activity, the appearances of growth and nourishment, and even of feeling and movement, are the effects of the physico-chemical forces,[2] of which the immanent principle of life makes use, but which do not exclude its controlling power, but, on the contrary, presuppose them. Only in this way can we explain why elements which are indifferent to this or that formation, form a particular organism, a particular kind and species, and no other. Hence we infer precisely the contrary of what material-

---

[1] "Reflex movements" in physiology are certain involuntary motions, caused by the irritation of a nerve, *e.g.*, sneezing, by the irritation of the mucous membrane of the nose.

[2] "Summa Theologica" i., qu. lxxviii., art. 1.: Etsi calidum et frigidum, humidum et siccum et aliæ hujusmodi qualitates pure corporeæ requirantur ad operationum sensus, non tamen ita, quod mediante virtute talium qualitatum operatio animæ sensitivæ procedat, sed requiruntur solum ad debitam dispositionem organi. Infirma operatio animæ fit per organum corporeum et virtute corporeæ qualitatis; hujusmodi autem operationes sunt ab intrinseco principio. Et talis est operatio animæ vegetativæ. Digestio et ea quæ sequuntur, fit instrumentaliter per actionem caloris.

ists assert; not the material qualities are the cause of the whole, but the whole, the principle of life, is the cause of the physico-chemical process, following its direction. "Life," says Cuvier, "acts very differently from chemical affinity on the material elements which it attracts and uses; hence, it cannot be their product."[1] "The body does not live because the physico-chemical forces are active," says Flourens, "but the forces are active because the body lives."[2] In another place the same author says: "It is not matter which lives; force lives in matter, moves and agitates it, and renews it continually." Even Burmeister admits: "In organic bodies matter is not the element which conditions the form, but rather the contrary; that is, the form of the organism is the essential element to which the material basis is subordinate."[3]

This power of organisms to control the chemical affinities of the matter which constitutes them—that is, the peculiar relations in which they stand to one another—is one side of those qualities which we designate by the word "life," and for which we accept the words "vital force." What this force is, we know as little as what force in general is. But it is enough for us to know that this vital force governs chemical affinity as long as it lasts. When the period within which the organism moves as a periodical body ends, death sets in. Then chemical affinity again controls the matter of the organism, and changes it by various processes—fermentation and corruption—into inorganic substances. According to Biot, man is able to excite dead matter to certain activities, to awake them, so to say, through the forces which operate within it or which he introduces from without;

---

[1] "Le Règne Animal," p. 17.
[2] "De la Vie et de l'Intelligence," vol. i., p. 156, and vol. ii., p. 98.
[3] "Geschichte der Schöpfung," 3d ed., p. 304.

but, with all his intelligence, man is unable to create the least atom; much less can he produce a living being by the combination of dead matter, or by the action of dynamic powers.[1]

Only by the unity of the principle of life can we explain the indivisible unity especially of the higher classes of living beings, the harmony of their functions, which acts in accordance with a plan and end. Finally, only by its means can we explain the peculiar laws which determine organic life, and which are quite different from those of mere matter both as regards the composition of bodies, and their form and shape, their origin and growth. Hence, we must either deny these unquestionable facts, or, since they cannot be explained as the effect of mere material forces, we must accept a higher principle—that is, a *soul*.

367. WHAT HOLY SCRIPTURE TELLS US ABOUT THE NATURE OF OUR SOUL.—After these somewhat dry and philosophical, but necessary, explanations of the principle of life—the soul—let us listen to what Holy Scripture tells us about the nature of our soul. The Abbé Vigouroux, says on this subject:[2]

"Nowhere in the Bible do we meet a didactic explanation of the nature of the soul—no more than a formal proof of its existence and of its distinctness from the body: the philosophical method, the subtle analysis, of which the Greeks have left to us the precept and the example, are not in accordance with the genius of the Orientals, who express themselves only by means of images, and who dread abstractions. But if we wish to know the ideas hidden under their metaphors, and, by stripping the thought of borrowed ornaments, contemplate the naked truth, it will be an easy matter for any

[1] Z. Ph. v. Martius, "Gedächtnissrede über Biot."
[2] "La Bible et les Découvertes Modernes," vol. iii., p. 112 *seq.*

person willing to see to obtain a clear knowledge of Hebrew psychology and to admire its precision.

"The whole of it is summed up on the first page of Genesis. According to the sacred narrative, God first formed the material part of man, his body, which He drew from the slime of the earth, *áfar min ha' ádámáh*. After this He breathed into it the breath of life, He imparted to it an immaterial spirit, *nišmat-haïm*. The union of this body and spirit, of this *áfar* and *nišmat*, forms man, the *néfeš hayah*, 'the living soul,' which receives the name Adam, or 'man.' The earthy body, although formed by the hands of God, is therefore at first only a lifeless statue; it becomes man only after a new element, the *nišmat-haïm*, has been added to the first, and these two elements form a single person. Can we desire a clearer affirmation of the soul's existence, as well as of the distinction between the body and the soul and the difference in their nature?

"However, Holy Writ adds a feature which makes these truths even more striking and palpable. Man is superior to the animal in body, for it is the work of the hands of God Himself; but his superiority lies especially in his soul, because his soul is made 'after the image and likeness' of God, its Creator. Men have admired, and with good reason, the disciple of Socrates when he called man a 'celestial plant;' and, nevertheless, what is the language of Plato in comparison with that of Genesis, which, in our soul, shows us the image of God? What a depth in this simple expression! The words of Moses have, and can have, but one meaning; in our cold and colorless, but more precise, language they mean: Man is composed of a body and a soul; his body has been formed from the earth, but his soul was created directly by God, and it is in the soul that man resembles his Creator. In his body he is not His image, for this is common to him and all other living beings, and, consequently, is no characteristic mark, or, as the philosophers express it, is not 'his specific difference;' he is God's image in his spiritual, intelligent, and free soul, which is his exclusive privilege, making him the king of creation and giving to him the right to command all nature.'

"All this has been said since Moses' time, in more abstract and, if you wish, in more precise words; but it has never been said more sublimely and more correctly. 'Again,' says Bossuet, 'God formed all the other animals by saying, "Let the earth, let the water, bring forth the plants and the animals,"' and thus they received both being and life. But after God had taken into His all-powerful hand the slime of which the human body was formed, Scripture does not say that He drew forth the soul therefrom, but Moses tells us that "He breathed into his body the breath of life, and it is thus that man became a living soul."'' The Lord brings forth all things from their principles: He produces from the earth the vegetables, trees, and animals—all of which have no other life than a purely earthly and animal life. But the soul of man is brought forth from another principle, namely, from God Himself. This is what the breath of life signifies, which God drew from His own mouth in order to animate man. That which is made after the image of God does not proceed from material things; and this image is not hidden in these low elements in order to go forth from them as a statue does from the marble or the wood. Man has two principles: as regards his body he comes from the earth, as regards his soul he comes from God alone; and this is the reason why Solomon says, 'Whilst the body returns to the earth whence it was, the spirit returns to God who gave it.''

¹ Gen. i. 28.   ² *Ib.*, i. 11, 20, 24.   ³ *Ib.*, ii. 7.   ⁴ Eccles. xii. 7.

368. THREE STEPS IN MAN'S CREATION.—"To sum up, there are three steps in man's creation: God first formed the material substance, the 'slime,' *âfar* or the 'flesh,' *bâsâr*, called 'the body.' Then He gave to this body 'the spirit' which animates the same, *nišmat*, His breath, which Scripture elsewhere calls *ruaḥ*—what the Greeks called *pneuma*, the Latins, *spiritus*. Finally, from the union of the spirit and matter the human person proceeds, the *néfeš ḥayah*, 'the living soul,' the one compound being—man, *psyche*, *anima*. The living soul, or man, is therefore not 'the spirit' alone, any more than the body alone; it is a compound of both—the *conjunctum*, as St. Thomas calls it, the personality which from two different substances forms one single individuality. Hence the custom, in Hebrew as well as in Arabic, of using *néfeš* for the reflexive pronoun 'oneself.'[1]

369. THE DISTINCTION BETWEEN BODY AND SOUL AND THEIR UNION ARE CLEARLY EXPRESSED IN HOLY SCRIPTURE.—" The sense of these different words, *bâsâr*, *ruaḥ*, *néfeš*, and their synonyms, is faithfully preserved in all the books of the Old and New Testaments,[2] in the original text as well as in the Septuagint and Latin Vulgate. 'Man's flesh' (*bâsâr*), says Job, 'shall have pain and his soul (*néfeš*) shall mourn.'[3] 'Because my soul (*leb*) rejoices, my body (*bâsâr*) hopes,' sings the Psalmist.[4] The Proverbs say in the same sense, 'Health

---

[1] I Kings i. 15; Amos vi. 8; see Exod. xxiii. 9, the sense of person.

[2] This rule, however, admits of exceptions, like all rules of language; "*néfeš*" and "*ruaḥ*" are employed sometimes as synonyms (Job xii. 10), just as in English we often use soul for spirit.

[3] Job xiv. 12.

[4] Ps. xvi. 9.—The word *leb*, "heart," often designates in Hebrew the seat of intelligence, and in this sense is used as a synonym for "*néfeš*" or "*ruaḥ*." The Psalms are here cited

of body (*besârîm*) is the tranquillity of the soul.'¹ 'God,' says Job to his friends, 'holds in His hand the soul (*néfeš*) of every living thing, and the spirit (*ruaḥ*) of all flesh of man (*bâśâr*).'² 'The spirit (*psyche*) indeed is willing,' says Our Saviour in St. Matthew, 'but the flesh (*sarx*) is weak.'³ 'My soul (*psyche*) doth magnify the Lord, and my spirit (*pneuma*) hath rejoiced in God my Saviour,' chants the Blessed Virgin Mary.⁴ 'That your whole spirit (*pneuma*) and soul (*psyche*) and body (*sôma*) may be preserved blameless in the coming of Our Lord Jesus Christ,' writes St. Paul to the Thessalonians.⁵

"By a singular coincidence, the philosopher of Stagyra, in his 'Treatise on the Soul,' speaks just like the Bible; he also distinguishes in man the body, the spirit, and the soul, the *sôma*, the *nous*, and the *psyche*, and he also makes the spirit come from outside.⁶

"Thus the distinction between the soul and the body, and the intimate union of these two substances forming only a single person, are clearly expressed in the Bible. The Hebrew psychology also attributes very plainly to *néfeš* the faculties which we attribute to the human person: sensibility, intelligence, and will. It loves,⁷ it hates,⁸ it rejoices,⁹ it is afflicted;¹⁰ the sensations of

---

according to the Hebrew Bible, and the translation is from the French of Vigouroux.

¹ Prov. xiv. 30. See also Ps. xxxiv. 3.
² Job xii. 10. See also Num. xvi. 22. Compare also Is. x. 18, and xxxi. 3: "The Egyptians are only men and not gods, and their horses are only flesh (*bâśâr*) and no spirit (*ruaḥ*)."
³ Matt. xxvi. 41.   ⁴ Luke i. 46, 47.
⁵ I Thess. v. 23; cf. I. Cor. xv. 45, 46, 47, and Heb. iv. 12.
⁶ See the first chapter of the second book "De Anima," Aristoteles, Opera, Aureliæ Allobrogum, 1605, vol. i., p. 486.
⁷ Gen. xxxiv. 3; I Sam. xviii. 1; Cant. i. 7; Is. xlii. 1, etc.
⁸ Ps. xvii. 9; Is. i. 14; xlix. 7.   ⁹ Ps. lxxxvi. 4.
¹⁰ Job xxiv. 12; xxx. 16, 25; Ps. xlii. 6, 12; xliii. 5, etc.

pain¹ and pleasure,² hunger³ and thirst,⁴ are also ascribed to it, as well as the feelings of fear⁵ and hope,⁶ of strength⁷ and weakness,⁸ the vices⁹ and virtues,¹⁰ desire¹¹ and disgust,¹² blessings¹³ and imprecations.¹⁴ It is this human personality which knows,¹⁵ thinks,¹⁶ remembers,¹⁷ and forgets;¹⁸ which wills¹⁹ and which wills not,²⁰ which forms resolutions and executes them.²¹ '*Arêk néfeš*²² corresponds word for word to 'longanimity,' *qâṣêr néfeš*²³ to 'pusillanimity.' The *ruaḥ* designating "the spirit," is naturally like *néfeš*, the principle of feelings and affections,²⁴ of the will²⁵ and intelligence.²⁶

370. THE PSYCHOLOGY OF THE ISRAELITES.—"The Bible nowhere tells us what is the essence of the *ruaḥ*. It has been claimed that to the Israelites the soul was

¹ Gen. xlii. 21; Num. xxi. 5; Job x. 1; Ps. lxxxviii. 4.
² Ezech. xxv. 6.   ³ Prov. x. 3.   ⁴ Prov. xxv. 25.
⁵ Is. xv. 4. Sentiments, dispositions in general, Exod. xxiii. 9.—1. Kings i. 15. To pour out one's soul, *i.e.*, everything one has on the heart, Ps. lvii. 2; cxxx. 5.
⁶ Ps. lvii. 2; cxxx. 5.   ⁷ Jud. v. 21.
⁸ Ps. cvi. 15; cxix. 18; Jer. iv. 31, etc.
⁹ Prov. xxviii. 25, of pride; Ezech. xxxvi. 5, of hatred against the people of God; Lev. iv. 2; v. 15, 17, etc., of sin.
¹⁰ Ps. lxxxvi. 4; cxliii. 8, of piety toward God.
¹¹ Deut. xii. 15; xiv. 26; xviii. 6; Is. xxxvi. 8, 9; Ps. xlii. 2; lxxxiv. 3; Mich. vii. 3.   ¹² Jud. xvi. 16.
¹³ Gen. xxvii. 4; Ps. ciii. 1, 2, etc.   ¹⁴ Job xxxi. 30.
¹⁵ Ps. cxxxix. 14; Prov. xix. 2. It speaks, Lament. iii. 24; it hears, Jer. iv. 9, in the sense of Ego, designating the person, I speak, I hear.   ¹⁶ I. Kings xx. 20.
¹⁷ Lament. iii. 20; Deut. iv. 9.   ¹⁸ Ps. ciii. 2.
¹⁹ Gen. xxiii. 8; I. Paral. xxviii. 9; cf. Col. iii. 23.
²⁰ Job vi. 7.   ²¹ Ps. cxix. 129.
²² Job vi. 11.   ²³ Num. xxi. 4.
²⁴ Prov. xxv. 28; xi. 13; xvii. 22; Gen. xxvi. 35; Ps. li. 12, 19, etc.
²⁵ Exod. xxviii. 21; II. Kings xix. 7; Is. xxxvii. 7.
²⁶ Exod. xxviii. 3; Deut. xxiv. 9; Is. xi. 2.

no spiritual being, because it is designated by names signifying 'breath' and 'wind.' This argument, borrowed from etymology, is without value. Human language has been obliged to make use of sensible and material images in order to express metaphysical ideas and to designate immaterial beings; this is a rule which admits of no exception. For most nations, perhaps because of an obscure remembrance of the old and primitive tradition of the origin of the soul, have considered 'the breath,' 'the wind,' as the image most expressive and most suitable to paint to the imagination and to express in words the spirit, the hidden and immaterial agent which our senses cannot perceive, as our eyes cannot see the invisible wind whose existence manifests itself only by its effects.' 'Soul,' 'spirit,' primitively had no other meaning than 'breath.' In Latin, in Greek, in Sanscrit, as well as in Hebrew and in Arabic, the same words designate the soul and the wind.

"The expressions, therefore, used by the Bible rather indicate the immaterial character of the thinking principle, because they designate it by the least gross and the most subtle terms that could be found, by terms identical with those employed by the most spiritualistic philosophers, such as Plato, St. Augustine, Leibnitz. Nowhere does the Bible say that the soul is a corporal being. True, it does not tell us that the soul is a pure spirit. It could not even tell us this, for it possessed no word to express the idea. The New Testament even does not tell us this.[2] But all that the Bible could do, it did: it has suggested spirituality of the soul. It speaks to us about the nature of the soul, as far as its simplicity is concerned, in the same terms in which it speaks of the nature of God. Nowhere does the Bible affirm explicitly that God is a pure spirit, but neither does it assert

[1] Ps. lxxviii. 39.   [2] However, see Luke xxiv. 39.

that God is flesh, body, matter.' Even in its boldest anthropomorphic metaphors it avoids expressions which might lead man to believe that God is a being like us. Thus it has taught the immateriality of God by way of reticence and suggestion, as far as the language in which it is written—imperfect and incomplete from the metaphysical point of view—permitted it.

"The same remarks apply to the notion of the spirituality of the soul. The soul, or the *ruaḥ*, is distinct from the body. The word *néfeš* is predicated of men and beasts, like our English 'soul,' because it does not exclude the body, and it often signifies 'life,'² but it cannot be used for God.³ The word *ruaḥ*, 'the spirit,' on the contrary, is used in Hebrew like 'spirit' in our language, of God and man, but not of animals.⁴ Hence between God and the *ruaḥ* there is some analogy in their natures which distinguishes the latter from material things. In fact, the *ruaḥ* is never confounded with the compound of earth which is called the body; it is even several times carefully distinguished therefrom. Ecclesiastes opposed the *ruaḥ*, which returns to God, its author, to the *áfar*, which returns to the earth from whence it was taken.⁵ Moses and Job also distinguish *ruaḥ* from *bāśār*,⁶ the spirit from the body. Man, when

---

¹ God is even put in opposition to flesh to express thereby that He has no body.—Ps. lvi. 5; Jer. xvii. 5. In the New Testament St. John says clearly, "God is a spirit."—John iv. 24.

² Hence the expression, "For the life (*néfeš*) of all flesh is in the blood."—Lev. xvii. 14, etc.

³ Amos vi. 8. *Néfeš* is said of God, but only in the sense of *Himself*, because the usage had rendered this word the reflex pronoun in Hebrew as well as in Arabic. See Job ix. 21.

⁴ It is used of animals in a different sense, that is, of the respiratory breath, of life (Gen. vii. 22), but never as the principle of animal acts.   ⁵ Eccles. xii. 7.

⁶ Num. xvi. 22; Job xii. 10.

he listens to his carnal passions, descends from his position of honor and becomes like to the beasts;' his better being is only a little less than the angels;² he is like to God. Now this likeness to God resides especially in the soul, in this 'breath of God,'³ this 'breath of intelligence,'⁴ which is in us the 'lamp of the Lord,'⁵ according to the expressions of the Bible, in the soul, which is endowed with reason; whilst animals are deprived thereof, according to the expression of the Psalmist.⁶

371. THE UNION BETWEEN SOUL AND BODY IS NOT INDISSOLUBLE. — "The union which exists between the body and the soul of man is not indissoluble; it is broken by death. The Hebrews looked on death as the separation of the soul from the body. Creatures cease to live, and become dust again, when God withdraws their souls, *ruḥam*.⁷ Again, 'to die,' with the sacred writers, is 'to strip his soul naked,'⁸ which seems to suggest that the body is, so to say, the soul's garment, of which death strips it.

"Resurrection is accomplished by the return of the soul into the body which it animated. While the prophet Elias was at Sarephta, the widow who gave him hospitality lost her only son. 'And she said to Elias: What have I to do with thee, thou man of God? Art thou come to me that my iniquities be remembered, and that thou shouldst kill my son? And he took the child and he cried out to the Lord and said: O Lord, my God! let the soul (*néfeš*) of this child return into his body. And the Lord heard the voice of Elias, and the

---

¹ Ps. xlix. (Vulgate xlviii.) 13, 21. ² Ps. viii. 6.
³ Gen. ii. 7. ⁴ Job xx. 3; xxxii. 8. ⁵ Prov. xx. 27.
⁶ Ps. xxxii. (xxxi.) 9. ⁷ Ps. civ. 29.
⁸ *He'erâh lammavet naf'sô*, "*nudavit per mortem animam suam*," Is. liii. 12. See also Ps. cxli. 8. and II. Cor. vi. 3. "The body is the house of the soul," Job iv. 19.

soul (*néfeš*) of the child returned into him, and he revived.'[1] In the same terms St. Luke relates the resurrection of the daughter of Jairus: 'At the voice of Jesus, her spirit (*pneuma*) returned into her.'[2] When Ezechiel, in his famous vision of the dry bones, had prophesied over them the first time, they took again their original form; nothing was wanting—nerves, flesh, skin—except life, because 'the soul (*ruah*) was not in them.' By the order of God, the prophet prophesied a second time. Then the soul came to animate the bodies and they 'lived anew, and they received motion.' "[3]

Therefore the life of man is the effect of the union between the body and the soul, and death is the rupture of this union. The body separated from the soul is buried in the bosom of the earth and returns into dust,[4] but will the soul separated from the body *die also? What will become of it?* These questions will form the subject of our next and last chapter.

After learning what is the *essence* and *nature* of our soul, we should now prove its existence from its manifestations. However, having sufficiently proved this in the chapters in which we examined the difference between man and animal, we refer the reader to the arguments there set forth. To conclude the present chapter we shall inquire into the principal objections materialism alleges against the existence of the soul.

372. OBJECTIONS AGAINST THE EXISTENCE OF THE SOUL.—Those who deny the existence of the soul base their denial on the great influence the body exercises on man's faculty of thinking. They tell us that the development of the spirit keeps even pace with that of the body, and that the greater the brain-mass is, the greater is the intelligence. The power of thought in

---

[1] I. (III.) Kings xvii. 18–23.
[2] Luke viii. 55.
[3] Ezech. xxxvii.
[4] Gen. iii. 19.

man, they say, disappears, or becomes disordered, if an abnormal change takes place in the brain, or if the brain is removed.

373. THE FLAW IN THESE OBJECTIONS.—These and similar objections rest on false premises. They are worthless because they confound the instrument, without which a power cannot work, with the power itself. If it were true that our soul is as dependent on the body and on the brain as is asserted, and even more so, still, this dependence would not do away with the soul as a substance free, self-conscious, self-existing, different and separable from the body. No doubt the soul is dependent in its activity on the body, and particularly on the brain. Still, it does not follow that "the soul is only the sum of the faculties and powers" of the corporal organs and their activities. Through God's almighty power the corporal organs and their activity are so intimately and mysteriously connected with the soul that they are in mutual need of each other. The body cannot exist without the soul, and the soul, to exercise its activity, is to a certain degree in need of corporal organs; without them, its normal activity is disturbed or impossible.

374. THE SOUL IS NO COMPLEXUS OF CORPORAL ORGANS.—But from this it does not by any means follow that the soul is only a complexus of corporal organs and their activities. In its dependence upon the body we can compare the soul with a player, who cannot play without his instrument. A master on the violin, or any other instrument, will bring forth the most sublime sounds from the instrument as long as this is in good order. But if the instrument is broken or damaged, the greatest virtuoso will produce only false notes. Still, who would assert that the instrument is the player because the player cannot show his skill without the

instrument? Or who would assert that the soft and tender sounds drawn from a violin, or the mighty tones of an organ, are only the work of the strings or keys the player touches with his bow or fingers? Without the spirit of the player, his thoughts, and the feelings he expresses in his playing, the best instrument cannot give forth a musical composition. So man's soul is certainly dependent on his corporal organs, and especially on his brain. But only a fool will believe that the soul is nothing more than the activity of the body.

375. **THE DEVELOPMENT OF THE SPIRIT KEEPS PACE WITH THAT OF THE BODY.**—The development of man's spirit will therefore keep pace with that of the body, or will be conditioned by it. As long as the brain is not yet developed the faculty of thinking, and the soul's activity in general, will be more or less dormant in a child, or will manifest itself only in an imperfect manner. But according as the brain grows the spirit develops. In old age the organs of the body become weaker, and the activities of the soul diminish. If the body is sick, its suffering may exercise a disturbing influence on the activity of the soul, and, in some cases, check it altogether. But it does not follow that the soul is the body, and that the soul's activity is a function of our corporal organs. The phenomena we have mentioned, and a hundred others, only prove that the soul is dependent on them in its workings and conditioned by them.

376. **EXCEPTIONS TO THE RULE.**—This becomes clearer to us if we point out cases in which mental and corporal development are not parallel. How often do we not notice in children a mental development and ripeness out of all proportion to their corporal development! We see aged men who, while their bodies decline,

surprise us by the wonderful freshness of their minds and their unusually clear mental powers.[1]

"Study," says Duihle, "a man of intelligence and talent, if you wish, a man of genius, on the point of death.... Behold him emaciated, broken down under the triple weight of work, age, and sickness. Death has already put his icy fingers upon every one of his limbs. A feather, a piece of paper, would be too heavy for his hand, which has not even the strength to tremble like the hand of an old man. At the same time the spirit is full of intelligence, the soul has preserved its full strength, all its life. What do I say! Its transports, raptures, manifestations, are more radiant than ever. Have we not read wonderful pages, masterpieces, dictated by the dying?"[2]

Indeed, how often does it happen that a sickness which attacks some part of the body has no influence whatever on the faculties of the spirit. We read of cases in which even a partial destruction of the brain caused no change whatsoever in the soul life. Clearness of mind, full consciousness until the last moment, are proofs that the soul is no function of the corporal organs, but a self-existing substance, different from the body. "How often," says Louergne,[3] a medical doctor, "have not the last wishes of the dying struck by-standers with wonder! How does it come that a man on the verge of the grave is so precise in his morality, so careful, that he seems superior to all that has taken place thus far; that in his extreme distress he is suddenly endowed with a

---

[1] We need only mention Socrates, Sophocles, Plato, A. v. Humboldt, Goethe, and Ranke the historian. Herder when dying said to his son: "Suggest to me some grand thought; this alone gives me a little strength."   [2] "Apologie Scientifique," p. 457.
[3] "De l'Agonie et de la Mort," vol. i., p. 75.

sense of prudence, of foresight, of localities, of relations, and of space; in possession of such a memory of absent and forgotten things and persons; filled with such rare wisdom, such supernatural aspirations—with the sentiments of religion, of God, and with firmness of character? We have said it already: The soul, released from the ties of matter, belongs altogether to itself; and in its isolation shows itself either altogether beautiful or altogether deformed."

Liebig, in his "Chemical Letters," says very truly of those who consider the soul the product of the brain or corporal organs:

"If you strip the argument of these people of its borrowed tinsel, of apparent reasons which in the eyes of the inquirer and thinker are nothing but illuminated mist, then all that remains is that the legs are to run and the brain to think, and that thinking has to be learned as well as the child has to learn to walk; that we cannot walk without legs nor think without brain; that an injury to the means of moving impairs the power to walk, and an injury to the instruments of the soul, the thinking powers. But the flesh and the bones of which the legs consist do not move, but are moved by a cause which is not flesh and bone; they are the instruments of a power; the soft mass called the brain is the instrument of the cause which produces the thoughts."

377. DISTURBANCES OF THE MIND DO NOT PROVE THAT THE SOUL IS THE PRODUCT OF THE CORPORAL ORGANS.—Materialists also appeal to mental disturbances—to madness—to prove that the soul is only the product of the corporal organs.

No doubt it is difficult to arrive at a satisfactory explanation of these phenomena. The most eminent physicians tell us that no final decision about the control of the soul's life has been arrived at. However, so much is certain, that there is no idiocy or madness, properly speaking. Our mind may err and deceive itself, it can sin; but it cannot be sick. What we call imbecility or madness is only a diseased change in the body, especially in the nervous system and in the brain. Grief, fright, fear, too great mental effort, cause disturbances in the circulation of the blood and digestion; and the organs of the body refuse their service to the mind, so that they lead it to incorrect representations.

378. DISTURBANCES OF THE MIND PROVE ONLY THAT OUR SOUL IS DEPENDENT UPON THE BODY.—These phenomena prove that our soul in its action is dependent upon the body as upon the instrument by means of which it operates. But do not the facts show that the soul is partially independent of our corporal organs? The faculty of thinking is not destroyed by madness. The soul continues to think even in the most violent cases of madness. The mind is only stopped from thinking correctly on account of the diseased condition of the body. We notice that madmen at times pass quite reasonable judgments; only one or other misconception they cannot avoid. Let us recall the old simile comparing man to the player of an instrument. Give to the virtuoso a violin on which one string is out of tune. He will play magnificently—will enrapture you. We can hear the virtuoso in every note. But as soon as he touches the ill-tuned string he will produce a false tone. And if all the strings are mistuned, then the greatest virtuoso can bring forth only false notes. And still he is the same master who will throw us into raptures with another instrument. So it is with man in whom one or other organ of the body to which the soul is tied, so far as its action goes, is mistuned—that is to say, diseased, or changed from its normal condition.

It is also a fact that madmen generally recover the full use of their intellectual faculties on their death-bed. They awake suddenly, as from a fainting or a heavy dream, and retain their full consciousness until the hour of death. This proves clearly that the soul's substance is different from the body, although dependent upon the latter in its action.'

379. CAN WE KNOW THE STATE OF A SOUL BY CERTAIN MARKS IN THE BODY?—Another objection is that there are peculiarities of the body by means of which we may know man's intellectual and moral qualities. By observing men's skulls Gall often succeeded in inferring their talents and inclinations. From the elevations and depressions in the skulls he recognized the presence or absence of certain qualities. From a man's features as well as from his corporal constitution inferences have been drawn as to his mental and moral peculiarities.

Materialists have made use of these experiments as arguments against the existence of the soul. But even if these experiments were as reliable as is claimed, they would only be another proof of the view we have advanced. They would show that the soul and the body are in intimate relation and connection; that the soul in its action depends on the condition of the body and its organs, and that the latter have a greater influence on the soul than is generally believed.

No sensible man will dare to infer the condition of the soul from that of the body, because it is well known how deceptive such inferences are. It may be that an elevation or depression in a certain place of the skull indicates an inclination to a certain virtue or vice; the statement may be confirmed in a hundred cases that a

' Cf Burdack, "Anthropologie," p. 613; Letourneau, "Philosophie des Passions," p. 157.

high arched forehead indicates eminent mental talents, or that large eyes indicate artistic talents, or that we may infer great intellectual power from a powerful fist. But who would dare to assert that great intelligence is found behind every beautifully-formed forehead, that large eyes are invariably the marks of artistic endowment, and that a powerful fist is always the sign of a strong mind? There are so many exceptions to all these rules that they are practically without value.

380. WE CAN ALWAYS OVERCOME OUR PASSIONS AND EVIL INCLINATIONS.—And even if it were true that we can ascertain talents and inclinations in the manner asserted, it would be equally true that we can rule our passions and evil inclinations *by free-will, with the help of the grace of God*. We can overcome and root out our vices and passions. No man is forced to commit a crime because it costs him a greater struggle to practise virtue than it costs his more favored fellow.

Therefore Holy Scripture tells us the truth when it says that man consists of two parts: of a body and a soul, which are united in us, and the union of which constitutes the unity of our being. Though there be many who in their blindness use their spirit to prove that they have no spirit, they will never succeed. They may desire this, in order to give themselves up without restraint to their sensual lust, their sins, and their vices; they will never succeed in killing their spirit-soul. For our soul is immortal, as we shall see in our next chapter. We glory in this immortal spirit, and say that in its possession lies our superiority over all other creatures and our dignity.

CHAPTER XVIII.

THE IMMORTALITY OF THE SOUL AND ITS FUTURE LIFE.

"And these shall go into everlasting punishment; but the just into everlasting life."—Matth. xxv. 46.

What will be the fate of man's soul after death?—Views of materialists.—Did the Hebrews believe in the immortality of the soul?—The Book of Wisdom.—Daniel.—Notions the Hebrews had of the soul's duration.—The Chaldeans also, the ancestors of the Hebrews, believed in the immortality of the soul.—Funeral customs and burial places.—Proof of the Babylonian belief in another life.—Descent of Ishtar into Hades.—Egyptian belief in another life.—Proof of the Hebrew belief in the immortality of the soul.—Sheol of the souls.—Belief of the Etruscans.—Iranians.—Indians.—Greeks.—Romans.—Ancient Germans.—Other nations.—Immortality clearly revealed.—Future life and the idea of God.—What is death?—Nothing can be annihilated.—Only two things possible with regard to the human soul.—Life the fundamental law of creation.—Without a future life man would be the most lamentable of beings.—Man's destiny from the standpoint of Christian doctrine.—Three factors.—Virtue must be rewarded and vice punished.—This world does not sufficiently reward virtue or punish vice.—Conclusion.

HAVING proved in the previous chapter the existence of our soul, it remains for us to inquire into its final destiny. We are aware of the progress of infidelity in our days. There are many who deny that the soul lives after death. Death is death, they tell us. With death all is ended! They degrade man to a mere animal, and infidelity, for this reason, if for no other, is forced to reject the continuation of life after death.

381. WHAT WILL BE THE SOUL'S FATE AFTER DEATH?—"He who fights," says Huxley, "for moral truth in this world of anguish and sin, is certainly stronger when he believes that sooner or later a vision of peace and happiness will take hold of his being. So also the one who works on the top of a mountain is more courageous when he sees awaiting him on the other side of the rocks and snows his home and rest.... If this fate were founded on a solid basis, certainly all mankind would cling to it just as obstinately as the sailor, when in danger of being drowned, clings to the buoy."

These words of one of the most famous chiefs of materialistic science deny the immortality of the soul and, at the same time, voice the irresistible aspirations of the human heart.

The teachings of faith on the destiny of man and on the future life are contained in this first lesson of the Catechism:

Q. Why has God created you?

A. To know God, love Him, serve Him, and thus obtain heaven, eternal life.

The highest and most rational metaphysics answers like faith.

382. MATERIALISM AND THE FATE OF OUR SOUL.— The desolating doctrine of total annihilation after death is found among the materialists. One of the foremost champions of the materialistic school, L. Büchner, has been most brutal in his denial of the immortality of the soul.

"A spirit without a body is as little conceivable as electricity without a metal; the naturalist, therefore, must protest against the idea of individual immortality; we cannot admit that the soul of a dead person continues to exist.... It is dead, to return no more."

Our pen revolts against setting down his odious blasphemies against the Christian cemetery, the blessed field where the seed of immortality germinates, the mysterious resting-place where sleep the faithful departed—according to the symbolic language of our faith, the "God's acre," where so many beloved await the signal of awakening. Büchner sees in the veneration of tombs nothing but an obstacle to public welfare, to rural economy, to the free circulation of fertilizing matter! He says: "The best, the most useful thing which man can do when dying is to leave behind him the greatest quantity of rare and rich phosphate of lime and salt, destined to form a richer association of molecules, and thereby increase the well-being of mankind."[1] Behold materialism in its grandeur and glory!

"The pretended arguments for the existence of a God and the so-called immortality of the soul are generally considered as the strongest basis of religion. What gives us the right to contradict the senses, which see man in his entirety marching toward death, and to ascribe eternal life to a part of us which we can see nowhere? ....The *ego* of man is his body, which after death is destroyed by the corruption of the grave, the dog, or vultures.... The so-called faculties of the soul develop, increase, and grow strong with the body, particularly with their most immediate organ, the brain; they decrease with old age. That which is so intimately united with corporal organs ceases to be the centre of the circle when the circumference is no more. Only that is incorporeal which is not corporal. Whoever is not inflated with pride knows that he has no right to any life beyond the grave; the idea of eternity causes us to shiver."[2]

This is what materialism has to say about the immor-

[1] Büchner, "Kraft und Stoff," p. 360 *seq*.
[2] D. Strauss, "Alter und neuer Glaube," chap. xli.

tality of our soul. The idea, the prospect of immortality, makes the infidel shiver. No wonder that this is the case, when men like Strauss, who have all their lives abused the faculties of their immortal soul, are summoned to enter eternity in order to render an account of the use they made of their talents and gifts.

But again let us ask, What will be the fate of our soul after death? Holy Scripture and the traditions of mankind tell us that it will continue to live. Our soul itself tells us this, for it carries within itself the idea of immortality—a mighty, inextinguishable craving for everlasting life. Nothing can satisfy it except the everlasting, the unchangeable, and the eternal.

383. THE BELIEF OF THE HEBREWS IN THE IMMORTALITY OF THE SOUL.—The "Academy of Inscriptions and Fine Arts" in Paris devoted several sessions in 1873 to the question whether the Hebrews believed in the immortality of the soul. J. Halévy, the learned and intrepid explorer of Yemen, began this discussion. In an essay which he had read before the Academy he drew attention to some passages from an inscription of Eshmunazar, king of Sidon, which he translated thus: "I have been carried off before my time into the midst of those who are separated from me to-day; besides my grandeur (literally 'elevation') I have been pious, a son of immortality."[1] The deceased on whose lips these words are placed, a little further on expresses the hope that the God to whom he addresses his prayer "may make him behold the Astarte of the magnificent gods."[2] In another place this hope is expressed again in almost similar terms. "He will

[1] J. Halévy, "Melanges d'Archéologie et d'Épigraphie Sémitiques," 1874, p. 8.
[2] *Op. cit.*, p. 9. Cf. Vigouroux, "La Bible et les Découvertes Modernes," vol. iii., p. 123 *seq.*

make me live with Astarte, with the magnificent gods." From these very explicit passages M. Halévy drew the conclusion that the Phœnicians, in the seventh century before our era, believed in a future life; and he took occasion from this to oppose those who refused to the Semites of Palestine, contemporaries and neighbors of the subjects of Eshmunazar, this consoling faith in a future life, which is the foundation of all religion, morality, and virtue.

In the sessions of February 28 and March 17, 1873, M. Derenbourg, a Jewish member of the "Academy of Inscriptions and Fine Arts," attacked the interpretation of the inscription of Eshmunazar given by his coreligionist, M. Halévy, and especially the conclusions he had drawn therefrom in favor of the belief of the Hebrews in the immortality of the soul. According to M. Derenbourg, the Old Testament knew nothing of this doctrine, and the Jews learned it only afterward, through their contact with strangers, especially the Greeks. All the passages of the Sacred Books thought to contain allusions to a future life have been misinterpreted. It is only by forcing or exaggerating the literal sense of these passages that this doctrine has been found therein. "No text exists in the Scriptures from which we can reasonably infer that the Hebrews believed in the immortality of the soul."[1]

M. Renan, without going quite as far as his friend M. Derenbourg, nevertheless supported him in the debate which M. Derenbourg's thesis provoked among the members of the Academy.[2] Mgr. Freppel took occasion to answer them by two short but solid papers; Halévy tried to support his views in a second memoir.

The discussion, after remaining dormant for nearly ten years, was taken up anew by the same gentlemen

[1] "Journal officiel" of April 16, 1873, p. 2618.   [2] *Ibid.*

toward the end of the year 1882. M. Halévy, in a memoir read before the Academy, enlarged the question by including in his inquiry all the Semitic peoples. They all believed in the immortality of the soul, and particularly the Assyrians. The Hebrews had the same belief on this point. But M. Derenbourg continued to maintain that his ancestors rejected this capital truth. "The Book of Job," he says, "keeps silence thereon; the *Refaïm* in the *'sc'ôl*, to which our attention is called, do not enjoy a real life; Ecclesiastes speaks of another life only in order to combat it; the Jews adopted this dogma only after the conquests of Alexander the Great; it is a belief they borrowed from the philosophy of Plato, through the Alexandrians and Syrians."[1]

M. Derenbourg was not the first to assert that the Hebrews did not know the doctrine of the immortality of the soul. Voltaire, in 1776, wrote: "Turn where you will, Jewish gentlemen, you will find in your sacred books no clear statement about hell or the immortality of the soul."[2] Voltaire in speaking thus was only the echo of a certain number of infidels, or nominal Christians. Since Voltaire, it is especially Salvador and Cahen, both Jews, who, saturated with rationalistic views, maintained that the ancient Hebrews had no knowledge of the immortality of the soul. They acknowledge that after the Babylonian captivity the doctrine of remuneration after death is clearly expressed in both the Deuter-

[1] "La Croyance de l'Immortalité de l'Âme chez les Sémites," by J. Halévy, "Journal officiel," Sept. 14, 1882, pp. 5055-5057, and "Académie des Inscriptions et Belles Lettres," Comptes rendus 1882, pp. 210-213; "L'Immortalité de l'Âme chez les Juifs," by J. Derenbourg, *Ibid.*, pp. 213-219, and "Journal officiel," Sept. 18, 1882, p. 519. Cf. Vigouroux, "La Bible et les Découvertes Modernes," vol. iii., pp. 100-105.

[2] Voltaire, "Un Chretien contre six Juifs," Œuvres, vol. xlviii., p. 512, edit. Bouchet.

onomical books and in the Talmud, but the period which followed the first destruction of Jerusalem is set down by them as the date when this doctrine was engrafted on Jewish theology.

384. THE CONSTANT BELIEF OF THE JEWS IN THE IMMORTALITY OF THE SOUL.—Let us note this acknowledgment. It is certain that the Talmudist Jews believed both in rewards and punishments in the other life; that is, both in a heaven and a hell. The treatise Sanhedrin is very explicit on this subject.[1] Josephus believed in the immortality of the soul,[2] and he affirms that the Pharisees[3] and Essenes[4] alike taught this doctrine. We find the same belief clearly expressed in the last books of the Old Testament. The victims of the persecutions of Antiochus suffer the torments of the present life in order to escape those of the life to come,[5] and thus merit an eternal reward.[6] The author of the Second Book of Machabees teaches that the prayers of the living can relieve the souls of the dead in purgatory.[7] The Book of Wisdom affirms the dogma of the immortality of the soul, and of rewards and punishments, in the clearest terms. Death, it tells us, is the fruit of sin, but it is not annihilation.

"The impious have said, reasoning with themselves, but not right: The time of our life is short and tedious, and in the end of a man there is no remedy, and no man hath been known to have returned from hell. . . .

"For our time is as the passing of a shadow, and there is no going back of our end: for it is fast sealed and no man returneth.

[1] See folios 90, b.; 91, a.; 92, b.; 94, a., etc.
[2] Josephus, "De Bello Judaico," iii., viii., in his discourse to the soldiers.   [3] *Ibid.*, ii., viii., 14.
[4] Josephus, "Antiquitates Judaicoe," xviii., i. 3; "De Bello Judaico," ii., viii., p. 11.   [5] II. Mach. iii. 26.
[6] *Ibid.*, vii. 11, 14, 28; xiv. 42.   [7] *Ibid.*, xii. 46.

"Come, therefore, and let us enjoy the good things that are present, and let us speedily use the creatures as in youth.

"Let us fill ourselves with costly wine, and ointments: and let not the flower of the time pass by us.

"Let us crown ourselves with roses, before they be withered: let no meadow escape our riot.

"Let none of us go without his part in luxury, let us everywhere leave tokens of joy: for this is our portion and this is our lot....

"These things they (the impious) thought, and were deceived: for their own malice blinded them.

"And they knew not the secrets of God, nor hoped for the wages of justice, nor esteemed the honor of holy souls.

"For God created man incorruptible, and to the image of His own likeness He made him.

"But by the envy of the devil death came into the world: and they follow him that are of his side.

"But the souls of the just are in the hand of God, and the torment of death shall not touch them.

"In the sight of the unwise they seemed to die: and their departure was taken for misery....

"Though in the sight of men they suffered torments, their hope is full of immortality....

"The just shall shine, and shall run to and fro like sparks among the reeds....

"But the wicked shall be punished according to their own devices: who have neglected the just and have revolted from the Lord....

"Then shall the just stand with great constancy against those who have afflicted them, and taken away their labors.

"These seeing it shall be troubled with terrible fear and shall be amazed at the suddenness of their unexpected salvation.

"Saying within themselves, repenting, and groaning for anguish of spirit: These are they whom we had some time in derision, and for a parable of reproach.

"We fools esteemed their life madness, and their end without honor.

"Behold, how they are numbered among the children of God, and their lot is among the saints....

"Such things as these the sinners said in hell....

"But the just shall live forevermore: and their reward is with the Lord and the care of them with the Most High."[1]

The prophet Daniel sums up in a few words what we have quoted from the author of the Book of Wisdom.

"At that time (at the end of time) a time shall come," he says, "such as never was from the time that nation began until that time. And at that time shall thy people (the Jewish people) be saved, every one that shall be found written in the book (of life). And many of those that sleep in the dust of the earth shall awake, some unto life everlasting (*ḥayê'ôlam*) and others unto reproach, to see it always. But they that are learned shall shine as the brightness of the firmament: and they that instruct many to justice, as stars for all eternity."[2]

It is therefore clearly proved that the Jews, after the captivity, had an explicit belief in the life to come. We shall now examine what the Hebrews believed about the soul and its destiny after death from their beginnings as a people until they were carried off to Chaldea.

To avoid all misunderstanding, we shall examine successively the opinions the Hebrews held (1) on the soul's duration, or its immortality; (2) on the *sĕ'ôl*, or place of sojourn of the soul after death; (3) on the future life and the idea of God.

[1] Wisdom ii., iii., v.
[2] Daniel xii. 1-3.

385. THE SOUL'S DURATION, OR ITS IMMORTALITY, AMONG THE CHALDEANS.—According to the belief of the Hebrews at all times, the soul does not die; it is immortal.

"From the very beginning the Hebrew race steadily adhered to the doctrine of the immortality of the soul as to a first principle. For them, as a people, it required no proof, as being a truth which could not be gainsaid; moreover, it underlay all Hebrew tradition, and was assumed by the doctors of the law as an undeniable postulate. The Hebrews knew that death was a punishment for sin, and not the complete annihilation of man. This their firm belief they manifested in various ways."[1]

On account of the surroundings from which the Hebrews went forth, and among which they lived since Abraham, the father of their race, until Moses, their lawgiver, it was impossible, says Halévy, that they should have been ignorant of this great truth. All men have known this fundamental dogma. Maury says: "It is absurd to be obliged to prove to-day that among all races of men, with a few insignificant exceptions, there exists a unanimous belief that the life of man continues after death, whatever form it may take. It is more than eighty years since a German *savant*, W. Flügge, put this in its proper light by passing under review all the creeds and traditions of mankind. It is an undeniable fact that the Hebrews held the general belief on this question."[2]

Indeed, how could they be ignorant of this doctrine? We cannot doubt any longer that the Chaldeans, the ancestors of the Hebrews, believed in the immortality of the soul. Assurbanipal, relating in one of his inscrip-

[1] Ronayne, "God Knowable and Known," p. 326.
[2] "Journal officiel," April 16, 1873, p. 2618.

tions the death of Tahraka, king of Egypt, says of him: *Illik muz musi-su*, "he went into his country (the land) of the night."[1] This expression, which must be very ancient, and must have been common to the inhabitants of Chaldea as well as to those of Syria, implies not only that men's souls survive after death, but also that they meet after death in a place appointed for them.

386. BURIAL PLACES AND FUNERAL CUSTOMS AMONG THE CHALDEANS.—Among the most significant indications of a people's belief regarding man's fate after death are its funeral customs. All the nations of the earth show a tender care for the dead; and this not only through affection for the friends and survivors of the dead; the spirits were looked upon as a blessing to the living. Their dwellings were adorned and venerated; the dead were thought to be living in another world. Among some pagan nations it was a duty to defend and protect the graves of their ancestors as well as the altars of the gods. The Chaldeans must have had ideas of this kind, as modern excavations prove. George Rawlinson says on this subject:

"Next to their (Chaldean) edifices, the most remarkable of the remains which the Chaldeans have left to after ages are their burial places. While ancient tombs are of very rare occurrence in Assyria and Upper Babylonia, Chaldea proper abounds with them. It has been conjectured, with some show of reason, that the Assyrians in the time of their power may have made the sacred land of Chaldea the general depository of their dead— much in the same way as the Persians even now use Kerbela and Nedjif, or Meshed Ali, as special cemetery cities, to which thousands of corpses are brought annually. At any rate, the quantity of human relics accumulated upon certain Chaldean sites is enormous, and

[1] Geo. Smith, "Zeitschrift für Egyptische Sprache," 1868, p. 113.

seems to be quite beyond what the mere population of the surrounding district could furnish. At Warka, for instance, excepting the triangular space between the three principal ruins, the whole remainder of the platform, the whole space within the walls, and an unknown extent of desert beyond them, are everywhere filled with human bones and sepulchres. In places, coffins are piled upon coffins, certainly to the depth of thirty, probably to the depth of sixty feet; and for miles on every side of the ruins the traveller walks upon a soil teeming with the relics of ancient, and now probably extinct, races. Sometimes these relics manifestly belong to a number of distinct and widely separate eras, but there are places where it is otherwise. However we may account for it—and no account has been yet given which is altogether satisfactory—it seems clear from the comparative homogeneousness of the remains in some places that they belong to a single race, and if not to a single period, at any rate to only two, or, at the most, three distinct periods; so that it is no longer very difficult to distinguish the more ancient from the later relics. Such is the character of the remains at Mugheir, which are thought to contain nothing of later date than the close of the Babylonian period, 538 B.C.; and such is, still more remarkably, the character of the ruins at Abu-Shahrein and Tel-el-Lahm, which seem to be entirely, or almost entirely, Chaldean. In the following account of the coffins and mode of burial employed by the early Chaldeans, examples will be drawn from these places only; since otherwise we should be liable to confound together the productions of very different ages and peoples.

"The tombs to which an archaic character most certainly attaches are of three kinds—brick vaults, clay coffins shaped like a dish-cover, and coffins in the same material formed of two large jars placed mouth to mouth and cemented together with bitumen. The brick vaults are found chiefly at Mugheir. They are seven feet long, three feet seven inches broad, and five feet high, composed of sun-dried bricks imbedded in mud, and exhibit a very remarkable form and construction of the arch. The side walls of the vaults slope outwards as they ascend, and the arch is formed, like those in Egyptian buildings and Scythian tombs, by each successive layer of bricks, from the point where the arch begins, a little overlapping the last, till the two sides of the roof are brought so near together that the aperture may be closed by a single brick. The floor of the vaults was paved with brick similar to that used for the roof and sides; on this floor was commonly spread a matting of reeds, and the body was laid upon the matting. It was commonly turned on the left side, the right arm falling towards the left, and the fingers resting on the edge of a copper bowl, usually placed on the palm of the left hand. The head was pillowed on a single sun-dried brick. Various articles of ornament and use were interred with each body, which will be more particularly described hereafter. Food seems often to have been placed in the tombs, and jars or other drinking vessels are universal. The brick vaults appear to have been family sepulchres; they have often received three or four bodies, and in one case a single vault contained eleven skeletons.

"The clay coffins shaped like a dish-cover are among the most curious of the sepulchral remains of antiquity. On a platform of sun-dried brick is laid a mat exactly similar to those in common use among the Arabs of the country at the present day, and thereon lies the skeleton, disposed as in the brick vaults, and surrounded by utensils and ornaments. Mat, skeleton, and utensils are then concealed by a huge cover in burnt clay, formed of a single piece, which is commonly seven feet long, two or three feet high, and two feet and a half broad at the bottom. It is rarely that modern potters produce articles of half the size. Externally the covers have commonly some slight ornament, such as rims and shallow indentations. Internally they are plain. Not more than two skeletons have ever been found under a single cover, and in these cases they were the skeletons of a male and a female. Children were interred separately, under covers about half the size of those for adults. Tombs of this kind commonly occur at some considerable depth. None were discovered at Mugheir nearer the surface than seven or eight feet.

"The third kind of tomb, common both at Mugheir and at Tel-el-Lahm, is almost as eccentric as the preceding. Two large open-mouthed jars, shaped like the largest of the water-jars at present in use at Bagdad, are taken, and the body is disposed inside them with the usual accompaniments of dishes, vases, and ornaments. The jars average from two and a half feet to three feet in depth, and have a diameter of about two feet; so that they would readily contain a full-sized corpse if it was slightly bent at the knees. Sometimes the two jars are of equal size, and are simply united at their mouths by a layer of bitumen; but more commonly one is slightly larger than the other, and the smaller mouth is inserted into the larger one for a depth of three or four inches, while a coating of bitumen is still applied externally at the juncture. In each coffin there is an air-hole at one extremity, to allow the escape of the gases generated during decomposition.

"Besides the coffins themselves, some other curious features are found in the burial places. The dead are commonly buried, not underneath the natural surface of the ground, but in extensive artificial mounds, each mound containing a vast number of coffins. The coffins are arranged side by side, often in several layers, and occasionally strips of masonry crossing each other at right angles separate the set of coffins from their neighbors. The surface of the mounds is sometimes paved with brick, and a similar pavement often separates the layers of coffins one from another. But the most remarkable feature in the tomb-mounds is their system of drainage. Long shafts of baked clay extend from the surface of the mound to its base, composed of a succession of rings two feet in diameter and about a foot and a half in breadth, joined together by thin layers of bitumen. To give the rings additional strength, the sides have a slight concave curve; and still further to resist external pressure, the shafts are filled from bottom to top with a loose mass of brick pottery. At the top the shaft contracts rapidly by means of a ring of a peculiar shape, and above this ring are a series of perforated bricks leading up to the top of the mound, the surface of which is so arranged as to conduct the rain-water into these orifices. For the still more effectual drainage of the mound, the top piece of the shaft, immediately below the perforated bricks, and also the first rings, are full of small holes to admit any stray moisture; and besides this, for the space of a foot every way, the shafts are surrounded with broken pottery, so that the real diameter of each drain is as much as four feet. By these arrangements the piles have been kept perfectly dry; and the consequence is the preservation to the present day not only of the utensils and ornaments placed in the tombs, but of the very skeletons themselves, which are seen perfect on opening a tomb, though they generally crumble to dust at the first touch." [1]

[1] George Rawlinson, "Ancient Monarchies," vol. i., pp. 85-90.

The care these peoples took of their sepulchres and the corpses of their dead, placing nourishment and water near them, as the jars and vessels prove,[1] are so many indications of the belief of the Assyrio-Chaldeans in the immortality of the soul.

387. WHAT WE KNOW OF THE BURIAL OF THE FIRST HEBREW PATRIARCHS.—The little we know of the burial of the first Hebrew patriarchs in the land of Canaan is sufficient to teach us the importance they attached to their sepulchres. Abraham, desirous of having a family tomb, bought one at a very high price. Here he buried Sara, his wife, and was buried there himself, as well as Isaac, his son, together with Rebecca, the wife of Isaac.[2] Jacob buried his spouse Lia in the same place, and on his death-bed bade his children to bury him there; which prayer they faithfully carried out.[3] Joseph also commanded his body to be taken to the Promised Land, after his people had taken possession thereof; and his descendants buried him at Sichem.[4] Everything goes to show that the Chaldean branch transplanted from the shores of the Euphrates to Palestine rendered to the mortal remains of their departed

[1] We find similar customs among all ancient nations; for instance, the Greeks, Latins, Etruscans, ancient Germans, as well as among our American Indians. Even to-day this custom is known to some extent. The Lapps bury with the corpse flint, steel, and tinder to supply light for the dark journey. The Chippewas light fires on the graves for four successive nights after the burial, in order to light the dead on his journey, which, as they believe, lasts four days. The Greenlanders have a touching custom: they bury with a child a dog as guide, for, say they, a dog will find his way anywhere. The "obolus" the ancient Greeks put in the dead man's mouth to pay Charon and the coin the Irish used to place in his hand are well known. The Indian practice of depositing weapons and food with the dead was universal in ancient Europe.   [2] Gen. xxv. 27-29; xlix. 31.
[3] *Ib.*, xlix. 31; l. 13.   [4] *Ib.*, l. 24; Exod. viii. 19.

honors similar to those rendered to them in their mother country, and attached to the ceremonies the same meaning as to the life of the soul after death.

388. DIRECT PROOF OF THE BABYLONIAN BELIEF IN ANOTHER LIFE.— Besides these funeral customs, the account of the Deluge Berosus has preserved furnishes us with direct and positive proof of the Babylonian belief in another life. Xisuthrus, after the drying of the earth, as soon as he had offered a sacrifice to the gods, disappeared with those who had accompanied him. "When those who had remained in the boat did not see him coming back any more, they also disembarked and began to seek him by shouting his name. But they could see him no more; and a voice was heard from on high saying to them: Honor the gods. Xisuthrus, in recompense for his piety, has been removed to live henceforth with the gods, as also his wife, his daughters, and the pilot of the boat."[1]

The cuneiform tablets of the Deluge published by George Smith, which we have quoted in another chapter, confirm in the main this feature in the account of Berosus, and thus warrant its high antiquity: they teach us that man, saved from the great Flood, received from the gods the gift of immortality. Izdhubar goes to find him (Xisuthrus) at the mouth of the rivers, in order to learn from him the secret of immortality. Hasisadra ends the account of the great inundation by saying to him: "Behold, Hasisadra and his wife, in order to live like the gods, have been removed; and Hasisadra will dwell in a place apart, at the mouth of the rivers. They asked me, and in a place apart, at the mouth of the rivers, they have placed me."[2]

[1] Berosus, "Fragmenta," Fragm. 7 in "Historicorum Græcorum Fragmenta," edit. Didot, ii., p. 501.
[2] Rawlinson, "Ancient Religions," p. 54.

These passages do not set forth explicitly the faith of the Chaldeans in the immortality of the soul, but we can see, at least, that the Chaldeans believed in the possibility of man's immortality; and, what is more, they considered this immortality the reward of virtue.

Other passages are more explicit. The Assyrians worshipped their gods, as was usual in the ancient world, by prayer, praise, and sacrifice. Prayer was offered for one's self and others. The "sinfulness of sin" was deeply felt, and the divine anger deprecated with much earnestness. "O my Lord!" says a suppliant, "my sins are many, my trespasses are great; and the wrath of the gods has plagued me with disease, sickness, and sorrow. I fainted, but no one stretched forth his hand; I groaned, but no one drew nigh; I cried aloud, but no one heard. O Lord, do not Thou abandon thy servant! In the waters of the great storm do Thou lay hold of his hand. The sins which he has committed, do Thou turn to righteousness."[1]

Special intercession was made for the Assyrian kings. The gods were besought to grant them "length of days, a strong sword, extended years of glory, pre-eminence among monarchs, and an enlargement of the bounds of the empire."[2] Their happiness in a future state was prayed for, as the following prayer, for instance, shows: "May he (the king) attain an old age, and after the gift of the (present) days enter the feasts of the mountain of silver, the celestial hearts, the dwelling of felicity, into the light Elysian fields; may he lead an eternal, holy life in the presence of the gods which inhabit Assyria."[3] This last passage expresses distinctly

---

[1] "Records of the Past," vol. iii., p. 133.

[2] Fox Talbot, "Transactions of the Society of Biblical Archæology," vol. i., p. 107.

[3] "Records of the Past," vol. iii., pp. 137, 138.

the belief of the Assyrians in the immortality of the soul.

The Assyrio-Chaldean heaven is described, we are told by Mr. Chad Boscawen, who refers to several inscriptions, as the "dwelling of felicity, the house of life, the land of life." The life of the blessed is represented as agreeable: they rest on beds, drinking pure drinks in the company of their friends and their parents. The warrior has around him all the spoils which he has taken in his combats—the prisoners included—and he gives grand feasts in his tent.[1]

389. THE ASSYRIO-CHALDEAN BELIEF IN ANOTHER LIFE PROVED BY THE DESCENT OF ISHTAR INTO HELL.—The most important text which has been discovered thus far on the belief of the Assyrio-Chaldeans in another life is that of the descent of Ishtar into hell. This very strange poem gives us a great number of details, from which we learn the theological ideas of the ancestors of the Hebrews.

The descent of Ishtar[2] into Hades, perhaps in search of Tammuz, is related as follows:[3]

"In the land of Hades, the land of her desire, Ishtar, daughter of the moon god Sin, turned her mind. The daughter of Sin fixed her mind to go to the house where all meet—the dwelling of the god Iskalla, to the house which men enter, but cannot depart from, the abode of darkness, of famine; where earth is their food, their nourishment clay; where light is not seen, but in darkness they dwell; where ghosts, like birds, flutter their wings, and on the door and the door-posts the dust lies undisturbed.

---

[1] "Transactions of the Society of Biblical Archæology," vol. v., 1877, p. 565.   [2] The queen of love and beauty.
[3] "Transactions," vol. iii., pp. 119–124, and "Records of the Past," vol. i., pp. 143–149.

"When Ishtar arrived at the gate of Hades, to the keeper of the gate a word she spake: 'O keeper of the entrance, open thy gate! Open thy gate, I say again, that I may enter! If thou openest not thy gate, if I do not enter, I will assault the door, the gate I will break down, I will attack the entrance, I will split open the portals. I will raise the dead to be the devourers of the living! Upon the living the dead shall prey.' Then the porter opened his mouth and spake, and thus he said to the great Ishtar: 'Stay, lady, do not shake down the door; I will go and inform Queen Nin-ki-gal.' So the porter went in to Nin-ki-gal and said: 'These curses thy sister Ishtar utters; yea, she blasphemes thee with fearful curses!' And Nin-ki-gal, hearing the words, grew pale like a flower when cut from the stem —like the stalk of a reed she shook. And she said, 'I will cure her rage; I will speedily cure her fury. Her curses I will repay. Light up consuming flames! Light up a blaze of straw! Be her doom with the husbands who left their wives; be her doom with the wives who forsook their lords; be her doom with the youths of dishonored lives. Go, porter, and open the gate for her; but strip her, as some have been stripped ere now.' The porter went and opened the gate. 'Lady of Tiggaba, enter,' he said. 'Enter. It is permitted. The Queen of Hades to meet thee comes.' So the first gate let her in; but she was stopped, and there the great crown was taken from her head. 'Excuse it, lady; the Queen of the Land insists upon its removal.' The next gate let her in; but she was stopped, and there the ear-rings were taken from her ears. 'Keeper, do not take off from me the ear-rings from my ears!' 'Excuse it, lady; the Queen of the Land insists upon their removal.' The third gate let her in; but she was stopped, and there the precious stones were taken from her head.

'Keeper, do not take off from me the gems that adorn my head!' 'Excuse it, lady; the Queen of the Land insists upon their removal.' The fourth gate let her in; but she was stopped, and there the small jewels were taken from her brow. 'Keeper, do not take off from me the small jewels that deck my brow!' 'Excuse it, lady; the Queen of the Land insists upon their removal.' The fifth gate let her in; but she was stopped, and there the girdle was taken from her waist. 'Keeper, do not take off from me the girdle that girds my waist!' 'Excuse it, lady; the Queen of the Land insists upon its removal.' The sixth gate let her in; but she was stopped, and here the gold rings were taken from her hands and feet. 'Keeper, do not take off from me the gold rings of my hands and feet!' 'Excuse it, lady; the Queen of the Land insists upon their removal.' The seventh gate let her in; but she was stopped, and there the last garment was taken from her body. 'Keeper, do not take off, I pray, the last garment from my body!' 'Excuse it, lady; the Queen of the Land insists upon its removal.'

"After Mother Ishtar had descended into Hades, Nin-ki-gal saw and derided her to her face. Then Ishtar lost her reason, and heaped curses upon the other. Nin-ki-gal hereupon opened her mouth and spake: 'Go, Namtar,....bring her out of punishment,.... afflict her with disease of the eye, the side, the feet, the heart, the head' (some lines effaced)....

"The divine messenger lacerated his face before them. The assembly of the gods was full....The Sun came, along with the Moon, his father, and, weeping, he spake thus unto Hea, the king: 'Ishtar has descended into the earth, and has not risen again; and ever since the time that Mother Ishtar descended into hell, ... the master has ceased to command, the slave has ceased to obey!'

Then the god Hea in the depth of his mind formed a design; he modelled for her escape the figure of a man, of clay. 'Go save her, Phantom; present thyself at the portal of Hades; the seven gates of Hades will all open before thee; Nin-ki-gal will see thee, and take pleasure because of thee. When her mind has grown calm and her anger has worn itself away, awe her with the names of the great gods! Then prepare thy frauds! Fix on deceitful tricks thy mind! Use the chiefest of thy tricks! Bring forth fish out of an empty vessel! That will astonish Nin-ki-gal, and to Ishtar she will restore her clothing. The reward—a great reward—for these things shall not fail. Go, Phantom, save her; and the great assembly of the people shall crown thee! Meats, the best in the city, shall be thy food! Wine, the most delicious in the city, shall be thy drink! A royal palace shall be thy dwelling, a throne of state shall be thy seat! Magician and conjuror shall kiss the hem of thy garment!'

"Nin-ki-gal opened her mouth and spake; to her messenger, Namtar, commands she gave: 'Go, Namtar, the Temple of Justice adorn! Deck the images! Deck the altars! Bring out Anunnak, and let him take his seat on a throne of gold! Pour out for Ishtar the water of life; from my realms let her depart.' Namtar obeyed; he adorned the temple; decked the images; decked the altars; brought out Anunnak, and let him take his seat on a throne of gold; poured out for Ishtar the water of life, and suffered her to depart. Then the first gate let her out and gave her back the garment of her form. The next gate let her out and gave her back the jewels for hands and feet. The third gate let her out and gave her back the girdle of her waist. The fourth gate let her out and gave her back the small gems she had worn upon her brow. The fifth gate let her out and gave her back the precious stones that had been upon her head. The sixth gate let her out and gave her back the earrings that were taken from her ears. And the seventh gate let her out and gave her back the crown she had carried on her head."

Such is this ancient poem; singular in its details and some of its ideas, but important for us, as they attest very clearly the belief of Abraham's countrymen in another life. M. Oppert fixes the general meaning of the legend as follows:

"The Aral, the unchangeable country, the region of the dead of the Babylonians and Assyrians, corresponds to the Hades of the most ancient Greek poets. The belief of the Chaldeans in another life is thus definitely established. They believed in a dwelling of the dead, an immutable country from which there is no return—a place of obscurity and darkness, where the souls flutter like birds, and where they have no nourishment but dust. In order to enter there, one has to strip himself of everything. The goddess reigning there as sovereign is inexorable, even for the other gods, and particularly for Ishtar, the goddess of life."

390. THE BELIEF IN ANOTHER LIFE AMONG THE EGYPTIANS.—When we pass from Chaldea, where Abraham was born, to Egypt, where his descendants became a nation, we enter the land whose inhabitants, according to the Greeks, were the first who taught the immortality of the soul.[1] The origin of this doctrine is lost in the darkness of antiquity. The papyrus of Ebers recently discovered, which dates from the seventeenth century, before Christ, and appears to be a copy of a much more ancient document, deals with diseases, the relations between the soul and the body, and proves the antiquity of psychological studies in the valley of

[1] Herodotus, ii., p. 123: edit. Didot, p. 112.

the Nile. Everybody knows to-day that the Egyptians always believed "in the immortality of the soul, completed by the doctrine of punishments and rewards."[1]

391. THE JUDGMENT OF THE SOUL AFTER DEATH.— The belief in another life was a cardinal principle of the Egyptian religion. Immediately after death the soul, it was taught, descended into the lower world (*Amenti*) and was conducted to the "Hall of Truth," where it was judged in the presence of Osiris and his forty-two assessors, the "Lords of Truth" and judges of the dead. Anubis, the son of Osiris, who was called "the director of the weighing," brought forth a pair of scales, and placing on one scale a figure or emblem of truth, set on the other a vase containing the good deeds of the deceased, Thoth standing by with a tablet in his hand, whereon to record the result.[2] If the good deeds were sufficient, if they weighed down the scale wherein they were placed, then the happy soul was permitted to enter "the boat of the sun," and was conducted by good spirits to the Elysian fields (*Aahlu*), to the "Pools of Peace," and the dwelling-places of the blest. If, on the contrary, the good deeds were insufficient, if the scale remained suspended in the air, then the unhappy soul was sentenced, according to the degree of its evil deeds, to go through a round of transmigrations into the bodies of animals more or less unclean; the number, nature, and duration of the transmigrations depended on the demerits of the deceased, and the consequent length and severity of the punishment which he deserved, or the purification which he needed.

[1] Cf. de Rougé, "Études sur le Rituel Funéraire des Anciens Égyptiens," in the "Revue Archéologique," 1860, vol. i., p. 73.
[2] Wilkinson, "Ancient Egyptians," vol. v., p. 314. Representations of the scene are frequent in the tombs and in the many copies of the "Ritual of the Dead."

Ultimately, if after many trials sufficient purity was not attained, the wicked soul which had proved itself incurable underwent a final sentence at the hands of Osiris, judge of the dead, and, being condemned to complete and absolute annihilation, was destroyed upon the steps of heaven by Shu, the Lord of Light.¹ The good soul, having first been freed from its infirmities by passing through the basin of purgatorial fire, guarded by four ape-faced genii, was made the companion of Osiris for a period of three thousand years, after which it returned from Amenti, re-entered its former body, rose from the dead, and lived once more a human life upon the earth. This process was gone through again and again, until a certain mystic cycle of years became complete, when, to crown all, the good and blessed attained the final joy of union with God—being absorbed into the divine essence from which they had once emanated, and attaining the full perfection and true end of their existence.

392. EMBALMING AMONG THE EGYPTIANS. — With their belief in a future life and their opinions regarding the fate of good and bad souls were connected very closely their treatment of corpses and their careful and elaborate preparation of tombs. As each man hoped to be among those who would be received into Aahlu, and after dwelling with Osiris for three thousand years to return to earth and re-enter their old bodies, it was necessary that this body should be enabled to resist decay for this long period. Hence their custom of embalming the bodies, of swathing them in linen, and then burying them in stone sarcophagi covered with lids that it was scarcely possible to lift or even to move. Hence, if a man was wealthy, he spent enormous sums to build a safe and commodious, an elegant and well-deco-

¹ Birch, " Guide to Museum," pp. 14, 15.

rated tomb, either piling a pyramid on his sarcophagus, or excavating deep into the solid rock and preparing for his resting-place a remote chamber at the end of a long series of galleries. With the notion, probably, that it would be of use to him in his passage through Amenti to Aahlu, he took care to have the most important passages from the sacred book—entitled the "Ritual of the Dead"—either inscribed on the inner part of the coffin in which he was to lie, or painted on his mummy bandages, or engraved upon the inner walls of his tomb.[1] Sometimes he even had a complete copy of the book buried with him—no doubt for reference if his memory failed to supply him with the right invocation or prayer at the dangerous parts of his long journey.

The thought of death, of judgment, of a sentence to happiness or misery, according to the life he had led on earth, was thus familiar to the ordinary Egyptian. His theological notions were confused and fantastical; but he had a strong and abiding conviction that his fate after death would depend on his conduct during his life on earth, and especially on his observance of the moral law and the performance of his various duties.[2]

393. THE EGYPTIAN BELIEF IN A FUTURE LIFE KNOWN TO THE HEBREWS. — The Hebrews lived a long time among the Egyptians. Therefore, no man can doubt that the ideas of the Egyptians in regard to a future life were known to them. They saw the funeral rites themselves; they often listened to the description of the judgment of the souls; they even embalmed Jacob and Joseph according to the Egyptian custom, and held in honor of Jacob obsequies similar to those of a person of distinction at the court of the Pharaos.[3] How, then, can we doubt that the

[1] Bunsen, "Egypt's Place," vol. v., pp. 127-129.   [2] Cf. George Rawlinson, "Ancient Religions," pp. 28-30.   [3] Gen. l.

Israelites were cognizant of the immortality of tne soul? If they knew it, they accepted it. Nowhere do we meet the repudiation of this belief. Had they rejected it, we would find traces of their denial in the sacred books. The Pentateuch reproves and condemns in detail all the errors and reprehensible customs of the nations with whom the Israelites came in contact. But Moses did not write a word against the doctrine of the immortality of the soul.

394. DIRECT PROOFS OF HEBREW BELIEF IN THE SOUL'S IMMORTALITY.—But we have also direct proof of the Hebrew belief in the immortality of the soul. They believed in it, because they regarded death as the punishment of original sin, and held that Adam and Eve would never have ceased to live had they not disobeyed God's command.[1] Death itself, according to their ideas, was not a complete and total annihilation of man.[2] Death, the ancient Hebrews thought, put an end to this earthly pilgrimage. In their sight death was a "returning to their fathers, a gathering to their people." These remarkable expressions we can read in all the books of the Hebrew Bible, and especially in the Pentateuch;[3] they mean something more than ordinary interment, says Delitzsch. So also when it is said that the patriarchs died full of days, this expresses not only their disgust with the miseries of this life, but also the gathering of the patriarchs to their fathers.

Hence these expressions are an undeniable proof of the belief of the Hebrews in the immortality of the soul. They distinguish very clearly death, the sepul-

---

[1] Gen. ii. 17; iii. 3, 19, 22.
[2] I. Chron. xix. 15; Ps. xxxiv. 13; cxix. 19, 54; Gen. xlvii. 9.
[3] Gen. xv. 15; xxv. 8, 17; xxxv. 29; xlix. 29, 33; Num. xx. 24, 26; xxvii. 13; xxi. 2; Deut. xxi. 16; xxxii. 50; Jud. ii. 10; II. (IV.) Kings xxii. 20; Jer. viii. 2; Ezech. xxxiii. 50.

chre, and the gathering to their fathers. Infidels wish
to make us believe that the "gathering to his people,"
"returning to his fathers," had no meaning except
that the patriarchs were buried in the tombs or among
the graves of their fathers. This interpretation, plausible enough at first sight, is contrary to the facts.
Abraham, "who was gathered to his people,"[1] was
buried in Hebron, while his father, Thare, died at
Haran, in Syria; Abraham's ancestors died and were
buried in Chaldea. Ismael "was gathered to his people,"[2] although he was not buried in the tomb of his
father, Isaac. Jacob died in Egypt, and months elapsed
before his body was buried in Mambre, in the land of
Canaan; and yet Moses writes of his death, "and he was
gathered to his people."[3] Aaron died on Mount Horeb
and was buried there, away from every Israelite; Moses
himself died on Mount Nebo, but the place of his burial
was not known; and still both Aaron and Moses are said
to have been gathered to their people.[4] These and
many similar texts clearly prove that to the Hebrew
mind the aforesaid phrase meant that the souls of deceased friends lived on beyond the grave.

395. SHEOL, THE PLACE OF THE SOJOURN OF SOULS.
—Not only did the Hebrews believe that death was not
the end of man, but they knew the place where he continued his existence beyond the grave; and the sacred
authors have left us a description thereof. In Hebrew
it was called *sheol* (*sĕ'ôl*), the Latin *infernus*, and the
English *hell*. In the books of the Old Testament, which
were written before the Babylonian captivity, the word,
it has been found, occurs sixty-five times; in the Pentateuch alone it occurs seven times. The Septuagint version
of the Scriptures translates the word sheol by the Greek

[1] Gen. xxv. 8. [2] Gen. xxv. 17. [3] Gen. xlix. 33.
[4] Num. xx. 24; Deut. xxxii. 50; xxxiv. 6.

hades, the place which the Greeks assigned for the dwelling of the souls of the dead; only twice does the Septuagint translate the word "death." Sheol is indeed a general term, not designating especially the abode of the just or that of the unjust. Hence, even in the Apostles' Creed, we say of Christ that "He descended into hell," that is, into limbo, where the souls of the just under the Old Dispensation were detained. When Jacob, misled by the false report given him, thought that his son Joseph had been devoured by a wild beast, he exclaimed: "I will go down to my son into hell (sheol), mourning." Not, certainly, into the hell of the wicked, since he and his son were just men. On the other hand, it is written of Core and Abiron, who with their followers rebelled against Moses, "that the earth broke asunder under their feet, and, opening her mouth, devoured them with their tents and all their substance. And they went down alive into hell"[1]—clearly the hell of the damned. But the Hebrew faith in the different states of the just and unjust in another world, and the rewards that are assigned to them, is given at length in the fifth chapter of the Book of Wisdom, as we saw before.[2]

"In other books of the Old Testament, such as the Books of Kings, Job, the Psalter of King David, Ecclesiasticus, the Prophecy of Isaias, allusions are often made to the doctrine of the immortality of the soul—not of purpose, as if it were a matter of controversy, but incidentally, and, as it were, as unquestioned convictions that spring up naturally from a common, settled, national belief. Indeed, so popular and so absorbing, even for the Hebrew mind, was the doctrine of immortality, that some persons, in spite of all prohibitions, grossly exaggerated it and fell into superstition. The Israelites

[1] Num. xvi. 31–33.
[2] Cf. Ronayne, "God Knowable and Known," p. 328.

believed not only in the survival of the souls of the dead, but some among them by superstitious rites evoked and consulted them, and even made offerings to them, as if they were adorable. This practice is expressly mentioned and condemned in the Book of Deuteronomy; it is also spoken of in Leviticus, in the Books of Kings, in the Prophecy of Isaias. Sinful, undoubtedly, as it was in itself, as being a superstition, the practice points directly to the faith in the soul's immortality; it was, indeed, a corruption of that faith, but even by its extravagance it speaks to us of the vividness with which men then believed in the future existence of souls."[1]

Before the Babylonian captivity we find unquestionable traces of the faith of the Hebrews in the immortality of the soul. After the Babylonian captivity also we find ample testimony in the sacred books to the Hebrew belief on this point. In all, throughout the ages, the same voice, in grave, strong undertones, seems continually to repeat: "It is therefore a holy and wholesome thought to pray for the dead, that they may be loosed from sins."[2]

396. THE BELIEF IN ANOTHER LIFE AMONG OTHER NATIONS. THE ETRUSCANS.—We find this same belief and conviction among other nations. Among the Etruscans, for instance, over the dark realms of the dead ruled Mantus and Mania, king and queen of Hades. Immediately connected with these deities—their prime-minister and most active agent, cruel, hideous, half human, half animal, the chief figure in almost all the representations of the lower world—is the demon Charun, in name no doubt identical with the Stygian ferryman of the Greeks. At the death of man he holds the horse on which the departed soul is to take its journey to the other world, bids the spirit mount, leads away the horse by the bridle,

[1] Ronayne, *op. cit.*, p. 329. [2] II. Mach. xii. 46.

or drives it before him, and thus conducts the deceased into the grim kingdom of the dead. In that kingdom he is one of the tormentors of the guilty souls, whom he strikes with his mallet, or with a sword, while they kneel before him and implore for mercy. Various attendant demons and furies, some male, some female, act under his orders and inflict such tortures as he is pleased to prescribe.

397. BELIEF OF THE IRANIANS.—The Iranians were devout and earnest believers in the immortality of the soul, and of a conscious future existence. They were taught that immediately after death the souls of men, both good and bad, proceeded together along an appointed path to the "bridge of the gatherer." There was a narrow road conducting to heaven, or paradise, over which the souls of the good alone could pass, while the wicked fell from it into the gulf below, where they found themselves in the place of punishment. The pious soul was assisted across the bridge by the angel Serosh, "the happy, well-formed, swift, tall Serosh," who went out to meet the weary wayfarer, and sustained his steps as he effected the difficult passage. The prayers of his friends in this world much availed the deceased, and helped him forward greatly in his journey. As he entered, the angel Vohu-mano rose from his throne and greeted him with the words: "How happy art thou who hast come here to us, exchanging mortality for immortality!" Then the good soul went joyfully onward to the golden throne, to paradise. As for the wicked, when they fell into the gulf they found themselves in outer darkness, in the kingdom of Angro-Mainyus or Ahriman, where they were forced to remain in a sad and wretched condition.

398. BELIEF OF THE HINDOOS.—The Rig-Veda taught the Hindoos that "he who gives alms goes to

the highest place in heaven; he goes to the gods." "Thou, Agni, hast announced heaven to Manu," says a poet; which is explained to mean that Agni revealed to Manu the fact that heaven is to be gained by pious works. "Pious sacrificers," proclaims a third, "enjoy a residence in the heaven of Indra; pious sacrificers dwell in the presence of the gods." Conversely, it is said that "Indra casts into the pit those who offer no sacrifice, and that the wicked who are false in thought and false in speech are born for the deep abyss of hell." In the following hymn there is clear evidence that the early Vedic poets had aspirations after immortality:

"Where there is eternal light, in the world where the sun is placed,

In that immortal, imperishable world, place me, O Soma!

"Where King Vaivaswata reigns, where the secret place of heaven is,

Where the mighty waters are—there make me immortal!

"Where life is free, in the third heaven of heavens,

Where the worlds are radiant—there make me immortal!

"Where wishes and desires are, where the place of the bright sun is,

Where there is freedom and delight—there make me immortal!

"Where is happiness and delight, where joy and pleasure reside,

Where the desires of our heart are attained—there make me immortal!"[1]

399. BELIEF OF THE GREEKS AND ROMANS.—To the Greeks the present life was everything. According to

[1] The translation is Prof. Max Müller's, "Chips," vol. i., p. 40. Cf. G. Rawlinson, "Ancient Religions," pp. 28-31, 53-54, 74-75, 96-99, 124-126, 171.

them there is another world, but it is a world of horrors, and Hades was the most hated among the gods: lamenting and weeping do the souls of the dead descend into his kingdom. Achilles prefers to be a laborer in the light of the sun, rather than a king among the shades.[1]

The belief in the immortality of the soul and future life was not confined to the uncultivated masses, for it was taught by the most eminent writers, poets, and philosophers of Greece and Rome. Socrates, Plato, Aristotle, Cicero, Seneca, Plutarch, Homer, Virgil, Ovid, and other sages of pagan antiquity, guided by the light of reason, proclaimed their belief in the soul's immortality. In Rome this belief began to weaken only in the time of Cicero and Cæsar. Hence the former says:

"Nor do I believe with those that have lately begun to advance the opinion that the soul dies together with the body, and that all things are annihilated by death. The authority of the ancients has more weight with me—both that of our own ancestors who paid such sacred honors to the dead, which surely they would not have done if they thought those honors in no way affected them; and that of those who once lived in this country and enlightened by their institutions and instructions Magna Græcia (which now, indeed, is destroyed, but then flourished); and of him who was pronounced by the oracle of Apollo to be the wisest of men, who did not express first one opinion and then another, as on most questions, but always maintained the same, namely, that the souls of men are divine, and that when they have departed from the body a return to heaven is opened to them—speedy in proportion as each has been virtuous and just."[2]

"These eloquent words," says Cardinal Gibbons, "convey the sentiments not only of Cicero himself, but

[1] Homer, "Iliad," iii., 276.   [2] Cicero, "De Amicitia," chap. iv.

also of the great sages of Greece and Rome."[1] "This belief which we hold" (in the immortality of the soul), says Plutarch, "is so old that we cannot trace its author or its origin, and it dates back to the most remote antiquity."[2]

400. BELIEF OF THE ANCIENT GERMANS.—We find the same faith and conviction among the ancient Germans, who believed that the brave who fall in battle enter Walhalla, the dwelling of Odin, and continue there to live a life similar to their life on earth, only much happier. The others were thrown into the mournful dwelling of Hel.[3]

401. BELIEF OF THE GAULS, BRITONS, LAPPS, FINNS, AFRICANS, AND AMERICANS.—Space forbids us to speak in detail of this belief among many other nations, as the Gauls, the Britons, the Lapps, the Finns, the African tribes, the inhabitants of South and Central America. About the Patagonians P. Manuel Garcia writes: "All believe that the soul is immortal."[4] If we question the Indian of the North, he will tell us of the happy hunting-grounds reserved in after-life for the brave. Cardinal Gibbons says very truly:

"We may find nations without cities, without the arts and sciences, without mechanical inventions, or any of the refinements of civilized life; but a nation without some presentiment of the existence of a future state we shall search for in vain. Even idolatry itself involved an implied recognition of the immortality of the soul; for how could men pay divine honors to departed heroes, whom they worshipped as gods, if they believed that death is the end of man's existence? We may, indeed,

[1] "Our Christian Heritage," p. 202.
[2] "De Consolatione ad Apollonium."
[3] Grimm, "Die Germanen. Mythologie," p. 484.
[4] Cf. P. Charlevoix, "Histoire du Paraguay," p. 238.

find a man here and there who pretends to deny the existence of a future state; but like the fool that says in his heart 'There is no God,' this man's 'wish is father to his thought;' for if there is in the life to come a place of retribution, he feels that it will be so much the worse for him. Or even should we encounter one who really has no faith in a future life, we should have no more right to take him as a type of our intellectual and moral nature than to take the Siamese twins as types of our physical organization. The exception always proves the rule."[1]

Now, whence this universal belief in the immortality of the soul? Is it not the surest proof that there is an immortal being in us? For everything that surrounds us shows us death and perishableness. If mankind always carried within its bosom the idea and belief of the immortality of the soul, this proves most clearly its reality. The world cannot be built upon a lie and a dream. The consensus of all men and all nations cannot bear witness to a falsehood.

402. WHAT THE HEBREWS AND OTHER NATIONS BELIEVED REVEALED BY CHRIST.—And, indeed, what the Hebrews had believed, and what all other nations had regarded as a part of their faith, was clearly revealed to us by our Redeemer, Jesus Christ. The words of Job, which must have stirred the heart of every Jew: "I know that my Redeemer liveth, and in the last day I shall rise out of the earth. And I shall be clothed again with my skin, and in my flesh I shall see my God. Whom I myself shall see, and my eyes shall behold and not another: this my hope is laid up in my bosom"[2]— these words of the pious Job, whereby he expresses his conviction and faith in a future life, were confirmed in a clear and distinct manner by the Redeemer in whom

[1] "Our Christian Heritage," p. 203.   [2] Job xix. 25-27.

he hoped. Numberless times did the Saviour and His Apostles bear witness to this truth. The Redeemer said: "Fear ye not them that kill the body and are not able to kill the soul."[1] Speaking of the final judgment, He says: "These shall go into everlasting punishment; but the just into life everlasting."[2] And St. Paul writes: "This corruptible must put on incorruption, and this mortal must put on immortality; and when this mortal hath put on immortality, then shall come to pass the saying that is written: Death is swallowed up in victory."[3]

403. THE FUTURE LIFE AND THE IDEA OF GOD.—By its nature the soul cannot die. We have seen that the human soul is an immaterial, spiritual substance, that is, acts as a spirit independent of and superior to the body, and consequently has not, as the brute sensitive soul, been educed by vital seminal action from the potency of matter. As an invisible being, a spiritual substance, is one and indivisible like God, who created it after His image and likeness, it is one and indivisible like the consciousness by which it reveals itself. For it is nonsense to assume that our spirit can be split up and divided into parts. Therefore the soul cannot die.

404. DEATH IS NOT ANNIHILATION.—In fact, what is death? What we call death is not the annihilation of the living being, but the dissolution, the falling apart, of its elements. Death, if it means that something ceases to exist altogether, is not found in nature; the constituent parts of things pass into new forms of life and continue to live in them. Thus at death the

[1] Matth. x. 28. [2] Matth. xxv. 46.
[3] I. Cor. xv. 53-54; see also I. Cor. xxii. 23; Luke x. 35; John v. 21; vi. 39; xi. 24; Acts xxiv. 15; II. Cor. iv. 14; v.; Col. iii. 4; Philipp. iii. 21; iv. 3; I. Thess. iv. 13; II. Tim. ii. 11; Apoc. xx. 12.

body falls to pieces, but no part thereof ceases to exist. They mingle with the earth, or give nourishment to other forms of nature. The dead plant is not annihilated; it is ploughed under the ground and forms the manure which increases the fruitfulness of the soil and produces stronger life from its bosom. The same is true of animal bodies. A fundamental law pervades all nature, and this law is a law of life, not of death.

Nothing can be annihilated even by force. One may grind and crush a stone to the finest atoms, but none of these atoms is annihilated. Chemistry can dissolve compounds into their elements, but cannot annihilate a single atom. Fire, a most powerful agent, tends to break up everything, but when it has done its worst, gases and ashes remain. The mote swimming in the air cannot be annihilated.

But if what we call death is not the annihilation of a thing, but only its dissolution into its elements, what will become of our soul, which is an indivisible, spiritual being? Only two things are possible: either God annihilates our soul or it continues to live for all eternity.

405. GOD CANNOT ANNIHILATE THE SOUL.—Will God annihilate the soul? Astronomers agree that our satellite, after having been an incandescent globe, cooled off gradually; perhaps for a time it was able to shelter life, then, cooling more and more, it became a dead mass, receiving from the sun the melancholy light which it sends to us. Some day, perhaps, our earth, now so full of life, will again become an immense glacier. Now we understand these beautiful words of the poet Richter:

"When, after thousands and thousands of years, our earth will perish from age and cold, when all sounds of life will be buried in her bowels, can the immortal spirit, can God her Creator, looking down upon this dumb globe, say to Himself when contemplating this great field of the dead: 'Upon this glacial earth numberless shades have lived, have wept, doing good or evil; now everything has disappeared forever'? No; for then even the tortured worm would turn towards its Creator and say to Him: 'Thou couldst not have created me to suffer, and Thou art not indifferent to vice and to virtue; Thou shouldst not, yea, Thou canst not, be indifferent.' And He who gives to the worm the right to speak thus is the Almighty Himself, who has endowed us with the spirit of justice and of goodness, which awakens in our souls the aspirations and the transports of hope towards Him.

"I am not one of those," continues Richter, "whom faith has touched, of those who are happy in their faith. I envy their happiness. . . . I hold that for nations as for individuals, spiritualism is life, and materialism is death. To give to the soul a transient existence, to confine it to the combats and the deceptions of the present life, to make it perish with the matter which envelops it and which the soul enlightens, to forbid it to hope in a recompense, to forbid it to dread a punishment, to promise it annihilation, to degrade it below the molecules of the visible world, which transform themselves and which never disappear—this is to take away from man the divine breath and condemn him to a forced bestial state."

"I know only one trust and one refuge," says George Sand: "faith in God and in our immortality. . . . It is strange, it is almost painful, to be obliged to defend these doctrines; they have been the glory of humanity. . . . Without them nations are nothing but cattle struggling for existence — according to the expression of Darwin, devouring one another, eating and enjoying themselves, and then perishing instead of dying."[1]

God cannot annihilate the human soul. Only a pagan

[1] Maxime Du Camp, "Revue des Deux Mondes," April 1, 1883.

idol can do that; he, like Saturn, may devour his own children. God carries the fulness of life within Himself from all eternity; He has created our soul as His most perfect work; He has breathed into us the breath of life and filled our heart with the longing after it. He has inspired us with the thought of immortality, and has given it to our soul as a joyful hope; can God, then, annihilate our soul? Is the soul the only exception to the fundamental law of the world? Never; for man's soul crowns the universe and impresses it with the stamp of living truth.

406. WHY IS THE LAW OF CREATION LIFE AND NOT DEATH?—Why can nothing be entirely destroyed? Why is the fundamental law of creation life and not death? Every being the Lord formed is the embodiment of His infinity, a word from His mouth, taking visible shape. Every being is a work created for His honor and glory, a product of His love. Hence none of them can be annihilated. For no thought of His will ever prove false, and no word of His mouth will ever perish; He does not weary of the glory He receives from His works, nor can they show Him too much honor. The Lord will not withdraw a benefit which in His infinite love He granted to His creatures. He is not good at one moment to be cruel at the next. God cannot destroy the human soul. It is His greatest and noblest work, the most sublime thought He has realized in this world. From the soul He receives honor and glory. How could He annihilate this work of His infinite love, this soul destined to announce His greatness for all eternity?

Look at the soul's destiny, and this truth will become even clearer. We need not prove that we have a destiny. This follows from the idea of God as our infinitely wise and reasonable Creator. No reasonable being acts without an end and without wishing to attain that end; God, above all, cannot act without an end. Hence He who is infinitely good and wise and powerful cannot assign to us a destiny which we can never attain.

407. MAN DOES NOT ATTAIN HIS FINAL DESTINY IN THIS WORLD.—Is there any man that attains his destiny in this world? Where are the happy men in this world? We can find men that are content, but there are no truly happy men in this valley of tears. Knock at the gates of the rich or at the doors of the poor; stop all you meet and ask them whether they are happy. Not a man will answer with an unconditional "Yes!" All are uneasy and dissatisfied; they begin one thing, then begin another, and abandon everything, discouraged. Man's eye is continually directed toward the future; in the future he hopes for rest and peace; the future, he hopes, will grant what the present refuses him; and when the future has come, he is richer by a new disappointment. Again the dark and bitter present gnaws at his heart. Everything upon earth is a striving without attaining; and man's life will forever remain a wrestling and struggling, even when he has apparently reached the highest earthly good. Let us look at our own heart and life. Whether we stand on the threshold of our days or have already carried the heavy burden of life, can we say that we have found rest for our desires—some definite end, and in it our perfection and happiness? Everything upon earth is but a beginning, and will always remain a beginning, even when we stand at death's door.

408. WITHOUT A FUTURE LIFE, MAN WOULD BE MOST UNHAPPY.—Now, were there no future life, we would be the most lamentable of beings. Why all our life? Why all this struggle, if it leads to no victory? Why so much suffering for the sake of a winding-sheet, so many efforts for the sake of a narrow grave?

If there be no future life, we have reason to envy the animal; if there be no future life, it is no sin to curse the hour of our birth!

"What is the most ardent desire of man," asks Hettinger,[1] "the first and last wish of our soul? Ask all the millions who have moved on the earth since the creation of the first man, for what did they strive, for what did they struggle? Ask yourself, lay your hand upon your own heart, listen to its innermost, its truest word—what does it desire? Happiness. 'Happy,' said St. Augustine,[2] 'we all wish to be; and we abhor unhappiness, yea, we cannot wish for it.' Before man hears of virtue, before he knows anything of duty and sacrifice, he longs after happiness. Call it egotism, call it whatever you please—it is so. But where is happiness? We have a name for it, we seek it; it cannot be unknown to us altogether; it cannot be a stranger upon earth. It appears upon earth, accompanies us for a moment, then it disappears—we know not whence it came nor whither it has gone. Who can say that he never caught a glimpse of happiness? But we see it only for a moment; then it vanishes. . . . However, man craves to be happy; he wishes not for momentary happiness, but for happiness that lasts, that never ends, and that all must be able to attain. True happiness must be universal, must be eternal."

409. THE END OF OUR CREATION.—But let us consider the question of our end from the standpoint of truth and Christianity. Faith teaches us that our end is "to know God, to love Him, and to serve Him in this world, and be happy with Him in the next." Men deny that this is our destiny; it is a fact that we have no other. Our soul is created for God; it is His child, His

---

[1] "Apologie," vol. i., 1. p. 185.
[2] "De Trinit.," xiii., 4.

bride, and is eternally bent in love toward Him, wishing to be with Him.

But if this is our end and destiny, do we attain it here upon earth? If there be no future life, we must attain our end here. Still, no man can reach this high destiny in the present life. On earth we can neither know nor love God as perfectly as His Being deserves and our spirit and heart desire; hence we do not find in His knowledge and love our perfect happiness.

We know the knowledge of the truth is a difficult, a wearisome duty for man; and he never will know it fully. Even the greatest mind is limited. If we can know God's works only imperfectly, how can we rise to the knowledge of His Being? If we are incapable of reading His greatness in His works, how can we know Him, the Infinite, the Mysterious? Here below we behold Him only in a mirror, and the thoughts of the wisest are but the stammering of a child. The same is true of love, with which we cherish Him, our Creator and Father. No soul truly and honestly striving to love Him will say that it can do this as God and His perfections deserve, and according to its own desires. It feels the distance, the abyss, which exists between its best and highest efforts and the end after which it strives.

Therefore there must be an eternal life where we can see God face to face, as far as this is possible for our spirit; where God's grace will enable us to love Him with a love worthy of Him, with all the love of which our heart is capable. Another country awaits us, in which everything earthly is completed, and in which our knowledge and love of God will be glorified. Otherwise, those who refuse to turn their eye towards Him would be the most happy; otherwise, those would be blessed who see their end in the goods of this world, and who mock and despise the knowledge and love of God; otherwise, the wicked should be applauded, and the good would deserve to be pitied. The virtuous must bear the pain and struggles of their soul, and descend into the grave bearing with them their grief and the discord of their being.

410. SOCIETY COULD NOT EXIST IF MAN'S LIFE WERE NOT ETERNAL.—The society in which we live also requires eternal life; it must fall to pieces if the soul dies with the body. If there be no eternity to steady our present life, it must become a ruin; peace is no longer possible.

To make life on earth peaceable and well-regulated, three factors must conspire: evil and sin, as disorders, must be sufficiently chastised to keep them in check; good must be rewarded, so that men will love and prize it; and virtue must be practised to lighten the pains and burdens of life. But these three conditions cannot be realized, unless there be an eternity.

It is true that even in this life evil and sin bring pain and punishment to all who are so unfortunate as to stain themselves with them. Remorse of conscience is the chastisement of the evil-doer; he brings on himself the contempt of his fellow-men and stands disgraced in their eyes. Earthly justice makes every effort to discover crime and to punish it according to desert. But what are earthly punishments without the punishment of eternity? They cannot prevent capital crimes, or punish them as they deserve to be punished.

A wicked man controlled by powerful passion despises the warnings of his conscience; he can even suppress them for a while. When inflamed by passion, what does he care for the judgment of his fellow-men? He laughs at them and scorns their opinions. What can earthly justice do? Much evil and the greatest abominations it often cannot punish. Secret sins and sins of thought it cannot reach; the cunning and the powerful often escape its punishments. But suppose that all crimes were discovered by earthly justice and punished; the punishment it inflicts on the evil-doer, were it never so severe, is insufficient to chastise him according to his deserts. Eternal punishment is the last wall which surrounds and protects every other expression of divine justice upon earth. Without it vice would triumph over virtue.

Again, virtue demands eternal life for its reward. The good must be rewarded because divine justice demands it and because reward animates man to practise virtue in spite of the great difficulties with which the virtuous must often contend. We often hear that virtue must be practised for its own sake. Man will do nothing without a motive, and this motive cannot be the thing we do; it must be outside of that thing. The reward of a good action is the most powerful inducement to perform it.

But can the world reward virtue according to its merit? No, for the world knows and hears very little of the good done upon earth. The noblest and greatest sacrifices are made in secret; the truly virtuous neither desire nor seek earthly reward. Must their good actions and sacrifices therefore go unrewarded? Besides, the world does not reward some virtues, for it neither esteems them nor holds them worthy of reward. The evangelical virtues which spring from the mysterious soil of grace are despised by the world. And, after all, what reward can the world offer to the virtuous? All its honors and rewards, all its gold and silver, are but a slender recompense for their struggles and self-denial. Eternity is necessary, in order that all good may be brought to light and rewarded according to its desert. Without eternity the strongest motive for good actions would be wanting, and the noblest sacrifices would go unrewarded.

Again, without the hope of a better and an everlasting life the spirit of self-sacrifice cannot exist, and the world must become a desert. Even if the strictest order reigned in the present life, order alone could not preserve society if men ceased to encourage and console one another by mutual sacrifice. Worldly glory and innate goodness might move some to practise heroic acts of charity; but to awaken and strengthen the Christian spirit of self-sacrifice the rewards of this world are inadequate. Only the thought of a higher and everlasting life can inspire us with enthusiasm for great deeds. Without eternity mankind, at best, would be commonplace; and soon would follow the reign of sin and vice.

The immortality of our soul and the future life are our hope in every situation of life. The present life is but a preparation for it. Death is the gate of the life to come. God grant that we may there find never-ending bliss.

THE END.

INDEX.

The numbers correspond to the sections.

ACEROTHERIUM, Age of the, 182, 185-187.
Age of the acerotherium, 182, 185-187; of bronze, 199, 200; of Elephas meridionalis, 184, 189; of halitherium, 183, 188; of iron, 199, 200; of mammoth and reindeer, 176; of stone, 197-200.
Alluvions, 161.
America, Archæological monuments of, 140; Chinese annals referring to, 289; mythology referring to, 290; records and legends of, 285.
Americans, their origin, 283; their history, 285; Americans and the races of the world, 286; and the traditions of Central America, 284.
Anatomy, Comparative, 48, 49.
Ape, Anthropoid, 84, 91.
Apes, Catarrhine, man's ancestors, 85, 94.
Asiatic countries, Civilization of, 139.
Atavism, 52.
Arameans, Traditions of, 323.
Ararat of Genesis, 318, 342.
Ark, Size of, 351.
Armenia, 318, 342.
Art, Objects of, and human bones, 164.
Aryans, Traditions of, 324.
Atrophy, 48.

BARBARISM in Europe, 139.
Bathybius, Story of the, 17.
Bible, Chronology of, 146-149; and the antiquity of mankind, 158; and the Deluge, 340-342.
Books, Ancient, of China, 212.
Bone caves and osseous breccias, 330.
Bones, Human, and objects of art, 164.

Bonnet, Redi, and Vallisnieri, Experiments of, in spontaneous generation, 8.
Brain, Influence of size on the, 268–271; weight of, 270; intelligence measured by weight of, 267; volume of, 268–271.
Breccias, Osseous, 330.
Bronze, Age of, 199, 200.
Bushmen and Hottentots, 136.

CALCULATIONS, Astronomical, of China, 213.
Catastrophes in pliocene and post-pliocene periods, 193.
Caves, Bone, 330.
Celts, Traditions of the, 324.
Cenozoic, or new life, p. 23.
Chaldea, Chronology of, 226–228; and the cylinder of Nabonidos, 229, 230.
Chaldeans, their belief in the immortality of the soul, 385–389; cosmic days of, 157.
Characters distinguishing man from beast, 95, 105; physical, 96–100; psychological, 106–113; characters in races not specific, 241–244, 306.
China, Annals of, 214; astronomical calculations of, 213; monuments of, 215.
Chronologists and geologists, their agreement as to the antiquity of man, 144.
Chronology of the Bible, 146–149; consequences resulting therefrom, 150; discrepancies, 148, 149; omissions, 152, 153; and the cosmic days of the Chaldeans, 157.
 of Chaldea, 226, 227; and cuneiform accounts, 228; and the cylinder of Nabonidos, 229–232.
 of China, 210–215.
 of Egypt, 216; chief authorities for, 217–222; not complete, 223–225.
 of India, 205–209.
Civilization in Asiatic countries, 139.
Climate, Writers on, 172.
Climatic changes, 168; greatly exaggerated, 169.
Color of the skin, 250–252; cause of, 253, 254; no specific character in man, 255.
Comparative anatomy, 148.
Cosmic days in the Chaldean and Biblical chronologies, 157.
Creation of man, 368; end of, 409.

Cuneiform accounts of Chaldea, 228.
Cylinder of Nabonidos, 229, 230.

DARWIN, System of, 31, 51, 53, 60, 61; his view on man's descent, 86-90; struggle of life, 88; definition of races and varieties, 39; and Lamarck, 33.
Darwinism criticised, 26, 35, 90, 124; is an anti-Genesis, 37.
Death is not annihilation, 404.
Deluge, Meaning of, 310; universality of, 333, 340, 344; absolute universality, 335; restricted universality, 336, 337, 338, 344-346; aim of, 341; duration, 343; causes, 353-357; torrential rains, 354; invasion of the seas, 355; upheavals and depressions, 356; objections, 347-352.
  and the Biblical account, 311.
  and the traditions of the Egyptians, 313; of the Chaldeans, 316-320; of the Arameans, 323; of the Hindoos, Iranians, Aryans, Persians, Celts, Scandinavians, 324; of the Americans, 325; these traditions compared with Genesis, 314, 321, 326.
  and geology, 327, 328; and erratic rocks, 329; bone caves and osseous breccias, 330; tufaceous limestone, 331.
Depressions and upheavals, 165, 356.
Descent of man, see *Darwin* and *Mivart*.
Development, Bodily, 100; embryological, 102; development to higher culture possible only through Christianity, 141.
Diluvial and quaternary man, 195.
Discrepancies in the tables of Genesis, 148.

EGYPT, Chronology of, 216, 223; monuments of, 221; Greek writers on, 218.
Egyptians, Traditions of, 313; their belief in the immortality of the soul, 390-393.
Elephas meridionalis, Age of, 184, 189.
Embryological development, 102.
Embryology, 45-47.
Environment, Influence of, 245, 246.
Eozoon Canadense, 77.
Etruscans, their belief in the immortality of the soul, 396.
Europe, Barbarism in, 139.
Evolutionists and the difference between man and beast, 119-124.
Experiments in spontaneous generation, 8-10; and Haeckel's monera, 18, 19.

INDEX.

FACULTIES of man and animals, 114-119.
Faith and the origin of life, 1; and the origin of man, 70-73, 81-83, 359; harmony between science and, 73.
Fauna, Changes of, and the antiquity of man, 174; tertiary, 58; of Egypt, 56.
Fecundity, Interracial, 296.
Flora of Egypt, 56; tertiary, 57.
Fuegeans, 133.

GENERATION, Spontaneous, 4-10; history of, 5; experiments in, 8-10; adherents of, 11, 12; in earlier periods, 24-26.
Genesis, Genealogical tables of, 147, 154; and natural selection, 36.
Genus, Definition of, 38.
Geography, Physical, and the antiquity of man, 165.
Geologists and chronologists, their agreement as to the antiquity of man, 144.
Geology and the Deluge, 327, 328; confirms the permanency of species, 54.
Germans, Belief of the ancient, in the immortality of the soul, 400.
Glaciers, 171.
Golden age, The, 138.

HAECKEL and the first monera, 16; his system, 30; criticised, 80.
Hair, Character of, 256-259; no specific character in man, 257.
Halitherium, Age of, 182, 187.
Hebrews, their belief in the immortality of the soul, 383, 384, 393-395.
Heredity, Influence of, 247, 248.
Hindoos, Chronology of, 206; literature of, 209; their traditions about the deluge, 324; belief in the immortality of the soul, 398.
History confirms the permanency of species, 54.
Hottentots and Bushmen, 136.
Hybrids, Sterility of, 60.

ICE age, The, and the antiquity of man, 194.
Immortality of the soul, see *Soul*.
India, Chronology of, 205, 206; history of, 208; literature of, 209.
Indians (American) capable of civilization, 307; their belief in the immortality of the soul, 398.

INDEX. 573

Infidelity and the primitive state of man, 119–131.
Instinct and intelligence, 115–119.
Intelligence and reason distinguished, 106, 107.
Intelligence measured according to the capacity of the skull, 267.
Iraneans, Traditions of, 324; their belief in the immortality of the soul, 397.
Iron age, 199, 200.

LAMARCK, 33.
Lamarckism perfected by Darwin, 34.
Language, what we owe to it, 109, 110.
Languages, Differences in, 272; no argument against monogenism, 273; classification of, 274; causes of the many languages, 276; relation of, 277; and savage peoples, 275; the Mosaic account confirmed, 278.
Liberty, what we owe to it, 110.
Life, 1–3, 360; development of, 29, 30; different kinds of, 361; highest form of, 362; organic principle of, 363; future life and the idea of God, 403; eternal life and the welfare of society, 410.
Limestone, Tufaceous, 331.
Linnæus and the classification of genus, species, and variety, 38.

MAMMOTH and reindeer, Age of, 176.
Man, what he is, 69; origin of, according to faith and Scripture, 70–73, 81–83, 359; and philology, 109, 110; his ancestors, 78; pseudo-scientific systems about man, 74–77, 81–83; belief of, in God, 125; primitive state of, and infidelity, 129–132; created in a perfect state, 142; over 8,000 years old, 154; contemporary with the reindeer, 177; with many extinct animals, 178; his existence in the tertiary and quaternary age, 190, 191; toward the end of the ice age, 194; in quaternary and diluvian time, 195; more ancient than formerly believed, 203, anatomical organization of, 294; objections against the specific character of, 120; types of primitive, 198; man a social being, 302; his religious sentiment, 305; not limited to one kind of food, 295; can live under all climatic conditions, 300; endowed with reason and intelligence, 301; his destination, 407, 408.
— antiquity of, according to the Bible, 158; the tables of Genesis, 146; science, 149; geology, 160, climatic changes, 168–173;

changes of fauna, 174-178; tertiary and quaternary findings, 179, 180; progress of his industry, 196-203; according to the chronology of China, 210-215; of Chaldea, 226-232; of Egypt, 216-223; of India, 205-209.

Manetho, History of, 219, 220.

Mankind descended from one pair, 70; specific unity of, 293-299, its rapid increase no argument against monogenism, 279 fecundity of interracial marriages, 296-299.

Materialism and the nature of man, 74.

Menes, Date of, not clearly established, 225.

Mesozoic, or middle life, p. 24.

Mivart, System of, on the bodily origin of man, 81, 82.

Moneron of Haeckel, 15, 16, 60.

Monism, 13, 18, 20, 21, 64-68; an improvement on Darwinism, 14; last argument of, 21.

Monogenism, Objections to, 279-281.

Monogenists, who they are, 239.

Monuments of America, 140; of India, 207; of China, 212-215; of Egypt, 221-224.

Mortillet's types of primitive man, 198.

NABONIDOS, Cylinder of, 229, 230.

Naturalists, 33, 239.

Negroes, many are the peers of the white man, 308.

Neolithic age, 201.

ORGANS, Rudimentary, 48, 50.

Organism, Definition of, 364.

Osseous breccias, 330.

PALÆOZOIC, or ancient life, p. 24.

Paleolithic age, 201.

Peat-moors, 162.

Persians, Traditions among, 324.

Physical characters in man, 96-100.

Pithecoid theory, 86-90.

Pliocene and post-pliocene, Relation between, 192.

Polygenism, 234, 236.

Polygenists, Arguments of, 235; errors of, 240; polygenists of the United States, 237, 238.

Polynesians, Origin of, 282.
Prehistoric times and Darwinism, 59.
Psychological characters in man, 106–113.
Psychology of the Israelites. 370.

QUATERNARY man, 180, 191, 195; findings, 179.

REASON, what we owe to it, 110; distinguished from intelligence, 106, 107.
Redi, Vallisnieri, and Bonnet, Experiments of, in spontaneous generation, 8.
Reindeer and mammoth, Age of the, 176.
Rocks, Erratic, 329.
Romans, their belief in the immortality of the soul, 399.
Rudimentary organs, 48, 50; formations, 101.

SAVAGE races victims of wars and invasions, 130–133.
Scandinavians, Traditions of, 324.
Science, Harmony between faith and, 73; and the origin of life, 2, 3; and the antiquity of man, 159.
Senses, The, 104.
Septuagint, The, its venerable authority, 149, 204; and the cylinder of Nabonidos, 232.
Shame, Sense of, and the animals, 112.
Sheol, 395.
Shipwrecks in ancient and modern times, 287.
Skin, Color of, 250–255; no specific character in man, 255.
Skull, Form of, 260–266; custom of tying up, 262; no specific character in man, 261; subject to change, 263; influence of mode of life on, 264; its type in the first generations, 265.
Soul, The, not a complexus of corporal organs, 374–377; and disturbances of the mind, 378, its fate after death, 381; the soul and materialism, 382; its immortality and the belief of the Hebrews, 383–384, 393–395; of the Chaldeans, 385–389; of the Egyptians, 390–392; of other nations, 396–401; its immortality divinely revealed, 402.
Species, Definition of, 38; variability of, limited, 42–44, 60, 61.
Spontaneous generation, see *Generation*.
Stalagmites, 163.
Sterility of hybrids, 60.
Stone age, 197–200.

Struggle for life, 88.
Survival of the fittest, 87.

TABLES, Genealogical, of Genesis, 147, 154; chronological, of the ten antediluvian kings, 156.
Tables showing successive appearance of living things in successive geological periods, p. 23.
Tasmanians, 111.
Tertiary man, 180, 181; findings, 179.
Traditions about the Deluge, 311; among the Americans, 325; Arameans, 323; Aryans, 324; Celts, 324; Central America, 284; Chaldeans, 316-320, 385-389; Egyptians, 313, 390-392; Hebrews, 383, 384, 393-395, Hindoos, Iranians, Persians, Scandinavians, 324.
Types of primitive man, 198.

UNITY of the human species, 233, 249; specific unity, 293-299; teaching of faith and science on, 73.
Upheavals and depressions, 356.

VALLISNIERI, Bonnet, and Redi, Experiments of, in spontaneous generation, 8.
Variability of species, 41-44.
Variety, definition of, 38.

www.ingramcontent.com/pod-product-compliance
Lightning Source LLC
Chambersburg PA
CBHW031936290426
44108CB00011B/582